ANATOMY OF A FRAUD

□□□

*Inside the Finances of the
PTL Ministries*

GARY L. TIDWELL

John Wiley & Sons, Inc.

New York • Chichester • Brisbane • Toronto • Singapore

#26636225

This text is printed on acid-free paper.

This publication is designed to provide accurate and authoritative information in regard to the subject matter covered. It is sold with the understanding that the publisher is not engaged in rendering legal, accounting, or other professional services. If legal advice or other expert assistance is required, the services of a competent professional person should be sought. *From a Declaration of Principles jointly adopted by a Committee of the American Bar Association and a Committee of Publishers.*

Library of Congress Cataloging-in-Publication Data
Tidwell, Gary.
    Anatomy of a fraud : inside the finances of the PTL ministries /
Gary Tidwell.
        p.   cm.
    Includes index.
    ISBN 0-471-57110-5 (alk. paper)
    1. Bakker, Jim, 1940–   – Trials, litigation, etc. 2. PTL (Organization)—
Corrupt practices. I. Title.
BV3785.B3T53   1993
364.1'63'0973—dc20   92-31966
                                                                              CIP

Printed in the United States of America

10 9 8 7 6 5 4 3 2 1

Acknowledgments

MY STUDENTS AT THE COLLEGE OF CHARLESTON made this book possible. Without their enthusiasm and support for the special topics course, "Ethics and Evangelism," I would have had neither the stamina nor the desire to continue doing research on the business aspects of PTL. While I hope that I motivated students to understand the business transactions and the ethical and legal responses of various professionals at PTL, the students showed an excitement and genuine interest that continually prompted me to forge ahead with my research. The students' quizzical expressions and their basic yet probing questions caused me to delve more deeply into the records and court exhibits in order to respond to their questions and concerns.

Although it would be impossible to name all 225 students in the four classes of "Ethics and Evangelism," some of the "shining stars" included:

Reid Adams
William Baehr
Matt Baughman
Chris Bernard
Katherine Black
Ellen Brittain
Jonathan Bruckner
Michael Burkhold
Michelle Carlisle
Todd Combs
Michelle Derecho
Brude Doyle
Kathryn Edwards
Coleman Edmunds
Mark Ellwanger

Kevin Gates
Billy Gorman
Stephanie Gubacsi
Scott Guise
Chris Haborak
Brent Herlong
Daniel Hiers
Kevin Jackson
Ryan Kurtz
Finley Merry
Woodard Middleton
Scott Miramonti
Richard Mitchell
Elizabeth Newitt
Eric Nichols

Bill Parker
William Pitt
Fred Riesen
Doug Rodgers
Rhetta Rowland
J. C. Shaw
Bailey Smith
Tim Smith
Matt Sjostrom
Grady Thomas
Edward Tuccio
Robert Vinson
Eddie Whiddon

Special thanks go to the independent study students who not only took the course but also voluntarily worked with me in researching the business aspects of PTL. The fruits of their labor are incorporated in this book, and those students who helped me so much include: Thomas Boulware, Chris Brady, Allan Dove, Jenny Foresterling, Eric Hawkins, Michael Hussey, Jordan Liatos, Mike Schmitt, Jennifer Walter, Brian Wichlei, Lisa Wickstrom, and Laura Wolfe.

The independent study efforts and research of several students clearly went beyond the call of duty and were more than I could ever have expected. David Archer worked on accounting issues and gathered documents not only in Charleston, South Carolina, but also in Charlotte, North Carolina. Adam Cooper painstakingly researched the oversale of lifetime partnerships. Chris Jankowski and Matt Kappel did extensive research in Charlotte, North Carolina, where they examined Morris Cerullo's purchase of PTL. Chris Long not only provided valuable insight concerning Morris Cerullo's purchase of PTL, but also did extensive research examining documents filed with the Federal Court.

Beau Garverick and Beau Schweikert spent an entire summer working with me on the accounting issues related to PTL. They helped to set the standards for the independent study students that followed.

Jennifer Grindstaff, especially, made the independent studies such a success. Her tenacity, long hours, and dedication were unbelievable. I appreciate all her efforts as she worked not only in Charleston, South Carolina, but also spent her entire Christmas break doing research and gathering documents in Charlotte, North Carolina.

Carole Cox, a former legal correspondent for the Charleston, South Carolina, CBS affiliate, was a real pleasure to work with. She introduced me to people I would not have met otherwise, and she and I shared those early morning hours waiting in front of the Federal District Court hoping to get a seat for the Bakker criminal trial.

Ann Campbell obviously possessed special skills that allowed her not only to comprehend my dictation but to literally work around the clock preparing the manuscript. I truly appreciate her tireless efforts and dedication to getting this book written.

My editors, Tracy King and Susan Barry, have shown patience and commitment to this undertaking. I appreciate their suggestions and comments and, as usual, their reviews only strengthened the manuscript. The copyeditor, Greg Everitt, and Mary Ray and Joyce Jackson of Impressions made numerous and valuable contributions to the original manuscript. It was a real pleasure to work with them.

Lee Blue, Lynn Graham, Gray and Kim Johnson, Amy Stutsman, and Cathy Walsh are true personal friends who gave me the encouragement and support to write this book in the hectic spring and summer of 1992. My thanks go to them.

Finally, I want to thank all who were, in one way or another, involved with PTL and who took the time to speak to me and/or my class. To the lifetime partners, the trustees of the bankrupt PTL corporation, and the former employees of PTL: You may never know what a profound impact you had on my students when speaking to them either on the PTL property or while waiting in line to attend one of the many judicial proceedings concerning PTL. Thank you for sharing your thoughts and for turning the unfortunate events at PTL into a learning experience, thereby helping to ensure that what transpired at PTL is not repeated.

To all who gave so much to PTL, I dedicate this book to you.

Gary L. Tidwell
Charleston, South Carolina

Contents

1   Introduction   1

2   Jim and Tammy: Their Background and Beliefs   8

3   Rags to Riches and the Birth of PTL   21

4   "Four Days and Three Nights"   29
     The Grand Hotel Partnership Fraud   31
     The Towers Hotel Partnership Frauds   45
     The Bunkhouse Partnership Fraud   67
     The 1100 Club   69
     Gift Promotionals: David and Goliath   74
     The Bottom Line   76

5   United States v. Bakker and Overview of Related Proceedings   77
     The Bankruptcy Proceedings   78
     United States v. Taggart   89
     United States v. Bakker   94

6   Where Were the Corporate Officers?   113
     The Chief Financial Officer   113
     The Senior Executive Vice-President, Corporate Executive Director, and Co-Pastor   137
     The Administrative Assistant to the President   147
     The Vice-President of World Outreach   153
     Other PTL Employees   156

7   Where Was the Board of Directors?   162
     Tangible Observations at PTL   163
     The Board of Directors' Legal Responsibilities   165

The PTL Board of Directors Prior to December
 1982 166
Board Meetings Subsequent to December 1982 171
Bonuses 179
PTL's Last Hours 191

8 Insights into the Civil Trial 192
The Plaintiffs 194
The Defendants 195
What Was Litigated? 197
Issues Not Litigated 200

9 Where Were the Auditors? 204
What Do Auditors Do? 204
The PTL Audits and Oversale of Lifetime
 Partnerships 209
PTL and Issues Relating to Solvency 224
Auditor Independence 224
PTL's Attorneys and Their Relationship with
 PTL's Auditors and Corporate Officers 231
The Change in PTL's Auditors 236
What the Lifetime Partners Saw 243
Where Do We Go from Here? 245

10 Where Was the ECFA? 248
Background of the ECFA 249
PTL and the ECFA 250
The ECFA's Response to PTL's Demise 261

11 The Purchase of PTL: Reverend Morris Cerullo and
Arthur Andersen 263
Who Is Morris Cerullo? 264
The "Take It Back from the Devil" Telethon and
 Arthur Andersen 266
The Acquisition of PTL Assets 268
The Gold and Platinum Card Programs 270
The Litigation 276

12 Epilogue 287

Appendix 291

Index 349

CHAPTER ONE

─────────────── □□□ ───────────────

Introduction

You say, "Oh, but Jim, look at all the money you are personally making off PTL." Well, I have news for you, my church pays my salary . . . so no one can say Jim and Tammy are in it for the money.

James O. Bakker, "Jim Bakker Television Program," April 9, 1981

AT THREE O'CLOCK IN THE AFTERNOON on October 24, 1989, television evangelist and PTL founder Jim Bakker heard U.S. Federal District Judge Robert Potter deliver his opinion that "those of us who do have a religion are ridiculed as being saps [for] money-grubbing preachers or priests, but worst of all, it appears that Mr. Bakker thinks he deserves . . . all of his gain received from the little people who sent in their savings." With that said, Judge Potter proceeded to sentence him to serve 45 years in prison and pay a $500,000 fine. Although subsequently reduced to 18 years, this sentence effectively ended the television ministry of Bakker, then 49 years old.

This also ended the well-publicized, opulent lifestyle that Jim Bakker and his wife, Tammy Faye, had enjoyed for years. As Judge Potter summarized at the time of sentencing, their holdings included a $600,000 house in Palm Desert, California; a $149,500 house in Gatlinburg, Tennessee, for which an additional $340,000 was spent on renovations; a $600,000 condominium in Florida, complete with a $5,000 Christmas tree; a $449,000 house in Palm Springs, California; a collection of Rolex watches worth $11,900; three Mercedes automobiles worth $150,000; and $265,000 that was designated to be received by Jessica Hahn. From 1984 until May 1987 the Bakkers received total cash compensation of $4,760,660 in the form of salaries, bonuses, and contributions to Jim Bakker's Ministers' Benefit Association retirement plan.

But this extravagant lifestyle, funded by what most people would say was excessive financial compensation, was not the reason why Bakker was sentenced so severely. Clearly the tales of opulence, excess, and avarice were critical and moving portions of the criminal trial as well as the principal focus of media coverage. Nor was he convicted of having had an affair with the now infamous Jessica Hahn. What he was convicted of was wire and mail fraud and conspiracy to commit wire and mail fraud.

Moreover, this was not just any wire and mail fraud contended the government, this was "one of the largest, if not *the* largest, consumer fraud prosecuted as a federal mail fraud violation to date in this country." The magnitude of Bakker's crimes is phenomenal and cannot be understated. Specifically, Jim Bakker was convicted of having sold 152,903 fully paid lodging partnerships that produced income of approximately $158 million. This was a fraud that, according to the government and what was accepted by the *Bakker* jury, commenced by at least July 7, 1984, and continued until May 1987.

As Assistant U.S. Attorney Jerry Miller argued before Judge Potter at Bakker's sentencing hearing: "[t]his is a case of 158 million dollars of fraud. . . . Any concept that Mr. Bakker over the last five years was acting out of a calling from God needs to be stripped away in the light of day and the truth [is] that the jury found in this case that this man is a con man . . . a common criminal. The only thing uncommon about him was the mechanism that he chose and the vehicle that he used to perpetuate the fraud. The motives are all the same. It's not a bit different than any other fraud that's been perpetrated . . . anywhere in this country. It's motivated by greed, by selfishness, by a lust for power."

The details of the lodging frauds will be examined in subsequent chapters. To put it simply, Bakker used his television show and mailings to solicit literally millions of people to become "lifetime partners" at PTL's Heritage USA in Charlotte, North Carolina, where PTL members and their families could go for vacations and for religious activities. Unfortunately, this also became the site of the $158 million fraud.

From February 1984 through May 1987 Bakker solicited lifetime partners on the PTL Television Network and various commercial television affiliates. In January 1984 he also began soliciting through the mail by sending glossy full-color promotional brochures and letters outlining the benefits of becoming a PTL lifetime partner. For example, a "gift" of $1,000 granted a lifetime partnership in the Grand Hotel program. For that $1,000, the lifetime partner and his or her immediate family would be able to stay for free in the Grand Hotel at Heritage USA for four days and three nights each year for the rest of his or her life.

Bakker and others offered eleven different lifetime partnership programs from 1984 through 1987. These programs cost from $500 to $10,000, and eight of them boasted a package of benefits that included free lodging in one of the Heritage USA facilities. He promised television viewers across the country (and the thousands of people who received mailed solicitations) that the number of Grand Hotel lifetime partnerships would be limited to 25,000 because of the finite number of rooms in the hotel.

However, rather than selling 25,000 partnerships and raising $25 million as he had promised, Bakker sold 66,683 fully paid lodging partnerships in the Grand Hotel, thereby raising approximately $66.9 million. Furthermore, only 52 percent of the $66.9 million that was raised for the Grand Hotel partnership program was actually used for the construction of the facility. No funds were set aside to provide a reserve for covering the cost of providing free lodging for the balance of each lifetime partner's life. Instead, the funds were drawn down almost instantaneously to meet daily operational expenses, which, of course, included the executive compensation and other perks paid to the Bakkers.

In another lodging fraud, Bakker and others at PTL promised, again through television and mailed solicitations, to raise money for the building of the Towers Hotel. As in the previous fundraising scheme, there would be a limited number of partnerships available for this program. The Towers Hotel program would be limited to 30,000 lifetime partners; at $1,000 each, the partnerships would produce the target sum of $30 million.

As represented and explained by Bakker in the nationally televised announcement for the Towers Hotel, there would actually be $15 million remaining after the $30 million had been raised because the Towers would only cost $15 million to build. However, Bakker and others at PTL did not just sell 30,000 lifetime partnerships for the Towers and thus raise $30 million. Rather, 68,755 fully paid partnerships were sold. These lifetime partners contributed not $30 million but $74.2 million only 15.4 percent of which was actually used for the construction of the Towers Hotel, which was never even completed.

Just like nearly all other funds raised at PTL for the lifetime partnership program, these funds were used for other purposes, and no reserve was set aside to fulfill the promises made to the PTL faithful. As Jerry Miller said at the time of Bakker's sentencing: "[t]his crime was such that hour by hour, day by day, week by week, month by month and year by year Jim Bakker consciously violated the law. He consciously made the decision to lie to people on TV every single time he opened his mouth about that lifetime partnership program. It was a fraud time in and time out perpetrated in the guise of religion."

Eventually Jim Bakker; his executive vice-president and coconspirator, Richard Dortch; and the vice-president of administration, David Taggart went to prison. The IRS revoked PTL's tax-exempt status on April 22, 1988, after PTL had declared bankruptcy on June 12, 1987.

Those who are familiar with PTL and Jim Bakker, may contend that the now well-publicized tryst that Jim Bakker had with former church secretary Jessica Hahn brought about the downfall of Bakker and PTL. Such, however, is not the case.

PTL was living on borrowed time and in fact was only able to survive as long as it did because of the continued, fraudulent oversell of lifetime partnerships—an oversell that occurred at least by July 7, 1984.

At the time of Bakker's resignation, PTL was employing over 2,000 people. During the last year the Bakkers were at PTL, over $129 million was raised. PTL had corporate officers other than Bakker, it had a functioning board of directors, and it had attorneys and auditors who rendered advice and were well paid for their professional services.

From 1977 to 1984 the well-respected accounting firm of Deloitte, Haskins & Sells acted as independent auditor for PTL. During those years Deloitte was one of the "Big Eight" accounting firms; Deloitte has now merged with the firm Touche and Ross and is today Deloitte Touche, the third-largest accounting firm in the United States.

From 1985 to 1986 PTL hired Laventhol and Horwath, regarded by many in the hotel industry as the premier auditing firm. Laventhol, like Deloitte, acted as PTL's independent auditor; it has since declared bankruptcy and disbanded.

Yet neither accounting firm detected nor noted the massive fraud that was occurring at PTL. Where were the auditors?

Was the PTL board of directors given access to meaningful corporate information that would have allowed them to function properly and to fulfill their legal obligations? Did they justifiably or unjustifiably rely on others in making their decisions?

The Evangelical Council for Financial Accountability (ECFA) provides a sort of "good housekeeping seal" for certain religious organizations. Yet PTL had been a member of ECFA during the very time Bakker was committing a massive wire and mail fraud. Was the ECFA aware of this fraud? Did the ECFA fulfill its obligations to the contributing public?

Many questions must now be asked: How could all of this have happened? Where were the outside professionals employed by PTL? Didn't they have sufficient information to allow them to detect the fraud and other management irregularities that were taking place at PTL? Where were the corporate officers and directors during the time this massive deception was occurring? Where were the national accounting firms hired by PTL to conduct "independent" audits every year that these crimes were committed?

These questions are especially troubling given not only the magnitude of the fraud but also the fact that it continued for nearly three years. Could the oversell of lifetime partnerships have been detected early on, thus preventing literally tens of thousands of people from losing their money to the lifetime partnership program?

These are some of the questions that are addressed during the course of this book. Although I provide an analysis of various parties' actions or inactions, my primary objective is to provide you, the readers, with facts, allowing you to make your own judgment as to the propriety of what actually happened.

Consistent with that objective, the Appendix to this book contains a number of documents that were admitted into evidence in one of the civil or criminal proceedings involving PTL or Jim Bakker. As well, in each chapter I have quoted extensively from court exhibits, trial testimony, or sworn depositions.

The specific judicial proceedings to which I will refer include the criminal trials of *United States v. Bakker*, *United States v. Dortch*, *United States v. Taggart*, and *United States v. Johnson*. I have incorporated documents, depositions, and testimony from the bankruptcy proceedings involving not only the matters regarding *Heritage Village Church and Missionary Fellowship, Inc.*, but also all aspects of the related adversarial proceedings, including *Benton v. Bakker*. Finally, extensive documents that were admitted into evidence in the class action lawsuit of *Teague v. Bakker* have been examined and incorporated into the text. All the exhibits within the text and the appendices are photocopies of the original court exhibits. Due to this fact, the quality of reproduction of these exhibits may at times be less than perfect.

I have relied heavily on documents admitted into evidence because their accuracy will not fade or fail with time. I have also incorporated much sworn testimony from the various civil and criminal proceedings mentioned above. Because it was given under the penalty of perjury, these statements should be highly reliable.

I have examined not only the actions but also the ethics of various professionals who played a significant role in the business operation of PTL. Those of us who are members of the business world have an obligation to ensure that we obey the law and, in addition, strive for the highest of ethical standards.

The purpose of this book is twofold. First, it is very important that history accurately record the tragic downfall of the PTL facility. Although many good books that discuss PTL and the Bakkers have been written, nothing substantial has been written concerning the business practices of PTL. Therefore, this book critically examines PTL's finances and the actions of those professionals who had a responsibility not only to the corporation and the hundreds of thousands of PTL contributors but also to Jim Bakker.

Second, it is crucial that we learn the lessons of history. As I tell my students, one of the most important reasons to study history is to prevent certain events from being repeated. The tragedy that occurred at PTL can ill afford to happen again. Yet amazingly, as discussed in Chapter 11, there was nearly a repeat of the PTL debacle when television evangelist Morris Cerullo attempted to purchase the PTL property by soliciting his followers to buy "Gold Cards." Although no criminal charges were ever brought against Cerullo, and a federal court found no civil wrong doing, Cerullo's card program had a striking resemblance to Bakker's lifetime partnership program.

As we look at the savings and loan and the banking crises in the United States today, I believe that we may be asking some of the same questions that I have attempted to address in this book. Namely, where were the auditors and accountants and corporate officers during the entire time that these institutions were failing due to mismanagement or fraud?

I have often been asked, "How did you decide to do extensive research on the PTL case?" I respond by indicating that prior to my coming to Charleston, South Carolina, in August 1986, I had never really followed PTL. I came to Charleston after having worked in the Division of Enforcement of the U.S. Securities and Exchange Commission in Washington, D.C. In that capacity I was responsible for investigating fairly complex securities fraud cases and taking the depositions of numerous corporate officers, directors, lawyers, and public accountants. I never had any reason to examine PTL while I was at the SEC.

Bakker's resignation occurred in March 1987, and everything that I was reading in the press about how the corporation operated, including the statements that were being made by corporate officers, was totally inconsistent with anything I had ever seen or heard about during my tenure at the SEC. My interest quickly led me to a massive research project, which has allowed me to personally attend most of the civil and criminal litigation that followed the downfall of Jim Bakker and PTL. I have been able to interview and communicate with many of the key players involved in the business operation of PTL as well as those involved in both the civil and criminal litigation.

Finally, I want to make one thing very clear. There were a lot of people in the PTL organization who gave their hearts and souls to make the PTL concept and facility work. These were people who had strong religious beliefs; they were motivated by their desire to help others. The vast majority of the good that was being done at PTL was carried out by literally thousands of volunteers. The vast majority of PTL employees worked for meager salaries because of their sincere and strong religious beliefs.

While the business practices of certain professionals and of certain former PTL executives may be tainted by examining the facts relating to the business operation of PTL, this taint should in no way be inferred to also be applicable to the good and honest people who gave their all to the PTL dream.

CHAPTER TWO

□□□

Jim and Tammy:
Their Background and Beliefs

I'm sincere. I would not lie to you about anything.
James O. Bakker, "Jim Bakker Television Program," May 7, 1984

WE ARE THE PRODUCTS of our upbringing. Our childhood experiences have an impact on our actions, perceptions, and responses. To better understand why someone acts in a certain way, it is important to have some knowledge about that person's past. His or her family, home life, educational background, and past business experiences all become very relevant to this end. And in Jim Bakker's case it is also crucial to delve into his religious beliefs—or at least what he professes his beliefs to be.

Although not intended to be an exhaustive examination of the Bakkers' backgrounds or beliefs, this chapter and the next do provide a framework for analyzing what would later come to pass at PTL. It is significant that virtually all of the major events in Jim Bakker's life that I discuss in these two chapters are also included in his autobiography, *Move That Mountain*, published in 1976. Obviously, Jim Bakker thought that these events were significant as well. This, then, sets the stage for examining the fraudulent business practices at Heritage USA.

Jim Bakker was born in Muskegon, Michigan, on January 2, 1940. He was the fourth and final child of Raleigh and Furn Bakker. His father, a blue-collar worker, had a job in a piston-ring plant; his mother was a housewife. Raleigh finally retired from his job at the plant in 1969, after having worked there for 43 years. By the time that he retired from the plant, "Raleigh Bakker had never earned more than fourteen thousand dollars a year."[1]

By way of comparison, in 1986, the last full year the Bakkers were in power at PTL, it took them just four days to more than match what had taken Jim's father one full year to earn.

Jim had two older brothers, Bob and Norman, and an older sister, Donna. In his autobiography, Jim candidly writes that he "felt safe with Donna. She was my closest friend and as her little brother she tended to 'mother' me."[2] At least eight relatives of Jim and Tammy were eventually given paid positions on the PTL staff, but Donna was to be the only family member to work in the PTL corporate headquarters. This gave her access to the inner sanctum of PTL and to sensitive information concerning the Bakkers' income.

When Jim was asked on cross-examination at his trial about the large number of family members on the PTL payroll, he stated that "we believe that family should work together. We believe that is the scriptural thing to do, and that is what we were following."

Norman also ended up working at PTL; he attended virtually every day of his brother's trial. Norman was born with a small tumor on his right leg. As a result of medical treatment, his leg was stunted, and his right side weakened. When Jim was nine years old, Norman had to have his right leg amputated above the knee.

Bob was the oldest child in the Bakker family, and although he was rebellious as a youth, he graduated from North Central Bible College, the same school Jim would attend in later years. He was more than 15 years older than Jim, who describes him as the "brother I had never really known."[3] After serving as the pastor of a small church for several years, Bob Bakker would eventually leave his wife and reject the Christianity he once professed. He died from a rare kidney disease in February 1973.

Jim saw his brother Bob as someone who had natural skills and tremendous potential—certainly much more than Jim believed he himself had. Once it became clear that his brother had abandoned his religious activities, Jim felt it became incumbent upon him to attempt to pick up where his brother left off.

In his autobiography Jim Bakker describes in a very unflattering way his childhood home in Muskegon Heights, Michigan; he remembers it as a cement block structure that looked like an oversized Florida citrus fruit. According to Bakker, "the house had been painted with what daddy thought would be buff-colored paint. It turned out to be orange!"[4] His embarrassment about the house even extended to asking his friends to drop him off several blocks away so they wouldn't see it.

If his family house was an embarrassment, his elementary school experiences did even less to raise his self-esteem. Having never performed well in grammar school, Jim was labeled a "slow learner" by his teachers. Because he was such a poor speller, other students did not want him on their spelling team. Jim describes his inferiority complex in the following fashion:

> It seemed like anything I had was inferior to what other kids had. Year after year, I wore the same tattered blue baseball jacket with prominent white stitching, until the stitching unraveled completely. From the orange house to my dilapidated jacket to my poor school grades, I became filled with deep-seated feelings of inferiority.[5]

Jim's suggestion of a poor, if not impoverished, upbringing would be echoed later in televised appearances and published material in which he would recall his humble beginning.

The PTL employees who became aware of the Bakkers' excesses cited their "humble" background in an attempt to justify what would have certainly appeared to be inappropriate expenditures for ministers. As one of the former PTL bodyguards told me: "the Bakkers grew up poor and never had much money early in life. When the money started rolling in at PTL, they just did not know how to handle it." Although this reasoning probably does not justify their lifestyle, it certainly does not justify the fraud ultimately committed by Jim Bakker. Rationalizations such as this one, however, did help to make what one saw on TV every day more palatable in comparison to what one saw of the Bakkers' lifestyle when the cameras were not around. And most people on the PTL staff wanted to believe that what the Bakkers were doing was good and in the name of religion.

By the time Jim Bakker got to junior high and high school, things had started changing for him. He found two new interests: photography and speech. His interest in these important and powerful forms of communication would serve him well in later years.

Although in his autobiography he describes himself as a shy, lonely boy during these years, his high school photography teacher remembered him as outgoing and someone with an inborn talent for photography. Throughout Jim Bakker's professional career, many others would also be amazed at his skilled use of communications media.

Jim enjoyed speech class so much that he persuaded his father to buy him a reel-to-reel tape recorder, which he carried to and from school so as to be able to work on his diction. He was a perfectionist.

Jim Bakker went on to own a hand-held, miniature tape recorder at PTL, but he did not use it to practice his diction. Instead, he barked orders into it. These orders were then transcribed and, as discussed in future chapters, carried out without question. As employees at PTL often said, "Jim Bakker knows of every blade of grass that grows at PTL."

The comments that Jim Bakker made on his PTL tape recorder showed a wide variety of interests. They were obviously spontaneous and sometimes dictatorial. Some examples are:

> Would you make sure that all the housekeepers know that my good suits are to be hung on wooden hangers. They've got them on metal hangers. And they've been hanging them backwards on the hangers, which make the back of them pop out. Somebody's just going to have to give them a lesson on how to take care of clothes.
>
> I must find my bifocal glasses. Please everybody look for them. I can't even find one pair of them now. Shirley, [Jim Bakker's secretary], get yourself a new three-way bulb for your lamp on your desk, please. Just call maintenance and they'll do that.
>
> Find out why they took the air conditioning out of Jamie's tree house and get them to put it back in immediately.

If Jim Bakker had a problem with being shy or having a poor self-image in elementary school, he was well on his way to overcoming those problems while he was in high school. After being asked to emcee the photography club's annual dance, he became known as *the* disc jockey to have at school functions. Jim Bakker describes himself as having been "obsessed with popularity" in high school and adds that he "would do almost anything to get it."[6] His popularity increased to the extent that 400 kids from his high school, along with the current Miss Michigan, came over to the new Bakker home after a variety show.

The Bakker family had moved, and in his autobiography Jim mentions that his new house had formerly been a lumber mansion; it was located on a boulevard where a number of millionaires had once lived. As if to mitigate that fact, Bakker quickly adds that "over the years, the houses had decreased in value and now were modestly priced."[7]

It was also in high school that Jim had a religious experience that led him into the ministry. One wintry Sunday night in 1958, he took a girlfriend for a ride in his father's 1952 Cadillac. This joy ride occurred during the end of the Sunday night church service, at the time of the altar call. When they returned to the church, the big Cadillac hit what Jim thought was the curb but was instead a little boy. Jim got out of the car to see the arms of the little boy go limp. His lungs had been crushed, having been run over by both wheels of the car. Jim thought he had killed the boy. A police car arrived and raced off with the boy in what Jim thought would be a "futile trip to the hospital."

He went home that night totally distraught. As Jim tells the story, he continued to read his Bible and was repeatedly attracted to one verse: "And he commanded us to preach . . ." (Acts 10:42).

The little boy survived. This is the event that Jim Bakker points to as his initial calling into the ministry by God. He considered the boy's survival a miracle, and he went on to preach.

Jim followed in his brother's footsteps by attending North Central Bible College in Minneapolis, Minnesota. He writes that when his high school friends learned of his plans to do so, they said, "Yeah, I can just see Jim Bakker's church now. He'll probably have a full orchestra in it. Man, that'll be some church."[8] Those words turned out to be somewhat prophetic, given the music ministry that would later exist at PTL.

One day in September 1960, during his second year at North Central Bible College, Jim Bakker met his future wife, Tammy Faye LaValley:

> One day I passed a girl in the school's hallway. . . . my neck almost broke as I turned to watch her walk away. She was absolutely the cutest girl I had ever seen. . . . Even without makeup, she was a little doll . . . She was engaged and the wedding date had already been set.[9]

Eventually, Tammy broke her engagement, and Jim began dating her. It was a fast romance, and despite Jim's parents' objections, they walked down the aisle together on April 1, 1961. Raleigh and Furn Bakker had hoped that their son would complete his course of study before he got married.

Jim had to endure a meager lifestyle immediately before their marriage and thereafter. For example, Tammy had to lend Jim 50 dollars for the down payment for her engagement ring. And there were no pictures of the wedding because the minister's camera did not work, and they couldn't afford a honeymoon trip.

Another example of the Bakkers' modest beginnings is Jim's story of how he met Tammy's parents.

According to Jim, they had been married a few weeks when Tammy became upset because she realized that he had never met her parents. At the time, he thought she was upset because of their tight finances. Jim explains that until then he had believed Tammy to be an only child. Instead, it turned out that she had seven brothers and sisters. Although he claims he was under this impression because Tammy always looked so well groomed, he never indicates whether or not Tammy had actually said anything that would have led him to this belief. In any case, Jim went to visit Tammy's family in the small, paper-mill town of International Falls, Minnesota. It was only then that he realized the house had an outdoor toilet. This is an area of the country where the winter temperature can reach −40°F.

If the outdoor toilet wasn't primitive enough, Jim tells of taking a bath during his first visit to Tammy's house:

> Tammy brought in two large galvanized tubs filled with steaming water. I just looked at them.
> "What do I do with them?" I scratched my head.
> "Silly," she laughed, "you bathe in them."
> I had never had any experience with such things having been accustomed to the worldly luxuries of a bathtub. So I promptly sat my bottom down in one tub and my feet in the other and started bathing.
> Tammy laughed so hard that tears streamed down her face. "No," she howled, "you sponge off. You don't get in the tub. You wash in one tub of water and rinse with the other."[10]

This story that Jim and Tammy have shared can be viewed in two different ways. First, it shows how they both had real hard-life experiences, and that someone listening to or reading about the Bakkers' life stories could come away with the impression that they grew up in a naive, sheltered world. This background information on the Bakkers can be presented in such a way as to not only be disarming but also displace any skepticism that a listener or reader might have concerning the Bakkers. Consequently, in the eyes of the people the Bakkers were ministering to, the Bakkers could be seen as someone you could believe in, trust, and associate with. These are, obviously, very important characteristics for someone in the ministry.

On the other hand, as Jim Bakker reached high school and Bible College he was a very popular student. He was fortunate to have grown up in at least a middle-class neighborhood with family, friends, and teachers who took a special interest in him. To that extent, one could argue that Jim Bakker's childhood was indistinguishable and no different from the childhood of millions of other adolescents.

Once Jim and Tammy married, their formal education ended. They were forced to leave North Central Bible College because it had a rule prohibiting students from marrying while attending school. Jim Bakker, therefore, had completed only a year and a half of college by the time he got married, during which time he did not take any courses in business. Although a diploma is certainly no prerequisite to being successful in any chosen profession, including business or the ministry, a structured education does help provide a sound basis for the decisions that are made and practices that are implemented. Divorced from any further formalized education, the Bakkers would now only receive on-the-job training, which began when they were hired as youth directors at the Minneapolis Evangelistic Auditorium.

After taking on the job, Jim Bakker asked the co-pastor of the ministry a very basic question: "What is the key to success as an evangelist?" Bakker records in his autobiography what he considered a valuable response: "If you want to be a successful evangelist and have churches call you, you must get results. It's nice to have a theory, but only results will demonstrate the value of the theory."[11]

That advice, and its literal application, stayed with Jim Bakker. Everything he did was with an expectation of results. As will be seen with his sale of lifetime partnerships, these results were often gotten at the expense of the truth. There was a time at the PTL ministry when results were measured in terms of the goals that had been set for the sale of lifetime partnerships.

Another very significant event occurred while Jim was still in Minnesota. The Bakkers were given an opportunity to preach in a revival at a church in Burlington, North Carolina, in hopes of raising money for a mission trip to South America.

The Bakkers sold some furniture, consolidated their outstanding bills, and had just enough money to buy a bus ticket to get from Minneapolis to the church in Burlington. It was at that time that the other co-pastor of the Minneapolis Evangelistic Auditorium told Jim that he would be too tired to conduct the revival if he took the bus. Saying, "I think the Lord can take care of this," he reached into his pocket and gave Jim enough money for two first-class plane tickets to North Carolina.[12]

Although this would certainly appear, at first blush, to be an innocent and harmless gesture, an attempt by the co-pastor to reward his hard-working assistant, it may have sent the wrong message to Jim and Tammy Bakker.

Rather than living and exemplifying a modest and humble lifestyle, the Bakkers tried to do everything first-class. The austere upbringing that Jim and Tammy both originally experienced in their youth seemed to have been forgotten. The Bakkers would expect the religious organizations of which they were a part to meet more and more of their worldly needs.

The lifestyle that the Bakkers wanted was consistent with their belief in prosperity theology. Very simply stated, prosperity theology posits that God will make one rich if one will first give him money as a token of faith. Luke 6:38 is one of the verses cited to support prosperity theology: "Give that it may be given to you."

Prosperity theology justified asking the faithful to give so that they might receive. It also helped the Bakkers to justify what would eventually become an unbelievably lavish lifestyle. Prosperity theology allows its proponents to be beneficiaries; that is, they can demonstrate that the theology works. If ministers or other proponents of prosperity theology are seen to be rich, then their theology must have a basis in truth. The belief in prosperity theology became a subtle, if not central, part of the Bakker message.

Jim Bakker soon realized that not only is truth important, but also the public's perceptions of what the truth is. As Jim tells the story:

> A few months after I had preached in one small town, word filtered back that we had received an extra large financial gift from the couple with whom Tammy and I had been staying while there. The money was supposed to have been in addition to the church's love gift. I was stunned by the news since it wasn't true and the implication was that Tammy and I had taken advantage of this elderly couple. . . . That established a precedent for Tammy and me. Never again would we stay in the homes of church members while we were leading meetings. We would stay instead with the pastors—and only visit a private home when the pastor accompanied us.[13]

The need to avoid even the appearance of impropriety cannot be understated, and the Bakkers knew this. When one assumes a position as a public figure, there is a certain amount of loss of privacy and a higher level of public scrutiny. This is especially true for televangelists. The Bakkers were well aware of their need to be sensitive to problems as well as to perceptions. While at PTL the Bakkers either forgot or chose to ignore this very basic principle.

In his on-the-job training, Jim Bakker learned another skill that he would use repeatedly at PTL—the concept of crisis fundraising. If everything is going well and there are no problems, there is a reluctance to provide charitable donations. If, however, there is a crisis, especially one that threatens the very existence of the ministry, then the donations roll in. Sometimes the crisis would take the form of a personal misfortune; on other occasions a crisis would have to be fabricated—or at least exaggerated—to ensure the flow of donations.

A classic example of Jim Bakker using crisis fundraising occurred in the early 1960s. The Bakkers put a down payment on a 28-foot travel trailer to use in their revival travels. The trailer was pulled by the couple's 1959 Cadillac. While traveling to a revival, the trailer came loose and slammed into a utility pole.

At the revival service the next day, the Bakkers relayed their misfortune to the congregation. Tammy tried to sing, but after one verse she was too shocked to continue; Jim writes that "she laid her head on her accordion and began sobbing. . . . All over the auditorium, ladies popped open their purses in search of tissues while men coughed uncomfortably in the sensitive atmosphere."[14]

Jim Bakker writes in his autobiography that he and Tammy really did not care for that particular model trailer anyway because it had square corners. They had originally wanted a trailer with rounded corners, which are more aerodynamically suitable. The dealer ultimately admitted liability, and the Bakkers received a replacement trailer with rounded corners—for free.

These types of personal crises would be presented again and again to the PTL viewing audience, who would be told of an imminent financial disaster that could only be forestalled by their responding immediately. The financial crisis would often be wrapped around the selling of lifetime partnerships, which would make the contributors' sacrifice much less painful. This was a sales technique that Bakker would use again and again at PTL.

Of course this raises some very important questions. Was there really a financial crisis at PTL? If there was a crisis, were there other ways to alleviate it? And if there was no real crisis, then where were the other corporate executives and what was their response to the statements that Bakker was making to the contributing public?

Jim and Tammy continued their road show of revivals and added a new twist to their sermons by using puppets. Tammy had developed the idea of having a puppet ministry aimed primarily at children. The "Susie Moppet" puppet family turned out to be a real hit with the kids on the revival circuit, and it was also therapeutic for Tammy to be able to express her emotions through her puppet, Susie Moppet. The puppets also landed Jim and Tammy with an opportunity to join Pat Robertson and the Christian Broadcasting Network (CBN).

By September 1965, Jim and Tammy had acquiesced to Pat Robertson's request to join him at CBN. Robertson, the son of Virginia's senior senator and himself a future presidential candidate, had just started broadcasting out of a shabby, rundown area of Portsmouth, Virginia. Robertson wanted the Bakkers to do their puppet show on his newly formed and developing CBN station. Bakker made his acceptance expressly conditional on his being able to do a late-night talk show; he indicated that the talk show was very important to him because he had already questioned why Christians couldn't have a talk show similar to Johnny Carson's secular "Tonight Show."

Much later in his career, while under investigation by a federal grand jury, Jim Bakker would again rely on his Johnny Carson analogy. He compared Carson's schedule and salary with his own schedule and compensation package, contending that this provided sufficient justification for the compensation he received from the PTL, a tax-exempt organization.

Jim Bakker's work at CBN would eventually propel him into his position at PTL. However, several events transpired at the Portsmouth, Virginia, operation that would again effect the business practices and the mind-set of the Bakkers at PTL.

Although CBN was a struggling station and the Bakkers were only making $150 a week, that did not deter them from desiring secular comforts. Because they would be doing the Lord's work in the community, Jim reasoned that they "should live somewhere nice."

Consequently, he and Tammy inquired about living in an exclusive high-rise complex near the Elizabeth River in Portsmouth. Although Jim originally wondered whether they could afford such an expensive apartment, he "felt God leading" them there. They ultimately rented an efficiency at $150 a month. However, it was not long until Tammy expressed embarrassment about living in a mere seventh-floor efficiency. As Jim told the story concerning their move up the social ladder:

> The eighteenth floor was the most expensive in the high rise. We were perfectly satisfied in our efficiency on the seventh floor, but within a year God had changed our financial situation so radically that we were able to move to the eighteenth floor ourselves.[15]

The Bakkers had arrived in September, but by November CBN was making plans for its first telethon in an attempt to reach its budget of $10,000 a month. CBN may have been struggling, and contributors may have been asked to make personal sacrifices by giving, but that certainly did not stop the Bakkers from seeking the luxuries of the secular world. Such spending was also consistent with prosperity theology, and what Bakker contended was the will of God.

Bakker now had a first-class house to match that first-class ticket he had received years earlier. The lifestyle illustrated by this event would continue as the Bakkers bought home after home with the financial assistance of the PTL corporation.

If Bakker's desire for a more affluent lifestyle was solidified while at CBN, then his use of crisis fundraising was likewise solidified. In fact, Bakker appears to have perfected, if not mastered, the technique while he was at CBN.

Prior to Bakker's joining the CBN staff, its television crew had been instructed not to tell the viewing audience that the station was in debt to the tune of more than $40,000. Jim Bakker did not agree with that philosophy. Instead, near the end of what had been a fairly uneventful telethon, Bakker, on camera, broke down and began crying. "Our entire purpose had been to serve the Lord Jesus Christ through radio and television," he said, "but we've fallen far short. We need $10,000 a month or we'll be off the air."[16] As the tears ran down his face, Bakker told the viewing audience that unless the funds were raised, Christian television would be all over and gone.

People responded massively by phone, and the CBN studio was filled with people who could not get through the phone lines. The telethon finally ended at 2:30 A.M., but not before all of the past bills of CBN had been paid, and the next year's budget had been fully underwritten.

Jim recognized what he believed to be a God-given talent to raise money:

> From the moment that I stepped before a television camera at CBN, God began to anoint me to raise money for Christian television. I realized it the night I wept during the first "700 Club" telethon. Many times since then, God similarly anointed me.[17]

While at CBN, Jim was given the chance to develop the late-night program he had requested prior to his accepting the position at the network. The first program, titled the "700 Club," was aired at 10:00 P.M. on November 28, 1966.

The program served as the prototype for the PTL program. The talk show featured guests who were often other revivalists passing through the Portsmouth, Virginia, area. Sometimes the show would even include interviews with the television camera operators.

The show was certainly not as sophisticated as the television program that would be aired from PTL, but it did continue to give Jim valuable on-the-job training.

While at CBN, Jim and Tammy both had health and emotional problems. These problems would resurface not only during their years at PTL but also during Jim's criminal trial. While at CBN, Jim Bakker nearly had a nervous breakdown, which was attributed to his relentless efforts and responsibilities at CBN. He was only 29 years old and realized that he was much too young to be having such serious problems with his nerves.

While Jim was recovering, Tammy went to the doctor for a physical. Surprisingly, the doctor recommended that she get pregnant to get Jim's mind off his work. The Bakkers had a daughter, Tammy Sue, and immediately afterwards Tammy began experiencing emotional problems of her own.

At first the medical personnel thought Tammy was reacting adversely to drugs. She thought that spiders were crawling over the drapes and that there were mice under the bed. Tammy would later say that she could not have licked this problem herself; she needed psychiatric help.

While looking in the phone book for competent psychiatric care, she heard the Lord speak: "Tammy, let me be your psychiatrist." Tammy phoned Jim, relayed this experience, and then determined that she would weather the storm.

By November 8, 1972, Jim's relationship had deteriorated with Pat Robertson, and Jim felt he was being led by God to resign his position at CBN. Robertson had become tired of Bakker's bickering with staff and what he saw as immaturity on the part of the Bakkers. According to Bakker, Robertson told him that he did not want him to leave and that the board of directors had just voted him a pay raise.

The decision was final, and that night the Bakkers watched taped reruns of the "700 Club" while they contemplated their next move. Thus, the Bakkers ended seven years of service that had given them valuable experience in religious broadcasting.

The Bakkers would now be off to California and then to Charlotte, North Carolina, and PTL.

Notes

1. Charles E. Shepard, *Forgiven* (New York: Atlantic Monthly Press, 1989), 7.
2. Jim Bakker with Robert Paul Lamb, *Move That Mountain* (Plainfield, N.J.: Logos International, 1976), 2.
3. *Ibid.*, 98.
4. *Ibid.*, 3.
5. *Ibid.*
6. *Ibid.*, 6.
7. *Ibid.*
8. *Ibid.*, 17.
9. *Ibid.*, 19–20.
10. *Ibid.*, 26.
11. *Ibid.*, 27–28.
12. *Ibid.*, 31.
13. *Ibid.*, 37, 38.
14. *Ibid.*, 45.
15. *Ibid.*, 56.
16. *Ibid.*, 58.
17. *Ibid.*, 63.

CHAPTER THREE

□□□

Rags to Riches and the Birth of PTL

You can't lie to people to send you money—it's that simple.
What unfolded before you over the past month was a tale of
corruption—immense corruption. . . . What was revealed here
was that Mr. Bakker was a world-class master of lies and half-
truths.

Deborah Smith, Trial Attorney, Criminal Fraud Section,
U.S. Department of Justice, in her closing argument
to the jury in *United States v. Bakker.*

ONE OF THE FIRST THINGS JIM BAKKER did after he left CBN was to
establish a nonprofit corporation to house his ministry. The Bakkers,
along with some friends from Charlotte met in Portsmouth, Virginia,
in late 1972 and formed the Trinity Broadcasting Systems [TBS],
which was the forerunner to PTL.

On December 7, 1972, TBS opened its first bank account in Charlotte, North Carolina, with a $52 deposit. Amazingly, it would be from
this modest deposit that PTL got its beginning—and from which
hundreds of millions of dollars would ultimately pour into Heritage
USA.

TBS, in its embryonic stage, was incorporated as a nonprofit organization on February 21, 1973. Included within the legal documents
filed with the state of South Carolina was the stated purpose of TBS
to engage in all forms of broadcast activity of a religious nature.

By April 8, 1973, TBS had applied for tax-exempt status. The IRS
issued a letter dated May 17, 1973, recognizing TBS as a religious
organization exempt from federal income taxes pursuant to the IRS
Code Section 501(c)3; this letter also advised TBS that if its sources

of support, purposes, charter, or method of operation were to change, it would need to inform the IRS so that the agency could consider what effect that might have on its tax-exempt status. This is the same tax-exempt status that PTL would ultimately lose because of what the IRS found to be excessive compensation being paid to Jim and Tammy Bakker.

The Bakkers did not immediately go to Charlotte to begin the PTL ministry. Rather, they traveled for several months, during which time they renewed an old friendship with Paul and Jan Crouch. Paul Crouch had been assistant pastor of Bakker's home church in Muskegon, Michigan and was now working as general manager of a Christian television station in Los Angeles, California.

Jim indicated to Crouch his dislike of being on the road all the time. After learning that their ideas concerning Christian television were compatible, the two friends discussed the possibility of starting a new television venture in California. It was ultimately agreed that Crouch would run the business operation and Bakker would be responsible for the ministering aspects of the television program.

Bakker wanted to continue with the same type of show format he had done while at CBN; that is, Jim Bakker would host a Christian talk show that would serve as the benchmark for the newly formed network. The talk show would combine interviews, music, and appeals for viewers to call the network to make known their prayer requests or special needs. Viewers could also, of course, make financial pledges to the network.

The Crouches and the Bakkers came up with the name of the talk show: "Praise the Lord." They also agreed that the program would be known by a shorter code name, PTL, so as not to offend or turn off nonreligious viewers. It was also decided that Jim Bakker would be president of TBS and that the Crouches would head up operations in Los Angeles.

Crouch and Bakker were ultimately able to make the necessary arrangements for operating the station from Santa Ana, California. They were almost ready to begin their broadcasting near the end of May 1973 when, as Jim explains, "we realized there was a missing ingredient in our plans: no television cameras!"[1]

This is a peculiar admission by someone who had just spent seven years at CBN. It also, of course, speaks volumes about the degree of business sophistication and long-range (not to mention short-range) planning skills that Bakker possessed.

When the television studio was finally operational, it was decided that Jim Bakker would host the television program which would be named "The PTL Club." It originated from KBSA, Channel 46 in Santa Ana, and tapes of the show were duplicated and sent to WRET, Channel 36 in Charlotte. The tapes were aired three days a week for two hours. The remaining slots were filled by a Charlotte-based replica of the "The PTL Club".

Only one year after the departure from CBN, the same dispute that had developed between the Bakkers and Pat Robertson developed between the Bakkers and the Crouches. Although Paul Crouch has been reluctant to publicly discuss the details concerning the falling out between the two families, it seems that Jim Bakker wanted the ministry to expand much more quickly than did the more cautious Crouch.

The Bakkers (and a large percentage of the staff) resigned and left TBS in November of 1973, which allowed them to prove themselves once again to be innovative entrepreneurs. Jim had always maintained contact with the folks involved with the Charlotte version of "The PTL Club" by making occasional guest appearances on WRET, and so in January 1974 the Bakkers were asked to handle their annual fundraising effort. The Bakkers arrived on January 13, 1974, and expected to be in Charlotte for only two weeks. They were well received by a crowd of over 2,400 in Charlotte's Ovens Auditorium, and as a result they called several of the former TBS staff members who had resigned with Bakker and encouraged them to come to Charlotte.

As Bakker would later say in a PTL press release concerning his opening night in Charlotte: "I don't believe I've ever had as exciting a night as that. The tumors and cancers just dropped off bodies that night as we prayed. It was as if God had said, 'How much clearer can I make it Jim? Stay here.' "

Although their plan was to stay in Charlotte for the next six months and help the station build a new studio, Jim and Tammy Bakker ended up staying for over 13 years. All of the apparent successes of the future were now just a matter of time.

The first stop on the road to building the PTL empire was a converted furniture showroom on Charlotte's East Independence Boulevard. Jim Moss, a layman who operated a successful janitorial firm and eventually rose to the position of executive vice-president of PTL, said, "We started from nothing. WRET-TV was the only station we were on and they advanced us air time." PTL occupied the converted showroom from February 1974 until July 1976 during which time the network expanded to include 46 stations.

The growth of PTL was phenomenal. Viewers not only in Charlotte but also around the country were responding to the televised pleas being made by Jim Bakker. Television affiliates were more than happy to sell early morning air time to PTL, and although PTL's viewing audience was relatively small from a market share standpoint, PTL programming was now being broadcast to a faithful following across the country.

PTL had outgrown its furniture showroom and was ready to move again. In September 1975 it paid $375,000 for a 25-acre tract of land, complete with an elegant three-story mansion built in the Georgian style. The mansion quickly became the site of PTL's executive offices. The question remained as to what to do with the rest of the land. According to Jim Bakker, the answer came from God.

"I've got it, I've got it," Jim remembers shouting from his sleep, "God wants us to build a village, a miniature version of Colonial Williamsburg."[2]

Bakker broke ground for what he would call Heritage Village, an ambitious $4 million project, on October 30, 1975. Construction soon began on its International Counseling and Broadcast Center. The steeple on the church-styled studio was really a 102-foot broadcast antenna designed to beam what was now called "The PTL Club" television program to WRET, which in turn broadcast the program to the surrounding area. Bakker's television program would be called, at various times over the years, "The PTL Club", "The Jim Bakker Show," and "The Jim and Tammy Show."

Plans were also made to construct a large complex of mock Williamsburg–style buildings on the property, all of which were to be connected by "prayer paths and formal gardens."

To expedite construction, workers used a giant 200- by 300-foot polyester fiber tent stretched over the construction site. According to the contractor, this was the first time a tent like that had been used in North Carolina, and as a result the studio building went up in record time.

In a PTL press release, Jim Bakker stated that "part of the miracle of PTL's construction project is that cash has been paid on it. We haven't financed one penny of construction on this building. . . . and anybody connected with business today will tell you that's a feat unheard of."

Bakker made similar statements again and again when PTL was making its final move from Heritage Village to the 2200-acre Heritage USA facility. Certainly this representation would seem to provide comfort and a sense of financial stability to PTL contributors. As discussed in the next chapter, Bakker falsely claimed that the facilities at Heritage USA were debt free and tried to explain at his trial that when he made these statements on national television, he believed them to be true.

The new studio was dedicated at Heritage Village on July 4, 1976, the nation's bicentennial. The success of PTL now took on a tangible form. Viewers and the studio audience could see how Bakker had transformed the property, and how everything had been built so quickly. The phone counselors, who were virtually all volunteers, gave reports to the television audience of miraculous healings that were being called in by television viewers and also recorded the pledges and contributions that were now rolling in. Jim often said that God's hand was behind all the good works PTL was doing.

PTL had truly come of its own. It was recognized not only in Charlotte but also within the evangelical movement in the United States. By July 1976, PTL had a network of approximately 70 television stations and about 20 cable TV systems broadcasting its daily "PTL Club" in the United States, Canada, and Mexico. PTL's growth could also clearly be seen in increased contributions. Between April 1975 and March 1976 PTL had received almost $5.5 million; during the previous year it had been given a mere $817,000. PTL's net worth had increased from $129,000 to more than $2 million.

By fall of 1977 "The PTL Club" was being broadcast in 11 major cities in the United States including New York; Washington D.C.; Philadelphia; Denver; and Los Angeles. It was also in 1977 that PTL and Jim Bakker signed an agreement for the purchase of equipment that would offer the capability of sending a television signal from Charlotte to any point in the world by way of satellite. The timing was to PTL's advantage, because television stations were just beginning to make the switch from video tapes to satellite equipment. Ultimately, the FCC awarded PTL a private satellite broadcasting network license, and on April 3, 1978, PTL hooked up to a $1 million satellite system that allowed for around-the-clock religious programming.

This was very significant for PTL. The corporation could broadcast whatever events it desired and at the time it elected; the balance of available air time could be sold, at a profit, to selected religious organizations. This arrangement would also allow PTL to purchase air time from local television stations, and thus "The PTL Club" could be seen not only on the satellite network but also on independent affiliated stations.

Jim Bakker testified that PTL soon outgrew the Hertiage Village property: "we were no longer able to even seat the studio audience in the studio and the inefficiency of having staff located in seven locations throughout the city was taking its toll as well. We realized we would have to do something." The "something" Bakker was referring to was to relocate once again.

Prior to relocating, the Charlotte operation made a total and complete break with its California roots on November 16, 1976. PTL had its corporate charter amended to reflect its legal name change from Trinity Broadcasting Systems, Inc., to Heritage Village Church and Missionary Fellowship, Inc. (HVCMF).

The corporate charter was also amended to reflect the purposes of the newly named corporation, which were as follows: (1) to establish and maintain a church, and (2) to engage in all types of religious activity, including evangelism; religious instruction; publishing and distributing Bibles and other religious publications, missionary work, both domestic and foreign; and establishing and operating Bible schools and Bible training centers.

Amending the corporate charter to reflect a wide variety of religious purposes was essential in obtaining a tax-exempt status from the IRS. Being able "to engage in all types of religious activity" certainly gave the corporation some latitude as to what it could and couldn't do. Although Jim Bakker interpreted the language in the corporate charter very broadly, the IRS would eventually take a much more restrictive view.

On January 2, 1978, Jim Bakker's thirty-eighth birthday, PTL broke ground for its final move to the Heritage USA facility. The events leading up to the final move are again probably best described in Jim Bakker's sworn testimony in his criminal trial:

> Well, as we began to realize we had to leave Heritage Village, that it would not contain the ministry, we wanted to find a piece of property that would be big enough this time that we wouldn't have to move again. We wanted to find something that would contain all of the parts of the ministry and we could bring everybody together and that it would be large enough to fulfill the vision that God had laid on my heart, and the vision for a people place that would be like the old-fashion campgrounds, only be modern and up to date. . . . I called it in the early days, a Total Living Center, a place for the old and a place for the young, and to bring the camp meeting into the 21st Century, and that was my vision and dream from God.

Although the September 12, 1984, minutes of the PTL board of directors reflected an offer to buy Heritage Village for $13 million, the facility was eventually sold for approximately $5 million in 1985.

The land that would become the site of Heritage USA is located on the border between North and South Carolina. It was an abandoned industrial park with three artesian wells, a water tower, and a few rough roads. Initially, PTL purchased roughly 1200 acres, but eventually owned approximately 2200 acres. PTL was now prepared to begin a massive construction and capital development project.

The initial facility at Heritage USA was to be the Total Living Center, which would be used as a training site for the growing ranks of PTL volunteers who served as phone counselors and in other ministering capacities. It would be the hub of PTL's worldwide evangelistic efforts.

Also in the works was the Heritage University and School of Evangelism, which Bakker expected to become a four-year degree-awarding institution. "This is the most important project in PTL's history," said Jim Bakker as he watched construction workers stake off footing for the first classroom building. Bakker, who had assumed the position of president of Heritage University, announced in March 1978 that he expected classes to start the following December.

Heritage University never fully materialized, and the three-story, pyramid-shaped edifice that was to have housed the first student classrooms was eventually made into the PTL executive office building. Officially named the World Outreach Center, it opened in the spring of 1980.

What did materialize was Fort Heritage Center, a retreat with 1600 campground sites, as well as facilities for swimming, tennis, and other outdoor recreational activities. Chalets were built, as were eating establishments and an open-air amphitheater. A state-of-the-art television studio was built, along with what became known as the "Big Barn Auditorium." The Barn seated over 2,000 people and was the site of the Sunday morning Heritage Village church worship services and of camp meeting services. It was also the site of some of Jim Bakker's most successful telethons.

The most elaborate and expensive projects to be undertaken at PTL were yet to come. The building and promotion of the 504-room Heritage Grand Hotel and the 500-room Heritage Towers Hotel was on the horizon of Jim Bakker's plans. These were to be the projects that would set into motion the $158 million wire and mail fraud committed at PTL.

Although the legal, business, and ethical considerations concerning PTL's response to charges made by Jessica Hahn will be discussed in subsequent chapters, it was in 1980 that Jim Bakker had his one-time sexual encounter with Jessica Hahn. Their versions of what actually happened differ remarkably, but what is uncontested is that on December 6, 1980, Jim Bakker had a sexual encounter with Jessica Hahn in Room 538 of the Sheraton Sand Key Resort in Clearwater Beach, Florida. This "indiscretion," as Bakker described it in 1987 would eventually come back to haunt him.

However, his affair with Hahn would not be a principal cause of the demise of Jim Bakker's ministry. Shady business practices, especially the decision to exceed promised limits in lodging facilities at PTL, would send Jim Bakker to jail.

Notes

1. Jim Baker with Robert Paul Lamb, *Move That Mountain* (Plainfield, N.J.: Logos International, 1976), 121.
2. *Ibid.*, 171.

CHAPTER FOUR

□ □ □

"Four Days and Three Nights"

I was going to say please stop giving. I can't say that. I need
help.

James O. Bakker, "Jim Bakker Television Program,"
August 23, 1984

WHEN JIM BAKKER resigned from his position as president and chair
of the board of Heritage Village Church and Missionary Fellowship,
Inc., on March 19, 1987, he made the following statement by telephone to the *Charlotte Observer*: "I categorically deny that I've ever
sexually assaulted or harassed anyone. . . . I was wickedly manipulated
by treacherous former friends."

With those words spoken, he ended his reign at PTL. This marked
not only the beginning of the public demise of Jim Bakker but also
the beginning of the end of the PTL organization.

Although at first blush it may appear that Jim Bakker's admission
concerning Jessica Hahn caused the downfall of both Bakker and PTL,
nothing could be further from the truth. The failure of the PTL organization was not caused by the alleged one-time indiscretion of its
leader back in 1980.

PTL's own gross mismanagement and lack of ability to conserve
and wisely use corporate assets certainly contributed to its collapse.
However, the downfall of Bakker and PTL was primarily caused by
the massive wire and mail fraud committed at PTL by Jim Bakker

and Richard Dortch, PTL's executive vice-president. This fraud, which involved a massive oversale of lodging partnerships that eventually raised at least $158 million for PTL, began on July 7, 1984, and did not end until May 31, 1987.

As a result, Bakker and three of his top aides went to prison, and the actions (and inactions) of many distinguished business people and two highly respected national accounting firms were called into question.

False statements and material omissions were often made by Bakker and Dortch concerning various "lifetime partnership" programs. These fraudulent representations were made from January 7, 1984 until May 1987, not only in mailed solicitations but also on PTL's Satellite Network.

The PTL Satellite Network began 24-hour Christian programming on April 3, 1978. Eventually, over 1,300 cable systems carried the PTL Satellite Network into more than 12 million homes, and about 2 million backyard "dish" owners could receive it as well. The PTL Satellite Network was at various times known as The PTL Television Network and The Inspirational Network.

The PTL Satellite Network originated television programs featuring Jim and Tammy Bakker. As previously mentioned, this program was entitled "The PTL Club," but over the years the name changed to "The Jim Bakker Show" and "The Jim and Tammy Show." This program, along with various telethons, provided the vehicle for Bakker and others to consummate the lodging partnership frauds.

These programs were broadcast live on the PTL Satellite Network and to affiliate stations. Other stations, especially in the earlier years, received them by means of a tape delay. Ultimately, Jim and Tammy Bakker's television show saturated 95 percent of the continental United States and also reached audiences in Canada, the U.S. Virgin Islands, Alaska, and Hawaii.

Television programming was the lifeline that allowed PTL to have direct contact with its financial supporters. It was in this setting that the PTL empire—at least outwardly—flourished.

What follows is a factual chronology of the four major frauds that occurred at PTL: the Grand Hotel Partnership Fraud, the Towers Hotel Partnership Fraud, the Family Heritage Club (Bunkhouse) Partnership Fraud, and the 1100 Club Partnership Fraud. These promotional stategies were presented in brochures mailed to hundreds of thousands of people and were also explained, in detail, to the viewing audience over PTL's satellite and affiliate viewing stations.

The Grand Hotel Partnership Fraud

> Man, you can't beat that. You can't lose on it.
>
> Tammy Bakker, "Jim Bakker Television Program," February 20, 1984

In November of 1983, Jim Bakker unveiled to the PTL executives a plan to build a 504-room hotel on the Heritage USA property. Funding for this project was to be obtained by offering "lifetime partnerships" in the hotel, and up to one-half of the rooms in the hotel were to be set aside for use by lifetime partners. That is, for a one-time "gift" to the ministry of $1,000, donors and their immediate families would be able to come to Heritage USA and stay in a first-class, Christian environment for four days and three nights, each year, for the rest of their lives.

The catch, as Bakker explained, was that there could only be a limited number of lifetime partners. Once that number was reached, that would be it. This limit was intended as the bait that would entice followers in.

Jim and Tammy Bakker unveiled this program to PTL's television audience on February 20, 1984. With Jim in his tuxedo and Tammy in her bright blue dress, Jim unveiled what he called "the most exciting project ever undertaken in the history of Christianity. . . . We want to share with you what God has given to us."

In introducing the program, Bakker explained that almost two million people came to Heritage USA from all over the world in 1983 and that the main concern these people had expressed was that they could not stay there. Instead, they had been obliged to stay in motels away from the facilities and the religious environment that were available at the village.

And so, as the orchestra played and the curtain rose, Jim and Tammy unveiled the "PTL Partner Center," which would ultimately be known as the Grand Hotel. Construction of this facility had actually begun in December 1983; it was planned to include a gigantic fellowship hall, a cafeteria, and numerous meeting rooms for PTL followers. Jim Bakker declared that this would be "the largest Christian center of its kind in the history of the world."

Bakker then gave the audience a seemingly straightforward explanation as to how the lifetime partnership program would serve to finance the Grand Hotel while providing perks for donors. As Tammy listened, Jim said

And then for a very short period of time, and I believe in God, Tammy, for a miracle. I believe in God that we have a club called the Lifetime Partnership [Club], and I believe in God that all we need is 25,000 people to fulfill for the Partner Center, the lifetime memberships. That's all the memberships we can have in the Heritage Grand Hotel, and we believe in God that in two weeks, the memberships will be closed. We haven't even announced it on television, and we already have around 1,000 lifetime members before the telethon started. That means there's only 24,000 memberships left, only one percent of the people who write me can join the lifetime memberships, and two and a half percent of my partners can join as lifetime partners.

When you give $1,000, you become a lifetime member with PTL. Now, when the memberships are gone, I can't give any more out, because we can only go to the physical amount, because we are only going to offer lifetime memberships up to 50 percent occupancy any one night at the hotel, so that we can maintain the hotel and have it taken care of.

When the 25,000 memberships in the Heritage Grand [Hotel] are gone, we cannot have any more [than] 25,000 [members] for the Heritage Grand [Hotel]. So when they are gone, we must stop. And we will have to actually refund your money if they come in after they are all gone.

When we reach the cut-off number, we will have to refund those gifts, and then you will just—if you want to give, you will just have to give without your lifetime membership. And that's just the only way we can do it to be honest, and we cannot allow any more memberships than we can physically take care of here at Heritage USA, and I think you understand that, don't you?

Please call right now. After we go off the air today, night and day, be sure and get these calls through, because when we get to the 25,000 [lifetime partnerships] of the Heritage Grand [Hotel], we [will] have to stop.

Time and again, Jim Bakker not only mentioned and explained the 25,000-member cap that had to be placed on Grand Hotel lifetime partnerships but also indicated the extreme urgency of the situation. Again, from his February 20, 1984, grand unveiling of the lifetime partnership program:

There [are] only 25,000 memberships. That means 23,000 and some partnerships [are] left, and I believe that maybe within this hour, we could be at 10 percent of our goal for the lifetime partners, and once that membership number is reached, we can no longer accept any more [lifetime] partners. . . .

Now, remember, you must mail your pledge in, because we are going to take them in the order that they come in the mail. You call your reservations in. We are going to take the memberships, and when we get to the limit, we will have to refund those [partnerships] if we have any over. So we cannot go over the [25,000] amount. The

Heritage Grand [Hotel] can only handle 25,000 lifetime members, because what we are doing is only going to give lifetime memberships up to 50 percent occupancy of the hotel, because we need the other 50 percent to clean the rooms and to run the place and to keep it going. You can't operate a hotel without some income. You have got to understand that, don't you?

So if you want to be a lifetime member, you need to call now and get your check in the mail right away, or you can put it on Master Charge or Visa or American Express, and say, "I want to guarantee my membership in the lifetime membership in the PTL Partner Center."

The solicitation for the Grand Hotel was certainly done in grand style. Nothing was spared, everything looked great, and people were encouraged to send in their money almost instantaneously. Even Tammy Bakker explained to the television audience that the partnership program had "unbelievable possibilities." That was very true. She explained, "Man, you can't beat that. You can't lose on it." One could write to PTL, or one could call their 1-704 telephone number to purchase a Grand Hotel lifetime partnership by credit card. PTL even had a toll-free number; quite appropriately, it was 1-800-CALL-JIM.

At his criminal trial, Bakker elaborated as to what he had envisioned PTL might become and what he had been attempting to build. Bakker testified that he wanted to service the needs of a modern generation and provide a Christian alternative to Disneyland and Disney World. Bakker remembered all of the discomforts of the old-time Christian "camp meetings" held in remote locations without modern conveniences. As he testified at his criminal trial, Heritage USA "had to meet a full spectrum of needs, from food to Bible bookstores, to whatever the needs of a modern person would be today to bring the campground up to date."

To help make that vision a reality, Bakker contracted with Roe Messner, a church contractor whose headquarters is in Wichita, Kansas. Bakker testified that Messner had the ability to transfer Bakker's sketches to reality:

Most people can't even tell what my sketches are, but Roe Messner, for some reason, could catch it. I sketched it out, and he grasped the concept of the Partner Center, and he went back to Wichita, Kansas, and in about two weeks, he had preliminary rough sketches and an artist's concept for me. I made changes in that.

Messner was later to play a major role not only in building the PTL facilities but also in promoting the lifetime partnerships. Standing at Bakker's side and responding, "that's right, Jim," to all of his statements, Roe Messner lent credence to Bakker's claims of great progress being made on PTL lodging projects.

Jim Bakker always contended that the lifetime partnership program was an inspiration given to him by God. As he testified in his criminal trial:

> People were complaining they didn't want to stay out on the highway. They didn't want to stay in town. They wanted to stay at a Christian retreat center. . . . They didn't come to be at a motel on the highway and we needed to build, and so I—in the middle of the night, or in the night I woke up and it was like a vision or a dream—I don't know what it was—but the concept, God gave me the concept of the Heritage Grand Partner Center and the Lifetime Partners. And I got up and I began to sketch and write it all down. . . . what I had felt was the dream and the vision for that and the Main Street Heritage USA. . . .

Bakker went on to say, "I brought that lifetime [partnership] concept to some of the staff people, [to the PTL] vice-presidents, and I introduced it to them, and I talked to some of the accountants, and I said, is this something that would work, and they said, yes."

Although Jim Bakker contends that his vision for the lifetime partnership program came in a vision from God in late 1983, it is very interesting to note that a somewhat similar project was considered by Jim Bakker on April 19, 1979. The PTL board of directors' minutes note that "[Bakker] has faith in his heart for a special project that will bring $10 million from the approaching telethon: If 10,000 people gave $1,000, it would mean $10 million to the ministry."

Moreover, in a promotional brochure signed by Bakker and dated June 8, 1983 (six months before his "vision" from God), he stated, "Every year for the rest of your life, I want you to come and stay as my guest for a week at Heritage USA. If you call me in advance, I will do my best to see that you stay in your room." Bakker proceeded to ask people for contributions of $15,000 with the understanding that every year the contributor could stay in that room for one week. The similarity between this and the Grand Hotel lifetime partnership program is uncanny.

In his criminal trial, Bakker went on to testify that he believed "with all [his] heart that the Lord gave [him] the total program," which, of course, included the idea of reserving 50 percent of the rooms at the Grand Hotel for lifetime partners. Bakker acknowledged this. The issue of Jim Bakker's vision from God concerning the lifetime partnership program is not critical in addressing the wire and mail fraud; it does, however, provide some evidence relative to Jim Bakker's truthfulness and veracity. Certainly the jury weighed this heavily when deliberating.

Pursuant to Bakker's plans, PTL entered into a legal and binding contract with the Brock Hotel Corporation, which managed the Grand Hotel. This contract indicated that only 50 percent of the rooms in the Grand Hotel were to be used for the lifetime partners. However, PTL, under the management of Jim Bakker, eventually approached the Brock Corporation and specifically requested to be allowed to exceed the publicized 50 percent limitation. The request was granted.

At this point, it is necessary to have a basic understanding as to what exactly constitutes wire and mail fraud. Federal statutes prohibit using the mails (or wire) for the purpose of executing a scheme or artifice with the intention to defraud the public in order to obtain money or property. Although federal law does not define the term *defraud*, the courts have interpreted it very broadly. The term *a scheme or artifice* generally refers to some type of plan or trick. This means that one can commit wire or mail fraud in one of two ways: by making a false statement about a material or an important fact by using the wire (television or radio) or the mails, or by not mentioning a material fact that is necessary to make one's statements true and complete.

For the government to be successful in its prosecution of a person under the federal mail or wire fraud statutes, it must establish that the scheme or artifice was reasonably calculated to deceive persons of ordinary prudence and intelligence in order to bring about some harm or to obtain some undeserved advantage.

And so, in its criminal indictment against Jim Bakker and Richard Dortch, the government stated that "Bakker and Dortch knew at the time that the pretenses, representations and promises [they made] would be and were false when made."

For example, on February 22, 1984, Bakker said the following on his PTL television program:

> You know, it is so important that if you want a lifetime membership, that you call as soon as possible, because there will only be 25,000 lifetime memberships in the Heritage Grand [Hotel] project. We must limit it, because of the size of the hotel. So we can only have two and a half percent of our total partnership join with lifetime

members. So when we reach the cut-off stage [of 25,000 partner-
ships], we will literally have to say, "We cannot receive any more
lifetime members.

Once again, Bakker had clearly indicated that there could only be
25,000 lifetime partners and that once the limit was reached, there
could be no new lifetime partners. On the previous day's program
Bakker claimed that 3,067 lifetime partnerships had already been
taken. However, PTL's computer records showed that as of that date,
the total number of lifetime partnerships that had been fully or partially paid was 1,145; the number of partnerships that had been
pledged but not paid was 105. So as of February 21, 1984, the total
number of pledged partnerships was only 1,250, not 3,067.

On February 28, 1984, Bakker had this to say:

Almost 50 percent of all of the lifetime memberships are already
gone and we can only have a limited number. So if you want to have
a lifetime partnership with PTL, I want you right now to call me and
say, "Jim, I want to stay at the Heritage Grand the rest of my life."
    The memberships will be gone within a few days, and it will be
too late then [for you to obtain a membership]. We can only take a
limited number [of memberships], because we have a limited number
of rooms in the Heritage Grand. . . .
    So right now, if you want to join a lifetime membership, we are
almost half through our membership drive. Almost half of the memberships have already been taken.

Once again, PTL's own computer records were reflecting something
entirely different. When Bakker made this pitch, the number of fully
and partially paid Grand Hotel partnerships totaled only 3,816—far
from the 12,500 that he maintained had been taken.

On the very next day, Bakker was explaining that PTL was able
to provide the lifetime partnership program because "this is a Christian retreat center and we don't have profit motivations." It was also
on that day that he announced that the total number of lifetime partnerships was 11,108; this figure was also displayed on an electronic
board in the studio. Again, PTL's own computer printouts showed
something entirely different. As of that date, the number of lifetime
partnerships that had been either fully or partially paid totaled only
4,293.

The government contended that Bakker's overstatements of the
number of lifetime partnerships sold was designed to create a demand
for the partnerships. Clearly PTL's own computer records reflected
sales far lower than those Bakker was announcing on television.

Jim Bakker was charged and convicted not only of wire fraud but also of mail fraud (Exhibit A-1.) As an example of this latter offense, on January 7, 1984, Jim Bakker directed PTL to mail a promotional brochure touting the Grand Hotel partnerships. It was sent to 140,282 individuals. Included within the brochure was a description of the lifetime partnership program and its 25,000-member limit. This was the same spiel that Mr. Bakker would later give on television. Included within the glossy promotional brochure was the following promise: "After we hear from 25,000 lifetime partners and receive their investment of $1,000, lifetime membership in the PTL Partner Center will be closed!" (Exhibit A-2.)

Yet another promotional letter went out in March, 1984, promoting the benefits and stressing the urgency of obtaining a Grand Hotel lifetime partnership. This letter was mailed to 570,874 individuals; it also expressly stated, "There are only 25,000 Lifetime Partnerships available!" (Exhibit A-3.)

By May 7, 1984, there was an attempt to convert the pledges that Bakker had received for lifetime partnerships into firm commitments. At that time, he indicated that "this is perhaps the highest return we have ever seen on pledges in our history. It is just a tremendous thing [that's] happening." Then, Bakker made a statement suggesting that the viewers ". . . do what I have done and I'm sincere. I would not lie to you about anything. And I made a pledge to become a lifetime partner . . . and I received a letter from Brother Dortch who is the co-chairman of the finance committee for the Heritage Grand, and it said, 'You haven't paid yours.' I suddenly realized that I had not paid my lifetime membership." Dressed in a light blue suit and seated at his desk in the executive offices of the World Outreach Center at Heritage USA, Bakker displayed his MasterCard and said, "Well, I just don't have the funds this month to do it. I really don't. I'm good for them. Mr. IRS got to me first and I had to pay my taxes and it took everything that we could scrape together to pay our taxes this year, and so we just didn't have an extra $1,000 that we could pay at this time." Bakker then looked rather sheepishly at his MasterCard and added, "And so this morning, I got out my MasterCard and I put it on the MasterCard account and, next month, I'll be able to take care of this, but this month is just real bad for me. So there are others who perhaps would like to say, 'Jim, I want to be guaranteed one of those lifetime memberships,' and you will receive your PTL membership card. But this is a lifetime membership with you and I together here in the Partner Center."

Bakker's statement that he did not have $1,000 for a Grand Hotel partnership is particularly interesting given the fact that for the fiscal year ending May 31, 1984, Jim Bakker's compensation totaled $1,032,512, which included $640,000 in bonuses. Tammy Bakker had received $194,355 during the same time period, including $100,000 in bonuses. The Bakkers' compensation is discussed fully in the next chapter.

Jim Bakker and others at PTL continued to understate the number of Grand Hotel lifetime partnerships that were obtained until July 7, 1984. PTL's records reflected that on that date the Grand Hotel's lifetime partnership program reached (and exceeded) its promised limit; to be more specific, the number of fully paid Grand Hotel partnerships was 25,303. The number of partially paid lifetime partnerships was 1,568, and the number of pledges that had been accepted by PTL as of July 7, 1984 was 13,102. Therefore, the total number of members of the public who had answered the Grand Hotel promotion as of July 7, 1984, either in the form of pledged, fully paid, or partially paid lifetime partnerships was 39,973. According to the mailed and televised promises, the promotion of Grand Hotel partnerships should have stopped before then. Unfortunately, it did not.

On July 25, 1984, Bakker mentioned on his PTL television program that there were 150 Grand Hotel partnerships left. PTL's own computer records showed that this was definitely not the case. In fact, the number of fully paid Grand Hotel partnerships totaled 28,430. Instead of a deficit of 150, there had been an oversell of 3,430, which meant approximately $3.4 million for PTL.

But problems other than this understatement loomed on two different fronts. First, Bakker had promised that the target date for opening the Grand Hotel would be July 4th, 1984. That day had come and gone. He also announced that he had spent approximately $23 million on building the Grand Hotel but that he still needed $10 million more to complete it. Therefore, even with 25,000 lifetime partners who had paid $1,000 each and thus raised $25 million, he was, by his own estimate, $8 million short. How would PTL pay for these lifetime partners who expected to be able to use the lodging facility for four days and three nights each year for life? Bakker always contended that the other one-half of the hotel, devoted to the "paying guests," would pay for current expenses.

Second, Jim Bakker was also receiving pressure from the TV affiliates because of the daily operational expenses of the PTL organization. Tammy Bakker probably said it best on August 1, 1984, when she said on the PTL television program, "All the thousands and thousands of dollars the lifetime members have given are being used to build the Grand. It is not being used to pay bills. So now, we need some paying-the-bills money, OK?" Unfortunately, the majority of this "paying-the-bills money" came from lifetime partnership funds that not only should have been used to build the facility but also should have been set aside as a reserve to pay for the lifetime partners' lodging.

Finally, on August 23, 1984, Jim Bakker stated clearly and emphatically that the Grand Hotel lifetime partnership program was closed. Sitting on a couch beside him was Richard Dortch, later to be a fellow defendant in the government action against Jim Bakker. As Bakker put it:

> This Heritage Grand is something very, very special. There [are] no more lifetime memberships left . . . . There will never be another lifetime membership in the Heritage Grand . . . . We are at our full extent and so please, ah, oh, I was going to say please stop giving. I can't say that. I need help. But there cannot be [any] more lifetime memberships in the Grand. We are at full 50 percent occupancy of the Grand, and we cannot go any further. So, thank you who've joined. You have a lifetime with us in the Grand. There is no more left. There will never be anymore. They're gone . . . .

How much clearer could he have made it? The Grand Hotel lifetime partnership program had reached its goal, and that was that. The PTL computer records, however, reflected that the cumulative number of fully paid lodging partnerships in the Grand Hotel as of August 23, 1984, was 29,949, or $4,949,000 over the promised limit.

This did not end the saga of the Grand Hotel lifetime partnership program. On April 11, 1985, Jim and Tammy Bakker made a startling revelation to the studio and television viewing audience: 900 checks from people who had originally purchased a partnership in the Grand Hotel had not gone through. As a result, Jim was now reopening the program in order to fulfill the original goal of 25,000 lifetime partners.

PTL records once again told an entirely different story. On April 11, 1985, there were in fact only 511 "bad" checks and invalid charges, not 900 as Bakker had said; furthermore, as of that same day, PTL and Jim Bakker had committed 34,983 fully paid lodging partnerships to the Grand Hotel.

On July 8, 1985, Jim Bakker, on his television program, now called, "The Jim and Tammy Show," said that the Grand Hotel Partnerships were closed. One of his guests, Lulu Roman, purchased what were supposed to have been the last two lodging partnerships. By that date, the total number of fully paid lodging partnerships in the Grand was up to 58,748, and the cumulative number of bad checks and invalid charges was only 770.

Therefore, as was outlined in the government's indictment of both Jim Bakker and Richard Dortch and as was presented to the jury in the Bakker criminal trial, the contention that 900 partners had paid for Grand Hotel partnerships with invalid credit cards and bad checks was used repeatedly as a rationale by both Bakker and Dortch to justify the sale of more than 20,000 additional Grand partnerships. The chart shown as Exhibit 4-1 was prepared and used by the government at the time of Jim Bakker's resentencing. It shows how Bakker's televised claims differed remarkably from PTL's own computer records.

Bakker also sent out promotional letters concerning the reopening of the Grand Hotel partnership program, the first of which was mailed on March 28, 1985, to 19,264 individuals. A second letter went out to 594,794 individuals; it was signed by Bakker and dated April 29, 1985. These letters reiterated what TV viewers had been previously told by both Jim and Tammy: "A couple of weeks ago, I received a final tabulation on the lifetime partnerships and was shocked to discover that because of checks and credit card payments that did not go through, over 900 lifetime partnerships were still needed to meet our goal." (Exhibit A-4.)

Jim Bakker wasn't the only one saying that because checks had bounced and credit cards had not gone through, there were 900 remaining Grand Hotel partnerships. Richard Dortch, a member of the board of directors of PTL as well as its senior vice-president, also made that same pitch. On June 6, 1985, he repeated what Jim Bakker said concerning the availability of Grand Hotel partnerships. With the assistance of a guest on the PTL program, Dortch solicited viewers to send in their $1,000 to purchase a lifetime partnership in the hotel. He even suggested that viewers should write on the outside of the envelope "prayer is the key." During the same show, Dortch pointed out what a good deal the Grand Hotel partnerships were compared to the Towers memberships (another lifetime partnership that is explained later in this chapter), which were selling at $2,000 each. Dortch concluded his solicitation by saying, "This is a bonus time, really."

Richard Dortch had said that prayer was the key to obtaining a Grand Hotel lifetime partnership; Jim Bakker maintained that these few remaining Grand Hotel partnerships were, in fact, answers to prayer:

Grand Hotel Lifetime Partnerships
(Advertised Limit of 25,000)

Televised Announcements	Fully Paid Partnerships (Cumulative)	Bad Checks and Invalid Charges (Cumulative)
July 25, 1984 Bakker Says 150 Grand Partnerships Left	28,430	439
August 23, 1984 Bakker Says No More Partnerships Available in Grand Hotel	29,949	469
April 11, 1985 Bakker Reopens Grand Partnership, Says 900 Checks Did Not Go Through	34,983	511
July 8, 1985 Bakker Says Partnership Closed; Lulu Roman Last Two Partnerships	58,748	770
May 31, 1987	66,683	935

Exhibit 4-1   Comparison of Bakker's Televised Statements with PTL'a Computer Records

41

Well, I don't know how many people told me they had prayed that they could get a lifetime membership for $1,000. I don't know, but you must have prayed some other people out, because almost a thousand people didn't take their memberships because their credit card didn't work, or their checks didn't go through, or something happened to them. And so we opened up the final membership. These are the last $1,000 memberships, and I promise you, ever in the history of the Heritage Grand Partner Center. There will never be any more. There can't be anymore. This is the final, final, final countdown. This was an unexpected thing and when we finish, we're almost there, we need a few more to finish paying for the Heritage Grand Partner Center. Not only will it be finished on victory day, but we will have it paid for on victory day. So it must be postmarked no later than 20 days from today. So if you are going to take a $1,000 membership to stay there for four days and three nights in the Heritage Grand, this is the final countdown. Twenty days to go and that number is going to go down and down and down. And the people that are here tell me, Jim, the Grand is better than you said. It is far nicer. We can't believe Heritage USA and you're not going to believe what you see when we finish all of this in the next, oh, really, 20 days.

Grand Hotel lifetime partnerships continued to be offered by Bakker and others at PTL. By May 31, 1987, PTL and Bakker had received a total of $66,938,820 from the Grand Hotel lifetime partnership offerings, and the number of lifetime partnerships that had been sold totaled 66,683.

Furthermore, of that $66,938,820, only $35,365,201 was actually spent on construction of the promised facilities. (Exhibit A-5.) The balance of the funds were drawn down almost instantaneously to meet daily operational expenses, which included the enormous salaries received by Jim and Tammy Bakker and selected others at PTL. These salaries would be the subject not only of much publicity but also of an IRS investigation.

Exhibit 4-2, which was used at the resentencing of Jim Bakker, shows in tabular form the gross oversale of the Grand Hotel lifetime partnerships.

Although more fully discussed in Chapter 9, it should be noted that there were some serious questions raised by certain professionals concerning the underlying premises of the entire lifetime partnership program. For example, PTL's outside counsel, John Yorke of the Charlotte, North Carolina, law firm of Wardlow, Knox, Knox, Freeman and Scofield, expressed his concerns in a letter to Richard Dortch on January 6, 1984, the day before the 140,282 mailings of the Grand Hotel lifetime partnerships were to go out.

Grand Hotel

- **First Introduced — January 7, 1984**
- **Number of Rooms Available for Lifetime Partnerships — 250**
- **Original Advertised Limit — 25,000**

Promotion	*TV Announcement Date*	*Required Payment*	*Fully Paid*	*Pledged But Not Paid*	*Total Dollars Paid**
Grand	**Feb. 20, 1984**	$ 1,000	66,683	16,989	$66,938,820
	Totals:		**66,683**	**16,989**	**$66,938,820**

* Includes Partially Paid.

Exhibit 4-2   A Breakdown of the Paid Grand Hotel Promotion

In his letter to Dortch, Yorke indicated that he had not had sufficient opportunity to review the mailing and therefore he ". . . [could] not give a legal opinion in this short amount of time as to whether this is regulated by any of the securities laws." He also indicated that it was his opinion "that this offering [came] within the purview of the South Carolina Time Share Statute and [required] a registration with the South Carolina Real Estate Commission." Yorke concluded his letter to Dortch by indicating that the mailing would go out that day "notwithstanding our opinion" because of PTL's "financial pressures." (Exhibit A-6.)

Yorke's concerns regarding potential securities and time share law violations were shared by other attorneys. Thomas Givens of the Rock Hill, South Carolina, law firm of McKinney and Givens stated in a confirming letter to Yorke dated January 20, 1984, that ". . . we both felt in view of the circumstances that Attorney Bill Pridgen of Myrtle Beach should look into the matter for possible 'time share' problems. You and I both agree that it would be in the best interests of PTL to hold off soliciting the $1,000 donation from 25,000 partners. Peter Bailey, and other officials at PTL acknowledged the potential problems and felt that in view of the amount owed on the construction of the Grand Hotel, they had no choice but to go ahead and mail out the solicitations." It should be noted that Peter Bailey was the senior financial officer of PTL. His role in the PTL operation will be discussed more fully in Chapters 6 and 9.

The attorney to whom Givens made reference in his January 20 memo was contacted by Yorke. In a memo to John Yorke dated January 23, 1984, concerning the Heritage USA brochure and sale of hotel accommodations, Bill Pridgen had this to say: "However, I have some concern that because the broad terms of offer contained in the brochure . . . coupled with the fact that there is no mechanism for assessments for ongoing operational expenses and capital reserves, someone could take [the] position that the offering is per se a violation of the general regulations as being fraudulent or misleading." He added: "The above concern is one that I have over and above the South Carolina Time-Sharings Statute. I feel that the terms of the offer being made by Fort Heritage should be made more detailed and less open-ended."

Obviously, there were many other substantial business problems concerning the lifetime partnerships in addition to the oversale. These problems included not only how the funds were actually being used and whether or not a reserve was set aside for the future but also whether or not the offering could be considered a common law fraud, a securities law violation, or a violation of the South Carolina time share laws. These were areas that should have been fully explored prior to the offering mailed on January 7, 1984, and the television promotions broadcast on February 20, 1984. However, Givens quoted a PTL officer as saying that PTL was under tremendous financial pressure to help pay for the Grand Hotel's construction.

The Towers Hotel Partnership Frauds

> People, when I introduced this to an audience last week, the first time, they literally ran out of the audience and shoved the money in my hand and said, please, I thought I missed it for life. And when this Tower is finished, or when this Tower opens, there is no more. That's all we can have. I'm believing God in 30 days the Tower memberships also will be gone.
>
> James O. Bakker, "Jim Bakker Show," televised September 17, 1984.

Towers at $1,000

On September 17, 1984, Jim Bakker announced the Towers lifetime partnership. On stage with him in an outdoor amphitheater were Tammy Bakker; Richard Dortch, the senior vice-president of PTL; Roe Messner, the builder and general contractor of PTL; and Dr. Fred Gross, the person to whom Jim Bakker confessed his affair with Jessica Hahn. Bakker was explaining the present status of the lifetime partnership program:

> Well, what are we going to do? All the partnerships are gone [in the Grand]. Every single one of the partnerships in the Heritage Grand are gone. We had to say stop, stop, you can't give anymore. Well, we still owe $9 million dollars to complete the Heritage Grand. Nine million dollars to go and it's paid for. And bankers can just go sit on their money.

At that point, the studio audience broke into loud applause. Two months later, however, PTL would receive a $10 million loan from Fairfax Savings and Loan of Fairfax, Virginia. The loan was for the completion of the Grand Hotel and also placed a lien on the Grand Hotel property.

Jim Bakker continued his discussion with the TV audience. He openly acknowledged once again that the Grand Hotel lifetime partnerships were gone. He was emphatic concerning the "fact" that there would never be another Grand Hotel lifetime partnership. And when confronted with the dilemma as to whether to continue offering lifetime partnerships, Jim Bakker said the following on September 17, 1984:

> There are no more lifetime memberships left in the Heritage Grand, in this main beautiful Grand. So that means in history there will never be another lifetime membership in the Heritage Grand. Now, what do you do?

Then Jim Bakker stalled and stuttered for a moment while his assistant, Uncle Henry Harrison, yelled out in Ed McMahon fashion, "What do you do, Jim?" to which Jim Bakker responded, "Well, when in doubt, build something more!" The audience cheered, and Richard Dortch yelled, "Amen!" Jim Bakker then proceeded to show the audience an artist's rendition of what he called the Heritage Towers, which would offer 500 additional rooms of lodging to PTL visitors.

Bakker solicited television viewers and his studio audiences to become Towers lifetime partners by indicating that some Grand Hotel lifetime partnerships were to be converted into Towers lifetime partnerships because of the former program's "overflow." Bakker never said whether or not this conversion was announced to, let alone approved by, those individuals who had sought to obtain a Grand Hotel lifetime partnership.

Bakker used a chalkboard on the set to explain exactly how the Towers lifetime membership was going to work. In my opinion, his "chalkboard talk" was probably one of the most devastating pieces of evidence to come out against him in his criminal trial. It was then that he not only explained how many lifetime partnerships would be available for the Towers Hotel but also outlined how the money raised from the partnerships was to be spent. At the top of the blackboard he wrote "30,000" and stated that 30,000 lifetime partners would produce a total of $30 million; the Towers lifetime partnerships would cost $1,000 each, just like the Grand Hotel lifetime partnerships. He then proceeded to explain that the Towers Hotel would cost $15 million. Because the Towers Hotel was not going to have a "main street" and all of the meeting facilities that the Grand Hotel had, it would be much less expensive than the Grand Hotel.

Thus, construction of the Towers Hotel would use up only half of the $30 million generated by the Towers lifetime partnership. Of the remaining $15 million, Bakker said that $9 million, or rather $10 million ("my math is not all that good," he added to explain his miscalculation) would be earmarked for completion of the Grand Hotel.

But these two projects still didn't account for the entire $30 million. "Lord, what will we do with five million left over?" Bakker shouted. At that point Tammy and others laughed in the background. Jim Bakker continued, "The five million left over will pay every TV station in America. . . . And PTL will have the hotel finished, will have the Towers paid for, and every TV station paid for, and we'll have a thousand-room partner center all completed, paid for, and not one banker entering the picture." Jim Bakker immediately turned to the studio audience and asked, "How many people here are going to take a Towers partnership?" He requested the audience to stand if they wanted a Tower membership and fill out a membership card for the Towers. Then he told the ushers just to pass out the cards to everyone. Sure enough, several people did sign up for Towers lifetime memberships, and Bakker said, "I believe this program will be closed in 30 days and that all of the 30,000 lifetime partnerships in the Towers will have been spoken for." He then told the viewing audience that if their money wasn't in for the Towers lifetime partnership program within the next 30 days, the cost of a partnership would go up to $1,500.

As I stated earlier, this "chalkboard talk" was probably one of the most damaging pieces of evidence introduced in the Bakker criminal trial. The jury viewed the tape of Jim Bakker's television program of September 17, 1984, in which he not only stated how the Towers lifetime partnership program would work but also used a chalkboard to show and to emphasize his calculations. Bakker's own television program was introduced into evidence, and it provided not only clear and convincing evidence as to the limit of the Towers lifetime partners, and how much money would be raised, but, possibly of even more significance, Bakker specifically indicated how the funds raised from the Towers lifetime partners would be spent.

Unfortunately for PTL and Jim Bakker, the promises made on September 17, 1984, were not kept. Instead, just like before, the lifetime partnership limit was exceeded, and the funds that were raised were used for other purposes.

On September 20, 1984, Bakker revealed that the Towers partnership, just like the Grand Hotel partnership, had been inspired by God. "And the Lord showed me in the Towers with 30,000 partners, many of them will be . . . lifetime members, and they will take number two. . . ." Bakker was promoting the idea of purchasing a second lifetime partnership; those who did so would be able to stay seven days and six nights a year at PTL.

Although the Grand was eventually built and did become functional, the Towers Hotel was never completed and has never housed any lifetime partners.

Promotion of the Towers Hotel partnerships followed the same general plan as the Grand Hotel scheme. The televised solicitation came first. Next, a promotional letter was mailed to 596,232 individuals from September 27 through October 5, 1984; it promised lodging for four days and three nights every year for the rest of each contributor's life.

In another promotional letter mailed to 596,865 individuals from October 15 through October 19, 1984, Jim Bakker confirmed that "twenty-five thousand people had joined with PTL as lifetime partners." That statement is true, although misleading. He seemed to be saying that there were *only* 25,000 lifetime partners for the Grand Hotel to date. (Exhibit A-7.) However, as indicated earlier, that number had been exceeded and continued to rise. In the same letter, Jim Bakker once again trumpeted, "There can only be 30,000 Heritage Grand Towers partners, so please be sure to write today!" Bakker was clearly making reference to the Towers lifetime partnership when he said the Heritage Grand Towers. As the total number of lodging programs grew at PTL, he would often merge the names of the different programs as he spoke live on camera to his viewing audience.

In addition to indicating that up to 50 percent of the rooms at the Towers Hotel were to be available at any given time for Towers members, this second letter also warned that Towers memberships would "soon be increased to $1,500." It boasted that the Towers would "house a health spa with complete professional health and fitness equipment, a theater featuring Christian and fine family films, lap pool, and family bowling lanes." Jim Bakker would later refer to the proposed bowling lane in the Towers as the "holy rollers bowling lane." Of course, neither the holy rollers bowling lane nor the Towers ever materialized.

In what was already Jim Bakker style, on September 25, 1984, he said to his TV audience: "They are just rolling in now, and when we get to 30,000 people, there is no more lifetime memberships in the Partner Center. It is over for history, forever."

Then, on September 28, 1984, Bakker made another televised statement regarding the limits, availability, and projected duration of the new Towers lifetime partnerships:

Since the memberships are all gone in the Partner Center, we have announced the new Towers, and it won't be long now and all of the Towers memberships will be gone. And so we need your help, and in about two more weeks, the memberships will go to $1,500. We have got about 14, [or] 15 more days to have the memberships at $1,000. And so if you want one of the final memberships at $1,000 for four days and three nights, sit down and write a letter to us and say, "Jim and Tammy, I want to be a part."

Such optimism on Bakker's part was characteristic of both the Grand Hotel promotion, and the Towers promotion. Statements to the effect that the goal would be met in two or three or four days became very common. For example, Jim Bakker predicted almost immediate success with the Towers, which was no different than what he had predicted with the Grand. In fact, when he first introduced the Grand on February 20, 1984, he said, "There is only 25,000 lifetime partners, and you know what, in three or four days, the lifetime partnerships could be all gone."

Again, all of this seems to have been done by Bakker in an attempt to create a demand for the partnership program. This was a technique that Jim Bakker would use repeatedly in his solicitations and in his prospecting for new lifetime members.

On the September 20, 1984, television program, Jim Bakker again asserted that the Grand Hotel and the Towers Hotel were being built without the assistance of bank financing. He prided himself on this fact, adding that if a loan were required to build the Grand Hotel, then the repayment cost of this loan would be $80 million. Because the Grand was being built on a pay-as-you-go basis, there were no financing charges. As a consequence, the lifetime partners would share in the benefits that were flowing to PTL as a result of PTL not having to finance the hotel.

When that statement was made, it was true. There was no bank loan or mortgage on the Grand Hotel. However, a $10 million construction loan for the purpose of completing the Grand Hotel was obtained by PTL on November 5, 1984, approximately 45 days after Bakker made that statement.

Bakker went on to explain the lifetime partnership program from a business perspective during that program:

They say, how can you afford for $1,000 to let people stay there every year of their life for four days and three nights? We couldn't do it if we were in business. It's a terrible business deal. It's a good deal for the partner, but it's a terrible business deal for PTL. You would have to figure that out. It's marvelous for you and for me and for the work of the Lord, because we are not [in] a profit mode. We don't believe in just raising things, and raising money to make a profit or to have PTL to make a profit. We are here to minister the Gospel. And so the partners are going to receive the benefit of a lifetime of staying in this great Partner Center instead of the bankers receiving the benefit.

In addition to the $1,000 Towers lifetime partnership that promised four days and three nights in the Towers Hotel each year, there were five other partnership programs that also offered lodging in the Towers Hotel, each of which is discussed in the following pages.

The Penthouse Promotional

On September 21, 1984, Jim Bakker announced that not only traditional lodging but also penthouse accomodations would be available at the Towers Hotel. As Bakker described it, a gift of $10,000 would allow donors to spend seven days and six nights in one of the eight two-bedroom penthouses on the 20th floor of the Towers Hotel. Each penthouse had a living room and, as Bakker described it, "mansion-height" ceilings. However, only five fully paid penthouse partnerships had been bought. Bakker would later say that because almost all of the Penthouse memberships were accounted for, the price of a Penthouse membership had been raised to $25,000.

No adjectives were spared in describing the lodging accommodations to the television audience. Richard Dortch said the following to Jim Bakker on the PTL program of September 21, 1984:

> Jim, can I just say this, you know for 17 years, one out of every two nights, I've stayed in hotels. That's a fact. For 17 years, one out of every two nights. And Jim Bakker, friend, there is no place in the world like this. I've stayed from the Taj Majal in India to Wolf Lake, Illinois, and this is unbelievable. It is. It is a world-class hotel. I've stayed in them in Switzerland. This is a world-class—this is not the hand-me-down. This is the best.

Bakker also explained how there could be a total of only 60,000 lifetime partners of both the Grand Hotel and the Towers Hotel. It is unclear how he arrived at the 60,000 figure, because he had originally indicated there could only be 25,000 members in the Grand and 30,000 in the Towers, which gives a total of 55,000. In any case, he stated that one-half of the rooms in each hotel would be open for use by lifetime partners. This was very important because the other half of the hotel's lodging would need to be available for full-paying guests. "You cannot go beyond 50 percent occupancy of the hotel for this, because we have to have the other 50 percent so we can make up your beds and take care of the place from the paid guests, because you won't be paying for the rest of your life,'' Bakker proclaimed.

On December 21, 1984, Jim Bakker explained how the 30,000 memberships in the Towers Hotel would cost $1,000 each for the first 10,000 memberships that were received, $1,500 for the next 10,000 memberships, and then $2,000 for the last 10,000 memberships. This explanation differs from the one offered on September 17, 1984, which promised that the 30,000 lifetime memberships in the Towers would all cost $1,000 each.

However, Bakker stated during this same program that "something [had] happened beyond [his] wildest dreams"—all of the $1,500 lifetime memberships in the Towers Hotel had been taken at $1,000 each. If such a response were to continue, Bakker said, then all of the $2,000 memberships would probably also be taken also at only $1,000 each.

What Bakker was indicating during this program was that at least 20,000 lifetime partnerships in the Towers Hotel lifetime partnership program had been taken as of December 21, 1984. Once again, PTL's own records show that as of that date, the total number of fully and partially paid Towers Hotel partnerships numbered only 12,086.

Using the same strategy he had employed with the Grand Hotel, Jim Bakker was attempting to create a false sense of urgency by making inflated claims about the program's success. What was being conveyed to the listening (and contributing) public over the television simply did not match with PTL's own numbers.

In the same program, Jim Bakker made an interesting statement concerning the safety of the PTL lodging facilities. These words would later come back to haunt him:

> I want to tell you something. If I would find anybody damaging anything at this place, or robbing or stealing, they're going to jail. I'll tell you, I have never prosecuted people for doing anything at Heritage USA, but this is going to be the safest place on earth. There will be no stealing. There will be no drugs. There will be no vandalism, because you are going to jail, and I will pay—I will pay up to $10,000—I'll pay at least $1,000 in a small case, [and] up to $10,000 for the arrest and conviction of anyone stealing at Heritage USA.

Towers at $2,000

By the end of December of 1984, Jim Bakker announced that all of the Towers memberships for $1,000 had been taken, as were all of the memberships originally to be offered for $1,500. These had also been sold at $1,000 each. Therefore, the only memberships that were left would now cost $2,000 each.

The PTL organization was at the time, and always, living way beyond its means. Although PTL was to obtain a $10 million construction loan for the Grand Hotel in November 1984, Bakker made the following plea on September 21, 1984: "The Heritage Grand is paid for already now, and we are moving in to pay for the Towers. And now, we can't spend that money for TV time, so we need some of you to order these baby dolls at $100 to pay for TV time."

After announcing that the Towers memberships were now going for $2,000 each and that the $1,000 lifetime partnership offer was over, Jim Bakker delivered what would eventually become a rather prophetic request: "Please help me to be honorable."

In January, 1985, the Grand Hotel opened with lifetime partners numbering far in excess of the promised 25,000 limit; it also carried a $10 million mortgage. Of course, neither of these critical facts had been disclosed to the contributing public.

By February 25, 1985, Bakker was back on TV promoting the Towers Hotel partnerships. He announced that only 3,925 of the $2,000 Towers lifetime partnerships were available. However, PTL's own records reflected that as of that date, the number of fully paid Towers Hotel partnerships totaled 17,977. There had also been 2,863 pledges received by that date.

Ultimately, Jim Bakker and PTL were able to sell only 91 fully paid Towers partnerships at the $2,000 price. 48 people pledged but did not pay for a Towers membership at the $2,000 price. The total amount raised by offering Towers memberships at $2,000 each was $187,657.

In addition to the $1,000 Towers promotional, the Penthouse promotional, and the $2,000 Towers promotional, three other programs also offered lodging in the Towers: the Silver 7000 Club, the Victory Warrior Club, and the Family Fun partnership. Although each of these programs will be discussed in the paragraphs that follow, Exhibit 4-3, introduced at Jim Bakker's resentencing, neatly summarizes the important facts and figures. In short, PTL and Jim Bakker did not raise just $30 million from the Towers lifetime partnership program; rather, they raised $74,292,751.

During the course of his promotional crusade, Bakker made some amazingly inconsistent statements concerning the operation and funding of the lifetime partnerships. For example, on June 20, 1985,

Towers Hotel

- First Introduced — September 17, 1984
- Number of Rooms Available for Lifetime Partnerships — 250
- Original Advertised Limit — 30,000

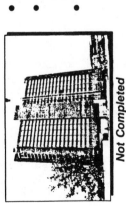

Not Completed

Promotion	TV Announcement Date	Required Payment	Fully Paid	Pledged But Not Paid	Total Dollars Paid*
Towers	Sept. 17, 1984	$ 1,000	26,981	5,057	$27,079,069
Towers	Feb. 19, 1985	$ 2,000	91	48	$ 187,657
Penthouse	Sept. 21, 1984	$10,000	5	0	$ 53,200
Silver 7000	Sept. 4, 1985	$ 3,000	2,344	1,385	$ 7,178,779
Victory Warrior	May 24, 1986	$ 1,000	35,984	4	$36,238,315
Family Fun	March 7, 1987	$900–1,000	3,350	1,955	$ 3,555,731
Totals:			**68,755**	**8,449**	**$74,292,751**

* *Includes Partially Paid.*

Exhibit 4-3   A Breakdown of the Paid Towers Hotel Promotion

53

Richard Dortch and Jim Bakker were speaking with Roe Messner on "The Jim Bakker Show." Messner, who was at the time considered to be the leading church builder in the United States, was the primary contractor for the lodging facilities at PTL. Dortch was attempting to explain how, over a 20-year pay-back period, a person generally pays back three times in interest what was borrowed. Roe Messner confirmed that statement. Dortch then told the viewing audience this means that if one makes a $1,000 contribution to the ministry in the form of a lifetime partnership, its actual worth to PTL is $4,000. Dortch had added the $1,000 gift to the supposed savings to PTL of $3,000 by not having to borrow $1,000 over a 20-year period and arrived at a $4,000 benefit to PTL. Jim Bakker then turned to Roe Messner and asked, "When the Towers and the Grand are finished, isn't it about a $60 million project, would you say Roe?" With a puzzled look, Messner faced Bakker and replied, "The Grand and the Towers, Jim?" Bakker answered, "Yes." Messner responded, "It's more than that, Jim, it's more like $70 million."

All three men began laughing, Bakker in a rather nervous, boyish, manner. He giggled, "Pardon my ignorance, it's much easier to live without knowing everything." Roe Messner then quickly added, "And that doesn't include the interest like Brother Dortch was talking about."

This dialog is very interesting in at least three respects. First, how did Roe Messner determine that the Towers and the Grand would cost $70 million? The Towers Hotel was clearly presented as costing $15 million when it was introduced on September 17, 1984; the Grand Hotel was supposed to cost approximately $35 million. And according to the September 17, 1984, "Jim Bakker Television Show," $10 million raised from the Towers partnership program was to be added to $25 million from the Grand Hotel's promotional to complete the Grand Hotel. Therefore, the total construction cost of the Towers and the Grand was $50 million, not $70 million. This $20 million over-calculation made by Messner is unexplained. Even Jim Bakker's quote of $60 million is $10 million more than what he originally stated on his television program ($15 million to build the Towers, plus $35 million to build the Grand). This is also unexplained.

Second, Messner indicates from his statement that PTL is being charged interest on his construction work. As the chief financial officer of PTL would later write in a memo to Bakker, PTL was paying a high rate of interest on all unpaid balances to Roe Messner.

Finally, one can only speculate as to Jim Bakker's actual knowledge of the cumulative costs for the Towers and the Grand. It is certainly difficult to comprehend how the chair of the board and president of an organization could believe that on-going construction totaled $60 million, when in fact on-going construction totaled $70 million plus interest. Is this faked ignorance on his part, or was this an example of leaving administrative and financial matters to others due to his lack of sophistication?

As is discussed in the next chapter, it could be viewed as either. The person who was primarily responsible for day-to-day operations was Richard Dortch. On the other hand, it is difficult to accept that, given all those pleas for money and goals he insisted they must meet, Jim Bakker did not comprehend the total cost of the project. Also baffling is the $20 million discrepancy not being explained or challenged by any of those who were at PTL and who presumably could have, and certainly should have, had their finger on the pulse of PTL's business operation.

Silver 7000

Bakker and Dortch announced another lifetime partnership program on September 4, 1985. According to Bakker, "There are only 7000 [partnerships] left in the Towers and we've called them the Silver 7000 Club." There were no more memberships in the Grand. Bakker and Dortch stated that upon payment of $3,000, a Silver 7000 Partner would enjoy six nights and seven days of free lodging in the Towers each year for life; year-round admission to various events at Heritage USA; and free admission to two self-improvement workshops each year held at Heritage USA.

This started the promotion for what would eventually turn out to be a very unsuccessful Silver 7000 Club.

Despite Bakker's assertion that there were only 7000 of the original 30,000 lifetime partnerships in the Towers still available, PTL's own computer records reflected that, as of September 4, 1985, there were actually 11,459 left.

The sales strategy for all lifetime partnership programs was to say that there were only a few more days in the particular partnership promotional, that thousands of people had already purchased their lifetime partnership, and that thousands more had been pledging to do the same. Also, viewers were continually bombarded with the message that there would never be another opportunity like the one at hand. In addition to all this, Jim Bakker was also promoting the monetary value of obtaining a lifetime partnership in the Silver 7000 Club.

Originally, when the Grand Hotel lifetime partnerships were first introduced, Bakker said that the Grand Hotel partnerships had been calculated to be worth between $20,000 and $40,000. The January 7, 1984, Grand Hotel partnership brochure represented the membership to be worth "approximately $19,500" over a 40-year period. However, these figures would go up exponentially when it came time to promote the Silver 7000 partnerships.

Mark Burgund, former vice-president and one-time budget director of PTL, testified in Jim Bakker's criminal trial that Bakker asked him "to make . . . a chart that would show the value of the 7000—Silver 7000 membership over a period of time." On July 26, 1985, Burgund delivered a memo to Bakker accomplishing what he thought Bakker had requested. Burgund determined that for a family of four using the Silver 7000 Club membership for a period of 30 years, assuming a 6 percent annual inflation rate, the Silver 7000 Club membership would be worth $84,735.

According to Burgund's testimony, he discussed this memo and his findings with Bakker. Bakker told Burgund that while he had the general idea, he wanted Burgund to show how a Silver 7000 Club membership would be worth a million dollars, and he sent Burgund back to do the necessary computations to reach that result.

Now knowing what Bakker wanted, Burgund simply had to work backwards. That is, what would one have to do in order to be able to contend, even theoretically, that a $3,000 Silver 7000 Club membership was worth over $1 million?

The first thing Burgund had to do was change the mythical family of four to a family of five. If the family of five did everything the family of four did, the membership would still be worth only $99,609 after 30 years of use. That is, the family of five must attend Heritage USA on their Silver 7000 Club membership for seven days and six nights each year for the next 30 years and spend as much time as possible while there engaging in recreational activities at PTL: every day of their visit for the next 30 years, they would have to be going to the skating rink, attending the PTL Passion Play, playing miniature golf, riding the carousel, utilizing PTL ground transportation, and swimming at the huge PTL water park. Unfortunately, this still was not enough.

If the family of five were to do all of the above for the next 50 years, the total value of the Silver 7000 Club partnership, according to Burgund, would be only $365,815, and that assumes a 6 percent annual rate of inflation.

Burgund eventually submitted documents to Bakker demonstrating that the Silver 7000 Club partnership would be worth $1,004,487 if a family of five came to PTL for seven days and six nights each year, and every day all of them went to the skating rink, played miniature golf, rode the carousel, took advantage of the ground transportation, and then—if they weren't too tired—went to the water park. They would also have to attend one PTL workshop and one Passion Play each year for the next 50 years. But the marathon wouldn't stop there. They would also have to come to Heritage USA for an additional 30 days every year. This meant the family either had to live within driving distance of Heritage USA or would have to stay in a hotel near the Heritage USA property. For their 30 additional days at Heritage USA, this family, every day, would be attending the waterpark, using the skating rink, playing miniature golf, riding the carousel, and using PTL ground transportation every day. They would need to attend two additional Passion Plays per year. If they did all this, the membership would be worth over a million dollars—assuming, as Burgund did, a 6 percent annual inflation rate.

On October 15, 1985, Jim Bakker went on TV and, with the assistance of Mark Burgund, attempted to explain how a Silver 7000 Club membership was worth over a million dollars. Displaying the data shown in the charts, Jim Bakker told his viewing audience, "It's valued at $1,004,487 for a $3,000 gift. Actually, the first year you have got back more benefits than you actually gave to build the Heritage Grand Towers and to be a partner of this ministry with this Christian retreat center." Turning to Mark Burgund, who was assisting him in explaining the chart, Bakker said, "Mark, this is so amazing, I guess you have to figure in the rate of inflation to understand what happens to things." Burgund responds, "That's right. The rate of inflation, if it is 6 percent a year, it doubles every 12 years, and, you know, accountants are often accused of being conservative and I tried to be conservative when I made this up." Bakker says, "You did. You had $8 [for waterpark tickets], and the tickets are going to be $10 for one thing." Burgund responded by saying, "I'd rather have you tell me that than the other way around, and someone saying, 'Oh, you tried to hyper-inflate this thing.' I could see somebody coming for 30 days easily taking in three or four Passion Plays because that's a religious experience just like going to church."

When Burgund was asked under oath at Bakker's criminal trial if he knew that it had been announced to the public on television by Mr. Bakker that Silver 7000 memberships were worth over a million dollars after 50 years of use, Burgund responded, "I don't know that." Prosecutor Deborah Smith also asked Burgund, "Mr. Burgund, did you appear on television and discuss these figures with Mr. Bakker?" His answer: "Not to my recollection."

Amazingly, on November 12, 1985, PTL accountant Mark Burgund wrote another memo for Bakker, which was an update on his previous one. Burgund testified he was requested to provide it "because we added bowling and the health spa in the benefits." Of course, neither the bowling alley nor the health spa were ever built, but it was announced on TV that these facilities would be built at a later time.

By Burgund's new calculation, if a family were to do all that was discussed above, and use the health spa and bowling alley over a 50-year period, the projected value of a $3,000 Silver 7000 Club membership would be $1,614,262.

Deborah Smith questioned Mark Burgund concerning his assumption and the physical liability of what he was suggesting:

> SMITH: So, now do you think a family, all five members, could do all these things in one day—go to the water park, go to all the recreational facilities, go bowling every day and go use the health spa if the bowling and health spa had been built?
> BURGUND: I believe they could if they chose to.
> SMITH: And do you think they could do that if they came and stayed in the area for 30 days and they did that every day they were here?
> BURGUND: I think they could physically do that.
> SMITH: And do you think if they did that every year for 50 years, the value would be what?
> BURGUND: $1,614,262.

Under additional questioning, Mr. Burgund could not name a family that had come to Heritage USA and done "all those things."

On October 18, 1985, after constantly promoting the Silver 7000 Club, Jim Bakker said, "The Silver 7000 Club has gone wild. Almost half of 'em are gone of the [Silver] 7,000. You better worry about gettin' in if you want one because there ain't gonna be no more after that. So quickly go to your phone. . . ." Again, PTL's own computer records put the lie to this claim: on October 18, 1985, the number of fully and partially paid Silver 7000s totaled only 408.

On October 22, 1985, Bakker said there were only a few hundred Silver 7000s left. However, according to PTL computer records that were admitted into evidence at the criminal trial, the number of fully and partially paid Silver 7000 Club memberships totaled 480. There were an additional 127 that had been pledged. This means the total response that had been received to date from the Silver 7000 partners was only 607.

Just as in the embryonic stages of the Grand and Towers Hotel lodging partnership, Jim Bakker was apparently trying to create a false sense of urgency in order to stimulate interest in the slow-moving Silver 7000 Club memberships.

Or was Jim Bakker being given erroneous information concerning the total number of partnerships that had been taken in the Silver 7000 Club? He always contended that at the time he made statements on the air, he believed them to be true.

Were there others at PTL who were aware of the untruths that were being conveyed to the contributing public? As discussed in the next chapter, Richard Dortch testified that there were others who knew the true number of sales of the lifetime partnership program. Assuming Dortch's testimony to be accurate, why didn't those corporate representatives take some action?

The Silver 7000 promotion simply was not going well. On November 11, 1985, PTL records reflected that there were 799 fully paid Silver 7000 club members. Another 294 individuals had partially paid on their 7000 membership, and there were 603 who had made pledges but had not yet paid. This meant that 1,696 individuals had taken some action toward becoming a Silver 7000 Club member.

However, during his "Jim Bakker Show" of November 11, 1985, Bakker said, "I don't know what happened. But all the Silver 7000s are gone. In fact, I looked at the list this morning and we have 7,300 . . ." Tammy Bakker frowned and with a quizzical, almost Lucille Ball–type look, mumbled "uh huh," at which time Jim completed his thoughts by saying, ". . . names on the Silver 7000 Club." Tammy, apparently spontaneously, said: "That's a little more than 7000, isn't it?" to which Jim responded, "Yeh, we have 300 more. Bbbut . . . those that are extra will get the first ones who don't take theirs by Friday . . ." Tammy, with a sigh of relief, says, "Oh, that's right." Jim Bakker's claim that the Silver 7000 list had 7,300 names simply does not match the PTL computer listing.

Amazingly, just eight days later, Jim Bakker reopened the Silver 7000 Club using the exact same pretense that he had used when he reopened the Grand Hotel lifetime partnerships. According to Bakker, the pledges that had been made were not being fulfilled.

But the PTL computer run dated November 19, 1985, reflected the following: 1,158 Silver 7000 Club memberships fully paid; 587

partially paid; 1,153 pledges not paid; and 2 bad checks. There had been a total of 2,900 total pledges.

Although the Silver 7000 Club offered a week in the Towers Hotel and free admission to events at Heritage USA, the next week saw Jim Bakker reneging on yet another promise he had made to the PTL faithful. Beginning on at least November 20, 1985, he offered to split the Silver 7000 membership; that is, for $3,000 one could get seven days and six nights in the Towers Hotel plus admission to all nonfood events, or one could give $1,000 and get four days and three nights for a traditional Towers lifetime membership.

On the PTL program aired on December 27, 1985, Jim and Tammy discussed how the projects were being completed with "no bank loans." Tammy's response was, "That's true." Then Jim said, "To this day, still no bank loans." Jim and Tammy paused significantly and said, ". . . and we've tried haven't we?" And the audience laughed. As previously stated, and as memos to Jim Bakker from the chief financial officer reflected, a $10 million construction loan for the Grand Hotel had been obtained from the Fairfax Savings and Loan in Virginia in November, 1984.

In addition to being misinformed concerning the financial status of the corporation, the PTL faithful were also being led to believe, based on representations made on TV, that the facilities were being built debt free when in fact they were not. The thousands of lifetime partners were now encountering difficulties in obtaining their promised lodging.

Of course, what Jim Bakker failed to let any of PTL's financial supporters know was that he had exceeded the number of lifetime partnerships that had been previously promised, which meant that the partners would be in fierce competition for the limited number of spaces available at the Grand Hotel.

Jim Bakker was well aware of that fact. On the PTL program of November 27, 1985, Bakker asked the audience members to raise their hands if they knew how hard it was to get a room in the inn there. He began to sing "The Impossible Dream" while the audience laughed in the background. Then he actually made a true statement. The impossible dream was to get a room at the Heritage Grand. "You can't get in," he said.

The last day the Silver 7000 Partnerships were promoted was May 21, 1986. Ultimately, in spite of Mr. Bakker's numerous statements to the contrary, the records reflect that the final number of fully paid Silver 7000s was only 2,344 and the number of pledged but not paid Silver 7000s totaled 1,385.

Although the Silver 7000s were a dismal failure from a marketing perspective, PTL and Jim Bakker were about to enter into the most successful fundraising effort in its history: the Victory Warrior program.

Victory Warrior

On May 24, 1986, Jim Bakker announced the Victory Warrior partnership program on the PTL Television Network. He explained that upon payment of $1,000, a Victory Warrior Partner would receive three nights and four days lodging in the Towers each year for life, free admission to nonfood events at PTL, and free admission to two self-improvement workshops each year. This was a partnership package that had originally been offered at PTL for $2,000 but now could be had for $1,000. Thereafter, Bakker and Dortch informed Victory Warrior lifetime partners that upon completion of the Towers Hotel they could choose to stay at the Towers, the Grand, the Heritage Inn Motel, a bunkhouse, or the PTL campground.

The Victory Warrior partnership program (or as it was known around PTL, "VW") was by far the most successful in PTL's history. PTL followers obtained a grand total of 35,984 fully paid Victory Warrior partnerships and paid $36,238,315 for their memberships. This partnership promotion alone exceeded the 30,000 limit originally placed on the Towers Hotel by Jim Bakker back on September 17, 1984. By July 10, 1986, just over six weeks after the Victory Warrior partnerships were first introduced, PTL's chief financial officer was writing to inform Jim Bakker that the total income received from the Victory Warriors as of that date was $34,908,076.

Prior to the May 24, 1986, television announcement of the Victory Warrior Partnership Program, PTL had already sold 28,837 lodging partnerships in the Towers Hotel. Just two days later, PTL had sold a total of 30,504 lodging partnerships, passing the original advertised limit of 30,000 that were to be sold in the Towers.

The development and the promotion of VW partnerships shows the total lack of sophistication of not only Jim Bakker but also the business operators who were employed at PTL and had responsibility for literally hundreds of millions of dollars.

A review of the PTL television programs shows what would at first appear to be an almost innocent "creeping up" and then oversell of the Towers Hotel while promoting VWs. It is important to realize that at this time the Grand Hotel had been drastically oversold but the Towers had not. It was the dramatic promotions of the Victory Warrior and yet other partnership programs relating to the Towers Hotel that resulted in the Towers Hotel being massively oversold as well.

Jim Bakker initially explained on his television program that the genesis of the Victory Warrior Club was when he realized that he owed Roe Messner, PTL's building contractor, eight million dollars. According to Bakker, he promised Messner a one million dollar payment "by faith." Consequently, he had to solicit contributions from the studio audience to be able to make this payment because he "was never going to offer this on TV"; he was able to raise approximately $460,000. Then, in an attempt to make up the difference, as Bakker describes it, "I'll just sneak on [the] satellite and just mention [this program] to a few satellite people to see if we can't get [the remaining funds for Roe Messner]." Jim Bakker elaborated, "We had a desperate need, and when you're desperate, you do desperate things." The phones started ringing, according to Bakker, and they would not stop. Jim Bakker also did not stop promoting VWs, but instead he promoted VWs for several weeks on the PTL sattelite network.

Just as Bakker believed that he had received guidance from God concerning the building of the Grand and of the Towers, so it was that he also received "divine guidance" concerning the Victory Warriors and PTL's bills.

"And the Lord said to me, and this is clear to the whole body, he said, Jim, I'm just as tired of these bills as you are. And enough is enough. I've had it and a miracle is taking place," Jim Bakker explained to his studio and TV audience. Jim Bakker later said that God had granted him a vision concerning the Victory Warriors from the Lord; Tammy replied, "I sure hope he did, honey."

In explaining the chronology of the Victory Warriors program to his TV audience, Bakker related a very interesting conversation he had with his vice-president of partner relations, Steve Nelson. Nelson became a very critical witness for the government against Jim Bakker, and it was Nelson's testimony, as discussed in the next chapter, that probably prompted Jim Bakker's panic attack. He provided some of the most graphic and damaging testimony in the government's wire and mail fraud case against Jim Bakker. It was Nelson's testimony that was used by the government, along with Dortch's, to prove Bakker acted with criminal intent.

Bakker told his television audience on May 26, 1986, that he had been encouraged by Steve Nelson to continue promoting the Victory Warrior partnerships. At Bakker's trial, Nelson testified he had gone to Bakker and told him he had to *stop* selling partnerships because he had exceeded the limit.

Another interesting aspect of the Victory Warrior promotional involved comments made by Doug Oldham, a jolly fellow with a round face and a robust voice who often sang and acted as a co-host on the "Jim Bakker Show." Although he was later identified by Richard Dortch during the criminal trial as a PTL employee who knew the actual number of partnerships sold, Oldham said the following on the PTL program of May 26, 1986:

> The reason I want you to do it, and you know me, I don't understand money, know anything about money, except for the pressure it puts on you. I don't care about it, but I do know this, here's an opportunity to grandparents to give to their kids, which means they're giving to their grand kids a heritage, and it also gives the young family, there are a lot of young families, I've got two young families of my own who can't afford to do what they'd like to do. And it gives them an opportunity to get involved and to get in and guarantee the vacation future of their home, and their kids as long as they are with them.

Money may not have meant much to Doug Oldham, nor may he have understood a lot about it, but in a subsequent civil litigation, Doug Oldham's W-2 form reflected that he had been paid in excess of $189,000 in 1986 alone.

During the same Victory Warrior promotional, Jim Bakker said that if all these VW partnerships were taken, not only would they be able to pay Roe Messner but they would also be current in their payments to their affiliate TV stations for the first time in 11 years. This sounded very familiar to the original Towers offering when Bakker was attempting to raise $30 million.

On May 26, 1986, Jim Bakker was emphatic that "the Victory Warrior Club closes for eternity in 58 minutes." Just as Bakker had said on numerous prior occasions, this final promotional would complete the Grand and Towers memberships. This Memorial Day weekend would, according to Bakker, be the greatest weekend in the history of Christian television.

On May 27, 1986, Jim Bakker, speaking to Richard Dortch, made some comments on the "Jim Bakker Show" that exposed the lack of sophistication and immaturity of the PTL corporation:

> I knew I was going too far [with the promotion]. Without you being here, you and I check with each other, we kind of use each other as a check-and-balance system. And then the board of directors. We check back and forth. But on the day-to-day operation, you and I check back and forth. And so . . . I asked Pastor Dortch about this. We had talked about the earlier part but then to extend on television then you know, it got a little frightening to me. . . . "

Finally, on May 29, 1986, it appeared that the Victory Warriors, Towers, and Grand lifetime partnership programs would be, once and for all, over. Dortch and Bakker's on-air conversation that day couldn't have been more clear:

> DORTCH: You know, Jim, I'm glad to announce there are no more lifetime partnerships left.
> BAKKER: What are you going to do now? I mean you're the chairman of the Lifetime Club, so you won't have nothing to do tomorrow. Four days and three nights is out of work now, so if anybody knows what to do with an unemployed lifetime chairman, we got plenty of work for Pastor Dortch here.

Dortch laughed as he explained that PTL staff members were coming up to him and asking him to say "four days and three nights" just one more time.

Two days later, Jim Bakker was back on TV to explain that he was going to reopen the Victory Warrior Club. He said that 15 percent of the credit cards that had been used to purchase Victory Warrior Club memberships were invalid.

PTL records, as usual, reflected a different story. As of the day that Bakker made that statement, the total number of partnerships designated for the Towers was 45,423, and the total number of invalid charges and bad checks on the Victory Warrior partnership program was zero.

Exhibit 4-4 shows the claims Bakker made concerning the Victory Warrior partnership promotion and the cumulative number of bad checks and invalid charges, as reflected by PTL's own computer records for various program dates.

Although more Victory Warrior partnerships would be bought, the last televised Victory Warrior promotion was on June 15, 1986. At that time, the total number of partnerships in the various programs that had obligated the Towers totaled 50,793, far exceeding the previously established 30,000 limit.

Amazingly, PTL's chief financial officer had informed Bakker that although the Victory Warriors program had raised $34,908,076 as of June 10, 1986, the current balance in the Victory Warrior account was $0. Every penny had been spent. Furthermore, only $6 million of the $34.9 million had been used as had been previously promised— that is, to pay Roe Messner and his corporation, Commercial Builders of Kansas.

Victory Warrior (Towers Hotel) Lifetime Partnerships Promotion

Televised Announcements	Pledged But Not Paid (Cumulative)	Bad Checks and Invalid Charges (Cumulative)
May 26, 1986 Jim Bakker Announces Victory Warrior Partnership on Jim and Tammy Show	0	0
May 29, 1986 Richard Dortch Announces, "No More Partnerships"	1	0
May 31, 1986 Program Pre-Recorded for June 9, 1986 Broadcast	1	0
June 9, 1986 Jim Bakker Reopens Victory Warrior, "15% of Credit Cards Did Not Go Through"	1	0
June 16, 1986 Jim Bakker Announces, "All Tower Partnerships Are Gone"	1	3
June 30, 1986	3	59

Exhibit 4-4   A Breakdown of Bad Checks and Invalid Charges for the Victory Warrior Promotion

65

Family Fun Special

Despite the fact that the Towers had been oversold by over 20,000 memberships, there was to be one more promotional concerning the Towers. In 1987, Richard Dortch introduced the $900 Family Fun Partnership Lifetime Program. The Family Fun Special was aired on the Inspirational Network during weekend telethons on March 7–8 and April 11–12 of that year. For $1,000, and later reduced to $900, one could become a lifetime partner in the Family Fun partnership program, which offered four days and three nights lodging in the Towers Hotel each year. Additionally, one received free admission to nonfood events and various promotional gift items; one could also attend one workshop each year.

PTL had already sold 65,533 lodging partnerships for the Towers. Although Jim Bakker resigned his position as president and chair of the board of the PTL Organization on March 19, 1987, he was still involved, according to the government, with the Family Fun partnerships. Specifically, a PTL employee testified that she had met with Jim Bakker prior to his resignation concerning a letter that would go out regarding the Family Fun partnership. That letter, mailed to 524,003 individuals from April 4 through April 8, 1987, stated in part, "I am very disappointed that some of those partners who had pledged to be a part of the Towers have not followed through on their commitment. I need several partners to help stand in the gap and make up the hedge for those who have fallen by the wayside and who have been unfaithful in their commitment. I believe that the devil had a master plan to destroy Jim and Tammy in the ministry of PTL, but God has defeated Satan's attack and His work will go on." Jim Bakker's signature and photograph accompany that brochure.

Ultimately, 3,350 individuals subscribed to the Family Fun partnership, and 1,955 individuals pledged but did not pay. The total amount raised in the Family Fun partnership was $3,555,731.

The Family Fun partnership was the last of six different promotional lifetime partnership programs that offered accommodations in the Towers Hotel. Jim Bakker had said on his September 17, 1984, "Jim Bakker Show" that there would be a limit of 30,000 Towers Hotel partners and that only one-half of the 500 rooms in the Towers would be available for partners. As of May 31, 1987, however, there were 68,755 fully paid lodging partnerships in the Towers. The total amount paid for various partnerships in the Towers hotel was $74,292,751.

Furthermore, of the $74,292,751 raised through these various partnerships, the amount spent on construction of the Towers was only $11,422,684. The Towers Hotel was never completed and currently stands as a monument to the mismanagement, waste, and excesses of the former PTL empire. The government presented evidence that the estimated amount still needed to complete construction on the Grand came to a total of $15,401,397. Exhibit 4-5 was used by the government in Bakker's criminal trial to show graphically the total amount of lifetime partnerships funds received and how only 15.2 percent of the funds received were used to begin construction on the Towers Hotel.

The Bunkhouse Partnership Fraud

> For which of you intending to build a tower, does not first sit down and count the cost, whether he has enough to complete it? Otherwise, when he has laid the foundation, and is not able to finish, all that see it begin to mock him.
>
> Luke 14:28–29, quoted by Deborah Smith, Criminal Fraud Section, Department of Justice in *United States v. Bakker.*

Although the Bunkhouse partnerships, sometimes known as the Family Heritage Club, were first mentioned by Jim Bakker on his television program of May 20, 1986, they were not actually promoted until August 4, 1986. Bunkhouse partnerships promised three days and two nights of lodging each year plus free admission to all nonfood events at PTL for the balance of the contributor's life. The Bunkhouse promised a more rustic environment, and this partnership cost not $1,000 but $500. Six people could stay in a Bunkhouse, which would be located in a more wooded area and away from the construction of the Towers and the Grand Hotels. Although there were no limitations placed on the number of members that could become members of the Bunkhouse Club, it was announced that there would be between 10 and 50 Bunkhouses built.

A promotional letter announcing the Bunkhouse partnership was mailed to 510,874 individuals from August 12 through August 17, 1986. Of critical importance, this mailing promised that 50 percent of the Bunkhouse lodging would always be reserved for Family Heritage Club members. Again, the Family Heritage Club was another name for the Bunkhouse partnership program.

In promoting the Bunkhouse memberships, it was not uncommon for Bakker and others to emphasize that the Grand and Towers partnerships were closed. For example, on August 5, 1986, Bakker an-

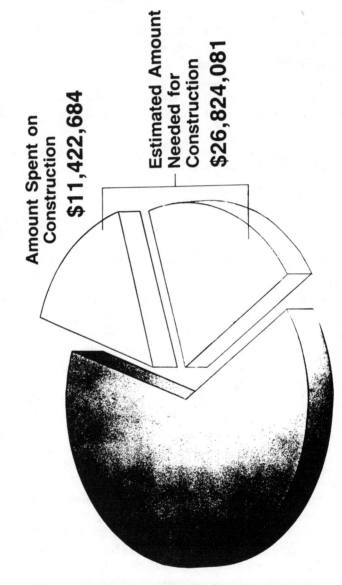

Towers Hotel
Total Lifetime Partnership Funds Received — $74,292,751

Amount Spent on
Construction
$11,422,684

Estimated Amount
Needed for
Construction
$26,824,081

Exhibit 4-5   A Breakdown of Total Towers Hotel Lifetime Partnership Funds Received

nounced that all the Grand and Towers partnerships were gone, and according to PTL's own documents, the number of fully paid Grand partnerships had reached a total of 66,283. Despite this contention, PTL continued to accept people's money for Grand partnerships even after this announcement. And by May 31, 1987, PTL had sold 400 more.

The same thing was happening with the Towers. By August 5, 1986, a total of 65,537 Towers partnerships had been sold by PTL. However, by May 31, 1987, PTL's computer records reveal that the total number of Towers partnerships sold had risen to 68,755, an increase of over 3,000 partnerships.

Despite Bakker's contention that PTL might build 50 bunkhouses, only one bunkhouse was being utilized at the time of Jim Bakker's resignation in March of 1987. As previously indicated, Bakker said that 50 percent of the bunkhouse units would be available for lifetime partners. The one completed bunkhouse had 16 rooms, meaning that 8 rooms were available for 9,682 fully paid Bunkhouse partners.

There were also 17,038 partially paid Bunkhouse partners, and 24,629 individuals who had pledged but not paid. The total amount raised through the Bunkhouse partnership program was $6,681,961. Exhibit 4-6 summarizes the program's history.

Furthermore, Jim Bakker was about to announce yet another lodging partnership program. In addition to other possible lodging accommodations, this program would also offer accommodations in the eight rooms available in the one bunkhouse. Finally, of the $6.6 million received from Bunkhouse partners, less than $1 million was designated for and actually spent on construction of the Bunkhouses. As the government contended, "with the full knowledge and consent of Bakker and Dortch, more than $5 million of Bunkhouse funds were used for PTL operating costs, including bonuses for the defendants."

The 1100 Club

Take your pick of lodging.

Promotional brochure for the 1100 Club Partnerships
mailed on January 7, 1987

The 1100 Club partnership program was promoted from November 24, 1986, to February 2, 1987. Jim Bakker again stated that the Grand, the Towers, and the Bunkhouse partnerships were closed. However, as previously indicated, partnerships continued to be sold for these "closed" programs. For example, even though Bakker stated that the

Bunkhouse

- First Introduced — May 20, 1986
- Number of Rooms Available for Lifetime Partnerships — 8
- Original Advertised Limit — None; Announced 10-50 Bunkhouses Might Be Built

Promotion	TV Announcement Date	Required Payment	Fully Paid	Partially Paid	Pledged But Not Paid	Total Dollars Paid*
Family Heritage Club	May 20, 1986	$500	9,682	17,038	24,629	$6,681,961
Totals:			**9,682**	**17,038**	**24,629**	**$6,681,961**

* Includes Partially Paid.

Exhibit 4-6 A Breakdown of Partnerships for the Family Heritage Club Promotion

Bunkhouse partnership programs were closed as of November 1, 1986, 1,622 additional Bunkhouses had been fully paid for by November 25. All of those were in addition to the 1100 Club memberships that offered bunkhouse accommodations.

Bakker and Dortch claimed in mailed brochures and on television that a donation of $1,100 would give partners their choice of four different places to stay: the bunkhouses, the Country Farm Inn, and The Heritage Grand Mansion, for four days and three nights each year for life; or the 1100 Club campground, for seven days and six nights each year for life. As well, partners would receive free admission to nonfood events at PTL while staying in lodging as an 1100 Club member and could attend one workshop per year free of charge.

According to the government and as found by the jury, the false claims made by Bakker and Dortch were no different than the other lodging partnership frauds. The government contended that Bakker and Dortch failed to fully inform the thousands of 1100 Club members that they would be in fierce competition with the thousands of Bunkhouse members for the use of the one completed bunkhouse, which contained a mere eight rooms reserved for use by lifetime partners. Furthermore, the government contended that "[t]he solicitation of lifetime partners by Bakker and Dortch without the full disclosure of the true numbers of partnerships being sold and the limited facilities available to accommodate them, constituted a knowing misrepresentation of material facts and concealment of material facts."

For example, in a brochure mailed on January 7, 1987, Dortch and Bakker made statements that created the impression that the Country Inn Farmhouse and the 1100 Club Mansion were constructed and available for immediate occupancy by 1100 Club members. In fact, they had not yet been built.

Furthermore, and of particular significance, the number of fully and partially paid Bunkhouse and 1100 Club members as of May 31, 1987, who were entitled to use the 8 rooms in the one completed bunkhouse was 42,162. Also, the money generated by the Bunkhouse and 1100 Club partnerships came to a total of $17,382,228. Only $864,911, or approximately 5.6 percent of that amount, was spent to construct the facilities promised to members. Exhibit 4-7 sums up the 1100 Club's finances; Exhibit 4-8 graphically illustrates the extent of the Bunkhouse and 1100 Club frauds.

Despite the millions of dollars that were raised by both the Bunkhouse and 1100 Club partnerships, neither the Country Inn Farmhouse, nor the Heritage Grand Mansion, nor the 1100 Club campgrounds were ever built.

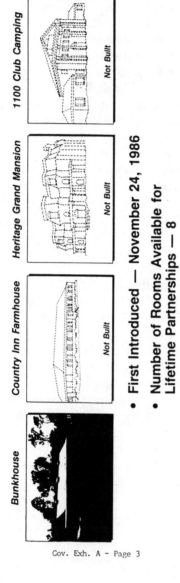

1100 Club

Bunkhouse

Country Inn Farmhouse

Not Built

Heritage Grand Mansion

Not Built

1100 Club Camping

Not Built

- First Introduced — November 24, 1986
- Number of Rooms Available for Lifetime Partnerships — 8
- Advertised Limit — None

Promotion	TV Announcement Date	Required Payment	Fully Paid	Partially Paid	Pledged But Not Paid	Total Dollars Paid*
1100 Club	Nov. 24, 1986	$1,100	7,783	7,659	11,059	$10,700,267
Totals:			**7,783**	**7,659**	**11,059**	**$10,700,267**

* Includes Partially Paid.

Gov. Exh. A – Page 3

Exhibit 4-7   A Breakdown of Partnerships for the 1100 Club Promotion

Bunkhouse and 1100 Club
Total Lifetime Partnership Funds Received — $17,382,228

Amount Spent on
Construction
$864,911

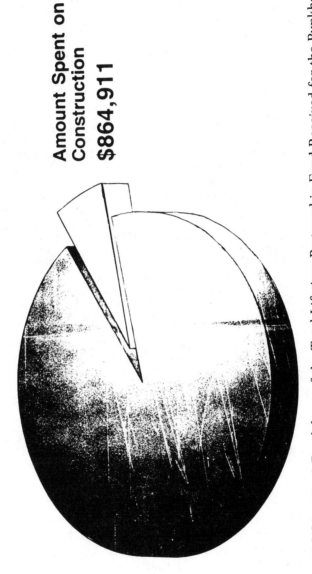

Exhibit 4-8   A Breakdown of the Total Lifetime Partnership Fund Received for the Bunkhouse
and 1100 Club Promotions

Gift Promotionals: David and Goliath

In addition to the lifetime partnerships, Jim Bakker also offered his followers certain promotional materials. These were given to contributors in addition to the yearly lodging perks. One example of this is the "David and Goliath" statue that was included in the original offering of the Grand Hotel lifetime partnership program. Jim and Tammy had the following interchange when they displayed the statue to their viewers on February 20, 1984:

> JIM: Few families could have this Heller piece, because that Heller piece in Mr. Heller's shop in Jerusalem sells for $10,000. That's why this security guard is right over there. His other pieces sell for—most of the pieces here are over $1,000 each, [they are] beautiful pieces.
>
> It's a limited edition number. It will be created for you. It is hand poured, hand finished, and it's a limited edition. You see a stamp on the back with the number 184. This is one that I have. There will only be 100,000 of these made, and the molds are going to be destroyed. This is pewter finished, and it is a beautiful piece. It is a signed Jacob Heller piece.
>
> This piece sells . . . the silver piece that is on my desk—for $1,200. This [same piece] has been recreated for us by special craftsmen here in the United States, and every lifetime member who gives $1,000 [can get one]. You must send your check in. . . .
>
> But we will begin creating your [art] piece. They are already beginning to manufacture these. It takes a little while to get them all—because they are crafted. It's not something that they go, stamp, stamp, stamp. This is poured. These are poured in molds.
>
> Maybe later on in the telethon, I will actually be able to show you—
>
> TAMMY: It is exciting how they do it, Jim. I was really excited.
>
> JIM: Somebody said, "My land, Jim, the Heller piece would be wonderful for a $1,000 gift by itself.

On "The Jim Bakker Show" of February 22, 1984, Bakker again discussed not only the four days and three nights that a lifetime partner could receive for the rest of his or her life but also said, "Plus, you are going to receive something that is worth, I think, $1,000 alone. It's the David and Goliath creation by Jacob Heller from Jerusalem."

The David and Goliath statue was also described and promoted as "a collector's item" in the original promotional letter for the Grand Hotel that was mailed on January 7, 1984.

PTL Lifetime Partnership Clubs

	Grand	Towers	Silver*	Silver 7000	Victory Warrior	Bunkhouse	1100 Club	Family Fun
Date Introduced	1/7/84	9/17/84	2/19/85	9/4/85	5/24/86	5/20/86	11/24/86	3/7/87
Contribution	$1,000	$1,000 or $2,000	$1,000	$3,000	$1,000	$500	$1,100	$900 or $1,000
Number Sold	66,683	27,072	7,630	2,344	35,984	9,682	7,783	3,350
Original Lodging Benefits	• Grand 4D/3N	• Towers 4D/3N	—None—	• Towers 7D/6N	• Towers 4D/3N	• Bunkhouse 3D/2N	• Bunkhouse 4D/3N • Country Inn 4D/3N • 1100 Club Man. 4D/3N • 1100 Club Camp. 7D/6N	• Towers 4D/3N
Original Non-Lodging Benefits	—None—	—None—	• Free Admiss. to Non-Food Events • Membership Pin • General Trans. • 2 Workshops Per Year	• Free Admiss. to Non-Food Events • Membership Pin • General Trans. • 2 Workshops Per Year	• Free Admiss. to Non-Food Events • General Trans. • 2 Workshops Per Year	• Free Admiss. to Limited Non-Food Events	• Free Admiss. to Limited Non-Food Events Only While Lodging at HUSA • 2 Workshops Per Year	• Free Admiss. to Non-Food Events • 1 Workshop Per Year • Various Promotional Gifts

* Gold and Diamond Non-Lodging Partnerships Are Not Included Here.

Exhibit 4-9   List of Prices and Benefits for the PTL Lifetime Partnership Clubs

Despite Jim Bakker's assertion that these David and Goliath statues were not produced mechanically, it turned out that this was in fact the case. Bakker's claims concerning the construction and actual intrinsic value of the statue was contradicted by the testimony of Richard Ball, PTL's vice-president of partner relations. Ball stated in court that the statues were mass produced, hollow pieces that cost PTL only $10 each, which was also reflected in the work papers of Deloitte, Haskins and Sells. (Exhibit A-8.) However, this accounting firm never raised the David and Goliath promotion as an issue with PTL; it served as PTL's outside and independent auditor for the fiscal year ending May 31, 1984.

The Bottom Line

Exhibit 4-9 reflects, in summary, the various PTL lifetime partnership clubs that were offered by Jim Bakker and others at PTL.

As of May 31, 1987, the number of fully paid memberships in the various programs included 68,755 Towers memberships, 66,683 Grand memberships, 9,682 Bunkhouse memberships, and 7,783 1100 Club memberships. For the four major lifetime partnership programs offered at PTL, the total number of fully paid lodging partnerships was 152,903, which produced at least $158 million in revenue for PTL.

These were the facts that were used in the prosecution of Jim Bakker for wire and mail fraud. The government submitted that the motive or purpose that provided the criminal intent for Jim Bakker to engage in this massive oversell of lodging partnerships was the vast income that he received over the years. In support of this charge, the government specified 42 overt acts that were carried out or initiated by Dortch and Bakker with the purpose of perpetrating and enjoying the fruits of the fraud.

The government spent two years investigating PTL's finances, but it only needed six weeks of trial to prove Bakker guilty.

□ □ □

CHAPTER FIVE

United States v. Bakker and Overview of Related Proceedings

In conforming with the religious overture of this case, this court observes that James Bakker either overlooked or ignored parts of the Bible, including I Timothy 6:10—"For the love of money is the root of all evil: which while some coveted after, they have erred from the faith and pierced themselves through with many sorrows." Now, however, we must apply Galatians 6:7—"Be not deceived; God is not mocked: for whatsoever a man soweth, that shall he also reap."

Federal Bankruptcy Judge Rufus W. Reynolds,
In Re Heritage Village Church and Missionary Fellowship

OVER TWO YEARS AFTER HE HAD RESIGNED FROM PTL, Jim Bakker finally faced his day of judgment in a U.S. Federal District Court. Over the years, Bakker had convinced thousands of followers to purchase lifetime partnerships; now he was hoping for just 12 more believers in the jury.

Bakker was facing 8 counts of mail fraud, 15 counts of wire fraud (3 from telephone use and 12 counts from use of television), and an additional count of conspiracy to commit wire and mail fraud with Richard Dortch, for a total of 24 counts. As Bakker's co-conspirator, Dortch was also charged with the same 23 counts of wire and mail fraud and 1 count of conspiracy to commit wire and mail fraud. In December 1988, after 16 months of testimony, a federal grand jury returned a bill of indictment against the two televangelists on all 24 counts. The stage was now set for the government to present its case.

This criminal case was the third of what were four significant judicial proceedings concerning the business operations of PTL. In the first of these, the U.S. Bankruptcy Court had handed Bakker and his wife a major setback by ordering them to reimburse the PTL corporation $5,603,639.47. This amount represented what the Bankruptcy Court found to be excessive compensation received by the Bakkers from PTL. The criminal case would later examine the illegal activities that occurred, but it was the Federal Bankruptcy Court that initially considered the exorbitant expenditures and management failures at PTL.

The second case had concerned charges of criminal tax evasion brought by the government against Bakker's administrative assistant, David Taggart, and his brother, James Taggart, who was PTL's interior decorator; both were convicted. These two proceedings revealed not only the excesses but also the shockingly poor business practices that existed at PTL. The organization was clearly teeming with fraudulent activities.

The remaining court proceeding was the civil case against PTL's auditors and selected officers and a director of the corporation. This case occurred subsequent to the Bakker criminal trial and is discussed later in this book.

The bankruptcy proceedings and the Taggarts' trial set the stage for the Bakker criminal case. It was also through these proceedings that corporate documents were entered into evidence and sworn testimony was obtained relative to the finances and the business practices of PTL.

The Bankruptcy Proceedings

After PTL declared bankruptcy in June 1987, Jim and Tammy Bakker filed a claim with the Federal Bankruptcy Court in September 1987 seeking "$1.3 million plus." The claim was premised on their alleged rights to recover the value of a parsonage and to recover money due from copyrights, trademarks, and other intangibles. David Taggart, Jim Bakker's personal assistant, also filed a claim with the Bankruptcy Court in October 1987, seeking recovery of $187,500 for employment services rendered under a contract he supposedly had with PTL.

The court-appointed trustee not only objected to these claims but also counterclaimed and alleged that each of the defendants engaged in corporate mismanagement and wrongdoing and that they had received inordinate personal benefits from PTL for fiscal years 1984 through 1987.

What emerged from these proceedings was a finding by the Court that the conduct of all of the defendants was not merely negligent; as Bankruptcy Judge Rufus W. Reynolds found: "In actuality, the conduct of the defendants . . . was intentional, wanton, capricious and reckless. The parties have failed to perform their duties honestly, in good faith, or with any reasonable amount of diligence or care."

PTL's fiscal years ended on May 31. A comparison of PTL's lifetime partnership revenue for each fiscal year end reflects that as lifetime partnership revenues increased, regular contributions declined. (See Exhibit 5-1.)

The Bankruptcy Court noted in its opinion of November 9, 1988, that as soon as funds for various building projects at PTL were placed into designated accounts, "most of the money was drawn out for operating and administrative purposes, including the payment of excessive salaries and bonuses, and for disbursements to cover the cost of extravagant travel and entertainment expenses [for certain PTL executives]."

The Bankruptcy Court found that from 1982 until 1987 PTL received $400 million in donations, which included approximately $160 million raised from the sale of lifetime partnerships. Concerning these funds and PTL's obligations, the court noted that "there was no cash set aside by PTL to take care of continuing obligations which would be incurred over the years by the lifetime partner program. All of the money was spent primarily for current operations, rather than being set aside to fund the cost of construction or expenses which would be created by furnishing four days and three nights of lodging for no additional payment."

To emphasize the critical financial situation of PTL, the court noted that at the time of Bakker's resignation in March 1987, PTL

Fiscal Year Ending	Free Will Donations	Lifetime Partnerships
1983	$48,236,282.00	0.00
1984	$52,932,581.00	$16,827,547.00
1985	$42,056,220.00	$49,486,462.00
1986	$43,691,001.00	$56,654,968.00
1987 (thru 3/87)	$26,104,422.00	$41,724,324.00

Exhibit 5-1   A Comparison of Free Will Donations and Lifetime Partnerships from 1983 through 1987

had a cash deficit of $323,766, current assets of $9,370,556, and current liabilities of $36,843,567. Although not addressing the over-sale of lifetime partnerships, the Bankruptcy Court noted that before construction had begun on the Towers Hotel, PTL had already raised over $20 million through promotion of the project. Once construction actually commenced, all but $2 million of the $20 million had been spent by PTL on general operational expenses.

Despite this financial crisis, extraordinary sums of money were paid to (at least) Jim Bakker, Tammy Bakker, David Taggart, and Richard Dortch. Exhibit 5-2 itemizes just the bonuses paid to these four individuals during the nine months previous to Bakker's resignation in March, 1987.

Just three months before Bakker's resignation, $845,000 was distributed between the three defendants—$450,000 to Bakker, $170,000 to Tammy Bakker, and $225,000 to Taggart. As the Court noted, "[s]uch extravagance is almost unlimited or at least it was until the funds gave out." Even after Bakker left Heritage USA in January, 1987, he was paid $450,000 in bonuses during a ten-day period.

Disbursement of corporate funds was accomplished by using three different checking accounts that were maintained by PTL executives. These accounts were the Executive Payroll Account, the Parsonage Account, and the Executive Account. The Bankruptcy Court noted that "[t]hese accounts were not subject to normal PTL audit procedures."

The Bankruptcy Court found that Jim Bakker received remuneration from PTL in the form of salary, bonuses, housing allowances,

BONUSES—June 1986 through March 17, 1987

	J.O. BAKKER	T.F. BAKKER	D.A. TAGGART	R. DORTCH
7/86			11,000.00	100,000.00
7/01/86			110,000.00	
7/16/86	350,000.00	115,000.00		
11/07/86	10,000.00			100,000.00
11/10/86	190,000.00	20,000.00		
11/20/86			125,000.00	
11/24/86		20,000.00		50,000.00
12/18/86	20,000.00	10,000.00		
12/19/86			22,700.00	
12/22/86	20,000.00			100,000.00
1/87				50,000.00
2/04/87	300,000.00	170,000.00		
2/13/87	150,000.00			
2/16/87			225,000.00	
3/87				53,010.00
TOTAL	$1,040,000.00	$335,000.00	$493,700.00	$453,010.00
GRAND TOTAL	$2,229,305.00			

Exhibit 5-2   A List of Bonuses for the Key PTL Personnel

and retirement contributions. Bakker's total remuneration from May 31, 1983, through May 31, 1987, was $4,326,169.39.

In addition to receiving a housing allowance of $2,000 per month, PTL also paid the utility bills for the parsonage occupied by the Bakkers. Because they wanted their outdoor pool heated to 90°F year round, these bills were quite high. The total amount of utility charges for the Bakker parsonage paid by PTL was $88,629.02. In one year alone the Bakkers' parsonage utility bills totaled $25,472.66.

The PTL parsonage was eventually sold to pizza parlor owner Robert Rubino for $685,000. The 10,000-square-foot house has six bedrooms large enough to hold two queen-size beds each; five and a half baths; a pool; and five decks overlooking the lake at Tega Cay, South Carolina, an exclusive community just south of Heritage USA. What used to be Tammy Bakker's closet was converted into a 19′ × 22′ bedroom.

A total of $610,000 was paid out of the parsonage account for the four fiscal years 1984 through 1987 for the use and benefit of Bakker and his family.

Expenditures of $118,001.05 were paid from the executive account for such personal items as limousine services, antiques, hotel accomodations, travel, cash advances, and jewelry. Other personal expenditures for which there is not sufficient documentation to justify them as business expenses came to a total of $147,462 from July 4, 1984, through October 10, 1985. These funds came from the general checking account of PTL.

Bakker was also charged by Judge Reynolds for the $363,700 that PTL expended on the Jessica Hahn settlement. (The trustee of the PTL property was eventually able to recover $185,049.66 from other sources, and therefore the judge reduced the charge by that amount.)

What the Bankruptcy Court characterized as the "unfettered and unchecked use of the PTL Saberliner airplane" also resulted in a charge of misusing of corporate assets. The value of Bakker's use of the plane in 1985 was $102,460.76; in 1985 he also incurred an additional $124,986.23 in expenses for other chartered aircraft during that same year.

Although the Court recognized that Bakker had reimbursed PTL a total of $72,755.61, it did find that the excessive spending at PTL was "shocking to the conscience to the extent that it is unbelievable that a religious ministry would be operated in such a manner."

The Court then listed what it characterized as "[a] few of the outrageous, unbelievable, and shocking expenditures" of Jim Bakker and his family:

☐ Rental of a jet plane for a two-week vacation in California at a cost to PTL of $124,000 (including the costs incurred while it sat idle on the ground)

☐ The purchase of an $8,500 waterslide by PTL for the Bakkers' residence (the PTL parsonage)

☐ $8,870 spent on decorating the Bakker's houseboat

☐ Approximately $5,900 spent on a multi-story playhouse for the Bakker children, equipped with electricity and heat

☐ The purchase of a $570 shower curtain for the Bakker's daughter at PTL's expense

The Bankruptcy Court admitted into evidence the result of an IRS investigation concerning Bakker's excessive compensation. The IRS had full-time agents at PTL for about three years; as many as 12 agents at a time were responsible for reviewing the corporate records and operation of PTL.

As Exhibit 5-3 reflects, the Bankruptcy Court made its own determination as to the amount and the propriety of Bakker's expenditures. The Court also determined, as did the IRS, what it believed to be reasonable compensation for Bakker. The difference between what Bakker actually received each year and what he should have received was found by the Court to be excessive compensation, or private inurement, which the Court ordered Bakker to give back to the bankrupt corporation.

Despite Tammy Bakker's assertion that she was not aware of the amounts of any of the bonuses, that she played the role of an ordinary housewife, and that she spent whatever money was put into her account, the Bankruptcy Court found her liable for $677,397.07. Exhibit 5-4 lists the specific findings of the Court relating to Tammy Bakker.

Tammy Bakker gave a sworn deposition on August 17, 1988, relating to the bankruptcy proceedings. Her testimony is interesting in that it not only gives insights into her understanding of the business affairs of PTL but also reflects her recollection of what she and her husband discussed concerning bonuses, and what actions she took:

Q: I'd like to ask you some questions about bonuses which you received, especially in the last couple of years.
A: Yes, sir.
Q: Do you remember the last bonus you received?
A: No, sir, I don't.
Q: Do you remember any bonuses that you received in '86 and '87?

Exhibit 5-3   A Comparison of the Court and IRS Findings of James O. Bakker's Compensation

DESCRIPTION	NOTES	1984		1985		1986		1987	
		Column #1 Findings of IRS	Column A Findings of COURT	Column #2 Findings of IRS	Column B Findings of COURT	Column #3 Findings of IRS	Column C Findings of COURT	Column #4 Findings of IRS	Column D Findings of COURT
Salary	1	228,486.16	228,486.16	291,425.28	291,425.28	264,996.00	264,996.00	278,158.00	264,999.96
Bonuses	2	640,000.00	640,000.00	450,000.00	400,000.00	600,000.00	600,000.00	1,167,000.00	1,040,000.00
Housing Allowance	3	24,000.00	24,000.00	24,360.00	24,360.00	25,440.00	25,440.00	23,320.00	25,440.00
Minister's Benefit Assn.	4	108,468.75	108,468.75	123,429.20	123,429.20	132,500.04	132,500.04	121,658.36	132,500.04
FRV of Parsonage	5	45,000.00	N/A	45,000.00	45,000.00	45,000.00	N/A	45,000.00	N/A
Parsonage Utilities	6	17,563.15	8,781.57	27,696.76	10,798.12	23,996.97	11,558.69	25,472.66	12,734.23
Housekeeping/Maint.	7	27,696.76	N/A	27,696.76	N/A	27,696.76	N/A	27,696.76	N/A
FRV of Florida Condo.	8	24,000.00	N/A	2,000.00	N/A	0.00	N/A	0.00	N/A
Condo. Utilities	9	924.78	N/A	150.41	N/A	0.00	N/A	0.00	N/A
Personal Use Aircraft	10	0.00	0.00	102,460.76	102,460.76	0.00	N/A	0.00	N/A
Personal Use of Auto	11	1,200.00	0.00	4,200.00	N/A	4,800.00	N/A	17,255.32	0.00
Personal Use of Pres. Suite, Heritage Grand Hotel									
Expend. for Personal Benefit of Bakker from Exec. Chk.	12	0.00	0.00	108,000.00	N/A	N/A	N/A	N/A	N/A
Personage Chk. Acct.	13	0.00	0.00	33,340.25	21,340.25	46,197.39	44,197.39	59,463.41	50,463.41
General Chk. Acct.	14	5,000.00	0.00	16,500.00	3,500.00	134,723.06	127,723.08	480,595.11	479,000.00
Write-off of Cash Adv.	15	30,000.00	0.00	81,264.03	33,264.03	38,198.88	13,296.88	0.00	0.00
Cash Adv.-MC & VISA	16	9,000.00	9,000.00	14,590.26	5,000.00	0.00	0.00	0.00	0.00
Amer. Express Charges	17	178,616.41	178,616.41	0.00	0.00	309,520.89	309,520.89	300,048.55	300,048.55
Exec. Air Fleet Pymts.	18	0.00	0.00	47,458.97	47,458.97	0.00	0.00	0.00	0.00
J. Bahn Related Pymts.	19	0.00	0.00	124,986.23	124,986.23	0.00	0.00	34,919.99	34,919.99
Other Expenditures	20	0.00	0.00	38,700.00	38,700.00	355,660.50	355,660.50	325,000.00	325,000.00
Other Expenditures	21			378,280.47	378,280.47				
Total for Bakker's Benefit	22	1,339,956.01	1,197,352.89	1,935,438.86	1,605,123.31	2,008,730.49	1,886,895.19	2,898,388.16	2,647,108.18
Less: Reasonable Comp.	23	(133,100.00)	(133,100.00)	(146,410.00)	(146,410.00)	(161,051.00)	(161,051.00)	(177,156.00)	(157,156.00)
Increment to J. Bakker	24	1,206,856.01	1,064,252.89	1,789,028.86	1,458,713.31	1,847,679.49	1,725,844.19	2,721,232.16	2,489,952.18

IRS FINDINGS (Columns 1, 2, 3, 4)

Total of Line 22	$8,182,513.52
Less: Total of Line 23	617,717.00
Total of Line 24	$7,564,796.52

COURT FINDINGS (Columns A, B, C, D)

Total of Line 22		$7,336,479.57
Less: Total of Line 23		597,717.00
Total of Line 24		$6,738,762.57
	185,049.66	(Bahn Recovery)
	72,775.61	(Reimbursements Proved)
		$6,480,937.30
	1,554,694.90	(Potential Joint Liability)
		$4,926,242.40

83

Description	Notes	8405	8505	8605	8705
Salary	(1)	$ 84,963.91	$142,586.04	$ 83,174.63	$ 92,478.96
Bonuses	(2)	130,000.00	115,000.00	200,000.00	336,000.00
Expenditures for the Benefit of Tammy Faye Bakker					
Exec. Check. Acct.	(3)		5,000.00	7,184.00	31,955.03
Parsonage Check Acct	(4)	6,000.00			
Total for T. Bakker's Benefit		$220,963.41	$262,586.04	$290,358.63	$459,433.99
Less: Reasonable Comp.		119,790.00	131,769.00	144,946.00	159,440.00
Inurement to T. Bakker		$101,173.41	$130,817.04	$145,412.63	$299,993.99
Total		$677,397.07			

Exhibit 5-4   Tamara Faye Bakker's Compensation

A: Not really. I know that they were substantial, but I never asked for them, and so therefore they weren't that important to me and I do not remember how many I received and I know we would get them at Christmas, and that's the only ones I can remember.

□ □ □

Q: The records seem to indicate that in July of '86, you received a gross bonus of a hundred and fifteen thousand dollars that netted out to about fifty. Do you recall?
A: I don't recall particular months. I promise you I don't. I don't. I just know they put them in my account, they were there, and I spent them, like a typical woman.

□ □ □

Q: How would you generally learn about your bonuses?
A: ". . .[Richard Dortch] always told me after the fact. He said, "We have given you—you've got a surprise coming," he would say to me, that kind of thing, "The board has voted you a bonus and you'll be getting it at such and such a time," and inadvertently I'd always say, "Brother Dortch, you don't have to do that."
Q: Were you ever made aware of the financial affairs of P.T.L.?
A: No, only when we were having telethons and needed money, and I was there helping, you know, singing and helping to be a part of raising the money, but I had absolutely no knowledge of the internal affairs of P.T.L. at all.

□ □ □

Q: How about the light bill, the electric bill, the phone bill?
A: I don't know who paid for that. I have no idea who paid for that, but I know we paid for the food. I know all of the little knickknacks and stuff we bought out of our own pocket, anything to decorate it with. You know, the little fun things that sit on counters and all. But I have no idea who paid the electric bill, I have no idea who paid the phone bill, I have no idea who paid any of the other bills. Because I wasn't ever in on it, I didn't have to worry about it.

□ □ □

Q: Who determined your pay?
A: I don't know. I honestly do not know who determined my pay.
Q: Did you ever talk to your husband about it?
A: Never. We never talked about my pay. I assume Reverend Dortch. They say don't assume, because that makes an a-s-s out of you and me, but I really don't know. I have no idea. All I know is I got it and I spent it like any woman would.
Q: When you would go on trips with Mr. Bakker, whether they were P.T.L. trips or otherwise, who would usually pick up the tab?
A: I don't know.

Q: Did you ever have anything to do with charging things on credit cards?

A: No, sir, I never use credit cards.

Q: Did you ever have one in your name, or one that you used?

A: No, I never had one that I used. I'm sure that I—I think there was one in my name, but I don't remember ever using the credit card.

□ □ □

Q: Do you know anything about P.T.L. paying personal bills for you and Mr. Bakker?

A: No, sir, because we were always very, very careful in the respect that anything that was personal to us, that was for our own personal benefit, that Jim Bakker paid for out of his own checkbook, and I've heard him say it a thousand times, "Make a check out from my own personal checkbook."

David Taggart served as vice-president of administration at PTL. In that capacity he served as Bakker's administrative assistant and not only supplied him with PTL funds but also made all the administrative arrangements for Bakker.

Initially employed in PTL's music department in 1978 at a salary of $200 a week, Taggart received the following compensation during fiscal years 1984 through 1987 according to the findings of the Bankruptcy Court:

1984	$ 60,662.08
1985	139,574.39
1986	210,042.29
1987	605,972.99
Total	$1,016,251.75

In his role as Jim Bakker's administrative assistant, Taggart had unlimited access to the executive checking account and the ability to receive numerous checks and obtain cash advances on PTL credit cards, often in the amounts of $5,000, $10,000, or $20,000. The court provided some specific examples of what it characterized as Taggart's unsubstantiated withdrawal of funds from PTL and undocumented utilization of PTL credit:

□ From 1984 through 1987, Taggart received $144,988.93 from the PTL Executive Account

□ During the fiscal years 1984 through 1986, Taggart received $24,000 from the PTL general checking account

☐ In 1984 and 1985, Taggart received cash advances from PTL amounting to $89,307.55. These advances were eventually written off by PTL.

☐ Taggart received three checks, signed in blank from Peter G. Bailey, PTL's chief financial officer. (The professional relationship between Taggart and Bailey and the latter's role in the PTL scandal is fully explored in subsequent chapters.) These checks were used by Taggart to pay his personal American Express account. The check numbers, date of the check and the amounts are:

Check #	Date	Amount
1929	2–16–87	$50,000
1930	3–28–87	$45,000
1931	4–16–87	$30,000

On April 16, 1987, check number 1060 was drawn on the PTL Executive Account for $15,000 and was made payable to the personal American Express account of David Taggart. The Court found that "[t]hese checks totalling $140,000 were not authorized by officers of PTL and documents to justify them as a PTL expense were not presented at trial."(Appendix A-9.)

☐ Taggart borrowed $75,007.51 from the Rock Hill National Bank of Rock Hill, South Carolina. This note was secured by a PTL certificate of deposit. On or about June 12, 1987, the proceeds from the PTL certificate of deposit were applied against the outstanding amount due on this loan of $75,515.19. This amount has never been repaid to PTL.

Exhibit 5-5 reflects the Bankruptcy Court's findings concerning the potential liability of David Taggart.

Finally, in addition to the previously mentioned amounts, the Bankruptcy Court found Bakker and Taggart jointly and severally liable for $1,036,000. This amount represents expenditures and cash advances on American Express, MasterCard, and Visa accounts that were for the benefit of either Bakker or Taggart. The Court dismissed the claims filed by the Bakkers and Taggart against PTL.

There was an appeal of the Bankruptcy Court's decision based on a statement that Judge Rufus Reynolds made after he had reached a decision in the case and had retired from the bench. In an interview with the *Charlotte Observer*, Judge Reynolds said, "What puzzled me was why people were interested in that little sawed-off runt . . . . It

Description	Notes	8405	8505	8605	8705
Salary	(1)	50,662.08	107,693.39	98,297.29	82,592.99
Bonuses	(2)	10,000.00	31,881.00	111,745.00	523,380.00
Expend. for Personal Benefit of Taggart from Exec. Check.	(3)	0.00	18,720.16	42,225.16	84,043.61
Parsonage Check Acct	(4)	1,948.73	8,832.90	14,000.00	0.00
General Checking	(5)	20,000.00	4,000.00	0.00	0.00
Unsubstan. Cash Advance	(6)	6,500.00	82,807.55	0.00	0.00
Cash Adv-M.C. & VISA	(7)	6,398.71	0.00	309,520.89	300,048.55
Amer. Express Charges	(8)	165,249.52	45,934.97	0.00	0.00
Exec. Air Fleet Pymts	(9)	0.00	0.00	11,537.62	21,426.27
Other Expenditures	(10)	0.00	378,280.47	355,660.50	0.00
Total for Taggart's Benefit		$260,759.04	$678,150.44	$942,086.46	$1,011,491.42
Less: Reasonable Comp.		(69,878.00)	(131,769.00)	(144,946.00)	(159,440.00)
Inurement to D. Taggart		$190,881.04	$546,381.44	$798,040.46	$852,051.42

Chart Total: $2,387,354.36
Plus: 75,515.59   (Rock Hill National Bank Note)
Plus: 140,000.00   (Personal American Express Payments)
Less: (1,554,694.90)   (Potential Joint Liability)

Total $1,048,175.05

Exhibit 5-5   David A. Taggart's Compensation

really shakes you up when you see a Christian like Jimmy Bakker, [Jimmy] Swaggart and all of them come in and have no conscience." Bakker's appeal was denied. The court appointed trustee found no assets to satisfy the judgment.

United States v. Taggart

The logical extension of the bankruptcy case was, did David Taggart pay taxes on all of the compensation he received while at PTL? A federal district court jury in Charlotte, North Carolina, answered no.

The same federal grand jury that investigated potential criminal wrongdoings in the PTL organization and that returned indictments against Jim Bakker and Richard Dortch for wire and mail fraud and conspiracy to commit same also indicted David Taggart, and his brother, James Taggart, for income tax evasion. As discussed later, James Taggart served as PTL's interior decorator. The indictments against all four defendants were filed in December 1988, and the Taggarts' trial was held in July 1989.

The jury found that 32-year-old David Taggart and his 35-year-old brother, James, had under-reported their income by approximately $1.1 million from 1984 to 1987 and thus failed to pay approximately $487,000 in taxes. Specifically mentioned within the indictment were the three checks Peter Bailey had signed in blank that David Taggart used to pay $125,000 in personal American Express charges.

Exhibit 5-6 reflects what David Taggart and James Taggart reported as income and what they paid in taxes for calendar years 1985 through 1987. Also shown is what the IRS contended and what the jury found to be the actual income of the Taggarts and what they really should have paid the IRS.

While the Taggart brothers were reporting a taxable income of $828,087 for the years 1984 through 1987, their combined net worth grew tenfold during the same four years, from $171,075 to $1,695,837.

The Taggarts' unreported income was primarily in the form of cash advances (for as much as $25,000) obtained by using the PTL Visa or MasterCard credit cards. Other unreported income was in the form of PTL checks used for cash advances and PTL checks used to pay the Taggarts' joint personal American Express card. On several occasions, David Taggart got a cash advance on the PTL credit card and, rather than receiving cash, instead had the bank issue a check

DAVID TAGGART

	REPORTED BY DAVID TAGGART			IRS CONTENTION	
YEAR	INCOME	TAXES PAID		ACTUAL INCOME	TAXES DUE
1984	$108,095.00	$36,420.00		$168,833.00	$64,954.00
1985	$74,762.00	$25,032.00		$212,729.00	$93,808.00
1986	$302,930.00	$138,446.00		$555,279.00	$264,621.00
1987	$242,453.00	$87,308.00		$485,203.00	$180,767.00

JAMES TAGGART

	REPORTED BY JAMES TAGGART			IRS CONTENTION	
YEAR	INCOME	TAXES PAID		ACTUAL INCOME	TAXES DUE
1984	$26,734.00	$4,906.00		$73,472.00	$21,948.00
1985	$22,432.00	$3,755.00		$180,471.00	$75,782.00
1986	$30,076.00	$5,856.00		$181,719.00	$77,841.00
1987	$20,605.00	$3,519.00		$48,910.00	$12,978.00
COMBINED AND GRAND TOTAL:	$828,087.00	$305,242.00		$1,906,616.00	$792,699.00

Exhibit 5-6　Income and Taxes Paid by David Taggart and James Taggart, 1984–1987

to be used to pay their personal American Express Card. Sometimes cash advances were used to purchase items from exclusive stores, such as Cartier's jewelry store in New York City.

IRS Agent Charles Mauney, an expert in tax-evasion cases, testified that the IRS did not challenge more than $320,000 in PTL payments to the Taggarts from 1984 through 1985. Of that amount, $208,000 represented cash advances on PTL credit cards that were used by the Taggarts to pay off their personal credit card accounts and to purchase personal items.

In 1985 alone, the Taggarts received $150,000 in cash advances on PTL credit cards that were used to pay off the Taggarts' American Express bill. In addition, the Taggarts received nearly $140,000 in PTL checks that were used for luxury hotel bills, designer clothes, furniture, jewelry, and other items. Agent Mauney testified that none of that income was reported.

This trial was a prelude to the Bakker–Dortch trials and offered a rare, behind-the-scenes glimpse of how PTL operated and how the television ministry's executives spent their followers' money. Just some of the luxuries the Taggarts enjoyed while they were employed at PTL included

☐ a $660,000 condo on New York's Fifth Avenue

☐ a $317,000 house in Charlotte, North Carolina

☐ Jaguar cars worth $87,765 that they gave each other for Christmas in 1986

The following items were purchased from Cartier's in New York City:

☐ a $96,000 diamond ring

☐ an $85,000 platinum, sapphire, and diamond pin

☐ a $75,000 platinum, sapphire, and diamond bracelet

☐ a $64,000 antique bracelet

The Taggarts also purchased a $10,000 Rolex watch with diamond markers, a $2,273 miniature silver tea set, $1,020 worth of Gucci bags for their mother, and books by Robert Frost and Walt Whitman for $1,087. A parade of store owners and sales clerks testified that the Taggarts spent about $35,000 at a New York fur shop on furs and mink coats for themselves and that from 1982 through 1986 they dropped nearly $100,000 on shoes.

Finally, two women who had worked at PTL testified that they had accompanied the Taggarts on trips to California, Florida, and London, during which the brothers picked up all the expenses, including $3,000 hotel bills and dinners costing as much as $600 each.

David Taggart continued to get cash advances, but despite repeated requests for support documentation for these advances, they were never provided to PTL. Finally, sometime between August 1985 and January 1986, Peter Bailey, PTL's finance director and vice-president of finance, made a journal entry writing off $215,578.44 of PTL cash advances to David Taggart.

The Taggarts' tax returns were prepared by Charlotte attorney Robert Gunst, who testified that David Taggart bought $100,000 worth of jewelry and $400,000 in other purchases in 1984, the same year he told the IRS his taxable income was $107,795.

"Did [David Taggart] ever tell you how he could purchase items worth $500,000 when his income was only $100,000?" Justice Department Prosecutor David Brown asked. "It looks like a mistake was made," said Gunst, who signed and prepared Taggart's 1984 tax return.

David's brother, James, was paid a retainer fee of $10,000 a month as PTL's interior decorator. He also had an employment contract that obligated PTL to pay his interior design corporation $250,000, with a minimum guarantee of $100,000; PTL had an additional $100,000 bid agreement with James Taggart's corporation.

The Taggarts' defense centered on whether or not the brothers had acted with the specific intent to avoid paying taxes. As Ben Cotton, the Washington, D.C., lawyer who represented the Taggarts, said in his opening statement: "This case is not about taxes. We concede at the outset there are some taxes owed by David and James . . . . This case is about authorization, intent and doubt." The prosecution countered by saying "[t]his case is about large amounts of income the defendants failed to report."

David Taggart testified that he left the PTL ministry in April 1983 but was persuaded by Bakker in October of that same year to come back to run Bakker's office. As a prerequisite for returning to PTL, Taggart testified that he told Bakker that he "wanted to have the same resources [Bakker] had." As a result, Taggart told the court that Bakker responded by saying, "David, you've killed yourself for the ministry for $25,000 a year [from 1978 to 1983, when Taggart served as an assistant music director and then as Bakker's personal assistant]. Now the ministry is in a different position and I'm willing to pay you $100,000 a year."

The prosecutors characterized Taggart's testimony as a "sweetheart deal," a lie concocted in a last-ditch effort to avoid a prison sentence. When asked by the prosecution how he could demand from Jim Bakker the same financial deal that Bakker enjoyed, Taggart replied, "I did not get everything Jim Bakker got. I think Jim Bakker had a better deal than I did."

Taggart admitted during cross-examination that proper record-keeping would have helped him determine whether certain sums of money that he drew on the PTL account were legitimate corporate expenses and therefore not subject to taxes.

James Taggart remarked in court that, "[t]here were no limitations on spending" and that he got whatever it took to get the job done while he was PTL's interior decorator. Taggart said items that had been purchased for the Towers and other lodging facilities were kept at the brothers' New York condo or in their Charlotte home while the Towers Hotel was being completed. He quoted Bakker as saying: "As far as I am concerned, you need to start now. You need to be buying. You need to be storing items."

Jim Bakker was called as a witness by the defendants. While the jury was out, Bakker nervously asserted his right to remain silent under the Fifth Amendment. In ten minutes, he was out of the court. Neither the "sweetheart deal" allegedly given to David, nor the instructions allegedly given to James could be further explored in court.

After a twelve-day trial, the jury took five hours to return a verdict of guilty on all counts. As one juror was quoted as saying, "There was no way I could walk out of that jury room and not find them guilty."

Living up to his nickname of "Maximum Bob," Judge Robert Potter gave David Taggart 18 years and 5 months, the longest prison sentence he could impose under the circumstances. James Taggart was sentenced to 17 years and 9 months. The Taggarts were fined $500,000 each and ordered to pay at least $525,000 in income taxes. Before handing out punishment, Judge Potter said, "White collar criminals in this country seem to get extremely light sentences. I feel like it's time to put a halt to that."

The Taggart trial served to expose how loosely PTL was run and how money intended for the ministry was taken by Jim Bakker and his assistants to fulfill their own selfish needs.

Never resolved by the Taggart trial was how David and James Taggart could have continued to take substantial amounts of money from PTL over four years' time. All this happened while PTL accountants complained about Taggart's failure to document his spending. More importantly, it continued to happen while PTL was being audited by national accounting firms.

United States v. Bakker

The ruling against Bakker in the November 1988 bankruptcy proceedings and the criminal conviction of the Taggarts on July 25, 1989, were certainly not a source of comfort for Jim Bakker and Richard Dortch. As if this were not enough, the U.S. Magistrate, with the support of Federal Judge Robert Potter, ruled that the criminal case against Bakker and Dortch would be heard in Charlotte, North Carolina over the objection of the defendants. The Federal Court was not persuaded by the defendants' claim of adverse pretrial publicity; they had attempted to have the trial moved elsewhere because over 2,000 articles had appeared from mid-1987 to May 1989 in the *Charlotte Observer* about Bakker, Dortch, or PTL. Neither was the Court swayed by two T-shirts making reference to Tammy Bakker that were introduced as evidence to back this claim. One read "Tammy-sses," which purported to be a take-off of the Egyptian Ramses exhibit in Charlotte in the winter of 1988. The other had blotches of ink across the front; it bore the slogan, "I ran into Tammy Faye at the mall." The government contended that the defense was looking for a jury "from another planet," and Judge Potter denied the request to change the location of the trial.

Of even less comfort to Bakker was Richard Dortch's decision to plead guilty to the charges against him: two counts of wire fraud, one count of mail fraud, and one count of conspiracy to commit wire and mail fraud. Dortch had a plea agreement with the government that required him to cooperate fully with federal prosecutors and to provide "truthful, complete and forthright information" to federal authorities, which included testifying against his co-conspirator, Jim Bakker. Judge Potter asked Dortch, "Are you in fact guilty of the crimes charged?" Dortch replied, "In the last few years, I have had a lot of time for reflection, and I am not proud of myself. And I plead guilty."

At the time of Dortch's sentencing, prosecutor Deborah Smith introduced charts showing that Dortch collected $1,128,735 in salaries, bonuses, and tax-deferred retirement payments between January 1984 and June 1987. Dortch had also lived rent-free in a $400,000 PTL-owned home.

As he pleaded for mercy, Dortch said, " . . . I cannot believe that I participated in this . . . in deceiving people, in doing something I knew was wrong . . . . I failed my Master, failed my family, and failed myself . . . . I lost the thing that I lived for—my ministry."

Representing the government, Smith said she would "take issue with the argument that Mr. Dortch wasn't keeping an eye on business or that he was seduced by Mr. Bakker" in committing the frauds at PTL. "The victims in this case are in the thousands," she said. "They are waiting for justice."

Although Dortch could have received a sentence of 10 years in prison and a $500,000 fine, Judge Potter sentenced him to 8 years and a $200,000 fine. Dortch, as part of his agreement with the government, promised to testify truthfully in the Bakker criminal case. But how much weight should be given to Dortch's testimony? On one hand, Dortch's promised testimony could be the result of his "selling his soul to save his hide," or, in the alternative, Dortch could be viewed as "the person with the keys to the safe, and he is about to open it." That is, in all cases where a co-defendant pleads guilty and agrees to cooperate with the government, there are questions concerning the truthfulness and veracity of the cooperating defendant.

The Bakkers had begun to ask their supporters to contribute over $1 million to help defend Jim Bakker against the fraud and conspiracy charges he was facing even before his criminal trial commenced at the end of August 1989. In a letter signed by Tammy Bakker that was mailed in July 1989, she pleaded, "Jim and I have no personal funds at all. We do not know what to do except share with you the terrible urgency of this situation and ask if you will please help us. We need $1 million plus for the defense fund. Half of that must be in Charlotte by the end of this month."

Since Bakker's resignation from PTL in March 1987, he and his wife had been attempting to restart their television ministry, first broadcasting out of a rented home in Pineville, North Carolina, and thereafter moving to a deserted shopping center in Orlando, Florida. It was from this Orlando shopping center that the "Jim and Tammy Show" was broadcast via satellite to approximately eight cities in the U.S. Before Jim Bakker's trial commenced, Tammy Bakker claimed that the couple had received many donations in response to her plea; she added, "Several of [our supporters] are sending thousands" and "some are sending hundreds." For most of the trial, Tammy Bakker elected to stay in Orlando, explaining that the new television ministry would not survive without her and that their son did not need to miss school. Jim Bakker was to face his trial with his daughter, Tammy Sue Chapman; his parents; a loyal following of friends; and his two attorneys.

Jim Bakker's lead defense counsel was 82-year-old George T. Davis from Honolulu, Hawaii. Davis' approach to the trial was feisty, often unorthodox, and frequently irritating to the trial judge. Davis was assisted by 47-year-old Harold Bender, a University of North Carolina Law School graduate and former federal prosecutor. Bender appeared to enjoy a better rapport with the trial judge than did lead counsel Davis; he had the task of cross-examining the key witnesses who testified against Bakker.

The Prosecutor for the government was Deborah Smith from the U.S. Department of Justice's Criminal Fraud Section. She had worked as a reporter in Fort Lauderdale, Florida and before had served as Alaska's Chief Assistant U.S. Attorney from 1985 to 1987, during which time she supervised and prosecuted many complicated white collar criminal cases. Deborah Smith seemed to be the ideal government prosecutor. She gave a masterful presentation and displayed a meticulous understanding of all the facts involved in this case.

Sharing responsibility for the prosecution of the government case was Jerry Miller. Miller gave powerful opening and closing arguments in the case. His characterization of Jim Bakker in his opening argument was especially incisive. He said that Jim Bakker "started a ministry to love people and to use things, but as the extravagances got so great, Mr. Bakker changed to a man who loved things and used people."

The trial judge was none other than Robert Potter, the same judge who had tried and sentenced the Taggart brothers and Richard Dortch.

The government's case against Jim Bakker was very similar to its case against the Taggart brothers. With the exception of the disruption caused by Hurricane Hugo in September and Jim Bakker's suffering a panic attack, during which time he saw news reporters outside the courtroom as huge, ferocious bugs, the prosecutors' presentation of the case against Bakker went smoothly. In typical fashion, the prosecutors conducted a meticulous, detailed, and methodical presentation of the evidence by calling over 90 witnesses and introducing thousands of documents into evidence. They continued not only to present a staggering case against Jim Bakker but also effectively chipped away at any possible defense that Bakker could raise.

Although it was clear from the outset that PTL had been mismanaged, the real question in the Bakker trial was whether or not there had been criminal intent in its mismanagement. The prosecution sought to prove that Jim Bakker knew he was making false and fraudulent statements on television and through the mails when the lifetime partnerships were oversold.

As George Davis said in his opening argument, "We will concede a great error was done. The issue in this case is whether Jim Bakker did or didn't do it with criminal intent." For a full hour and a half, he contended that the lifetime partnerships were not sold by Jim Bakker and PTL. He argued that the partnerships were given in exchange for donations made to the PTL ministry. He also argued that there was no intent to defraud and that when Jim Bakker made statements concerning the lifetime partnership programs, he believed them to be true.

The government indictment listed 42 overt acts that were alleged to have been committed by Jim Bakker and Richard Dortch in the course of their fraudulent, criminal activities at PTL. For example, the government contended that the Bakkers received over $3 million in bonuses from PTL from 1984 through 1987. According to the indictment, Bakker obtained the bonuses "with the full knowledge that PTL was in poor financial condition; and [that] the organization was experiencing severe cash flow problems; and [that] an insufficient amount of lifetime partnership funds had been designated and segregated from operating funds to ensure the completion of various lodging facilities promised to partners by Bakker and Dortch." The oversale of lifetime partnerships was necessary, according to the prosecution, to allow Bakker and Dortch to continue receiving the enormous salaries and bonuses that funded their opulent lifestyle.

The prosecution set out to prove that Jim Bakker was, in essence, running a pyramid scheme and that most of the money from the lifetime partnerships went into operating expenses of Heritage USA, including the executive payroll from which Bakker and Dortch received millions of dollars.

This pyramid scheme might more accurately be called a *ponzi* scheme. The operation of a ponzi scheme has been described as follows:

> In a ponzi scheme, a swindler promises a large return for investments made with him. The swindler actually pays the promised return on the initial investment in order to attract additional investors. The payments are not financed through the successes of the underlying venture, but are taken from the corpus of the newly attracted investments. The swindler then takes an appropriate time to abscond with the outstanding investments. As one author has described it, "He borrowed from Peter to pay Paul, and it worked . . . until Peter got wise." [*United States v. Rasheed*, 663 F. 2d, 843 (1981)]

The government contended that Bakker and Dortch were selling lifetime partnerships and then used the money for other purposes, including salaries and a lavish lifestyle for the Bakkers as well as construction of building projects that should have already been completed. Bakker contended the funds raised were unrestricted as to their use and that the lifetime partnerships had not been "sold." Again, the major hurdle in the government's case was to prove that Jim Bakker acted with criminal intent on television and through mass mailings. Did Jim Bakker know at the time that those statements he was making were indeed false?

Clearly there was evidence from which the jury could, and obviously did, draw the inference that Jim Bakker was acting with criminal intent. For example, as fully discussed in the next chapter, PTL's chief financial officer, Peter G. Bailey, wrote several memos to Jim Bakker reflecting PTL's continued cash crisis. Despite these memos, Jim Bakker, Tammy Bakker, and Richard Dortch continued to receive excessive bonuses from the corporation and continued their solicitations for lifetime partnerships.

The government also offered the chart shown in Exhibit 5-7 as evidence of the Bakkers' lavish income. As discussed in the next chapter, many of the bonuses Bakker received were obtained just days after his vice president of finance wrote doom-and-gloom memos telling of the financial crisis and impending demise of PTL.

Although maintaining this level of compensation might certainly be a reason to continue the perpetration of a wire and mail fraud and is circumstantial evidence of intent to commit same, is this enough evidence to prove intent beyond a reasonable doubt?

After the trial, Deborah Smith said that the most effective witness against Jim Bakker had been Jim Bakker—both in person during the criminal trial and on television.

Special Agent John R. Pearson of the FBI was given the task of reviewing various television programs that aired on the PTL Television Network, specifically programs that aired from February 20, 1984, through April 1987. Pearson testified that he viewed close to "200 hours of aired PTL programs." From these programs, he compiled 11 different "composite videos" for the Bakker jury to view. In compiling these composite videos, Pearson agreed that "there was no editing or splicing, or any change to the segments themselves once they were transferred onto the tapes that [he] prepared for composite viewing." Each of the composite tapes, as well as the full tape from which the segment was taken, was made available for Jim Bakker and his counsel to review. The tapes were admitted into evidence, and the jury viewed each of them.

SALARIES, BONUSES AND MBA CONTRIBUTIONS PAID BY PTL
TO OR ON BEHALF OF THE BAKKERS

JIM BAKKER

YEAR	SALARY[1]	BONUS	MBA	TOTAL
1984	270,822	640,000	121,690	1,032,512
1985	314,673	550,000	145,348	1,010,021
1986	313,567	790,000	132,500	1,236,067
1987	(NOT AVAILABLE)	450,000[2]	55,208	505,208
	899,062	2,430,000	454,746	3,783,808

TAMMY BAKKER

YEAR	SALARY[1]	BONUS	MBA	TOTAL
1984	94,355	100,000	—	194,355
1985	99,034	148,512	—	247,546
1986	99,951	265,000	—	364,951
1987	(NOT AVAILABLE)	170,000	—	170,000
	293,340	683,512	—	976,852

COMBINED

YEAR	SALARY[1]	BONUS	MBA	TOTAL
1984	365,177	740,000	121,690	1,226,867
1985	413,707	698,512	145,348	1,257,567
1986	413,518	1,055,000	132,500	1,601,018
1987	(NOT AVAILABLE)	620,000	55,208	675,208
	1,192,402	3,113,512	454,746	4,760,660

NOTES: (1) INCLUDES SALARY, HOUSING AND/OR AUTOMOBILE ALLOWANCES, EXCESS GROUP TERM LIFE INSURANCE PREMIUMS, ETC.

(2) INCLUDES $150,000 PAYMENT OBTAINED THROUGH DAVID TAGGART 3/87.

Exhibit 5-7   A List of Salaries, Bonuses, and MBA Contributions Paid by PTL to or on Behalf of the Bakkers

This testimony was, in my opinion, devastating. As discussed in Chapter 4, Jim Bakker made numerous statements on the television concerning the number of lodging partnerships that were currently available or had been taken. Additionally, he explained how funds were supposedly to be used. Periodically throughout Pearson's testimony, Deborah Smith would direct that the videotape be stopped. She would then ask Pearson to testify as to what PTL's own computer-generated records reflected.

Inevitably, there was a material difference between what Jim Bakker, Richard Dortch, and others said on television and what PTL's own records showed. These records, and how access to them was secured, are more fully discussed in the next chapter. Exhibit A-10 is a copy of one page from the PTL computer run that was admitted into evidence, that shows the cumulative number of lifetime partnerships that had been sold for each lifetime partnership promotional as of May 31, 1987. Although Agent Pearson's testimony was lengthy and sometimes tedious, this seemingly endless recitation of material inconsistencies between what Jim Bakker had said and what PTL's own records reflected helped to establish criminal intent.

Although the videotapes and the Bailey memos certainly provided at least circumstantial evidence relating to Bakker's fraudulent intent to sell lifetime partnerships, testimony from Steve Nelson and Richard Dortch provided direct evidence.

Steve Nelson came to PTL in the summer of 1985 as vice-president of World Outreach. His testimony was that in October 1985 he became aware that lifetime partnerships were being oversold. Nelson told the court that he "met with Pastor Dortch and explained to him that this information had come in and that I thought it was a problem, and that we had a situation here where we had oversold memberships, and he told me not to worry about it, that that was not really a problem, that the memberships really weren't oversold, and that I shouldn't be concerned about it at that point in time."

Not satisfied with Dortch's response, Nelson later discussed the issue with Jim Bakker; specifically, Nelson testified that he told Bakker, "I had seen these numbers and that there seemed to be a problem. . . ." Again, according to Nelson's testimony, Bakker responded that "this was not a problem, that these were not sales, but gifts and you could not sell something that was a gift."

Aware of the ever-increasing number of lifetime partners, Nelson said that he came to realize that the Grand Hotel simply could not accommodate all of the memberships that had been sold. Jerry Miller asked a question of Nelson that was objected to by George Davis but which seemed to summarize the dilemma that Nelson was in: "So you had a problem that was incurable in that you just had a hole that was too small [to] fit the partners into?"

Steve Nelson testified that he met with Dortch and Bakker regarding the Towers lifetime partnerships after the Victory Warrior promotion. Nelson went to Dortch first and told him "that someone could go to jail for this." He then went to Bakker with the same complaints and, according to Nelson, Bakker's response was, "Look, you know, the Lord's done a miracle for us here and there's not anything for you to be worried about or concerned about, you know, we can get room, we can have room for these people to get in here." In fact, Nelson revealed that after the Victory Warrior telethon, Jim Bakker had a meeting with all the vice-presidents in his office at which he talked about the large amount of money he had raised during the telethon and that "we should thank God a miracle had been performed."

Nelson also testified that he prepared reports reflecting the total number of lodging partnerships for the various lifetime partnership promotionals at PTL. These reports were prepared every week, and he normally forwarded the report to Jim Bakker, who would return it with his handwritten comments. Nelson stated in court that two to three weeks before Jim Bakker resigned, he was called by David Taggart and Richard Dortch. As a result of those phone calls, Nelson destroyed the weekly reports. Nelson testified, "Well, I got a call from Pastor Dortch, too. Told me to destroy the reports—destroy everything, but it was regarding—they thought there was an IRS agent on the property, they wanted to make sure to get rid of all of it."

Another absolutely devastating revelation by Steve Nelson concerned two sets of numbers that were kept at PTL regarding the total number of sales of lifetime partnerships. The lower numbers were shown on television to the viewing audience; the true, higher numbers were given to a select few. Nelson's testimony concerning this matter was as follows:

> A: We specifically had a person—for lack of a better term, I'll call them a total person, that their job was to—if I can give you a picture of this. There's a room maybe with a fifty to a hundred operators in it taking telephone calls. Before each one of these is a piece of paper with the different offers that are there so that you can take information down on and what would happen is, we would have—I call them a runner, go around picking up these pieces of paper to bring them to this total person and the total

person would sit there and add them up so that they could know how many of the gift offers or what kind of things were moving. This person in respect to lifetime memberships, at the direction of Mr. Bakker and Mr. Dortch, would let no one else know what those totals were on the lifetime memberships. This person knew—Brenda Smith knew—

Q: Excuse me. At whose direction was that?

A: Pastor Dortch's and Pastor Bakker's.

Q: And what was that instruction?

A: It was not to give that number to anyone else other than those that they had said to disseminate it to.

Q: And that was the numbers of lifetime partnerships that had the totals on those?

A: Right. The numbers that we give everybody else were a lot lower than the numbers that were on the sheet.

Q: So you had two sets of numbers?

A: Yes, sir, we did.

Q: One set for who?

A: One set that would go across and they might post on the other. The other set would be the numbers—the real numbers that had been sold.

Q: And who did the real numbers do go?

A: Pastor Dortch, Pastor Bakker, Peter Bailey, Mark Burgund, Wanda Burgund, Paul King.

Q: And how frequently during the telethons did these numbers get reported to Mr. Bakker and Mr. Dortch?

A: Every few minutes they would call, especially when they were promoting the offer.

It was shortly after this testimony that Defense Attorney Harold Bender began a rigorous cross-examination of Steve Nelson. He asked Nelson about a $30,000 bridge loan that he had acquired from PTL; it had been converted into a bonus by Richard Dortch. An affidavit previously sworn by Nelson failed to reflect the totality of remuneration that he had received while at PTL. While Nelson was being questioned concerning this matter, he collapsed on the witness stand.

This marked the first time that Bakker was directly confronted by a witness concerning the oversale of lifetime partnerships. This, coupled with Nelson's assertion of two different sets of numbers reflecting total lifetime partnership sales and his fainting on the stand, may have been too much for Bakker to handle in one session. Jim had what was later diagnosed as having been a panic attack.

If Steve Nelson's testimony was a shock, the testimony of Richard Dortch was a grand slam. Dortch proved to be the perfect government witness. He seriously considered every question that was asked by both the government and the defense, after which he slowly turned to look at the jury and provided incriminating evidence against Bakker. From the government's perspective, it could not have gone any better.

Dortch confirmed Steve Nelson's assertion that there were two sets of numbers being used regarding the lifetime partnership program. Specifically, Richard Dortch testified as follows concerning the sale of lifetime partnerships in the Victory Warrior promotional:

> Q: And Mr. Bakker—tell the jury whether or not Mr. Bakker gave you any instructions as to those numbers.
> A: Yes, sir, he did.
> Q: What did Mr. Bakker tell you about those numbers?
> A: We were given those numbers by Steve Nelson and there were two sets of numbers that were shown to me and to Mr. Bakker by Mr. Nelson, and I made the inquiry as to which set of numbers these were. I was told that these were the numbers that Steve Nelson had been using and also what was defined as the real numbers.
> Q: Who told you that?
> A: Steve Nelson.
> Q: And Mr. Bakker was present?
> A: He was present.
> Q: What did Mr. Bakker tell you about it?
> A: He asked me not to use those numbers and not to announce what those numbers were.
> Q: Which numbers?
> A: The real numbers.

Richard Dortch also read from notes he had prepared in either June or July of 1987, shortly after he left PTL. They had been written prior to criminal charges being brought against him and were later given to Dortch's attorney. These notes are found at Exhibit A-11. Dortch stated in court that he recalled Bakker indicating to him that "there was no limit to the amount of money that we could raise for the projects that we would need in the days to come, for the projects we would undertake." Asked by Miller, "And did Mr. Bakker ever tell you anything about his ability to control use of facilities?," Dortch responded, "Yes, we—that it was explained to me by Mr. Bakker was that I could control the use of that by getting the partners here when I want them to come and by keeping them away by talking to them daily on television when we don't want them to come."

Concerning the limits placed on the lifetime partnership program, Bakker allegedly said to Dortch, "There was no limit to the amount of people that we can offer these, too, because I can control the crowds of the people as they come."

Dortch admitted that there were limits placed on the various lodging partnerships. He admitted his guilt to the jury in Bakker's trial. He provided direct evidence of criminal intent to commit fraud by use of the wire and mail and of conspiracy to commit fraud. Moreover, the direct evidence he provided clearly implicated Bakker and supported the circumstantial evidence that had been offered by other witnesses and PTL documents. This testimony, combined with Steve Nelson's, left Bakker little room to maneuver.

Dortch testified that nothing was done by himself, Jim Bakker, or anyone else to let people who were buying partnerships know that because of the true number of partnerships sold, there was no way possible for them to all be accommodated in the facilities if they chose to use them the way they were entitled to. Despite that knowledge, when Dortch was asked, "And did you, at that point in time, knowing that had not been done, continue to participate in the sale of lifetime partnerships over television and PTL?" he responded, "Yes, Sir." Significantly, Dortch was also asked and responded as follows concerning the next question:

Q: And who participated in that with you?
A: Mr. Bakker, Steve Nelson; prior to that time Rich Ball, and Doug Oldham and several other people."

Although additional PTL employees will be examined in subsequent chapters, it is interesting to note the dialogue that occurred between prosecutor Jerry Miller and Richard Dortch concerning this critical part of the trial:

Q: Now, did Mr. Bakker, in your presence ever tell those people, such as Doug Oldham, and those other people who were pitching the programs, those true numbers that you were talking about that Steve Nelson was giving to you, was available? Did he give those numbers to Mr. Oldham?
A: I don't know whether he did privately, but Doug Oldham participated in meetings where those numbers were given.
Q: So at that point in time, Mr. Oldham and you and Mr. Bakker and Steve Nelson and Rich Ball, while he was there, all of you participated together in this agreement to use television to solicit these partnerships?
A: We knew what the numbers were, yes, Sir.
Q: In spite of that, you continued the solicitations without telling these people what the numbers were?
A: Yes, Sir.

Those were the last questions asked of Richard Dortch by the government in its direct examination of its star witness.

Intertwined throughout the proceedings were statements from contributors to PTL. These were the people who had sent in various amounts of money under the lodging partnership programs. After being interviewed by the FBI and having responded to a questionnaire, "victims" were chosen by the government to testify against Bakker. One of these was Garbrielle Betzer, a retiree living on Social Security, who had purchased two lifetime partnerships hoping for a much-needed vacation each year. She told the court that she never utilized her lifetime partnership at Heritage USA because "I called and called and it was a just a waste of my money on the telephone because they said they were all booked up. They had one bunkhouse completed and the other was just a shell. It wasn't completed inside, although they were supposed to have more than that." Betzer was presented by the government as one of the 9,682 fully paid bunkhouse partners who were competing for the use of eight rooms in the one completed bunkhouse.

Another government witness and victim was Larry Kerstetter, who also was retired and living on disability payments after having worked as a coal miner for 31 years. He purchased a Towers partnership for $1,000 and testified that if he had been informed of the true number of Towers partnerships sold by March 1987, he would not have joined. He was also unable to get a refund. Elizabeth Combs and her husband, who suffers from black lung disease, have 13 children. They purchased a Grand Hotel lifetime partnership in 1984 after visiting Heritage USA to make sure that the Grand Hotel was actually under construction. They used $1,000 from his medical disability payments to make that partnership purchase. Mrs. Combs testified that she had tried three to four times a year to get a reservation at the Grand but was unsuccessful.

One of the strongest statements made against Jim Bakker came from Pastor Allan Foor. As a clergyman, he made $18,600 yearly and had supported PTL for 12 years. He joined the Towers partnership in 1986, but a year later he wrote a letter to PTL requesting a refund. Pastor Foor was asked by Deborah Smith to read that letter in open court on what happened to be the first day that Tammy Bakker attended the trial. His letter, a portion of which follows, sums up many of the comments and sentiments expressed by other victims who testified at the criminal trial:

Dear folks:
I write this as a very concerned lifetime and monthly partner. I am quite distressed about the fall of Jim and Tammy and feel so sad

that things turned out as they did, but at the same time, I am not too surprised. I followed PTL for at least twelve years and have lent my support . . . . Jim and I are the same age. I have wanted to write for so long because of my concern for Jim and Tammy and their extravagant lifestyle and extravagant building . . . . Almost a year ago, Jim made a great appeal to get the ministry on sound financial ground with all bills paid for and the Towers Hotel paid for. For the final days of this appeal, he offered those who would send in $1000 a Tower membership with four days and three nights free for life, plus a Silver membership. I believe[d] so much in what he was doing that I borrowed $1000 for the Towers and Silver membership . . . . I still have not got to use [my membership], so return my $1000 please. . . . after almost a year, the Towers is still unfinished while Bunkhouses and other things have been built. Now here you are asking for more Towers memberships to finish the Towers. A year ago the Towers was to be paid for and membership closed forever and ever . . . . Now I've had it. I feel robbed and cheated. While Jim and PTL spent over a quarter of a million dollars for a sexual cover up, plus it has been revealed that Jim and Tammy own at least four properties amounting to millions of dollars and gold fixtured bathrooms, expensive jewelry, mink coats, limousines, Rolls Royces, plus the thousands of dollars spent on big birthday extravaganzas for Jim and Tammy with tuxedos and fine furs . . . . Now enough is enough. I for one am through. At least until I see a real change in the use of monies in this ministry. . . . I have a hard time dealing with what I feel is the misuse of my contributions which were to go for the work of the Lord, but rather seems to have gone to exalt Jim and Tammy's empire and cover ups. Jim and Tammy and everyone else better look at the humble life of Jesus Christ. Jesus didn't cheat or show a lavish or materialistic lifestyle as the teaching of PTL and some other ministries have. . . . Believe me when I say that I really appreciate what PTL has done and the good that it is doing, but I believe you can do so much better and use the peoples' contributions more efficiently and to benefit more people. . . . Now it will be interesting and if any of you even get this or read this before some secretary or volunteer throws it away. Again, I love you all in the spirit of Christ. I hope that sometime we will have the chance to sit down and allow Jesus to speak through and to each of us. Until then, may God's abundant love, Grace and Peace be with you.

Serving in Christ, Alan K. Foor.

P.S. I do care about the ministry taking place at PTL, but until I see a true repentance and that there will be a better honest use of the money, I will withhold. . . . We need to be building lives, not the biggest buildings. . . .

The real pressure point for the oversale of lifetime partnerships was at the front desk and at the reservation office of the Heritage Grand Hotel. William Mabrey was General Manager of the Grand Hotel pursuant to a management contract that PTL had with the Brock Hotel Corporation by which Brock was to receive a management fee for operating the Grand; the fee amounted to 5 percent of gross revenues derived from the paying customers. Brock Hotel Corporation was to receive nothing from the lifetime partners who stayed at the hotel, and the contract also specifically stated that Brock was obligated to make only half of the guest rooms in the hotel available for lifetime partners. Thus the contract was consistent with all the verbal and written representations that were being made to the lifetime partners concerning limits on the hotel.

Mabrey testified that in March 1985, his assistant showed him "a printout of lifetime partners, and after doing some calculations, we determined that if we were to accommodate every partner on that list in the Grand, we would have to run in excess of 100 percent occupancy 365 days a year just for the lifetime partners." Mabrey also testified that he discussed this major concern with Reverend Dortch and that Dortch told him: "Bill, you have to understand that one of three things may occur, that some people just purchase the lifetime partnerships merely as a donation to the ministry. Others may come once and never use it again, and yet others may be deceased before they ever use it. So don't worry about it. Get back to running the hotel."

Mabrey testified that to alleviate the pressure on the Grand Hotel to accommodate lifetime partners, PTL would sometimes allow 60 percent of the hotel to be occupied by lifetime partners, with PTL paying the management fee to Brock. Finally, Mabrey spoke about the high turnover rate that occurred in the reservations department. During one particular month, the turnover rate approached 40 percent because the reservation agents were, according to Mabrey's testimony, having to deal with "[i]rate partners demanding either accommodations or their money back."

The defense counsel continually objected to the prosecution making reference to Jim Bakker having "sold lifetime partnerships." Instead, Bakker's counsel contended that these partnerships were really gifts given by the ministry in return for financial contributions. As a result of the haggling over whether or not the partnerships were a sale, as the prosecution advocated, or a gift, as the defense advocated, the court instructed the parties to simply use a neutral phrase, such as "promote" rather than "sell." However, this contradicts the testimony of several witnesses called by the government, especially that of Dortch and Nelson. These witnesses testified that lifetime partnerships were, in fact, sold. Additionally, the promotional literature distributed by PTL indicates that potential lifetime partners were engaged in a sales transaction. For example, the original Grand Hotel brochure of January 7, 1984, stated that "tax receipts for a charitable purpose" will not be issued. If this truly were a gift, tax receipts would have been issued because PTL was recognized at that time by the IRS as a tax-exempt charitable organization. Furthermore, that same brochure included blatant sales pitches such as the following: "[There's] never been a better value for your investment," "You will not be able to find a better investment opportunity," and "We're only inviting the most faithful PTL partners to invest . . ."

Other brochures similarly reflected what appeared to have been a sale of lifetime partnerships as opposed to a request for the donation of funds for PTL's general use. The Grand Hotel partnership brochure of March 12, 1984, contained language that was only slightly different than the January 7th mailing. Specifically, while the January 7th mailing stated that "tax receipts for charitable purposes will not be issued," the March 12th mailing read, "Because of the value being invested in exchange for your payment of $1,000, no part of this $1,000 is a charitable contribution and should not be claimed as a tax deduction."

The Towers brochure that was mailed from September 25 through October 5, 1984, clearly stated, "Tax receipts for charitable purposes will not be issued for the $1,000 Towers membership gift." Such statements made in mailings and televised promotions seemed to indicate that contributors to PTL were buying a right to four days and three nights of yearly lodging as opposed to simply making a charitable contribution.

Bakker was asked during cross-examination in his criminal trial if he had ever used the term *sold* in his promotion of the lifetime partnership plans. Bakker's response: "If I did, it would have been a slip of the tongue."

Jim Bakker's defense consisted in part of showing several of his television programs in their entirety. These programs reflected the religious nature of PTL and the fact that lifetime partnership telethons were not the only events being promoted at the facility. In addition, no less than 42 PTL lifetime partners testified that they believed in Bakker and that any money they had given to PTL was to be disposed of as he saw fit. The defense had many more PTL supporters waiting in the wings to testify, but Judge Potter allowed only a certain number to testify, saying that these witnesses were repetitive and served only as character witnesses.

Jim Bakker testified on his own behalf that he believed all statements he made on his television program to have been true at the time. His testimony lasted two days. Bakker was asked at the end of his direct examination, "Did you ever intentionally knowingly commit in any way, or by any reference, a fraud and an intentional criminal act with reference to the subject of conspiracy?" His response was, "I absolutely did not."

Bakker had previously testified as to how the lifetime partnership program had been an inspiration from God. He said that he would have completed all of the building projects at PTL if he were still in charge of the facility and that the projects would be completed as soon as God supplied the finances. He added that his salary and bonuses were set by PTL's board of directors, not by himself, and that he had charged PTL nothing for his fundraising activities.

Bakker testified that he was running a ministry based on his faith in God supplying the needed resources. When Bakker was asked if he had confidence in his ability to raise money, Bakker responded, "I had confidence in God supplying it." Bakker also contended that the lifetime partners were always informed as to the status of the building projects at Heritage USA, and that the partners knew that their particular lodging facility had to be built before they could utilize their lifetime partnership rights.

Because the lifetime partner funds sent to PTL were unrestricted, the money could be used for financing the entire PTL ministry and not just to build a lodging facility, Bakker claimed in court. Segments from the "Jim Bakker Show" supported Bakker's assertion. Viewers were told that their lifetime partnership would help fund the various religious and business aspects of the PTL ministry.

Bakker's attorneys attempted to place into evidence certain charts reflecting Bakker's contention that there were lodging facilities available for the lifetime partners. The judge did not allow these charts into evidence, contending that they were misleading and did not accurately reflect the testimony received; they were subsequently mailed to some of the PTL faithful by Tammy Bakker after Jim Bakker's conviction. Exhibits A-12 and A-13 are copies of the charts, complete with what appears to be Tammy Bakker's handwritten notations, reflecting how there were adequate accommodations for the lifetime partners. However, during cross-examination, Bakker could produce no evidence, specifically no television tape, that announced the "expanded" lifetime partnership program described in the charts. Deborah Smith pushed Jim Bakker concerning this, asking him, "In fact, Mr. Bakker, your long list of what was available to the partners is a very recent fabrication done by you in direct response to these charges here. Isn't that true?" Bakker responded vehemently: "That is a lie! That is absolutely not true!" Smith continued interrogating Jim Bakker about how the expanded program was supposed to work. She asked, "Now in your mind, do you think it's fair to promise [PTL lifetime partners] Miss Angel and her 80-year-old mother that they can come and stay three nights each year for the rest of their life in the luxurious Grand Hotel, and then when they call or arrive for reservations, tell them that the room you have for them is in the rustic, undeveloped campground down the round, and maybe they could buy a pup tent. Do you think that's fair?" Bakker responded: "She would not, she would not be put in a campground when she arrived. She would call on the telephone and if she wanted to stay at the campground, she could choose to do so, but if she wanted to stay at the Inn, she would get an extra night. Have you ever gone to the Heritage Inn and seen the rooms there?"

Bakker took issue with not only the government's presentation of the number of lifetime partnerships that had been sold but also the reliability of PTL's own computer records. As Bakker testified: "I used the figures that were given to me on the show on a daily basis. Whenever anybody would give me the figures, that's the figures I worked from." He added, "What I said on the air, I believed to be true 100 percent at the time I said it . . . . I was working on information that was given to me."

Bakker's specific response concerning the computer records was: "If you believe the computer records of Heritage USA, I could sell you some land under water in Florida. The computer at Heritage USA has been a problem from day one at the beginning of the lifetime partnership program. . . ." He specifically denied Steve Nelson's allegation that Bakker had directed certain PTL records be destroyed.

Bakker's attention was drawn to a statement that he made while promoting the Grand Hotel partnership on February 22, 1984. Prosecutor Deborah Smith reminded Bakker that while promoting the David and Goliath creation of Jacob Heller, he had said, "Plus you are going to receive something that's worth, I think, a thousand dollars alone." "That's a bit of an overstatement there, in fact wouldn't you say, Mr. Bakker?" queried Smith. Bakker responded, "I believed that when I said it and it was a limited edition, and I think the spiritual value—I don't see how you can put a value on a biblical inspiration piece." Bakker went on to say, "I think it's an absolute phenomena that [the statue] could be manufactured that cheap." Later, during intense cross-examination, Deborah Smith returned to Bakker's estimation of the worth of the Jacob Heller sculpture, to which Bakker responded in a patronizing manner, "You really don't like that piece, do you?"

In short, Bakker had no recollection of many of the Peter Bailey memos or of ever having been informed of any irregularities in the lifetime partnership program. He steadfastly maintained that the statements he had made on television and through the mails were true. However, Bakker's memory did seem to improve when Deborah Smith indicated that one of Bakker's palm prints had been found on a particular Bailey memo that Bakker failed to remember having received. Smith asked, "So if the FBI analysis indicated two of your fingerprints were on that document, you would not dispute that?" Bakker answered, "No, not at all." From that point on, Bakker seemed to be slightly more tentative in his answers to Smith.

Bakker was chastised about his failed recollection by Prosecutor Deborah Smith. Bakker was questioned concerning a $50,000 bonus that PTL records reflected Bakker had received, but Bakker testified he had "no remembrance." Smith then said: "Mr. Bakker, had your lifestyle become so extravagant at that point that you would not notice a $50,000 deposit in your checking account? That would not even come to your attention?" Bakker responded: "I did not look at my checkbook for many years, and I know you're smiling. You find that hard to believe, but that's the truth."

Bakker testified that although he never had any training in book-keeping, accounting, or served on a board of directors prior to PTL, he always tried to compensate by hiring CPAs, accountants, and business people. Bakker said: "We spent millions of dollars on legal [fees] and on audits and all to make sure everything was done properly. . . . I wanted to make sure that everything was done properly, and that everything was done correctly. I hired the best people that I could find and hired what I felt to be the best firms and law firms to represent us."

Bakker never really focused on the fact that PTL's audits never detected any fraud that was occurring at the facility, but during cross-examination he did attempt to raise an interesting defense concerning intent and culpability. When questioned concerning his relationship with Richard Dortch, Bakker said, "He did his part of the management and I did mine." But when asked if he had had ultimate responsibility for the day-to-day, financial operation of PTL, Bakker's response was as follows, "No, that is not correct. . . . Reverend Dortch oversaw the day-to-day financial operation of the ministry and met with the division heads. . . . I did not, however, oversee the daily financial operations. I did not understand finances."

In the criminal trial, Bakker never really elaborated on testimony he had given in a previous bankruptcy deposition. Specifically, Bakker was asked what his reaction had been when he learned that the Towers account had been significantly if not completely outspent in February of 1985; his reply: "I was upset . . . because I had counted on that account to complete the Towers, but I had a man who I trusted as my executive vice-president and . . . Reverend Richard Dortch. And they were not designated funds, and so they were funds that could be used to pay the expenses of the ongoing of the ministry, and since he felt that it was necessary to spend those funds for other payments, I had to accept that fact that I had a vice-president and general manager that I had to trust and allow to fulfill his idea of what was proper to do in running the company. But I was very upset."

Bakker did seem to allude to this when Deborah Smith asked him, "And you constantly gave permission for those [lifetime partnership funds] to be used for operational expenses even after Mr. Bailey warned you over and over again that that meant there would be insufficient funds left to construct the Towers? Isn't that true?" "No!" Bakker responded. She continued, "Did you hear the testimony of David Taggart who indicated that he, in fact would convey your approvals over and over again to Mr. Bailey?" Bakker's answer: "Mr. Taggart was in the room and probably was the one who informed me that all the funds for the Tower had been depleted, and I was shocked."

The jury found Jim Bakker guilty on all charges. But how could the fraud that occurred at PTL ever have happened? More importantly, how could it have gone undetected, given its magnitude?

CHAPTER SIX

□□□

Where Were the Corporate Officers?

My main concern is the financial integrity of PTL or the lack of it. . . . This past week we issued payroll checks totalling over $800,000. These checks were issued, as usual, with no funds to cover them. The only source of funds is the Towers account.

Peter G. Bailey, Finance Director, in a memo to Jim Bakker and Richard Dortch, dated January 5, 1985

The Chief Financial Officer

Peter G. Bailey, a certified public accountant since 1967, began his career at PTL in June of 1979 at a starting salary of $18,000. Bailey was first employed at PTL as a staff accountant, and after several revisions of his job functions and responsibilities, he eventually became PTL's director of finance. In that position, he was, in effect, the chief financial officer of PTL. He was responsible for the day-to-day financial operations of the ministry, he oversaw financial reporting, and he supervised the PTL finance staff of approximately 45 individuals.

Peter Bailey also wrote voluminous, almost weekly memos to Jim Bakker and Richard Dortch outlining, in painful detail, the critical financial standing of the organization. These memos served as time-lapse snapshots of PTL's financial situation and proved to be very popular in court. Consequently, Bailey testified in all of the judicial proceedings concerning PTL, and his memos, which were introduced in chronological order, were used to track the financial dealings behind PTL's demise.

Prior to examining some of these memos, it is important to understand not only Peter Bailey's background but also the organizational structure of PTL's top echelon.

Peter Bailey came to PTL without a great deal of accounting experience. He had worked for a small CPA firm in Connecticut, had been a financial analyst for a tool manufacturing company, and eventually took a post as assistant controller for a clothing manufacturer; his experience in accounting relative to nonprofit organizations had been gained while serving as treasurer of the Michigan Baptist Foundation and as the business manager of the Christian Retreat Center. Bailey did not have "Big Eight" experience or extensive auditing experience.

Initially hired as an accountant at PTL, Bailey became an accounting manager in 1980. In that position he had been responsible for supervising accounting staff members and preparing financial statements.

By August of 1983, Peter Bailey became known as "one-third of Peter, Porter and Puckett"; that is, Peter Bailey, Porter Speakman, and Donna Puckett joined forces in PTL's three-person Finance Committee. Porter Speakman acted as budget director, Donna Puckett—Jim Bakker's sister—served as accounts payable supervisor, and Peter Bailey was responsible for general accounting. This committee attempted to run PTL's finances for one year, after which time Bailey's position was changed to vice-president of finance and later to finance director.

In May 1986 the financial division was split into four separate divisions, with each having its own director of finance. Bailey remained the overall supervisor, at least officially, of each of these divisions. At PTL, policy was often ignored, and that was clearly the case in the financial division. Although, Bailey, by virtue of his position, was supposed to have control over all of the financial aspects of PTL, such was not the practice. As Bailey recalled, "There was no direct line of authority between myself and those finance divisions. So it was pretty hard to enforce something when those finance people . . . were really reporting to another vice-president. . . . It just made it awkward for myself."

Although the chief financial officer has a great deal of power and commands the respect of most corporate officers, again such was not the case at PTL. Bailey acknowledged in the Taggart trial that PTL did not have a normal corporate structure. According to Bailey, the vice-president of finance is ordinarily one of the top four or five corporate officers. Hypothetically, if there were ten vice-presidents at PTL, Bailey viewed himself as "9th or 10th" from the top in terms of power. The reason being, "[s]imply because their priorities were to raise funds, minister to partners, and the television. The television was their main thing." Bailey added that he was considered by those at PTL to be a "numbers cruncher." Bakker oftened referred to his accounting staff as pencil pushers and opined, "[i]f the pencil pushers had their way we'd still be in tents." After hearing that last comment, Bailey reportedly said, "and at least they would be paid for."

From Bailey's perspective, Dortch was responsible for the day-to-day operations of PTL and was the general manager of the organization. Bailey had little contact with Jim Bakker and only slightly more contact with Richard Dortch. Bailey's immediate supervisor was David Taggart, who had the title of vice-president and administrative assistant to Jim Bakker. From a proper organizational point of view, Bailey should have reported to Richard Dortch, but Bailey testified that "it just didn't work that way."

Taggart testified that he had never taken any accounting courses. In fact, when asked, "Did you ever take any business, accounting or finance courses?", David Taggart responded, "I took in high school and in college Business 101 and 102. [I had] no accounting courses." Yet Taggart ended up being the senior executive with whom Bailey had the most contact.

It is important to understand that the executives at PTL had their offices in the World Outreach Center, or WOC, which is really a misnomer. The pyramid-shaped WOC building had little, if anything, to do with world outreach and everything to do with the business operation of PTL, that is, the continual shuffling of funds among its various checking accounts. On the first floor of the World Outreach Center, mail was received, and cash was counted. Some days, PTL received over a million dollars in donations. The PTL vault was located on the first floor, along with computer hardware and software that was used by PTL to keep track of its fundraising activities. The general financial business of PTL was conducted on the second floor, which also housed employees who had responsibility for the PTL Television Network's relationships with cable television systems and television affiliates. Peter Bailey had his office on this floor along with the other accountants on his staff.

The third floor of the World Outreach Center was where the real power of PTL was located; Jim Bakker, Tammy Bakker, David Taggart, Richard Dortch, Shirley Fulbright (Jim Bakker's secretary), and Patricia Harrison (Jim Bakker's personal bookkeeper) had their offices here. Access to the third floor by other employees was limited. A special card key had to be used to gain access to it, and the phrase "the third floor" had a special meaning for PTL employees. According to the Federal Bankruptcy Court, "[a] memorandum or a directive coming from 'the third floor' was to be complied with without question. It was 'the third floor' that determined PTL policy and direction and it was 'the third floor' that determined that PTL policies relating to documentation of cash advances and expenses would not apply to those individuals located at that level."

Bailey's primary personal contact on the third floor was David Taggart. While Bailey had fairly easy access to Taggart, his personal contact with Dortch and Bakker was much more limited. Memos from Bailey were delivered by himself or his secretary to the third floor, because Bailey's communication with Bakker and Dortch was primarily by memo.

Bakker never wanted to hear bad news because he always had to be "upbeat" while on the air. Negative news often resulted in his becoming silent and swinging his chair around to gaze out his third-floor office window for long periods of time. Consequently, Bailey's deeply felt misgivings about the state of PTL's finances were shared with Dortch and Bakker in memos, seldom face to face.

In addition to a lack of face-to-face meetings and a distorted chain of responsibility not only within the finance division but also between the finance division and the executive management of PTL, the organization also had an urgent need to update its internal accounting system. PTL hired an automatic data processing firm that accumulated its financial records and did the PTL general ledger but did not have an in-house computer system for sophisticated entry of financial transactions. For example, PTL, at the direction of either Bakker or Dortch, had 45 different checking accounts, most of which corresponded to various lifetime partnership programs or special projects. For example, there was a Grand Hotel account, a Towers Hotel account, and a Bunkhouse account. When funds came into PTL from lifetime partners who, for example, had purchased a Grand Hotel lifetime partnership, the $1,000 payment would be deposited in the Grand Hotel account. Bailey acknowledged that "[i]t might have been easier to consolidate the bank accounts" and separate the accounts on the general ledger. This would have reduced the time and expense of performing numerous bank reconciliations.

Interestingly, less than four months after Bailey urged consolidation of bank accounts and reducing cost in finance, the very opposite was done. According to Bailey, Richard Dortch took Bailey to lunch and told him that Jim Bakker wanted to break the finance division into four different areas: Retail, Heritage USA, Church, and Television. Obviously, this reorganization had the effect of lessening Peter Bailey's control and authority over finances. Each department had its own finance director, accounts payable, and bank accounts, and all of this was done in spite of the fact that overall payroll was still administered by Bailey's office.

PTL had as many as 45 different checking accounts, but there were at least three different checking accounts that Peter Bailey did not control. The executive payroll account, the executive checking account, and the parsonage account were all under the control of the third floor. Peter Bailey, even in his role as finance director, was generally not privy to details of the transactions conducted in these accounts. Control of these accounts gave certain individuals at the highest level of PTL access to almost unlimited funds. The IRS found that from 1985 through 1987, $3,791,653 was paid through the executive checking account and $5,494,545 through the parsonage account.

The third floor decided which individuals would be paid out of the executive payroll account. This account paid between 30 and 40 individuals on a bimonthly or monthly basis. The compensation of those paid out of the executive payroll account ranged from $21,000 a year to Jim Bakker's annual salary of approximately $290,000 a year. With the exception of Jim and Tammy Bakker, Richard Dortch, and David Taggart, most individuals on the PTL executive payroll made between $35,000 and $50,000.

As will be more fully explored later in this chapter, the executive payroll was maintained on the premises of PTL prior to Richard Dortch's arrival. Peter Bailey had control over the executive payroll and knew the various levels of compensation for all PTL employees. But upon his arrival as executive vice-president of PTL, Dortch instituted an executive payroll that was handled outside of the Heritage USA facility. Citing the need for confidentiality, Dortch arranged for outside accountants to maintain it, starting with Deloitte, Haskins and Sells and concluding with Laventhol and Horwath. The third floor notified the outside accounting firm of any changes to salaries and bonuses or special payment situations that would accrue to those listed on the PTL executive payroll. The accounting firm prepared the checks, which were then picked up by a PTL courier, delivered to the third floor, and distributed as necessary. The accounting firm would not sign the checks, but rather the payor's (PTL's) signature was affixed once the checks were returned to Heritage USA. The outside accounting firm also prepared each employee's 1099 form to reflect total wages paid to the employee by PTL.

Peter Bailey was notified by the accounting firm as to how much money should be deposited into the executive payroll account. As finance director, Bailey testified that he was not made privy to the salaries or bonuses of those who were paid out of the executive payroll account. Bailey specifically testified that he did not know anything about the salaries of Jim Bakker, Tammy Bakker, Richard Dortch, David Taggart, or Shirley Fulbright. He also did not have access to the information concerning the amount of bonuses to the Bakkers, Dortch or Taggart. Instead, the outside accounting firm periodically told Bailey or one of his assistants how much money should be deposited into the executive payroll account. Additionally, Bailey never received any of the minutes of the board of directors or any other documents reflecting authorization or approval of executive salaries or compensation.

Peter Bailey's testimony concerning where he secured the funds to place into the executive payroll account is particularly interesting:

> Q: Now, when you had received this call or letter from the outside auditing firm asking you to transfer funds, where would that money come from? Where would you get it to transfer into the executive payroll account?
> A: Wherever I could.
> Q: Basically, whatever account of the 45 that had money in it?
> A: That's right.
> Q: Would this include lifetime partner accounts?
> A: Yes
> Q: So if the, for example, the general fund, your general operating fund was low in funds or had no funds in them, or insufficient funds to cover the request, you would take it out of whatever account had money in it at that time?
> A: You had no choice, yes.
> Q: Was that frequently taken out of lifetime partner accounts that you've described, the Grand, the Towers, the Bunkhouse and the 1100 Club accounts?
> A: Yes, it was.

The executive checking account "was used for various expenditures by the third floor." As money was needed for it, funds were transferred from the general fund and various other PTL funds. Just as with the executive payroll account, neither Peter Bailey nor his staff were involved with reviewing or authorizing checks drawn on the executive checking account. Bailey testified that his understanding was that the executive checking account was handled out of the third floor rather than through the accounting area, for reasons of "expediency and for confidentiality."

The parsonage account also received funds from other accounts in order to maintain its viability and was used to pay expenses relating to the "parsonages" (that is, executive residences) that PTL owned. Exhibit A-14 shows how over $300,000 of PTL funds were used by just one contractor to construct additions to homes occupied by Bakker and Dortch.

In addition to the three executive bank accounts just discussed, there was another source of easy money for certain PTL executives: credit cards.

At one time, PTL had an American Express Card. According to Bailey's bankruptcy testimony, that card "was terminated on the part of American Express because we kept paying our bill late." "Why did you pay your bills late?" asked the attorney for the bankrupt PTL organization. "Because we were always one step ahead of the money coming in, and American Express is pretty strict," responded Peter Bailey. "They'll let you go maybe 30 days, but if you do that too often—they were probably the most strict account, and so after awhile they got tired of it, I think, and just terminated the—canceled our credit card." Consequently, PTL gave up their canceled American Express card and traded it in for a Visa card and a MasterCard; each card had a $100,000 limit. Payment of PTL's credit card bills was made through the executive checking account. Again, Bailey never received the actual credit card statements; those were received and maintained on the third floor under the guise of a need for confidentiality.

Richard Dortch, David Taggart, Shirley Fulbright, and Jim Bakker were all given a PTL credit card. Bailey was specifically asked what controls PTL had over these credit cards if the finance division at PTL didn't have access to any of the credit card records. Bailey responded, "Well, they had a $100,000 limit."

In his role as finance director, Peter Bailey prepared memos and weekly reports that were forwarded to Jim Bakker and Richard Dortch and delivered by Bailey or his secretary. Bailey testified that he kept Bakker fully informed about the cash flow problems at PTL as well as the overall decline in financial health that PTL was facing from week to week.

As I have previously stated, these memos were used in all of the judicial proceedings concerning PTL and Jim Bakker. They provided a monthly, if not weekly, assessment of PTL's chronic cash flow crisis.

For example, Peter Bailey wrote a memo dated January 19, 1983, in which he stated

> At the time we purchased the Florida condominium, we transferred $222,000 out of the gift savings and the balance of our regular savings. When the financing goes through on the condominium in five to six weeks, I will put $222,000 back into gift savings to pay off our vendors so that we will be current with them as we had told them originally. Just for your information, we are current on our tithe and we will remain so.

Bailey was asked to explain each memo to the jury and put its contents into proper perspective. For example, in his January 19, 1983, memo, Bailey confirmed that PTL was having to put off paying various vendors who had provided services and materials to PTL so that the Florida condominium for Jim Bakker could be purchased. PTL's vendors, who were already overdue for payment, had to wait an additional five to six weeks for payment, which was contingent on PTL's receiving financing for Jim Bakker's vacation home.

On March 21, 1983, Bailey had this to write in a memo to Bakker: "The Parsonage Checking Account is not able to sustain the cash outflow. We need $10,200 per week in church offerings to maintain the expenditures from the Parsonage Account. At present, the account is about $12,000 overdrawn. This is offset by telecast funds that were taken for the studio and now for various maintenance projects."

Bailey wrote a memo dated June 2, 1983, in which he stated, "On a temporary basis, we are asking all program guests to help PTL during its financial crisis by requesting them to pay for their own travel expenses when coming to PTL as a program guest." A month later, on July 4, 1983, the PTL board of directors voted in favor of granting a $100,000 bonus to Jim Bakker and a $50,000 bonus to Tammy Bakker. Bailey testified that he was not aware of this.

On September 2, 1983, in yet another memo to Bakker, Bailey made this report: "In the past three weeks, we have spent $2,921,000 from the general fund. We have received a total of $1,870,000 in general contributions and miscellaneous receipts." Bailey also emphasized the eternal cash flow crisis in this memo: "This week, I pulled out $200,000 from savings to keep us afloat. We are still maintaining $50,000 per day to TV time to keep them from slipping, but they are also in need of another shot in the arm as they are still 90 days past due on many bills."

PTL's general fund was now more than a million dollars short of expenditures and more than 90 days past due in paying its satellite television stations across the nation.

On September 16, 1983, Peter Bailey asked Jim Bakker a question that was to be repeated many times in the future: "There are not sufficient funds in the general fund. May I have your permission to pay from savings? Next week I must cover payroll from the general fund." Bakker answered in the affirmative, and so funds were taken out of savings to meet the bills that were due that day. Thereafter, Bailey often had to take funds out of savings or any of the 45 different PTL checking accounts to meet immediate expenditures, including bonuses, executive compensation, and PTL's own payroll. Just ten days later, on September 26, 1983, the PTL board of directors voted a $100,000 bonus to Jim Bakker and a $50,000 bonus to Tammy Bakker. Bailey testified that he was not aware of those bonuses.

On November 30, 1983, Bailey penned a memo to Bakker that began another constant theme: "Contributions in November were over $4.7 million, not including church tithes and offerings. We should be thankful for this; but, as you know, we spent more than we took in." On December 16, 1983, the board of directors of PTL voted another $100,000 bonus to Jim Bakker and an additional $50,000 bonus to Tammy Bakker. Per the now familiar pattern, Bailey testified that he was not informed that the Bakkers were receiving bonuses, nor was he aware of the amounts of this or any bonus.

On January 6, 1984, the day before the first massive mailing of the Grand Hotel lifetime partnership brochures, Dortch received a memo from Peter Bailey reflecting that it was costing $185,000 per day to operate PTL and that PTL had been running approximately $758,000 over its average income for the six-month period ending November 1983.

By January 16, 1984, Bailey wrote to Bakker and Dortch that PTL owed $714,807 to the company that provided it with its Bibles; of that amount, $205,000 was past due. This same memo reflected that PTL owed $75,515 to its own auditors, Deloitte, Haskins and Sells; of that amount, $50,525 was past due. Bailey concluded the memo by stating: "I respectfully suggest that we curtail as much future spending as possible for the next two months. We are not able to make commitments to anyone as our income is far less than our current spending. (Approximately $500,000 per month.) All savings accounts have been used."

Jim Bakker received another memo, dated February 24, 1984, which stated that for the first month of 1984, PTL had already lost $400,000.

Even more to the point was a memo dated March 12, 1984, from Bailey, which made the following grim pronouncements: "Our payroll is far too high and cannot be sustained by general funds any longer, as we had many other bills that we need to pay now. We have negotiated with vendors for months and felt that the telethon would provide the necessary funds. Our payroll is now running at an annual rate of $17 million." In the same memo, Bailey indicated that PTL owed American Express $85,000 and so had been "cut off" until payment was received and that gift payments were behind by $350,000. He added: "Blue Cross is behind and will not pay claims if not paid immediately. We have been able to pay only $25,000 a day on time charges. We need to pay $50,000 to stay even." (Exhibit A-15.)

The very next day, on March 13, 1984, the PTL board of directors awarded Jim Bakker a $390,000 bonus. The board never saw the Bailey memos, nor were they advised of PTL's critical financial situation as Bailey had discussed in his memos.

Just three days later, Peter Bailey wrote: "We still are not able to cover last pay period's payroll taxes, and now a new payroll is upon us. We need to get our payroll under control. . . . I really believe we need to seriously trim our payroll. Each day brings us into a deeper crisis. We continue to hire employees and increase our payroll; and at the same time, we are months behind on loan payments and television time."

PTL did eventually terminate its relationship with Blue Cross and on or about June 1, 1984, began using a local company, Fringe Benefit Corporation, which, according to Bailey, provided "more efficient service to our employees."

On June 29, 1984, Peter Bailey discussed another practice that PTL was frequently using: the floating of funds. In this memo, he said: "We have spent funds this week against next week's receipts. The total of $1,979,000 was spent with general contributions totaling $872,000. We transferred $384,000 from other PTL accounts to help cover the difference, with the remaining differences coming from next week's contributions. I am concerned that our budget cuts are not happening as we planned. We are still traveling, hiring people. It's a gut feeling that we need to do much more to cut back on our expenses." In the same memo, Bailey notified Dortch and Bakker that the IRS, which was now conducting an audit of PTL, had made over 120 separate document requests with numerous requests relating to each document. Despite this bleak picture, on July 3, 1984, the Board voted a $100,000 bonus for Jim Bakker and a $50,000 bonus for his wife. Again, Peter Bailey testified that he was unaware of this, which is not unlikely given that he was not asked to appear at the July 3, 1984, PTL board meeting or any other board meeting.

Just two and a half weeks later, Bailey projected an even more urgent tone in his memos to Dortch and Bakker: "Unless we quickly and seriously reduce our spending, we will not be able to pay future payrolls. . . . I feel we are definitely in a serious crisis."

Lack of cost controls and the failure to obtain firm bids from contractors was a major problem at PTL. According to Bailey, "PTL did not get competitive bidding." Instead, PTL got cost estimates, and when a project was finished, its final cost invariably exceeded the original estimates by a fairly large amount. As an example, the PTL home for unwed mothers had been estimated to cost $400,000, but the actual cost was in excess of $1 million. Cost overruns of 30 to 50 percent were not uncommon. In addition to cost overruns, PTL also made some very unwise purchases. For example, on July 11, 1984, a jet airplane was purchased for $965,000; it was sold on April 14, 1986, for $460,000. Originally, PTL had planned to use the plane and also rent it to other businesses to cover the plane's cost. This was never done. The mismanagement at PTL went far beyond failing to control construction costs and making unwise purchases.

On August 10, 1984, Bailey wrote again to Dortch: "We need to be in prayer for our next payroll. We must hold back on nearly all our expenditures in order to meet the payroll. . . . If I did not require my initials [on purchase orders and check requests], there would be an immediate cash crisis on our funds."

Five days later, Bailey was telling Dortch and Bakker that although the next payroll would be $700,000, he had been able to set aside only $70,000 toward it. In addition, he informed them that over a million dollars was due vendors, including $240,000 owed for 24,000 David and Goliath statues. These statues had not yet been shipped but had been promised by Jim Bakker to be a part of the benefits one could receive by joining the $1,000 Grand Hotel lifetime partnership. He concluded his memo by stating, "[w]e are in a serious crisis and must continue even more so to cut back our programs until our operations are in line with our income."

Peter Bailey's desperation concerning coverage of outstanding bills was reflected in his October 3, 1984, memo in which he addressed "the immediate emergencies that must be paid now." After listing a total of $685,000 worth of "immediate emergencies," Bailey wrote, "I do not have funds to pay these and many other bills. Please help."

Even more blunt is this memo to Bakker and Dortch on October 17, 1984: "To me, we are in a false euphoria. We must cut back on spending or continue to use Tower funds to maintain operations." Bailey also mentioned that $5.2 million had been raised for the Heritage Towers but no money had been set aside for construction. With the exception of $500,000, all had been spent on other projects.

As of November 9, 1984, Jim Bakker and PTL had raised $8.6 million from the Towers lifetime partnerships. As of that date, none of the funds raised had been put into an account or earmarked for construction of the Towers Hotel.

On November 16, 1984, Peter Bailey was writing of the expenses PTL continued to incur: "This means we must continue using hotel funds [to meet daily operational expenses] until we either raise contributions to our spending level or cut our level of operations and projects. We are in a very serious cash flow position." (Exhibit A-16.) On November 20, 1984, at another PTL board meeting, Jim Bakker received a $150,000 bonus, and Tammy Bakker received a $50,000 bonus. Again, Bakker did not inform Bailey of the bonuses.

Peter Bailey's memo to Dortch and Bakker of January 5, 1985, was, in my opinion, the most telling of all. It concerned "financial integrity," which is a rather curious topic to be discussing within a religious organization. What prompted this memo was Dortch's request to Bailey to come up with a system that would ensure that PTL's payroll checks would not bounce. After making three rather unprofound suggestions as to how to accomplish this goal, Bailey directly faced the problems that existed at PTL. (See Exhibit 6-1.)

If top management at PTL had only taken Peter Bailey's advice as outlined in such excruciating detail, the downfall of PTL might possibly have been avoided, although the oversell of Grand lifetime partnerships had begun six months earlier.

Bakker testified that he had no specific recollection of having received this memo, and no action was taken as a result of it. But how could any corporate officer forget a memo in which the director of finance is questioning the "financial integrity" of the corporation?

One may ask, should Peter Bailey have done more? Bailey was a prolific writer and clearly communicated the seriousness of PTL's financial crisis as well as his objections to how money was being handled to both Bakker and Dortch. But should he have notified others of his concerns? Should he have taken more drastic action? Also, if Peter Bailey was reaching these conclusions concerning PTL's financial integrity, what conclusions were PTL's outside auditing firms reaching?

Just five days later, on January 10, 1985, Bailey was again writing to Dortch and Bakker advising them of situations that needed their

PTL Television Network

Memo

To: Richard Dortch

From: Peter G. Bailey

Date: January 5, 1985

RE: Financial Integrity

CC: Jim Bakker

I have given much thought to your asking me to come up with a system that will guarantee that we do not bounce any checks.

Ever since I have been with PTL (almost 6 years) checks have been written on future deposits. That is what is called "float." This is a common practice especially with christian organizations. Your books, therefore, always show a negative cash balance. Checks written are dependent upon the deposits received over the next several days. If contributions fall or emergencies come up (which is continually) then the chances of bouncing a check becomes stronger.

The only bank account in which a bounced check has occurred is the Washington account for checks written for television time. I have stopped using that account and have set up a television time account with Security bank. Security Bank, up to now, will not bounce any of our checks on any of our accounts. If Security should change this policy and in order for PTL to guarantee that no checks bounce, the following system should be installed:

1. PTL should never write a check that will cause the cash book balance to go below zero. At present, our general fund accounts have a negative book balance of approximately ($500,000).

2. PTL first must reduce the amount of checks written, including payroll, to bring the (500,000) balance up to zero.

3. Next, PTL must only write checks that do not exceed that day's deposit.

Next, to accomplish the above, PTL's top management must have the financial integrity to stop approving expenditures that continually exceed our income. This is the root of our problem. No system will work unless top management assumes its responsibility of financial integrity.

DEPOSITION EXHIBIT
Group Ex # 3
Pg 1-84 (1985)

ENCL 4 ⓵

0334 009

Exhibit 6-1 A Memo from Peter Bailey to Richard Dortch Regarding PTL's Financial Integrity

Memo to Richard Dortch   -2-   January 5, 1985

The following are monthly expenditures that top management has approved:

Salaries	$ 1,300,000
Medical-Employees	100,000
Retirement	30,000
Social Security	90,000
Partner Expenses	850,000
Television Time	1,100,000
Tithe	400,000
Travel	50,000
Daily Operating Bills	400,000
Loans-RCA payments	70,000
Loans-Computer	23,000
Loans-Buses	13,000
Loans-Real Estate	50,000
Loans-Equipment	125,000
Insurance	45,000
Bond Interest	90,000
Line of credit-interest	12,000
Country Fairs & other specials	40,000
Electricity	50,000
Telephone	50,000
T.V. Tape duplication	60,000
Christmas City	80,000
Airplane	40,000
Other	40,000
Monthly Total	5,108,000

This does not include Brock Hotel and Morrisons deficits that PTL must fund, not capital expenditures.

Next December, PTL will have an additional $235,000 a month payment to Fairfax for the $10 million loan. The above list amounts to $1,200,000 a week. PTL has been receiving an average of $700,000 a week. This negative cash flow of ($500,000) a week has been funded by the hotel and tower account over the past few months, this must stop. This is not financial integrity. I agonize daily over this and the lack of action taken by top management to resolve this critical problem. We have the water park to finish as well as plans to build a 5,000 seat studio and a nursing center. Nursing centers do not pay for themselves.

We cannot afford to keep financing projects such as more television equipment, the water park, a nursing home or maybe even the west coast operation. On paper the west coast will make money but funding the project until it is running is questionable.

My main concern is the financial integrity of PTL or the lack of it. We constantly buy from local vendors knowing we cannot pay for it on time. Our system rewards those at PTL who get the job done whether or not it leaves PTL in the eyes of our vendors as being irresponsible. Our purchasing departmen does less purchasing then various people in television, Rich Ball, Jim Swaim or Charlotte Whiting

Exhibit 6-1 *Continued*

Memo. to Richard Dortch   -2-   January 5, 1985

Finance is looked upon as being in the way of progress by many in the ministry. In these last few months, I have found there is very little time given to me to talk to you about financial issues. Whenever my finance people try to do their jobs to enforce financial procedure, they are stopped from doing so by the third floor, especially in the area of cash advances and emergency check requests.

Getting back to the system to guaranteeing that checks don't bounce, please sit down with me and let's come up with a realistic priority of what can be paid and where we will cut back.

This past week we issued payroll checks totalling over $800,000. These checks were issued, as usual, with no funds to cover them. The only source of funds is the tower account.

/plg   PGB

Exhibit 6-1 *Continued*

attention. One of the bills that was listed as being "past due—up to six months" is PTL's bill to its outside auditor, Deloitte, Haskins and Sells. The amount of that bill? $161,270. PTL was having a hard time even being able to pay its outside auditor.

By January 14, 1985, Peter Bailey could clearly see the difficulty that PTL would have in trying to raise funds simply to do what it had originally promised: to build the Towers Hotel. Bailey wrote to Bakker and Dortch: "To date, PTL has used $20 million from the Towers account for Heritage Grand Hotel construction and expenses, TV time, payroll and water park. There remains about $2 million in the account, with approximately 9,000 lifetime partners remaining at $2,000 apiece. This will leave $20 million available to build the Towers. Per Mr. Messner's reports, it will cost $19.2 million to build the Towers." This means that Bailey recognized that being able to sell 9,000 additional Towers lifetime partnerships at $2,000 each would raise $18 million, the $2 million already in the Towers account would provide $20 million, which would be just enough to build the Towers.

Two points are critical concerning this memorandum. First, Peter Bailey recognized that there were "9,000 lifetime memberships remaining," which seems to indicate that Bailey recognized that there was a limited number of partnerships that could be sold for the Towers Hotel. Second, on September 17, 1984, Jim Bakker and PTL's contractor, Roe Messner, appeared on television and told the audience that the Towers would cost $15 million. Almost four months later, its cost was quoted as $19.2 million. This represents nearly a 33 percent increase in the construction cost of the Towers Hotel. How could it have increased by $4.2 million in less than four months?

Bailey continued in his memo to say that "what this means is that no longer will we be able to cover payroll, our loan maintenance costs, utilities, television time or partner expenses at the present level. This Friday, I will not issue payroll checks unless there are funds in the general account to pay the payroll unless approved in writing by Jim Bakker, David Taggart or Richard Dortch." This was, in effect, Peter Bailey's "drop dead" memo concerning the Towers Hotel. He seems to have been saying that raising funds for one purpose and using them for another would no longer be possible. Unfortunately, it was possible, but only by continuing to divert the funds for other uses, and through what would eventually be the massive overselling of the Towers just like the Grand Hotel was oversold. On the very date this memo went to Richard Dortch, $75,000 was approved by Dortch to pay James Taggart's interior decorating company. Bailey testified that after January 14, 1985, his practice was to contact either David Taggart or Richard Dortch for the authority to transfer funds from other accounts to be able to pay current operating expenses.

Four days later, on January 18, 1985, Bailey informed Dortch and Bakker that for seven months PTL had been experiencing a decrease in contributions of $11 million while expenses had increased by $5 million. This resulted in a loss of $9,704,055. Approximately two months later, on March 28, 1985, at a PTL board meeting, Jim Bakker received a $200,000 bonus, and Tammy Bakker received a $50,000 bonus. Prosecutor Deborah Smith asked Bailey, "Did Mr. Bakker ever come to you after that vote and discuss with you whether or not PTL could afford this or anything of that sort?" "No," replied Bailey.

Peter Bailey's June 30, 1985, memo to Richard Dortch and Jim Bakker reflected that the "Heritage Village Church and Missionary Fellowship, Incorporated, shows a year-to-date loss of ($20 million). This is because contributions this year were $40 million against $52 million last year due to the emphasis on lifetime partners. The balance of deferred income for lifetime partners is $65 million. This amount will be realized in income over the next several years." (Exhibit A-17)

The concept of deferred revenue was discussed by Peter Bailey in his testimony as it related to this memo: "The basic tenet of the American Institute of Certified Public Accountants [is] that all financial statements must match revenues with expenses in a current, [or] in the same period. In other words, you can't show a lot of income in one period if that income is going to benefit future periods. You've got to, as best you can, match up your income with your expenses for that period. So, therefore the $65 million is what I call—or not

I—but the term is called deferred revenue. In other words, it's put off showing on your financial statement as income until the [latter] years—[when] the expenses against the revenue is incurred." In other words, he was saying that it would be inappropriate to count all of the lifetime partnership contributions as current income. A lot of money would be required to take care of those lifetime partners in the future years, and money should have been reserved for that purpose. The money was not reserved, however, and as Peter Bailey indicated in his April 1985 memo, there was at that time a $348,000 negative cash flow from the Grand Hotel. Bailey was asked by Smith, "So even with a negative cash flow from the hotel, did PTL change its course of action or say, oh, we'd better start saving this lifetime partner funds to make sure it's here to build and service the hotel in the future?" Bailey's response was, "No."

On September 30, 1985, Peter Bailey was recommending a 40 percent cut in payroll expenses. But on November 12, 1985, Jim Bakker was voted a bonus of $200,000, and Tammy Bakker received a bonus of $100,000. The very next day, the IRS sent a report to PTL proposing that its tax-exempt status be revoked. According to Bailey, such an action by the IRS "would probably have a devastating effect."

PTL's lax business organization, with inadequate or nonexistent controls, also affected a number of PTL employees. For example, by September 30, 1985, Bailey wrote Bakker a memo that stated, "PTL employees have charged meals at our food services in the amount of $90,000 each for July and August." Bailey recommended that employees pay for their authorized business meals with cash or personal charge cards and then be reimbursed by PTL rather than simply going to the food services area and charging meals for themselves and their guests.

In his November 18, 1985, report to Bakker and Dortch, Bailey stated: "We must have $1.3 million contributions per week. Because of the drop in general funds and payroll not dropping ($1 million last pay period). We have had to cover $600,000 in payroll checks with funds other than general contributions. We still owe $1 million on payroll. We need to sit down and make necessary cuts in payroll costs." Peter Bailey's desperation comes out most strongly in the third paragraph of the memo: "We have a $200,000 payment due this week to Praise Unlimited which I don't feel we can meet. We owe the Galaxy Network $200,000 for October and $200,000 for November which must be paid shortly but, I don't believe we can. We owe two months to Finalco for the telecommunication system in the amount of

$148,000. These are some of the expenses facing us besides another payroll on Friday."

Bailey did not recall any specific conversation in which he discussed these issues with Jim Bakker.

More desperation set in on November 19, 1985. As usual, funds continued to be depleted from the various lodging partnership accounts. Now it was time for funds raised from the Silver 7000 promotional to be plundered. In this memo, Bailey said, "We are falling further behind on payroll. I need to draw $1 million from the Silver 7000 Club in order to cover what we are behind." Although Bailey did not recall receiving a written response from Jim Bakker, he believed that he received a verbal authorization by way of David Taggart to begin withdrawing funds from the Silver 7000 Club partnership fund, which was tapped for $774,188.87.

On March 25, 1986, Bailey gave Bakker a detailed warning concerning the fact that PTL's general operating fund had a negative balance of $1.6 million. At a board meeting approximately one week later, Jim Bakker was awarded a bonus of $200,000, and Tammy Bakker received a $100,000 bonus.

On April 16, 1986, Peter Bailey listed "real emergencies" and said: "We are continuing to operate far in excess of what is coming in. The contributions are flat. We can have all the financial controls in the world, but if we don't live within our means, it doesn't mean anything." (Exhibit A-18.) This memo is particularly devastating because it mentions that Fairfax Savings and Loan was owed $165,000 for April; he said, "They are very demanding and can put us in default." Bailey was referring to the lien that the Savings and Loan had on the Grand Hotel.

His April 21, 1986, memo verges on hysteria: "I am not writing checks this week unless it is an extreme emergency. . . . The most urgent crisis is payment on the bonds due this week for $600,000. We cannot afford the level we operate at based on our current income. We need to quit blaming finance for our difficulties and bite the bullet by cutting expenses and new fundraising ideas. We must survive!" Bailey received no response to this memo.

The memo of April 28, 1986, stated: "We are surviving because of the lifetime partnerships. Our budget is for operations only." On May 5, 1986, Peter Bailey made the following comment in a memo concerning the PTL float of $2.2 million: "This means we have $2,200,000 in checks written on future deposits." Obviously, Peter Bailey's memo regarding financial integrity and how to ensure that checks don't bounce, written one year and five months earlier, had had no effect on the business operations of PTL.

Bailey's June 2, 1986, memo to Jim Bakker reflected that parsonages owned by PTL located at Kiwi Point, Park Road, and Starbrook Road carried significant mortgages. Additionally, there was a $10 million mortgage on the Heritage Grand Hotel that was being carried by Fairfax Savings and Loan. When Bailey was asked, "When you watched the television program, did you ever hear any representations made by Mr. Bakker as to whether or not the various buildings at PTL and specifically the Grand were debt free?" Bailey responded, "Yes."

The Victory Warrior lifetime partnership promotional began toward the end of May 1986, and so Peter Bailey's June 6, 1986, memo reflected those lifetime partnership contributions. In this memo, Bailey showed how PTL had gone through more than $20 million of lifetime partner funds in only three weeks but still had $3.3 million of "uncovered float."

By June 9, 1986, PTL had raised $19,011,510.04 from people wanting to become a Victory Warrior and stay at the Towers Hotel. Bailey's memos bore witness (as did Bailey under oath) that PTL was spending the money as fast as it came in.

On July 2, 1986, Bailey wrote a memo to Bakker warning that there were insufficient funds reserved to build the Towers as of that date. The amount PTL needed to complete the Towers was $15,225,000, which included money owed to Roe Messner. PTL according to Bailey's memo, had $13,605,000 in "savings." Therefore, PTL was approximately $1.6 million short of funds needed to complete the Towers. The very next day, July 3, 1986, the PTL board of directors voted a $300,000 bonus to Jim Bakker and a $100,000 bonus for his wife.

Total Victory Warrior income, as of July 10, 1986, amounted to $34,908,076, and PTL had already spent every cent. Furthermore, PTL still owed Roe Messner $11,617,460. That is, even after raising nearly $35 million, PTL still did not have enough money to pay for construction of the Towers Hotel. (Exhibit A-19.) Clearly, there were some phenomenal fundraising days in the Victory Warrior lifetime partnership program. As Exhibit A-20 reflects, the total received on just one day, May 30, 1986, was nearly $6 million alone.

Jim Bakker wrote a two-paragraph memo to Steve Nelson and Wanda Burgund on May 30, 1986, in which he said the following:

> I really don't think that people in this Victory Warriors need the silver pen. They're expensive and let's just forget them for this time.

Let's just use them for those who have given $1,000 for the
Silver. The Victory Warrior Silvers do not need the silver pens. This
is very important!

From the government's perspective, this memo showed that Jim
Bakker was in fact concerned with minute financial details, although
he argued at trial that he had left the day-to-day operations of PTL
to other people.

On August 19, 1986, Bailey penned yet another memo to Bakker
and Dortch projecting that PTL would be unable to pay any bills in
three to four weeks. The savings account that had been set up to pay
the over $15 million necessary to complete the Towers had now dwin-
dled to $4.6 million. In addition to this bad news, Bailey also notified
Bakker and Dortch that PTL had a $3.6 million float of checks that
had been written but not cleared and that there was only $300,000
in the Bunkhouse lifetime partnership account.

Despite Peter Bailey's September 9, 1986, memo reflecting his
recommendation that $1 out of every $3 raised under the Bunkhouse
lifetime partnership program should be set aside for construction purposes, such was not done. Less than a month later, Peter Bailey was
recommending that his own advice be ignored. Fairfax Savings and
Loan was threatening to sue PTL over its $343,000 debt, and Bailey
was forced to ask Bakker on October 8 if that amount should be taken
from the Bunkhouse account.

PTL's critical financial situation was again the subject of another
memo from Bailey to Bakker, dated November 17, 1986: "We have
also been covering the excess expenditures over receipts from lifetime
donations. The balance in the Bunkhouse account is zero. We have
also used up our reserve account for taxes. We are going to get bids
on construction of the Crystal Towers." This last sentence refers to
a new project under consideration at the time, even though PTL
couldn't pay for previous ones.

Peter Bailey often concluded his memos on a religious note, indicative of his being a devout Christian. Bailey was specifically asked
in the civil case against PTL's auditors and others whether it was
"[his] belief that [his] Christian faith and Mr. Bakker's Christian faith
were the answers for the financial problems that [Bailey] would de-
scribe from time to time at PTL?" Bailey responded, "Yes." When
asked, "Why was that your belief relative to PTL?," Bailey made the
following assertion: "Because I've seen it happen many times. I've
seen God answer prayers in my own personal life and at PTL. Of

course, God expects us to work, and He just can't push buttons, but with proper work, God does answer prayers."

Peter Bailey was also questioned concerning whether or not he was surprised that the PTL ministry declared bankruptcy after Jim Bakker resigned from the ministry. Bailey responded that he was totally surprised that the ministry declared bankruptcy. He testified, "I was obviously very concerned with having the bills paid and how the money was being spent daily, but never in my wildest dream[s] would I think that PTL would ever go under, and you see, this is where I have to tie in my spiritual belief and my job, they were one. PTL was too big and too growing and appealed to too many people and had the ability to raise money, too much good was going on, that it would fold."

Bailey's strong religious beliefs clearly influenced him to believe that PTL would not go bankrupt. However, his memos were full of increasingly ominous statements concerning the state of PTL's finances. Although Jim Bakker had the ability to raise enormous amounts of funds, it was only by overselling lifetime partnerships that PTL was able to remain afloat. Again, the government indictment charged that the lifetime partnership program had raised approximately $158 million. If the stated limits on the Grand and the Towers had been strictly adhered to, then those two projects alone would have raised only $55 million. Conservatively, therefore, approximately $100 million in income was derived from the oversell of the two projects, and again, the Towers was never even completed. What was Peter Bailey's response to the oversell of the Towers and of the Grand Hotel? Surprisingly, Peter Bailey testified that he did not know that there had been any limits placed on the number of lifetime partnerships for the Towers or the Grand Hotel.

Peter Bailey's sworn testimony in the civil trial was very clear:

Q: Mr. Bailey, did you ever believe or understand that PTL had any obligation to make refunds above 20,000 or 25,000 Heritage Grand lifetime partners?

A: No.

Q: Or 30,000 Grand, Tower lifetime partners?

A: No.

Q: In fact, Mr. Bailey, you never understood that there was any legal limit if you will of 25,000 or 30,000 on the partnerships that could be accepted, did you?

A: Not a legal limit. PTL mentioned 50 percent, but it wasn't a legal limit. They could have gone 60, if they could financially afford it.

Q: In other words, PTL could have accepted this number of lifetime partners if they chose to do that?
A: Yes.
Q: Alright, and there was no limit such that you had to disclose any kind of contingency, right?
A: Right, there was no contingency that I know of.

Bailey was also questioned under oath concerning the promotional brochure mailed in January 1984 that mentioned the lifetime partnership limitation. Bailey's testimony in that regard was as follows:

Q: And we have heard testimony in this case that there was a brochure that went out that said that they were going to have only 25,000 lifetime partners in the Grand Hotel?
A: Yes.
Q: You have heard of that said?
A: I have heard that and I subsequently did see that brochure.
Q: I believe you said in your direct examination that the first time you ever saw such a brochure was in 1987. Was that right?
A: Yes.
Q: After you had left PTL?
A: Correct.
Q: After Mr. Bakker had resigned?
A: Yes.

□ □ □

Q: You never saw that brochure any time prior to that time, did you?
A: I don't recall. I did see it after I left though.

□ □ □

Q: You never told anybody from Laventhol [and Horwath, PTL's outside auditor] there was any 25,000 limit on the lifetime partners, did you?
A: No. I had heard of a 25,000 limit, but it was so, a blip on the screen because everything you heard about was 50 percent, using the 50 percent rule, so that must have, that must have been said in the initial stages, but it was quickly changed to 50 percent.

It is difficult to understand how Peter Bailey, PTL's chief financial officer, could have been unaware of the limitations that were placed on the Grand and Towers Hotels.

Bailey seemed to acknowledge the ponzi scheme that was occurring at PTL when Deborah Smith asked him, "Did you ever make any statements that Mr. Bakker's fundraising technique was to raise money for one building, and then use it to catch up on construction that had already been begun and promised?" Bailey's answer: "Well, that's what it was. They raise money—basically, you have other projects to raise money on because they had to pay off the previous projects." Prosecutor Smith continued, "It was necessary to begin promoting the Towers Hotel, wasn't it, in order to have enough money to finish the Grand Hotel?" "In actuality, yes," Bailey responded.

Prosecutor Deborah Smith continued in her questioning of Peter Bailey regarding his belief in and potential knowledge of a ponzi or pyramid scheme at PTL:

Q: It was also necessary to begin promoting the Bunkhouses, wasn't it, to obtain additional money to keep PTL running and to keep the Towers construction going?

A: The overall plan of PTL, I don't know the overall plan. Although I shouldn't say that. They had a big map of all the plans at PTL breaking out the land. The fact was that these projects that they started down the line, raising money for [projects], had to be used to pay off previous projects. I don't think the driving force to do these projects necessarily was to pay off previous projects, but that's the way it was, though.

Q: —The actuality of it was you had to start a new project to get some money to keep PTL running and continue construction. Is that correct?

A: That's really what happened, although I don't think the intent was that way, but that's what happened.

Q: Do you know, Mr. Bailey, what a pyramid scheme is?

A: I've heard of them. I'm not real familiar, but through the mail type of thing, where you go and get five other people, and they get five other people?

Q: Right.

A: The ones in the beginning make a lot and the ones in the bottom don't make anything?

Q: Right. The ones in the beginning can get what they were promised, and the ones later down the line are out of luck. Is that your understanding?

A: That's usually what happens.

Q: Isn't that, in fact, what happened here, where the people down the line who joined later were just out of luck, where the people who were in the door first with the Grand did, in fact, get to come and stay some before the scheme began to fall and crumble?

A: No, it wasn't a scheme. I mean, it really wasn't a scheme. It was a great plan. Let's put it this way, we may never know. I'm not suggesting anything, but Mr. Bakker was gone and Mr. Falwell came in and it was put in bankruptcy and everything was stopped.

Q: Now, everything stopped before that, didn't it, Mr. Bailey?

A: Yes.

Bailey would later admit, under intense examination by Deborah Smith, that "the bulk of the Towers money was, in fact, spent for operating expenses at PTL which included Mr. Bakker's salaries and bonuses."

Peter Bailey is certainly to be commended for the candor of his memos to Jim Bakker and Richard Dortch. It is unfortunate that the corporate officers did not heed his advice. Bailey recognized the importance of those memos and made copies of them prior to his being relieved of his duties by the Falwell administration.

Although it may simply have been coincidental, it should be noted that Peter Bailey also received increasingly lavish compensation for his work at PTL. The Federal Bankruptcy Court was certainly not charitable to Peter Bailey when it noted that "[a]lthough two signatures were required on all PTL accounts, Peter Bailey testified that he would, on occasions, sign blank checks and then deliver them to David Taggart. Peter Bailey's reward was substantial bonuses. In December 1986, he received a $30,000 bonus and another $34,000 bonus in January 1987, one month after the first."

"It wasn't until 1985 when I started making what I considered decent money," testified Peter Bailey; he was then making approximately $55,000 a year at PTL. However, as previously noted by the bankruptcy court, Peter Bailey did receive bonuses and loans in addition to his base salary. Specifically, Bailey testified that he received a $30,000 loan but "someone, thank the Lord, in 1987 after I left PTL, somebody at PTL decided to give it to me as a bonus. . . ." He also received a couple of other bonuses, one of which was a $30,000 Christmas bonus. PTL records reflect that Peter Bailey received a bonus in seven of the twelve calendar months of 1986. He also requested a $27,000 bonus from David Taggart in January 1987; to ensure that Bailey would not have to pay any taxes on it, PTL doubled the bonus. Therefore, Bailey was paid approximately $73,000 in the first four months of 1987.

In addition to cash bonuses, Bailey also received a new car. When asked to explain the circumstances surrounding receiving this new car, which was also considered a bonus and paid for out of the Executive Checking Account, Bailey testified, "The fact of the matter is, it was easier to get a bonus than it was to get a pay raise, and so I, instead of requesting a pay raise, requested a bonus and that is how I got it."

Bailey also received "around $10,000" to purchase a new wardrobe. At the instruction of Jim Bakker, David Taggart told Bailey that he wanted Bailey to "look like a Madison Avenue banker." "They were very conscious of their looks as they were on television every day, [and they] had a lot of visitors. . . ." testified Bailey.

Peter Bailey was eventually relieved of his duties in July 1987 by the Falwell Administration, which brought in the outside accounting firm of Arthur Andersen to examine PTL's finances; according to Bailey, "[t]hey ignored me."

What did Bailey do prior to his leaving PTL? "I made copies of memos that I had written to Jim Bakker." When asked, "Was there any particular reason why you kept those memos as opposed to any other ledgers?" Bailey responded that "[t]hey were my only written documentation [I had showing that] . . . I was trying to, you know, bring attention to the matter that we were in a crisis, financial crisis continually."

The Senior Executive Vice-President, Corporate Executive Director, and Co-Pastor

Richard W. Dortch served as PTL's senior executive vice-president, corporate executive director, and co-pastor. Along with Jim Bakker, David Taggart, Shirley Fulbright, and Pat Harrison, he enjoyed the elite status of having an office on the third floor of the World Outreach Center.

These titles make it sound as though Richard Dortch exercised unlimited power at PTL. In PTL's chain of command, he was second only to Bakker and was at least as powerful as David Taggart. Although Richard Dortch appeared to have primary responsibility for the nitty-gritty, day-to-day operation of PTL, the question remains: Was Richard Dortch pulling Bakker, or was Bakker pulling Dortch? Although this question may never be answered, a lot can be learned by examining Dortch's background and some of the business actions he took while he was at PTL.

Dortch possessed strong leadership skills and an ability to mediate disputes but didn't have much in the way of formal education and true business experience. Dortch never received a college diploma. Instead, like Bakker, he had dropped out of the North Central Bible Institute to become a traveling evangelist.

After pastoring churches in South Dakota and Kansas, he served as a missionary in Belgium. From there, he left to pastor a church in Illinois and eventually was elected District Superintendent of the Illinois District of the Assemblies of God Church. In this capacity he was responsible for overseeing approximately 700 ordained and licensed ministers in the Illinois area. Additionally, he was chosen for a seat on the denomination's 13-member executive presbytery, the Assemblies of God national governing board.

Jim Bakker's choosing Richard Dortch for a position on the PTL board and then as a corporate officer added a much-needed degree of credibility and respect for the PTL organization. And he brought some of his church associates from Illinois. Mark Burgund, who had served as Business Administrator for the Illinois District of the Assemblies of God, took a post as Budget Director; his wife became the Personnel Director of PTL.

According to Dortch's testimony, Bakker made it clear upon his arrival that although Dortch had the responsibility to help Jim Bakker fulfill his vision, ". . . [he] was to have the responsibility of operations and that, generally speaking, the staff was to be responsible to [him]." There were, however, certain staff members who did not report to Dortch, including Mr. Bakker's personal staff of David Taggart, Shirley Fulbright, Pat Harrison, and the other six or seven people who worked on the third floor.

Richard Dortch was named pastor, senior executive vice-president, and corporate executive director at a PTL board of directors meeting held on September 26, 1983. Although Dortch had been serving on the board since 1979, he was now also a corporate officer. Interestingly, at that same meeting, Tammy Bakker was given a $25,000 bonus, and Jim Bakker was given a $50,000 bonus. According to the minutes of that meeting, "Reverend Bakker stated to the Board a need for a new administrative officer for the ministry and suggested that Reverend Dortch be hired to fill the position. The matter was discussed, seconded and passed unanimously that Reverend Dortch be asked to accept the position of Co-Pastor and Senior Executive Vice President and Corporate Executive Director." The minutes reflect that the only board members besides Bakker and Dortch who were present at this meeting were Aimee Cortese and A.T. Lawing, Jr.

The vote may have been unanimous to make Richard Dortch a corporate officer in addition to retaining his status as a board member, but such unanimity did not exist on the part of PTL's outside attorneys. After Dortch failed to keep two different appointments with PTL's attorney, Eddie Knox, he took it upon himself to write a letter to Dortch on November 8, 1983, which states in part, "To get directly to the point, I'm afraid that problems will arise if you become a member of the staff at PTL and continue as a member of the Board of Directors. There are many angles to be considered, not the least of which is the tax status of the ministry. . . . Frankly, I can see no benefit from your staying on the Board, but I can see potential harm to the ministry should you continue in the capacity as a member of the Board and also as the number two staff person at PTL. I would not presume to pick and choose the members of the Board of Directors, but I do feel a continuing responsibility to give my best advice to you and to the other members of the Board of Directors." According to Knox, Bakker had agreed that Dortch should have resigned from the board once he became a corporate officer. Apparently, he didn't feel too strongly about this because Knox testified that he did not recall receiving any response to his November 1983 correspondence to Bakker and Dortch.

Three days later, John Yorke, another of PTL's attorneys, wrote Jim Bakker to recommend that the PTL board of directors be expanded: "I think that we can safely say that everyone concerned would be more comfortable with a larger Board of Directors. . . . The Board should be more familiar with the details of the financial picture of the ministry as well as the details of each of the projects they might consider from time to time. Persons with a solid background in business would be helpful to you now and will be especially helpful to you in the future as the ministry becomes more and more complex. . . . Of course, we continue the recommendation that Eddie [Knox] made long ago that a lawyer be present at the Board meetings. It would be appropriate and to your benefit to have both general counsel and tax counsel present for the Board meetings, but at least one should be available to answer questions and offer advice. Many of the problems of the past could have been avoided with a little advice up front." These letters and the concerns raised by the attorneys were never conveyed to the other members of PTL's board of directors.

John Yorke testified that his letter had no effect on PTL. He never attended a board of directors meeting. Instead, Richard Dortch was now at PTL to stay until he was fired on April 28, 1987. Everything was now in place to begin the lifetime partnership promotions.

Dortch was very secretive about issues relating to payroll. As previously stated, Dortch took the preparation of the executive payroll function out of the PTL finance department and gave it to an outside auditing firm. When Mark Burgund told Dortch that to obtain long-term financing through the issuance of a bond it would be necessary to prepare a prospectus listing the five most highly paid executives at PTL, Dortch balked. According to Burgund's testimony, Dortch stated "that the [PTL] Board had passed a resolution that there would be no salaries disclosed and that if that's what it required, we wouldn't do it."

Although Burgund was tapped less frequently than David Taggart, he did act as a facilitator to help provide certain perks to Jim Bakker and was often asked to help with special projects. Burgund eventually became one of the top executives at PTL, earning a salary of approximately $51,000.

Burgund, on one occasion, was asked by Dortch to drive a car—a 1929 Mercedes replica called a Gazelle—from Miami to Charlotte, North Carolina. PTL picked up the tab for all expenses incurred. At the insistence of the seller, the Gazelle was paid for by a cashier's check, which was itself paid for with PTL funds. The car was presented to Jim Bakker at the July 4, 1985, PTL celebration. According to Burgund, the idea to purchase the car for Bakker came from Richard Dortch and David Taggart. Burgund also related how on another occasion he obtained several Mercedes for Bakker and his entourage. According to Burgund's testimony, Dortch told him that Mrs. Oldham (the wife of a PTL singer) had wrecked Tammy's Cadillac. Jim Bakker was concerned about the safety of his family and wanted to get Tammy a Mercedes. Dortch directed Burgund to have Charles Woodall buy the car. (Woodall was a business associate who had previously assisted PTL in its failed attempt to secure a $50 million loan in Switzerland.) Dortch relayed to Burgund that when the Mercedes was brought out, "Tammy Faye didn't particularly like the way it looked, and so Jim decided that he would take that one and . . . bring another one out for her." As Deborah Smith pointed out on her examination of Burgund, "Now we're up to two Mercedes." Eventually, a Mercedes station wagon was obtained so the PTL security people could chauffeur the Bakker children.

And what financial arrangements were made to enable the Bakkers to purchase these three Mercedes? Burgund said, "I told Charles Woodall that Mr. Bakker wanted him to buy the cars. . . ." Woodall then purchased the cars with a check for $150,000 that Burgund gave to him. The $150,000 came from PTL funds. Woodall loaned the cars to PTL but kept the titles to them in his own trust account. Therefore, according to Burgund's testimony, the Bakkers used PTL funds to buy three Mercedes that were held in someone else's name; the cars were never legally either the Bakkers' or PTL's.

In the Bakker criminal trial, Burgund also provided some interesting testimony concerning the highly questionable way that Richard Dortch was handling some of his own personal affairs. Burgund described Dortch as being well versed in tax laws, certainly more knowledgeable than average; however, he admitted that Dortch had been making approximately $73,000 a year while holding a position with the Assemblies of God during the early 1980s. According to Burgund,

Dortch instructed him to complete a W-2 form for Dortch reflecting income totaling only $22,000 a year. A significant portion of the funds paid to Dortch by the Illinois District went to certificate of deposits that were not carried in Dortch's name but were carried in the name of the Illinois District Council. These certificates were estimated by Burgund to be worth between $65,000 and $70,000. Dortch did not pay taxes on these certificates in the year in which he received them. According to Dortch, all of this was proper because Dortch was not taking possession of the money and the money was still under the control of the Illinois District Council.

Richard Dortch's decision to defer recognition of income to later years by having certain funds carried in the name of the Illinois District Council and having his personal W-2 form reflect a reduction in income certainly appears to raise ethical if not legal issues concerning tax avoidance, not only for himself but for the Illinois District Council.

Dortch ushered a sense of confidentiality and privacy into the inner workings of PTL. He directed that the Executive Payroll Account be maintained by the outside auditors and that certain checking accounts be maintained on the third floor. He, along with David Taggart, seemed to control access to Jim Bakker.

Richard Dortch was a key player in the critical December 17, 1982, meeting of the PTL board of directors, at which certain business and board proceedings were established that set into motion what eventually proved to be very unwise practices and procedures.

Although the board of directors and the role it played at PTL will be examined in detail in Chapter 7, it is important to point out that prior to this time, the following procedures and practices had been implemented at all board meetings: 1) the amount of any bonuses given by the board always appeared in the minutes; 2) the name of the person making the motion for a bonus was recorded in the minutes; 3) PTL attorneys were welcomed and could attend board meetings; and 4) the vice-president of finance was welcomed and attended board meetings.

After the December 17, 1982, board meeting, all this changed. The amount of the bonuses did not appear in the minutes but rather appeared in "addendums" to the minutes. As discussed in Chapter 7, there is a question as to whether or not those addenda accurately reflected the bonuses awarded by the board. The person making the motion for a bonus was also not recorded in the minutes. Neither PTL attorneys nor the vice-president of finance were welcome at board meetings.

Whose idea was it to implement these changes? The minutes of that meeting reflect, in part, the following: "Reverend Dortch stated that he felt it was not necessary to have an attorney present at meetings of the Board of Directors at Heritage Village Church and Missionary Fellowship, Incorporated. Reverend Dortch stated that Board meetings should be times when the Board unites together in prayer and agreement with the President and seeks God's direction for the ministry for the future. This was seconded by [PTL board member] Charles Cookman and was passed."

With the attorneys out of the room, the perks, all at PTL's expense, really began to flow. First, "Reverend Dortch moved that the Board raise the President's MBA Retirement Fund to 50% of his yearly income." (The Ministers' Benefit Association, or MBA, provides a retirement fund for ministers within the Assemblies of God.) Although he later denied under oath that he made such a specific motion, the minutes reflect that "Reverend Cookman made a motion that the salary of the President of the Corporation be raised by 91.2%. A second motion was made by Reverend Cookman that Tammy Bakker's salary be raised by 53.8%." These percentage increases resulted in Jim and Tammy making $195,000 and $80,000 a year, respectively. The minutes also reflect that a motion was made by the board to show their appreciation to the Bakkers by granting both of them a bonus; Jim Bakker received a $75,000, and Tammy Bakker received $40,000. It was also "decided that bonus amounts would not be recorded in the Minutes[,] but would instead be kept in the files of the Assistant Secretary of the Corporation."

That was not all. The minutes also reflect that "Reverend Dortch reported that, pursuant to the instructions of the Board, a condominium in Florida had been located and purchased. Reverend Dortch moved that the furnishings and expenses necessary to furnish the condominium be paid for by the corporation. Charles Cookman seconded the motion and then it was passed. (Reverend Bakker abstained.)" What is not stated in the minutes (but is found in the IRS report) is that the condominium cost $390,000 and was furnished, in accordance with Bakker's preferences, at a cost of $202,566.14. These furnishings included $5,000 being spent for a Christmas tree. The total cost of this condominium was $592,566.14. The PTL board also passed a motion that PTL pay for "travel expenses to and from the condominium" and "that a car be purchased for use at the Florida condominium." The minutes reflect that the motion was made by Richard Dortch and seconded by Aimee Cortese; Bakker abstained from voting.

There is a conflict in testimony concerning the initial decision to no longer allow attorneys to attend board meetings of the PTL organization. As Richard Dortch testified at the Bakker trial: "I asked Mr. Bakker why Mr. Yorke [PTL's attorney] was there, and he explained to me that he wasn't quite sure, but that he was not generally pleased with him being there, and so I asked, 'Why is he here then?' And his response was, 'Well, let's ask him to leave.' " Thereafter, Dortch went to David Taggart and asked him to have Yorke absent himself from the meetings. However, Yorke testified that it was his understanding that Taggart wanted him to be present at the meetings of the PTL board of directors.

Nowhere do the board's minutes reflect that the decision to remove attorneys from board meetings was made by Jim Bakker. In fact, the board minutes reflect that the initiator of that decision was Richard Dortch.

Taggart testified that before the board meeting, Yorke was in his office. Dortch saw Yorke and asked what he was doing there. Taggart responded that Yorke was there because he had been advised to have an attorney present at all meetings. Dortch said attorneys were not to attend board meetings; he went to Bakker and got him to agree. Taggart had to tell Yorke to leave.

Yorke wrote a memo on December 20, 1982, concerning the December 17 board meeting:

> Pursuant to David Taggart's request and pursuant to your earlier suggestion, I went out to Heritage USA on Friday to attend the meeting of the Board of Directors of Heritage Village Church and Missionary Fellowship, Inc. Before the meeting started, David took me aside and said that Richard Dortch, a member of the Board, strongly objected to having an attorney present at the Board meetings and that he voiced his objections to Jim. Jim acquiesced and so I was not present at the Board meeting.
>
> David told me that you had stressed to him and to Jim the importance of having an attorney present so that the Board meetings could progress orderly and so that some of the problems that they have had in the past could be avoided. Unfortunately, they did not follow our advice this time.

This memo indicates that Richard Dortch was pulling Jim Bakker, at least this time.

There were a number of employees at PTL who simply did not trust Richard Dortch. Among them was Peter Bailey. "To put it bluntly, I just never really trusted Mr. Dortch," testified Peter Bailey in Federal Bankruptcy Court. When asked to explain his reasons,

Bailey testified, "[h]e just seemed to have his own agenda. . . . He was very smooth, very gracious. He worked hard. But [he] talk[ed] to not just me, but to people condescendingly [and he was] patronizing [to] people. He was very supportive of Mr. Bakker, at least outwardly. I just didn't trust him." Even more to the point, when Bailey was asked, "Did you think that it was on Dortch's agenda to take over PTL?" Bailey testified, "Oh, I imagine somewhere along the line it was, yes."

Bailey was also critical of Dortch's decision to exclude him from information concerning the executive payroll. Although he agreed that the payroll should be kept confidential, he also desired to have access to that information and felt that Dortch's decision to have the executive payroll maintained exclusively by the outside accounting firm was an example of what he had previously described as Dortch's devious and secret nature.

Bailey was clear in his testimony that the person in charge of the business side of PTL was Richard Dortch. Of significance, Bailey had delivered his professional judgment of PTL's financial status to Dortch, and it was Dortch who failed to notify the board of directors of PTL's financial crisis.

Bailey was asked to give an example of Richard Dortch's "secret and devious nature." Bailey responded as follows:

> While I was on the third floor of PTL near Dortch's office, he came up and put his arm around me and said, Peter, just so you know, Roe Messner will be doing work on our parsonage, where we live, but he is not going to charge PTL. I said, great, good, fine. Shortly after that, I got a bill from Roe Messner for work done on his home. So I took it to him and said, well, he's billing us. You said he wasn't going to. And he said, I know. Well, you'd better go see Roe Messner. So I went to see Roe Messner and this went on for about two or three months, and Roe Messner said, no, I never had that agreement. So I really don't know what was going on, but I got ping-ponged back and forth between Richard Dortch and Roe Messner. . . . We ended up having to pay for it. It was booked on our books. I'm not sure why he told me he wasn't going to charge us. I really don't know why, but stuff like that made you wonder where he was coming from. He told me he wanted some bills on the parsonage charged to other accounts.

What turned out to be one of the most controversial and disputed aspects of Richard Dortch's job at PTL was arranging for the payments to silence Jessica Hahn. Dortch told Bakker that he "had been dealing with the situation for several months for a person had called and told me that [Bakker] had raped and assaulted [and] kidnapped this individual." According to Dortch's testimony, Bakker responded, "Brother

Dortch, I've never assaulted or kidnapped or done anything like that in my life." Dortch responded, "I know that and I believe that." Then Bakker asked where the person was from. Dortch said New York. "What is her name?" Bakker asked. Dortch said, "Jessica Hahn." Then, according to Dortch, "in a reflective way, [Bakker] turned toward the window and for a period of time said nothing, and I remained silent, and after a period of some expanded time, he turned around and looked at me and said, 'I have not done those things. I have not raped anybody or assaulted anybody, but there is a problem.' "

Dortch and Bakker realized the gravity of Hahn's complaint. According to the by-laws of Heritage Village Church and Missionary Fellowship, Inc., dated December 14, 1978, Bakker was appointed and elected "President, Chief Executive Officer and General Manager" of the corporation. His appointment was for "the natural term of his life along with power of appointment of his successor." However, the same section of those amended by-laws stated that Jim Bakker could be removed for "any subsequent conviction of a criminal felony . . . or conduct which would be defined as immoral. . . ." Bakker's affair with Jessica Hahn was certainly immoral conduct in the eyes of PTL and, had it become known, would thus have given grounds for his removal from PTL.

The first thing Dortch did pursuant to this "problem" was have Aimee Cortese, a PTL board member from the Bronx, deliver $2,000 and later $10,000 to Jessica Hahn. The $10,000 had been part of $12,000 that Dortch had given to Cortese; she gave Hahn $10,000, and returned the remainder to Dortch.

According to Dortch, he kept Bakker fully appraised of the Hahn situation. Bakker's only response was that "the accusations she had made were not accurate, but there was a problem." Dortch testified, "when I realized the problem was not going to go away, I was getting telephone calls from Jessica Hahn and her pastor and other individuals, [and] I then, in Palm Springs, California, during the time Mr. Bakker was there, sent someone to call him out of a meeting that he was in and explain to him the problem we had and that it was going to have to be dealt with and [I] told him that a sum of money was going to have to be paid to her and his response was, I hate to give them anything, I hate to give them a dime, but do what you have to do to get this solved." Dortch responded that he made arrangements to settle the Hahn problem on February 27, 1985. A settlement conference took place before a retired judge in Los Angeles, California, and arrangements were made for Jessica Hahn to receive a settlement in her complaint against Jim Bakker; the settlement stipulated that Hahn was to receive $265,000. The issue now confronting Richard Dortch was how would he obtain $265,000. Dortch testified that "[t]here were a number of [people] at PTL [who] I thought possibly cared about staying in business there and [I] had decided that whichever of those [people] that I could come into contact with I would share with them the problem that I was trying to deal with. It happened that . . . I came upon Roe Messner first and shared with him what I believed to be as big a problem for him as it was [for] me, and he said that he would take care of it, and he did." Dortch continued, "I will have to be honest with you and tell you that in my mind, out of a $40 million project, I thought he'd get the money back somehow, and I didn't know how." Later, Richard Dortch learned that Messner was putting in a false invoice for $265,000 to be billed to the PTL Amphitheater for work related to the PTL Passion Play.

Completely in contradiction to Jim Bakker's assertions, Richard Dortch claimed to have told Bakker of the transfer of funds. According to Dortch: "When we were walking down Main Street, USA, and I approached Mr. Bakker and explained to him what had transpired in the California transaction, and told him the amount of money that we had settled the matter for, his response was, 'I don't want to know it, I don't want to know it, I don't want to hear it.' And I responded and said, 'Well, you will hear it because for us to do something like this, this is something you will know.' and [I] explained to him how the transaction took place."

In his bankruptcy deposition, Bakker denied approving the use of PTL funds to pay Jessica Hahn, and Roe Messner also tells a story different than Richard Dortch's. Messner testified that one day over lunch at Heritage USA, Dortch spoke vaguely about Jim Bakker having had a fling with an unnamed woman. "I said, who is it?, and [Dortch] said, 'Roe, it doesn't matter who it is.' " Messner claimed in court that he learned the woman's name "when [he] read it in the newspapers." He also recounted the following conversation with Dortch:

> I said, does Tammy know about this alleged affair, and he said, no. I said, does Jim Bakker know that you are asking me to loan PTL $265,000, and he said, no, I'm acting on my own. And he made a big point out of the fact that I'm the chief executive officer at PTL, we're doing over $100 million business a year, and I have the authority to make a $265,000 decision. He made a big point out of that, and so I said ok, I'll do it.

That did not end the discussion. Dortch said, according to Messner's sworn testimony, "[i]f you loan us the money and we pay you back on the next month's invoice—and he told me exactly where to bill it and how to do it." Dortch told Messner to "bill it under the Passion Play"; Messner agreed, and that was the way it was billed. Dortch also asked Messner to "create an invoice," and Messner said "I won't do that." Messner was asked in court to explain what Dortch meant: "He asked me to make up an invoice for brick and block and labor and, you know, materials and labor as if I was doing work, the specific amount of work out in the field, and I said, I won't do that, Brother Dortch, I will not create an invoice, but I will loan you the money."

Messner avoided this dilemma by making up a bill and writing on it, "per Richard Dortch." When Messner took the bill into the PTL finance division to be paid, he told those present, "[i]f you want to know about [this bill], you're going to have to go ask [Richard Dortch] because I'm not going to tell you."

The $265,000 PTL paid to settle the Hahn matter was included within a $5 million check, dated June 6, 1986, to Roe Messner and his company, Commercial Builders of Kansas. That check reflected funds raised from the Victory Warriors Campaign and is found at Exhibit A-21.

Along with Richard Dortch, David Taggart also had easy access to the inner sanctum of PTL.

The Administrative Assistant to the President

David Taggart was vice-president and administrative assistant to Jim Bakker. His duties and his functions have been described in various ways; Peter Bailey described Taggart as being the arms and legs of Jim Bakker, whereas PTL board member Charles Cookman described Taggart as being Jim Bakker's errand boy. John Yorke, outside counsel for PTL, testified that "David [Taggart] was never a power figure [at PTL]. He was just a mouthpiece for Jim [Bakker]."

As previously stated, David Taggart quickly rose through the ranks of PTL. Starting as an assistant in the music department at a salary of $200 a week, he eventually became Jim Bakker's administrative assistant, and his office was moved to the third floor of the World Outreach building. He resigned from PTL for a six-month period and was then rehired in November 1983 as administrative assistant and vice-president. His office was once again on the third floor, and this time his annual salary was approximately $90,000. Evidence from his criminal trial showed that David Taggart also had the function of being the facilitator of wealth for Jim Bakker; while procuring funds for Jim Bakker, Taggart also procured funds for himself and for his friends.

Don Hardister, Jim Bakker's former bodyguard, testified that David Taggart once carried $25,000 in a briefcase on a trip with the Bakkers. According to Hardister, it was Taggart's responsibility to make sure that Jim Bakker always had ten $100 bills. Hardister also testified that Taggart helped purchase clothing for Jim Bakker and for Hardister himself. "Jim Bakker didn't like what I was wearing," said Hardister; "it was under Jim's instructions" that Taggart helped him choose a wardrobe. Hardister confirmed that Taggart had told him on several occasions that his father owned Cadillac dealerships in Michigan and that he and his brother had inherited a $6 million trust fund from their grandmother's estate. (The trust fund story was later denied by Taggart's father, a retired service manager for a car dealership in Michigan.)

While the extravagance and the expenditures of David Taggart were detailed in the previous chapter, they cannot be understated. For example, an invoice from a plush New York clothier shows that David Taggart bought a smoking jacket for a total cost of $3,788.75. (Exhibit A-22.) Quite appropriately, the statement reflects that the smoking jacket was to be delivered to Trump Towers. David Taggart was also very generous in administering PTL funds. For example, an invoice dated May 25, 1985, reflects that PTL owed a total of $2,932 to Dynasty Limousine Service of Beverly Hills, California. Taggart directed that a $733 gratuity be added to that invoice. The PTL executive account check was signed by David Taggart and Pat Harrison.

During a three-night trip to New York City, the IRS found Taggart incurred expenses at the Waldorf Astoria Hotel of $3,571.05 plus $1,014 for "room service." During another two-night trip to the Waldorf Astoria, Taggart's expenses included $3,897 for room and tax, $677 room service, $405 for what the IRS listed as "florist." PTL funds were used to cover these expenses.

Taggart testified in the Jim Bakker criminal trial that he helped move the Bakkers from their parsonage in Tega Cay, South Carolina, to Palm Springs, California, in June 1984. He said the move, for which they used a private jet, cost PTL $105,000. Yet, while they were visiting Oral Roberts University, Bakker complained to Taggart that "he lived shabbily compared to Oral Roberts and other ministers."

Frequently, when traveling with Jim Bakker, Taggart obtained cash advances, which were used to pay for extravagant shopping sprees. The PTL credit cards were used to pay for the trips taken by Taggart or the Bakker family, during which they frequently stayed at exclusive lodging facilities. For example, the Bakkers took a vacation to Palm Beach, Florida, during June 1985. Arrangements were made for the Bakkers to stay at a two-story, seaside estate at a cost of $10,000 for one week.

In November 1982, Taggart traveled with Jim Bakker to Palm Springs, California, where both of them underwent plastic surgery. As usual, this surgery was paid for with PTL funds.

The Taggarts were flashy with their money while around PTL. They frequently bought expensive gifts for PTL employees, including a $4,000 mink coat as a Christmas present for Shirley Fulbright. The Taggarts led others to believe their money came from their parents, specifically from Taggart's father.

That assertion was clearly refuted by the testimony of their father, Henry Taggart, when he testified at his sons' criminal trial. "Let me put this to rest once and for all, I do not and never did own 7 Cadillac dealerships . . . . I did not and never did own one Cadillac dealership. I worked for a Cadillac dealership. That's it." The elder Taggart outlined his progression from being a mechanic to a body shop manager at a car dealership in Detroit, Michigan.

Taggart's close association with Jim Bakker allowed him to testify at various proceedings concerning conversations he was privy to regarding business decisions made between Bakker and others at PTL. For example, he testified that Bakker received the written reports prepared by Steve Nelson and Peter Bailey concerning the number of sales and total dollar amounts received from the lifetime partnership program. He also said that complaints were conveyed to Bakker from lifetime partners who were having difficulty getting reservations.

Taggart was present when Dortch discussed with Bakker the possibility of PTL selling bonds and issuing a prospectus in preparation for selling bonds. The prospectus, a sales document that had to be printed before the solicitation of bonds could begin, required a list of the salaries of PTL's top five executives, and because of that requirement, Dortch recommended against pursuing the bond issue; Bakker agreed.

Mark Burgund testified that when he approached Richard Dortch concerning the prospectus and the possible selling of bonds, he indicated a different reason for not wanting to pursue bonds as a form of financing. Dortch said it was the PTL board of directors who did not want to disclose the salaries of PTL's top executives and that was why PTL would not be pursuing the sale of bonds.

David Taggart's brother, James, was also reaping benefits from PTL. His interior decorating corporation, Panache, was paid $100,000 on March 16, 1987, in payment for designing the Towers Hotel; this was separate and apart from the $10,000 monthly retainer fee PTL paid James Taggart. The check was issued pursuant to instructions given by David Taggart and Richard Dortch, and the check was signed by Shirley Fulbright and David Taggart.

Apparently, the exorbitant expenditure of funds by and on behalf of personnel on the third floor was accomplished by avoiding the normal audit procedures and processes at PTL. Although PTL did not have an accounting manual, it did have written policies and procedures concerning travel and travel advances. All employees had to abide by those rather stringent procedures; however, the executives on the third floor never complied with any procedures relating to travel and related expenses. Whenever Bailey confronted Taggart concerning his travel expenses, Taggart always responded that the receipts were being maintained on the third floor for reasons of "confidentiality" or that the receipts were at home in a shoe box. Bailey and Pat Harrison were continually assured that this was the case. As of July 1987, when Bailey left PTL, he hadn't seen those receipts, although he continued to receive assurances from Taggart that they existed.

Peter Bailey reported to David Taggart, but Taggart would submit check requests to Bailey for work allegedly completed by James Taggart's company. Although PTL paid Panache hundreds of thousands of dollars, Peter Bailey testified that he could recall only "one occasion where they did submit an invoice to us upon my request." Bailey testified that despite his attempts over a three-to-four-year period to obtain invoices or documentation as to how PTL funds that had been disbursed to James Taggart's company were being spent, he was not successful. "How many of those years were you successful in obtaining such documentation as substantiation?" asked the government prosecutor in the Taggarts' criminal trial. Bailey's response: "Zero." The prosecutor became a little more feisty later on in Bailey's examination:

Q: Just so the jury understands how big we're talking about, what was the annual gross receipts, if you will, which is a corporate term, how much money [was PTL] bringing in through you?
A: In the top years when they were having the lifetime partnerships, it probably approached $175 million.
Q: $175 million a year?
A: Yes. Their budget is approximately $15 million a year to operate on.

Q: That's not, and I don't mean any offense by this term, but that's not what we would call in our business, Mr. Bailey, a mama and papa operation is it?

A: No, it was not.

Q: Alright, and are you the senior financial officer of that corporation?

A: That's right.

Q: Then you've got all those outlays of PTL funds to the defendants, David and James Taggart?

A: Right.

Q: Why didn't you demand from David Taggart to produce the documentation required for you to fulfill your responsibilities?

A: Well, we did the best we could. We tried to get the funds on— not funds, excuse me, the receipts on many occasions. The—Mr. Bakker's office had a lot of authority and you just couldn't—we just weren't able to produce them.

Q: Mr. Bailey, could you fire David Taggart?

A: No.

When Bailey was further questioned concerning why he didn't approach Jim Bakker or Richard Dortch to complain about the absence of documentation being produced by the Taggart brothers, Bailey testified that he thought that he "wouldn't get a lot of help." Bailey also was questioned in the bankruptcy court concerning his role as chief financial officer of PTL:

Q: You certainly weren't in any position as Financial Director and Vice President of Finance to be making demands on David Taggart anyway, were you?

A: Well, I got mean with him a few times. But to answer your question, technically, he was my boss. You can still tell your boss what you should do and make sure that he complies.

Q: So you had a situation where, other than relying on his good faith and honesty, he could be ripping the place off, PTL, and you wouldn't be able to know it?

A: Well, you're asking if the sun is going to shine tomorrow. We never doubted—- I don't know of anybody that thought he was ripping the place off. I mean, we did run this place on a lot of trust and a lot of faith in one another. That's the way PTL was. We did have the internal controls and I will admit that the third floor didn't comply with them as I'd like them to comply with them, but, yes, a lot of it was run on faith and trust.

Q: You had no internal controls over the third floor accounts, did you?

A: Not a whole lot other than just pestering them about receipts . . .

Bailey was also asked how the Taggarts were able to get away with carrying such large amounts of cash when they went on their trips. Bailey responded by saying that when David went with the Jim Bakker entourage, "he had to have cash a lot of times for what they did." When asked why, Bailey responded that they needed cash for "buying antiques, whatever. You can ask David because he would know more specifically. Buy things for the hotel, buying . . ." The examining attorney then became somewhat impatient and said, "Excuse me. Your background again, you're a CPA, and you were financial director of PTL?" to which Bailey responded in the affirmative. Then the question was asked, "[a]nd . . . you're saying it's alright to go out and pay cash to acquire items?" Bailey responded, "I didn't say it was alright, I said that's the way it was. I'm saying David had to take cash with him." To which Bailey was then asked, "Why did you let him [take cash with him]?" Bailey's candid response, "Well, number one, he didn't ask me. He just did it."

On another matter concerning David Taggart, Peter Bailey said he could not be certain whether or not he had signed an employment agreement with David Taggart dated December 10, 1985. That contract made David Taggart president of Heritage Village Church and Missionary Fellowship, Inc., The terms of compensation for David Taggart included a salary of $150,000 plus a bonus in December of each year. Bailey could not recall signing the document, but he could not state for certain that his signature was not on it. The document was attested to by Shirley Fulbright. It was this employment contract, however, that David Taggart used in asserting a claim against PTL in the bankruptcy court for compensation that he claimed was due him.

Peter Bailey also assisted David Taggart in obtaining a $75,000 loan by assigning a PTL certificate of deposit. According to Bailey's bankruptcy testimony, the CD was put up as collateral for a loan made by a South Carolina bank to David Taggart: "David asked me to get a loan for him at Rock Hill Bank, and so I called the bank and so they said, fine, that we would have to put up a CD of PTL's funds to do it. I told David that, and that was fine, and so that's what we did."

Bailey never knew why Taggart wanted the loan, why he didn't get the loan himself, or what he was going to use the money for. Bailey never discussed this matter with Dortch or Bakker, and the only corporate signatures appearing on the agreement to secure the loan with PTL assets were those of Peter Bailey and Shirley Fulbright.

Peter Bailey testified that he did not know whether or not Taggart ever repaid that loan to the bank. The bankruptcy court added $75,515.79 to the liability of David Taggart, which represented "a PTL certificate of deposit pledged to the Rock Hill National Bank to secure a personal note made by [him]." Three months after Bailey had pledged collateral to secure the Taggart loan, Bailey received a $54,000 bonus.

It was clear that the third floor of PTL's World Outreach had been awash in deceit. The bankruptcy judge, Rufus Reynolds, stated in his written opinion that "[t]his unauthorized and wrongful taking of funds [at PTL] centered around the activities and actions of James Bakker, Reverend Dortch, David Taggart and Shirley Fulbright. They worked in unison on the third floor of the WOC with all the attributes of a conspiracy." By working under cover of "confidentiality," giving repeated assurances that documents existed to legitimize their actions, and capitalizing on what turned out to be the unwarranted trust and faith that existed at PTL, the third-floor gang took over the organization.

David Taggart, Jim Bakker, and Richard Dortch took advantage of the misplaced trust and confidence that Peter Bailey had placed in them. And he should have had more professional skepticism as the chief financial officer of PTL.

The Vice-President of World Outreach

At PTL, the vice-president of World Outreach was primarily responsible for not only the distribution center but also promotion of the lifetime partnership programs at PTL. The distribution center was a large building from which gift items were shipped to various PTL partners around the world. Richard Ball was the first vice-president of World Outreach; he was succeeded in the fall of 1985 by Steve Nelson. Both Nelson and Ball were well aware of the advertised limit of 25,000 memberships in the Grand Hotel, and their testimony reflects that both complained to Jim Bakker about the oversell. Bakker denies that testimony, whereas Dortch's testimony maintained that he himself, Jim Bakker, Steve Nelson, Rich Ball, Doug Oldham, and several other people knew that there were two sets of numbers being kept at PTL.

Steve Nelson testified that the real numbers reflecting sales in the various PTL promotionals went to "Pastor Dortch, Pastor Bakker, Peter Bailey, Mark Burgund, Wanda Burgund, [and] Paul King." Furthermore, according to Nelson, these numbers were given to Jim Bakker every few minutes, especially when PTL was engaged in the promotion of the various offers.

At least two people who worked for Richard Ball and then Steve Nelson in PTL's computer operations area became well aware of the oversale of the partnerships. Hollis C. Rule, who began working at

PTL in 1980 as a computer programmer and rose in the ranks to serve as senior analyst and programming manager, expressed his concerns both orally and in writing to Richard Ball and to Steve Nelson.

Hollis Rule testified that his fear "was that we were overselling the Grand Hotel memberships, [and] that there would not be enough room to satisfy the needs of the partners." Rule expressed his concerns directly to Rich Ball and in meetings with others. Rule continued in his testimony, "[w]e had weekly status meetings, I talked to [Rich Ball] about it during these meetings, and I also talked to him about it privately, you know, one-on-one in his office." Eventually, he prepared correspondence reflecting his views on the problem. "I was concerned about the overselling of the memberships from, first off, from the advertised, you know, the promotional stand point," testified Rule. "I was concerned certainly about the overselling of the memberships from, the advertised, you know, the promotional standpoint. I was concerned . . . for the partners themselves, because in my heart, I knew that there [were] going to be some disappointments, based on what I saw there. Secondly, I was concerned, I wanted to do my job as a data processing, as head of data processing, to inform my superiors and get that information to Mr. Bakker so he could make some other decisions."

Exhibit A-23 is a copy of a memo that Rule sent to Nelson on September 3, 1985. This memo and other Hollis Rule memos are very telling. They reflect that the Grand Hotel was obligated beyond capacity with lifetime partners; that is, even if all paying guests were turned away at the door, the Grand Hotel could not house all the lifetime partners even if every room was reserved for a lifetime partner. These memos reflect the reality of what was transpiring at the Grand Hotel. Because of the greatly exceeded 25,000 cap that had originally been placed on the Grand, the partners were in fierce competition for lodging. This document shows that the promises made to the Grand Hotel lifetime partners could not be fulfilled even if 100 percent of the hotel's rooms were to be reserved for lifetime partners.

Jeff Eggen had worked in the computer department at PTL since July 1979. He was in charge of data research and was a member of the team that originally designed the partner system at PTL and the reporting structure for its computer. Eggen was primarily responsible for having produced a computer report that gave daily and cumulative totals relative to the different lifetime partnership promotionals. Eggen would later call that computer report "Everything You Always

Wanted to Know about Lifetime Partnerships but Were Afraid to Ask"; a page from that report is found in Exhibit A-24. By using this document, one could easily ascertain the number of fully and partially paid memberships in the various lifetime partnership programs as well as the total dollar amount raised by the various programs. It was the primary source for the government's assertions as to the amount of funds raised and the number of partnerships sold at PTL. Exhibit A-24 shows the PTL computer run dated July 7, 1984, which reflects that the number of fully paid memberships in the Grand Hotel was 25,303. Exhibit A-25 is a memo that Eggen sent to Peter Bailey, dated June 18, 1987, which shows the total number of lifetime partners.

In addition to his responsibilities in the computer department, he testified that he also handled lifetime partner complaints. Eggen had a discussion with Nelson in 1985 about the need for PTL to stop offering lifetime memberships. "Lots of partners were complaining that there was never any room, [and] they came down and they want to stay in the hotel and it is always booked up and they can't get in," testified Eggen as to why he complained to Nelson. Although Steve Nelson reported to Richard Dortch, Eggen told the court that Nelson told him (Eggen) not to divulge this oversell information to anybody. Eggen testified that he was afraid that the oversell information wasn't getting to Mr. Bakker.

Eggen never conducted any studies to determine the feasibility in terms of money and demographics of the lifetime partnership programs. Additionally, he was never asked by Dortch or Bakker to research the number of partners who might have died since joining.

There came an occasion when Eggen did, of his own volition, conduct some research as to the number of lifetime partners who might have died. Eggen testified that while watching "the program one day. . . . I believe it was Pastor Dortch that was offering Grand memberships after we had said that they were all closed. . . . and he said something to the effect that because we've had some deaths and people had passed away, we're now able to relinquish a few more memberships in the Grand Hotel, so that prompted me then—because I wasn't aware of it and it certainly could have been factual so I wanted to provide factual information to back that up . . . so I ran a report to see how many [lifetime partners] we showed on our computer file [who had died]." The computer files showed that there had been no deaths among the lifetime partners at the time Dortch made such claims on television.

Other PTL Employees

As I said in Chapter 1, the majority of PTL's employees had a strong and an unyielding faith not only in God but also in the concepts that PTL and Heritage Village USA embodied. They believed that this was a unique place, and they believed Jim Bakker when he said that he had received a vision from God and that he was doing God's will in developing the PTL properties. These were people similar to Eggen and Rule in the PTL computer department. They occasionally saw what they believed might have been an irregularity and, within the confines of lower-level management, brought it to the attention of their supervisor. Their supervisors, the corporate officers, had the responsibility not only to correct the action but also to bring these matters to the attention of people like the PTL board of directors.

Although many other hard-working and dedicated PTL employees who deserve to be commended for their work, their voluntary efforts, and their commitment to do what is right are not specifically mentioned by name in this book, at least three other PTL employees' actions deserve to be discussed not only for what they did but also to show the response of others who were in positions of authority.

Carol Price began working at PTL as a volunteer in 1978 and became a paid employee in 1980. She became assistant manager and then, in the middle of 1984, became manager of the President's Club, which was responsible for handling correspondence and questions from major contributors to PTL, including the lifetime partners. There were approximately 10 to 15 people who worked in that department with the primary responsibility of responding to lifetime partners' questions. As manager of the President's Club, Carol Price's home number was always readily available to the lifetime partners. "They were free to call me anytime day or night," she testified in the Bakker criminal proceedings. "Many times I did get called out at night if they had problems; if the partner needed someone to pray with; if they needed someone to talk to, if they had personal problems they wanted to talk about, it was my duty to be there for them for whatever they needed; if they needed to be picked up at the airport." She provided personal transportation to and from the airport for lifetime partners, and she would not be reimbursed for her time or for her mileage.

Her testimony was that "[w]e had problems almost from the onset. We ran into a situation where we had partners who could not get into the hotels. They would call for reservations and due to the fact there [were] no openings available, they would then turn around and call us and myself and the people that worked for me would try to do everything we could to assure them that they could get a room and we would interface with the hotel people and request [a room for them.]" Price was working under the assumption that half the hotel would be available for lifetime partners and that the Grand Hotel lifetime partnership program would be limited to 25,000 members. But, she "found out that there were so many lifetime partners that there were not enough rooms available for all of the people who wanted to get in." Price testified that sometimes lifetime partners had to wait as long as 18 months or more before they could stay at the Grand Hotel per the terms of their lifetime partnership.

Price knew of the 25,000-member cap placed on the Grand Hotel lifetime partnerships and was very concerned as to what was going to happen concerning that cap. "We were asking Mr. Dortch and Mr. Bakker and our superiors at the time, 'What do we do? When do we cut this off? When do we stop?' "

She testified that Bakker sometimes responded, "Well, [I] don't know. Sometimes he would say, 'Well, you know, all of the people are not going to come over here. You know, there are people in California, people in Arizona, wherever, a long ways away, and these people aren't going to come here every year." Bakker was saying this at the very time that Price and her department could not accommodate the lifetime partners. She was continually told by her superiors "not to be concerned." Her superiors included Richard Ball, later Steve Nelson, and always Richard Dortch and Jim Bakker.

Honestly believing that the memberships were going to be cut off at 25,000, they continued to express concern as early as May 1984 to Richard Ball about the increased numbers of people requesting and paying for lifetime partnerships.

People later called in and asked for refunds because they couldn't get a room. Price testified that "Mr. Nelson told us that we should discourage giving refunds, but if there were no other way, then we could go ahead and give the refund." Price admitted she didn't always follow Nelson's instructions because "my conscience would not allow me to do so."

As she started to cry on the witness stand during the Jim Bakker criminal trial, Price testified how she would often discourage people from purchasing a lifetime partnership. After a conference between the lawyers and the judge, the direct examination of Carol Price continued. "Let me ask you this question, Ms. Price," asked prosecutor Jerry Miller, "From the basis of talking to [a potential lifetime partner], what did you tell that woman about purchasing the lifetime partnership?" "I told her that I felt [that] selling a burial policy to get $1,000, when she was in her 70s, was not something she should do."

In the summer of 1985, Jim Bakker called a luncheon meeting with people in the President's Club and other executives at PTL; it became affectionately known as "the Cadillac meeting." Price testified at the civil trial that Bakker "just instructed us [to keep] selling lifetime memberships in the Grand Hotel and that as an incentive, because the sales at that point had lagged a little bit, . . . [he offered] a customized Cadillac to whomever would be able to sell the most memberships, . . . not just the group that was there, but anyone in the ministry who, in effect, had a way to sell . . . a membership." According to Price's sworn testimony, "[t]here were so many questions in our minds at that time because we already knew that we could not accommodate the people that were there. We knew that we were just overwhelmed at that point in trying to accommodate those people and yet, we were being encouraged to sell even more memberships."

At that point, another woman who worked for Carol Price, J'Tanya Adams Gibbs, confronted Jim Bakker in a way that few people had ever done before. Carol Price's testimony concerning what transpired next is as follows:

> [J'Tanya] stood up and said to him, "Mr. Bakker, you know, how are we going to do this if we're already oversold and we already got more memberships than we can accommodate; how are we going to do this?" and at this point, you could have heard a pin drop on this carpet because everyone in the room was aware that it took a very brave person to stand up and say that publicly, and Mr. Bakker said nothing to her for a moment. And he just kind of stood there and I think everyone was shocked, including him. That's just my opinion. And he then said to her, "Well, you know, there are going to be a lot of people that don't come, so, therefore, I don't feel like we have to worry about that. There are going to be people from all over, California, wherever that buy memberships that are not going to come every year and because they're not going to come every year, I don't think we have to worry about it."

As the number of lifetime partners increased, the situation only got worse. As part of what Carol Price described as a "last ditch effort," a letter dated March 6, 1985, went out to the current lifetime partners telling them that "[u]ntil the Towers are open, you will have the option of 10 nights and 11 days camping with your own camper, tent, or RV. . . ." As Price testified, "We were trying to grasp at anything to give them some room, to give them a place, to accommodate them in some way, and most of the people didn't want to stay in a tent. Most of them didn't have tents. Most of them weren't campers."

This letter caused a real dilemma. Price testified, "Well, whenever you get a call from an 80-year-old or a 70-year-old person, they are not going to stand there and tell you they want to camp, when they don't even know the front end of a camper from a back end or couldn't pop a tent if their life depended on it." Price said she got a lot of those phone calls but didn't blame the lifetime partners because "I wouldn't want to camp myself."

In an attempt to try to discourage any refunds, Dortch and Bakker approved a policy requiring that contributors should be talked out of their decision if at all possible. If they persisted in wanting a refund, they had to provide a copy of both sides of the check they had written to PTL. If a money order had been sent, then a copy of the partner's portion of the money order had to be sent to PTL. And if a charge card had been used to purchase the lifetime partnership, the partner had to send their credit card number and a copy of their charge receipt. Ms. Price testified that the purpose of this policy was to "discourage refunds because it made it almost impossible for [lifetime partners] to [obtain them]."

When J'Tanya Adams Gibbs testified, she too recalled that when the original Grand promotional was announced, there was a 25,000-member cap. She also recalled that Jim Bakker seemed to change the promotional in "kind of a roundabout way." As she described in her testimony, "[h]e just kept coming up with more rooms and more memberships."

Ms. Gibbs also found inconsistencies in Bakker's statements. For example, Bakker once commented on TV about how PTL had given out a lot of refunds and consequently had 500 more rooms available. According to Gibbs, "I [ran] back to Carol's office and [looked] in her bin to see if I actually saw 500 [refund requests]. She had a refund bin and there [weren't] any documents in there to be processed." She stated that they frequently attended the program because "we had to be consistent with what Bakker was saying, or be prepared to handle whatever he might say at a moment's notice. We got shocked regularly." Ms. Gibbs recalled the Cadillac meeting and Jim Bakker talking about selling lifetime partnerships. Bakker realized he should not have said PTL was selling lifetime partnerships. According to Gibbs, "then [Bakker] attempted to fix it. He said, 'oh, we are not supposed to say that.' " Gibbs testified that no Cadillac was ever given away by Jim Bakker. When she was asked, "Did you try and win that Cadillac?"

her response was as follows: "No, because it was a ministry and I viewed it as a commercial thing like sweepstakes, and we were dealing with people's lives, you know, trying to bring people into a holiness, and my conscience would not permit such a thing. My walk with Christ would not permit such a thing. I could not do that."

Within two to three months after the Cadillac meeting, Carol Price's department was disbanded. Some of the employees in the department were retained and others were dismissed, among them Carol Price. There was some evidence that members of the department had erroneously coded some lifetime memberships into PTL's computer.

According to Price's testimony, she went to Steve Nelson to talk about her dismissal and said to him, "Steve, I just want to know why. I know that this department has handled these memberships from the beginning and I know that this is not over and we're still six weeks behind. Why are we being let go?" Price testified that Steve Nelson then "leaned back in his chair and he looked at me and said, 'Carol, that's the price you pay for knowing too much and not keeping your mouth shut.' " Price then testified that she responded to him by saying, "Ok. I can understand that because, yes, indeed, I fought tooth and toenail for these partners and, yes, every opportunity that I had to tell Mr. Bakker what the situation was, I took it, and yes, I said here in that meeting with you that day and I told you that maybe that wasn't important to you, but it was certainly important to me because I was the one dealing with it. But why? Why are you taking it out on these other people. They love the Lord, they love the partners, and they give their hearts to this place. Why are you doing this?" Price testified that Nelson again, "leaned back and looked at me and he said, 'That's the price they pay for you knowing too much and keeping them too informed.' "

At that point in her testimony, Carol Price again started crying. She concluded by saying that "10 people lost their jobs because my conscience would not let me keep my mouth shut. . . . I have carried that on my head since this day."

That concluded Jerry Miller's examination of Carol Price, and no questions were asked by Bakker's counsels.

Connie Jenkins Brennecke testified that she worked at PTL from November 1983 until April 1986, first starting in partner research and then transferring to work in the President's Club. She testified that she recalled a meeting at which Richard Dortch was present, as were members of the President's Club and the reservation department at the Heritage Grand Hotel. Brennecke testified that Dortch was "specifically telling us not to use the word *oversold* [in our discussions with lifetime partners]." Brennecke resigned in April 1986. In her resignation letter to Steve Nelson, she stated her reason for doing so: "I could not stay at this ministry knowing that partners were having a hard time getting reservations and yet there were still more memberships being offered."

Although there was a plethora of financial, business, and ethical dilemmas facing PTL, Bakker and Dortch could have at least avoided criminal liability for the charges of wire and mail fraud if they had adhered to the promised membership limits of the various lifetime partnerships.

While Nelson, Ball, Dortch, Bailey, and Bakker were clearly aware of a variety of problems, what information was provided to the PTL Board of Directors that would have allowed it to make sound prudent business decisions?

□□□

CHAPTER SEVEN

Where Was the Board of Directors?

I have never asked for a penny for myself. . . . God has always
taken care of me.

James O. Bakker, "The Jim Bakker Television Program,"
December 3, 1985

BY JULY 7, 1984, the Grand Hotel was oversold. It was on that day
that PTL's own computer records reflected that 25,303 fully paid
lodging partnerships had been purchased, despite the fact that Jim
Bakker, Richard Dortch, and others on the PTL program had promised
that only 25,000 lifetime partnerships would be available for the
Grand. Every partnership sold after that day was in violation of the
promised limits; those people who purchased partnerships prior to
July 7, 1984, should have been told that the rules had been changed
and that an unlimited number of lifetime partnerships were up for
sale. Rather than competing against the promised number of lifetime
partners for the limited space that had been reserved for them, they
were now going to have to compete against many, many more. And
not only was the Grand oversold, misrepresentations were being made
concerning the true number of lifetime partnerships that had been
sold, in various other lodging programs, which ultimately resulted in
the Towers Hotel also being oversold. Furthermore, the Bunkhouses
and other lodging facilities described previously were being promoted
even though there was not enough money in the PTL coffers to allow
for the completion of these projects, let alone to keep the promises
that had been made to the various PTL partners.

Finally, the money resulting from the sale of partnerships was
being diverted for private purposes, including what many would con-

sider to be excessive salaries and bonuses for certain PTL executives. This excessive compensation, or private inurement, violated Section 501(c)(3) of the Internal Revenue Code and ultimately resulted in PTL losing its tax-exempt status.

How could all this have happened without the knowledge or participation of the PTL board of directors? Where was the PTL board of directors while these massive frauds were occurring? Exactly what are the legal obligations of a "nonprofit" corporation's board of directors? Before examining these questions, it is important to understand the dimensions and the magnitude of the religious and secular activities that were transpiring at PTL.

Tangible Observations at PTL

Certainly PTL was more than just Jim and Tammy Bakker and their television program. PTL owned in excess of 2,200 acres, roughly four square miles, on the border between North and South Carolina. Although much of the land remained untouched, approximately 400 acres had been developed. Included on the property was the Heritage Village Church, which cost in excess of $3.6 million to build and boasted an average weekly attendance of over 3,000 people. At a cost of $357,548, an Upper Room was built on the Heritage USA property. This room was built as a replica of the place where the Last Supper of Christ occurred. Prayer services were held in the Upper Room, and trained counselors were available on a 24-hour basis to minister to people in cubicles in the Upper Room.

Fort Hope, a missionary outreach house for homeless men, was also located at Heritage USA; it housed 36 men each year and had cost PTL $1.8 million to build.

The PTL Passion Play, a portrayal of the life of Christ, was presented in an outdoor amphitheater from May through October each year. In 1986, approximately 125,000 people attended the Passion Play. The theater cost $1.6 million to build.

A variety of musical and dramatic shows with religious themes were presented on a regular basis at the Grand Hall in the Heritage Grand Hotel. Admission was charged for the dinner performances, and the season attendance in 1986 was 77,000.

A number of religious workshops were presented throughout the year at Heritage USA. They were led by professionally trained counselors and covered such topics as marriage, counseling, and how to handle depression. At Christmas time, Heritage USA was the site of a lavish Yuletide display, complete with a nativity scene, colored lights, and dramatic musical productions. In 1986, over 1.5 million visitors were estimated to have viewed this pageantry.

Heritage USA also had attractions and facilities geared toward children. Heritage Academy provided religiously oriented education for students in grades K through 12; the academy building cost $2,277,000. There was also a daycare center for children whose parents were visiting or working at Heritage USA.

In addition to these overtly religious attractions, other facilities at Heritage USA were deemed by the IRS to be commercial in nature, although PTL contended that they were related to and in support of the more obviously religious activities. These suspect projects included

1. The four-story, 500-room Heritage Grand Hotel, which, in 1986, accommodated 317,459 guests
2. The 96-room Heritage Inn, which accommodated over 68,000 guests in 1986
3. The campgrounds, which accommodated over 210,000 guests in 1986
4. A variety of family housing, including high-rise condominiums and apartments that were under construction in 1986
5. A water park constructed at a cost of $13,940,000, with an attendance in 1987 of approximately 200,000. (On a typical day, 130 lifeguards were on duty.)
6. A wide variety of retail stores and recreational activities.

According to PTL, these resulted in Heritage USA being the third largest attraction of its kind in the United States after Disney World and Disneyland. PTL's records reflected that more than 6 million people visited Heritage USA in 1986; its water park alone ranked fifteenth in attendance.

PTL had organized a Prison Ministry with a volunteer staff of over 4,000 people and had also donated and installed satellite receiving systems in 39 prisons nationwide. This enabled prisoners in high-security correctional facilities to receive 24-hour Christian programs on the PTL Television Network. Each year, PTL distributed more than 25,000 Bibles and over a quarter of a million copies of other Christian books to prisoners. Thousands of inmates studied the Bible through PTL's correspondence courses. The Prison Ministry included visiting prisoners' families; helping prisoners find fellowship, encouragement, employment, and housing; and providing aftercare ministry to ex-convicts upon their release from prison.

As if all this were not enough, there was, of course, the PTL Satellite Network and its flagship broadcast, the Jim Bakker Television Program. PTL's television ministry allowed the board of directors to observe the religious activities that occurred at Heritage USA consistent with PTL's corporate charter.

Before discussing what transpired at the PTL board of directors meetings, it is important to understand the responsibilities and potential liabilities of a nonprofit organization's board of directors.

The Board of Directors' Legal Responsibilities

Although serving on the board of directors of a nonprofit corporation may be a commendable form of community service, members of the board may be personally liable for their actions or inactions, just like their counterparts in "for-profit" corporations.

Board members are in a position of trust and therefore owe *fiduciary duties* to their corporation, meaning that they must act in good faith and with due care toward the corporation.

Board members are enjoined to exercise *ordinary care and prudence*, which means that as long as they perform their duties with reasonable diligence and care, they generally remain free from personal liability even if their poor judgment actually causes loss or injury to the organization.

In properly evaluating the actions of PTL's board of directors, it is important to realize that board members are, in fact, presumed to have at least a general knowledge of the corporation. Generally, most boards of directors convene three or four times a year and serve in an oversight capacity.

The Model Business Corporation Act, which is designed to be a model statute for adoption by state legislatures, states

> (b) In discharging these duties, a director is entitled to rely on information, opinions, reports, or statements, including financial statements and other financial data, if prepared or presented by:
> (1) one or more officers or employees of the corporation whom the director reasonably believes to be reliable and competent in the matters presented;
> (2) legal counsel, public accountants, or other persons as to matters the director reasonably believes are within the person's professional or expert competence; or

(3) a committee of the board of directors of which he [or she] is
not a member if the director reasonably believes the committee
merits confidence.

This provision of the code allows board members to rely on representations made by officers or employees of the corporation, legal
counsel, public accountants, and committees of the board of directors
on the condition that they believe in good faith that those individuals
in whom they are relying are competent and reliable. Finally, a number of cases have established that a significant, although not absolutely
conclusive, factor in determining whether board members acted with
due care "has been the fact that company's books and records were
examined, during the period in which the directors were allegedly
negligent, by an outside expert who was able at that time to find
nothing wrong in them or in the accounting methods followed by the
company's officers and employees."

The PTL Board of Directors Prior to December 1982

In the beginning, the minutes of the board of directors of Heritage
Village Church and Missionary Fellowship, Inc., were very detailed
and reflected what actually happened at every meeting. They also
candidly reflected the salaries of a number of individuals. For example, the minutes from the board meeting of May 13, 1977, reported
that Jim Bakker was to receive a salary of $700 a week plus housing.
Two other PTL executives were to receive a weekly salary of $600,
another was to receive $500 a week, and yet two others were to receive
$450 a week. The minutes went on to note that the salaries of three
other corporate officers were to "stay where [they are]."

By 1978, the Federal Communications Commission was examining PTL and questioning the veracity of certain claims that it had
made on the air concerning its contributions to foreign missions. The
allegations against PTL were hotly debated but were essentially
thrown out in a split vote by the FCC. After considering whom PTL
should acquire as counsel for the FCC investigation, discussion at the
June 20, 1978, board meeting turned to Jim Bakker's salary. Dr.
Forbes M. Barton, Jr., stated "that a friend of his in Haskins and Sells
Audit Firm said that PTL is the cleanest outfit they have done in an
audit. Dr. Barton went on to say that he felt Mr. Bakker should not
cut his salary for public opinion." PTL board member Dr. James E.
Johnson "stated that Mr. Bakker would be making one-half million
dollars a year if he were in most organizations carrying the load he

carries." Johnson went on to note that "Walter Cronkite makes $750,000 a year and gives out bad news." Consequently, at that board meeting a resolution was passed unanimously adjusting Bakker's salary "from $700 a week to $1,000 a week, plus actual parsonage expenses [incurred] per month." Although the minutes note that Bakker "did not participate in the voting or the discussion [concerning his salary increase]," the minutes also note that "Bakker made a motion that we make a policy that we no longer distribute financial information to the Press."

Interestingly, on July 14, 1978, Jim Bakker wrote to his chief financial officer, then Herbert M. Moore, directing that he would not accept any increase in salary and, in fact, demanding that it be reduced to $600 a week. He did, however, request that his salary "be accrued on the books and payment shall not be made until such time that our cash flow is in a positive position rather than in the negative position that now exists." Bakker went on to indicate that when PTL's financial situation improved, he would accept the newly authorized salary.

At the board meeting on April 19, 1979, Richard Dortch was asking that a copy of the constitution and bylaws be mailed to him by the assistant secretary of the corporation. In later years, not only would the constitution and the bylaws not be mailed to board members, but the board members would never even see the addenda to the minutes that contained bonuses for Jim Bakker, Tammy Bakker, or Richard Dortch.

At the board meeting on June 20, 1979, Richard Dortch asked that certain perks be given to Jim Bakker. The following list provides the specifics:

1. "Richard W. Dortch made a motion that the Board confirm there is a one million dollar insurance policy [on Jim Bakker's life], and that $250,000 be assigned to James O. Bakker's estate."

2. "Richard W. Dortch made a motion that a $5,000 disability income policy per month go to Reverend James O. Bakker."

3. "Mr. Richard W. Dortch made a motion that the president be granted 10% on salary and benefits—[with those funds] to go into the Assemblies of God retirement fund."

4. "Richard W. Dortch made a motion that PTL pay for all transportation and transportation related expenses of

President James O. Bakker and wife, Tammy, and two
children, Tammy Sue and James Charles."

5. "Mr. Richard W. Dortch made a motion that Philip D. and
Ruth Egert act as official bodyguards to James O. and
Tammy Faye Bakker. . . ."

This board meeting was held at 7:30 P.M. in the home of Jim
Bakker. In addition to Bakker, the members of the PTL board of
directors were A.T. Lawing, an executive from Charlotte, North Carolina, who also acted as Treasurer and Secretary to the corporation,
and Richard Dortch, who was at that time only a member of the board.
The other board member, James E. Johnson, was absent from that
particular meeting. All of the motions relating to Jim Bakker's perks
were seconded by A.T. Lawing.

Was Richard Dortch attempting to cultivate a loyalty and a friendship with Jim Bakker that he could later use to his advantage? Although there is no direct evidence that such was the case, the minutes
clearly reflect that Dortch was always the instigator of motions to
award perks to Bakker. Dortch later directed that the assistant secretary not include in the minutes the name of the person making
motions concerning bonuses or salary adjustments.

At the meeting of the PTL board of directors, on November 12,
1979, only Richard Dortch and A.T. Lawing were physically present;
Jim Bakker took part in the meeting by way of a conference telephone
call. Several significant matters were again addressed by the three-
member PTL board of directors. First, Richard Dortch moved that
the board accept and adopt parsonage allowances for 16 PTL employees. Second, "A.T. Lawing made a motion that a set of guidelines
for the auditing committee of Heritage Village Church and Missionary
Fellowship, Inc. be set forth"; the auditing committee was to consist
of A.T. Lawing and Richard Dortch. Also, "Dortch made a motion
that travel/accident insurance be obtained for President James O.
Bakker," several other corporate officers, and the board of directors.
Third, "Richard W. Dortch made a motion that Reverend James O.
Bakker's salary be raised to $72,000 a year." Fourth, "Mr. Richard
W. Dortch made a motion that instead of the 10% agreed on for
Reverend James O. Bakker's Minister's Benefit Association pension
fund in the Assemblies of God, that it should be raised to 20%, and
also that Reverend James O. Bakker could put away any percent of
his salary into the Ministers Benefit Association that he so desired."

Also of interest, Dortch proposed that in the event of Jim Bakker's
death, he was to be succeeded by his wife, Tammy Bakker, and that

she was to serve as president and chair of the board as well as hostess of "The PTL Club." Jim Bakker then moved that if both he and his wife died at the same time, the board, with Dortch serving as chair, was to select a new president. As usual, all motions carried unanimously.

On December 5, 1979, three new members were nominated and elected to the PTL board of directors: Aimee Cortese, Charles A. Cookman, and Efrem Zimbalist, Jr.

Charles Cookman was the district superintendent of the North Carolina Assemblies of God, a position somewhat similar to that which Dortch had before coming to PTL. Aimee Cortese came from a less visible background; she was a pastor of Crossroads Tabernacle Church in the Bronx. After Bakker went to prison, Cortese was called to testify in federal court concerning, among other things, the facts surrounding her becoming a board member at PTL. She testified that she had been called by Richard Dortch in 1979 and that he had asked her to "come and help and be on the Board of PTL." When she explained that she did not have a great deal of knowledge concerning business, building programs, or large churches, Dortch replied that "he wanted [her] mainly for [her] expertise in the Bible, in teaching, and . . . expertise in spiritual affairs." Richard Dortch, according to Cortese, wanted someone to represent the ministerial rather than the secular side of PTL. Efrem Zimbalist, Jr. had played the role of Inspector Erskin on the popular TV show, "The FBI."

The October 23, 1980, board minutes reflected that one of the goals "of this corporation is to give 10% of its net income to world missions and world evangelism, recognizing, however, that it is not always possible to reach that goal, but it shall, nevertheless, be the goal." According to Peter Bailey's testimony, the last time PTL was actively involved in world missions was towards the end of 1985.

The December 10, 1980, board meeting reconsidered what would happen to PTL in the event of Jim Bakker's death. At that Board meeting, an amendment was added stating that in the event of Jim Bakker's death, Richard Dortch was to serve as president and chair of the board of directors of Heritage Village Church and Missionary Fellowship, Inc. The board of directors had the responsibility of selecting a new host for "The PTL Club." The minutes went on to reflect that "if ever a stalemate should come about on any situation or liquidation should occur, Mr. James O. Bakker would want the PTL program and Heritage Village Church and Missionary Fellowship, Inc. to go into the hands of the Assemblies of God. . . ." Evidently, this board meeting had the effect of excluding Tammy Bakker from any active involvement in PTL upon her husband's death. Jim Bakker made a motion that Deloitte, Haskins and Sells audit "all the books" of Heritage Village Church and Missionary Fellowship, Inc. (HVCMF), the legal name for the entire PTL parent corporation. This continued the official involvement of the "Big Eight" accounting firm, Deloitte, Haskins and Sells with Jim Bakker and PTL. Charles Cookman made another motion, which was seconded by Aimee Cortese, that the corporation pursue the possibility of borrowing $15 million for a long-range loan.

It was also at this December 1980 board meeting that a motion was made by Richard Dortch that the PTL corporation give one month's pay to Jim Bakker as a Christmas bonus; the motion was seconded by Charles Cookman and approved by the board. Dortch also moved "that 20% more money from the ministry be added to James O. Bakker's retirement fund for the MBA (Ministers Benefit Association) of Springfield, Missouri, bringing the amount to 40%, effective today." That motion was also seconded by Charles Cookman. Cookman then moved that proceedings begin to sell Bakker's parsonage, located in a fashionable Charlotte neighborhood, "in order to purchase something more suitable for the family."

The September 22, 1981, meeting of the board proved to be very good for the Bakker family. There was no old business, and the new business being reported was all positive, including a report from the chief financial officer that the net worth of PTL had doubled to $25 million and the debts of the organization would be cut in half. The minutes reflect that the board reviewed the audit report prepared by Deloitte, Haskins and Sells, and a motion was made and passed unanimously that the board "accept the financial report with extreme gratitude to God." Then the following transpired:

1. "Reverend Dortch moved that . . . [HVCMF] give a bonus to our President, James O. Bakker, in the amount of $50,000. . . ."
2. "Reverend Dortch moved that Charles Cookman be appointed to chair a committee to look into the matter of an option to purchase or contract to convey on the residence where Reverend Bakker now lives."
3. "Reverend Dortch made a motion that Reverend Bakker's salary be adjusted to $102,000 per year and 30% of the amount of this salary be put into the Ministers Benefit Association pension plan."

4. "Reverend Dortch made a motion that PTL purchase a company car to be furnished by the church for the president and that the church be responsible for the upkeep of the automobile. It is noted that the Board recommends either a Cadillac or Lincoln."

5. "A.T. Lawing made a motion that Tammy Bakker's salary be adjusted to $1,000 per week, along with their expression of the Board's appreciation for her services. . . .''

6. "Reverend Dortch made a motion that the Board pay for a vacation for Jim and Tammy when they feel they need it."

7. "Reverend Dortch made a motion that a committee be appointed by the Board to look for a residence in Florida for the ministry and Reverend Bakker. This residence would serve the President and his family for times of rest."

Of course, all motions passed unanimously.

The minutes of the board meeting of July 5, 1982, reflect that "Richard Dortch moved . . . [HVCMF] give a bonus to Reverend Bakker in the amount of $50,000 for his spiritual leadership and outstanding administration of the corporation over the past year." Such promptings from Richard Dortch had now become fairly common—so common that Dortch asked Sylvia Stephens, who was, as assistant secretary, responsible for maintaining the corporate minutes, not to record the name of the director making motions for bonuses. According to Sylvia Watson's (neé Stephens) testimony, "He told me to quit doing that—[he] asked me to quit doing that, to quit mailing copies [of the minutes] and to go back and clean up my minutes." Dortch never gave any reason for his request made to Watson. As a result of Dortch's request, Watson resigned from the position about three weeks later to be replaced by David A. Taggart.

Board Meetings Subsequent to December 1982

On December 17, 1982, Richard Dortch directed that PTL's lawyer not be present at that or future board meetings. The board then proceeded to give Jim and Tammy Bakker bonuses, pay raises, and a $390,000 condominium in Florida, plus over $202,000 in fixtures for it. This was one of many items that the Internal Revenue Service would later contend was an item of private inurement, thus causing PTL to lose its tax-exempt status.

With no official record of who was making or seconding motions, the environment was either consciously or unconsciously set for manipulation of PTL's own board of directors by Bakker and Dortch. In looking for a change in mindset of Jim Bakker and Richard Dortch, it clearly occurred by at least the December 17, 1982, meeting of the PTL board of directors. The scienter or the criminal intent to oversell the lodging programs at PTL may have occurred much later, but the December 1982 board meeting certainly set an environment that was conducive for top management and the inside directors of PTL to have a free hand in running the corporation and distributing its assets.

From January 1983 until December 1986, the PTL board of directors met at least five times each year. Meetings were not set for any particular date but were generally called by Jim Bakker. At the start of each meeting, the minutes of the previous board meeting were passed out and then collected, and board members were not allowed to take them home.

Nearly all of the minutes reflect that Jim Bakker usually gave an overview of the corporation at the beginning of each meeting. The testimony of board members generally reflects that Jim Bakker ran the meetings and made the significant reports concerning HVCMF to the board. The Federal Bankruptcy Court found that "[i]n all of Mr. Bakker's presentations to the Board, there was never any reason for any Board member to assume anything other than that things were going well."

Prior to Jim Bakker's resignation from PTL in March 1987, the PTL board of directors consisted of six to seven people. In addition to Bakker, Cookman, Cortese, Dortch, Lawing, and Zimbalist, all of whom have been previously introduced, Ernie Franzone became a member of the board of directors on November 20, 1984. Dr. Evelyn Carter Spencer became a board member on November 12, 1985, and Don George joined the board on January 28, 1986. Franzone was a vice-president of Brock Hotels, which was managing the Grand Hotel for PTL. Don George pastored Calvary Temple Church in Dallas, Texas, and Dr. Evelyn Carter Spencer was a pastor from California and a frequent guest and seminar leader at PTL.

Information concerning the finances of PTL that was given to the board, usually consisted of positive statements. For example, as one board member testified, Jim Bakker always said something like: "Since the last board meeting, our contributions are up. Our income has increased by 'x' number of dollars, and we are doing very well."

In addition to positive reports concerning the corporation and its financial status given by Jim Bakker and Richard Dortch, the minutes also reflected that outside independent auditors were examining PTL's financial data. Apparently, this provided the board of directors with a sense of security regarding the fulfillment of their fiduciary duties to the corporation.

For example, the minutes from April 11, 1983, stated: "Reverend Dortch reported that he met with representatives of the Charlotte office of Deloitte, Haskins and Sells and received a report on the financial status of the corporation. It was reported that progress was being made on the current audit and that on or before May 1, 1983, the [yearly] audit [of HVCMF] would be ready for a review. Reverend Dortch also reported that he is receiving financial information from the officers of the corporation each month." Then, at the meeting of the board of directors on January 3, 1985, "a copy of the financial statement approved by Deloitte, Haskins and Sells, with an authorized summary by Deloitte, Haskins and Sells was presented to the board for review. An in depth discussion of this report ensued."

Apparently, the board of directors was reviewing and discussing PTL's audited financial statements for the year ending May 31, 1984, and the auditor's report of those financial statements. There was no mention in the report of the oversale of the Grand Hotel, which had occurred by at least July 7, 1984. After discussing the "audit performance" of Deloitte, Haskins and Sells at a previous meeting, Jim Bakker announced at the July 5, 1985, meeting "that the firm of Laventhol and Horwath [had] taken over the auditing of the Corporation."

On January 28, 1986, "[t]he 1985 annual audit by Laventhol and Horwath, Certified Public Accountants, was presented to the board for review. A motion was made, seconded, and passed unanimously that the audit be accepted." The Laventhol auditor's report, unlike the previous one, was qualified. The qualification, as discussed in Chapter 9, concerned an ongoing IRS examination, but the auditor's report neither noted nor discussed the oversale of lifetime partnerships in the Grand Hotel.

A preliminary audit was presented to the board of directors for its consideration on November 3, 1986. PTL's financial statements for the year ending May 31, 1986, were apparently examined by the board of directors at their December 16, 1986 meeting. Those minutes stated that "a year-end audit was presented to the board for scrutiny. A motion was made, seconded, and passed unanimously that this audit be accepted." The auditor's report for the 1986 financial statements was dated November 17, 1986, and was, like the prior year's report, qualified to reflect an ongoing IRS examination. Again, nothing was said in the report, the financial statements, or the notes to those financial statements concerning the fraudulent oversale of lifetime partnerships in several of PTL's promotional programs.

On November 9, 1983, in addition to receiving audits completed by nationally recognized accounting firms, the board of directors approved an internal audit charter, which stated that the "objective of the establishment of the internal audit department is to provide additional assurances that ministry assets are used for intended purposes to the glory of our Lord, Jesus Christ." The internal audit department was to report to the president or the board of directors or its audit committee and ascertain the extent of compliance with established internal auditing procedures. Although the internal audit charter stated that the audit department "is granted access to all records and personnel necessary to carry out its objectives by the authorization of the board of directors of Heritage Village Church and Missionary Fellowship, Inc.," in reality, the person who served as PTL's internal auditor did not audit the various lifetime partnership programs; instead, the internal audits were limited primarily to examining the books and records of the stores, shops, and other smaller activities located at PTL.

Budgeting and financing were discussed at the meeting on November 20, 1984. Jim Bakker stated that his top priority was "to have a clean budget and to live within the budget areas."

PTL did have an audit committee, although it apparently did not actively function. Commencing November 12, 1979, Dortch and Lawing served as the audit committee of HVCMF. Evidently, PTL also had a finance committee. The minutes of May 22, 1984, also reflected that the "Finance Committee has the responsibility of approving the budget of Heritage Village Church and Missionary Fellowship, Inc.," and Charles Cookman and A.T. Lawing, Jr., were appointed members of the finance committee on that date. None of the minutes of the PTL board of directors ever reflected any report given, or discussion rendered, by either committee.

As discussed more fully later, the finance and audit committees apparently were formed at the request of the Evangelical Council for Financial Accountability (ECFA), an organization that attempts to ensure financial accountability among its voluntary members. PTL was a member of ECFA and as such was allowed to display the ECFA seal at the conclusion of its television program.

In addition to knowing there were audits performed by PTL's outside auditors, the board of directors continued to receive positive and upbeat financial information from Bakker and Dortch. As the Bankruptcy Court found, "[t]he board of directors was never informed that PTL was in any kind of precarious financial position. The board was never presented with the information contained in the numerous memos sent to Mr. Bakker by Peter Bailey, Vice President of Finance." The Bankruptcy Court's findings were confirmed by the sworn testimony in the Bakker criminal trial by PTL board members Charles Cookman; Aimee Cortese; Ernie Franzone; A.T. Lawing; Efrem Zimbalist, Jr.; Dr. Evelyn Carter Spencer; and Pastor Don George.

The board of directors also testified that they were never informed by Bakker, Dortch, or any other PTL officer that a decision had been made to continue promoting partnerships for the various lodging facilities at PTL beyond the original advertised promised limits.

Richard Dortch's testimony confirmed that the PTL board of directors was intentionally kept in the dark concerning the true financial status of the corporation. Dortch was asked: "Well, now, when [Jim Bakker] didn't [inform the PTL board of directors of the true financial status of PTL], and you heard the report of the status of the corporation, then did you interject and say, 'Mr. Bakker, we need to tell [the board] about these Bailey memorandum?' Did you ever do that yourself and report this information to the [PTL] board of directors?" Dortch responded, "No, sir, I did not." The questioning continued: "Well, Mr. Dortch, how was the board of directors supposed to know the financial condition of the corporation if the President and Executive Vice President were not reporting this information to the board?" Dortch testified, "[they] couldn't have known."

Jim Bakker stated in court that the board members were given free access not only to corporate books and records but also to all employees of the corporation. The board members were given tours of the facilities and could ask whatever questions they deemed appropriate, he added.

In addition to being misled about the true financial status of PTL by Richard Dortch and Jim Bakker, the board of directors was also deceived concerning the status of an ongoing IRS investigation of PTL, which had commenced in 1980. By August 3, 1982, PTL attorney Don Etheridge, in a letter to Deloitte, Haskins and Sells, was disclosing that not only was an ongoing preliminary audit in progress but also that the IRS was now requesting "a more complete audit" of PTL's books and records; that is, the IRS was examining the organization to determine whether or not there was excessive compensation, and whether or not there was any unrelated business income and whether it would be appropriate to revoke the tax-exempt status of the organization.

Very simply, Section 501(c)(3) of the IRS code states that excessive compensation, or private inurement, cannot be awarded to individuals of a tax-exempt organization. Compensation above what is deemed to be reasonable for a nonprofit organization could be found to be private inurement, and could ultimately lead to the revocation of the organization's tax-exempt status. Needless to say, revocation of PTL's tax-exempt status would have been a disaster because individuals who contributed to PTL would no longer be able to claim a tax deduction. As previously discussed in Chapter 5, the IRS did find that excessive compensation was being paid to Jim Bakker, Tammy Bakker, Richard Dortch, and David Taggart. The IRS began an on-site audit of PTL in October 1983, and in November 1985, the IRS notified PTL that its tax-exempt status had been retroactively revoked for the period June 1, 1980 to May 31, 1983. The IRS later filed a report revoking the tax-exempt status of PTL for the period May 31, 1983, through May 31, 1987. Both reports reflected that PTL "is not operated exclusively for exempt purposes, and part of its net income inures to the benefit of private individuals."

Two different memos written by John Yorke reflect his recollection of what transpired at meetings between other PTL attorneys and senior members of the Deloitte, Haskins and Sells audit team. The first memo, found in Exhibit A-26, reflects Yorke's recollection of a meeting that he had with Lloyd Caudle and Don Etheridge, two of PTL's tax attorneys, and Bob Brown and Evan Webster, the senior members of Deloitte, Haskins and Sells; it concerns not only a discussion of the private inurement problem that existed at PTL at least as early as January of 1983 but also exposes in excruciating detail the lack of internal controls and accountability that plagued PTL.

For example, John Yorke writes in his memo that "employee advances [are] also interesting. They regularly advance money to Jim and Tammy and other employees for travel. Apparently, they get a cash advance for the trip and then they pay for all their expenses on American Express and other charge cards and use the cash advances to go shopping. Over $23,000 was for wardrobe. Another $22,000 was just not accounted for. It was written off rather than charged to any account." The same memo stated that "under the American Express line, you can see that $59,000 was charged for Jim and Tammy under either clothes, magazines or miscellaneous." In another paragraph, John Yorke writes, "After Lloyd and Don [PTL's tax attorneys] left, Evan [Webster] and Bob Brown [auditors with Deloitte, Haskins and Sells] and I had further discussions about [cash advances and expenditures]. I told [them] that the alarming thing to me is that the suspect expenses are growing exponentially. Bob Brown said he thought Richard Dortch was part of the problem. It was interesting to me that he recognized that. I really didn't have time to go into it in depth with him, but it seems everyone is thinking the same thing on that point."

Things did not change over the next eighteen months. In another memo dated June 29, 1984, he again records a meeting that occurred between two tax attorneys for PTL (Lloyd Caudle and Don Etheridge) and three members of Deloitte, Haskins and Sells (Bob Brown, Guy Forcucci, and Ted Lineback). "One of the focal points of [the IRS] investigation is the amount of benefits—the total package of benefits— to Jim and Tammy. I don't think you are aware of how quickly the benefits to Jim and Tammy have accelerated in the past 18 months," wrote John Yorke to his senior partner, Eddie Knox. "According to what I was told by Deloitte, Haskins and Sells in a casual conversation, Jim and Tammy's wages and earnings statement showed income of more than $700,000 last year from PTL. Amazingly, it only showed an interest income of six hundred and some odd dollars. That includes interest drawn on their checking account. Apparently, the funds go through so quickly that they don't have time to draw interest. . . . We have advised Jim from the start, and Dortch since his arrival, that enormous sums of money were going to raise questions with the IRS. Don Etheridge has made it very clear that the central issue of the audit is going to be private inurement of benefits to Jim and Tammy." In that same memo, John Yorke admits to having "had several confrontations with Reverend Dortch, David Taggart and others [at PTL] because they are highly sensitive these days and had made passing comments about the fact that lawyers and accountants were all more concerned with protecting themselves than with protecting PTL. I pointed out to Dortch very clearly that one of the reasons they got this feeling was because they didn't follow the advice that was being given to them. I also pointed out the fact that they had done just the opposite and have rushed into build everything they can build. . . . I also pointed out to him that in spite of the ongoing audit, they have increased the benefits, the salaries of the people at the top, etc. I point this out to you to make you aware of this fact that there are some raw nerves out there about this. During my course of dealing with PTL, I had noticed that the further they get in debt, the more sensitive they get to a discussion of their problems."

On September 9, 1986, attorney Michael J. Wigton told Bakker in a letter, copies of which were furnished to Richard Dortch and David Taggart, that he was withdrawing as counsel to PTL and all church related activities. After outlining a litany of problems that Wigton had with PTL, he wrote the following: "I have repeatedly attempted to convince you all of the seriousness of the tax problems. I do not believe I have succeeded. My belief is based on the lack of responsiveness to requests for assistance and resistance to our advice. Let me reiterate what I have told you before. You have very serious problems in 1981–83, and based on what we have seen, even more serious problems in 1984–85." Wigton also wrote that "it appears that Reverend Dortch is making all the decisions without consulting the board with a representation that he is receiving input from you and other responsible fiduciaries. My calls to you have gone unreturned, and I have no indication that the board is aware of the specifics of what is going on."

Less than two months after that letter, the minutes of the PTL board of directors from November 3, 1986, reflect the following: "It was reported that [PTL's] response [due] by December 1, 1986, to the Atlanta office on the IRS audit is proceeding on schedule and there is every reason to be encouraged in this matter." It is difficult to reconcile Wigton's letter of September 9, 1986, with this statement. In addition, positive reports concerning the IRS audit were given to the PTL board of directors on July 3, 1984; September 12, 1984; November 20, 1984; July 5, 1985; and November 12, 1985. The assurances given to the members of the board at these meetings were treated by J. Don George, who testified that no one on the board made specific inquiries concerning the IRS audit because "Richard Dortch continued to assure us and reassure us that the investigation was going smoothly and that he had every hope that the investigation would be completed satisfactorily to the ministry and that everything was progressing on a positive note." George also testified that although "Mr. Bakker was the official chairman, he frequently left the meetings and Mr. Dortch actually did most of the talking during the board meetings."

Because the members of the board received information only from Dortch and Bakker, they did not have sufficient information to make proper business decisions. As found by the Bankruptcy Court, "Board members were lulled into a sense of security concerning the finances of PTL in that Mr. Bakker told them that PTL had excellent accountants, that it had internal control by certified public accountants, that it had external audits by reputable firms, and that the corporation employed lawyers. It never occurred to members of the board that anything other than financial integrity was practiced at PTL." Unfortunately, such simply was not the case. PTL's accountants and attorneys talked to Richard Dortch, David Taggart, and Jim Bakker. The concerns that they had were never directly shared with other members of the board of directors.

Bonuses

As previously discussed, the bonuses received by the Bakkers became a central issue of not only the bankruptcy proceedings but also Jim Bakker's criminal trial. The government contended that the oversale of lifetime partnerships was committed, in part, to enable Jim Bakker to receive the bonuses that he and his wife received during PTL's existence.

From June 1, 1983, through March 18, 1987, the date of Jim Bakker's resignation from PTL, the PTL board of directors held a total of 23 meetings. In 13 of those meetings, action was taken to approve bonuses for Jim Bakker; in 12 meetings, action was taken to approve bonuses for Tammy Bakker; and in 7 meetings, action was taken to approve bonuses for Richard Dortch. David Taggart, Richard Dortch, and the Bakkers also received PTL checks for bonuses in 1987. However, the board of directors met only on January 2, 1987, at which time, according to the minutes, no bonuses were approved or authorized; then the board met in executive session for the purpose of accepting Jim Bakker's resignation and for the resigning enmasse on March 18, 1987.

As Exhibit 7-1 reflects, substantial bonuses were awarded to Jim Bakker, Tammy Bakker, and David Taggart from July 1983 until February 1987. Again, these amounts reflect only bonuses, not gross salary or use of corporate funds for personal benefit.

As previously noted, Richard Dortch received $453,010 in bonuses in the nine-month period before Bakker's resignation.

Who made the decisions about whether or not to award bonuses, and how big they should be? There is a distinct difference in testimony concerning how these bonuses came about.

Jim Bakker swore in court that the board of directors set his and Tammy's salaries and that he always left the room during discussions

B O N U S E S

DATE	J.O. BAKKER	T.F. BAKKER	D.A. TAGGART
7/05/83	100,000.00		
7/11/83		50,000.00	
10/27/83		10,000.00	
11/04/83		2,000.00	
11/10/83		2,000.00	
11/18/83		2,000.00	
11/23/83		2,000.00	
12/01/83	50,000.00	32,000.00	
12/16/83			10,000.00
12/22/83	50,000.00	30,000.00	
12/29/83	50,000.00		
5/18/84	390,000.00		
7/10/84	100,000.00	50,000.00	18,182.00
11/30/84	150,000.00	50,000.00	
12/19/84			13,699.00
4/09/85	150,000.00	50,000.00	
5/14/85		15,000.00	
7/19/85	200,000.00	50,000.00	
11/26/85		50,000.00	
12/06/85			25,000.00
12/18/85	200,000.00		
2/19/86			29,680.00
3/25/86			85,000.00
4/21/86	200,000.00		
4/25/86		100,000.00	
5/01/86			1,774.92
6/17/86			11,000.00
7/01/86			110,000.00
7/16/86	350,000.00	115,000.00	
11/07/86	10,000.00		
11/10/86	190,000.00	20,000.00	
11/20/86			125,000.00
11/24/86		20,000.00	
12/18/86	20,000.00	10,000.00	
12/19/86			22,700.00
12/22/86	20,000.00		
2/04/87	300,000.00	170,000.00	
2/13/87	150,000.00		
2/16/87			225,000.00

Exhibit 7-1   A List of Bonuses Given to PTL's Key Personnel from July 1983 to February 1987

concerning his salary or bonuses. The minutes of the PTL board of directors bore him out; they reflect that at meetings during which a bonus for Jim Bakker was being discussed, he would leave the room, and the bonus would ultimately be approved. Bakker testified that it would be necessary to talk to the board members about what happened in any meeting concerning bonuses, because he simply was not present when bonuses were discussed. In fact, many of the board minutes reflect that Jim Bakker voted against his receiving a bonus.

After he resigned from PTL, Jim Bakker was questioned about what appeared to be the staggering amount of his compensation. Bakker said: "[t]he Board had placed $40 million to $50 million in insurance on me. They would often say to me 'If you are worth $40 million dead, you are surely worth what we pay you alive.' "

The April 2, 1986, minutes do reflect board approval to purchase a $50 million policy for Jim Bakker. The minutes also stated a reason for the purchase: "This amount of insurance was required to obtain the $50 million loan [for PTL]."

Richard Dortch testified as to the mechanics of how Bakker and his wife received bonuses from the board of directors. From time to time, "David Taggart would come to me and tell me that Mr. Bakker needed a certain amount of money, and on those occasions I would talk to one of the board members and communicate that message," he said. The board member, according to Dortch, virtually always made a motion at the meeting that Jim Bakker should receive a bonus for the amount that had been previously supplied by Richard Dortch. Dortch verified that Bakker left the room any time a bonus for him was being discussed with the board. Dortch was asked whether, after Bakker had left the room, he told "the board of directors about the content of those Bailey memoranda and say that Mr. Bakker may be needing this but the ministry can't afford to give it to him?" "Regretfully, no," Dortch responded. "You should have done that, shouldn't you?" the prosecutor inquired. "Yes, sir, I should have," Dortch replied.

The Dortch version of the story behind the bonuses seems to be supported by the testimony of Robert Dash, a fraud-detection specialist in the U.S. postal inspection service with 19 years experience. Inspector Dash scrutinized PTL's bank and financial records. He analyzed not only the flow of funds into the 45 different PTL bank accounts but also the flow of lifetime partnership contributions and, significantly, the flow of the Bakker bonuses.

Dash testified that total deposits received by PTL from lifetime partners from January 1984 through May 31, 1987, amounted to

$172,180,011.13. Adjustments due to refunds, invalid checks, bad checks, and loan defaults totaled $8,066,664.24, which means that net deposits received by PTL from lifetime partners from January 1984 through May 31, 1987, totaled $164,113,346.89.

After tracing the flow of PTL's lifetime partnership contributions, Dash also analyzed the various bonus checks and wire transfers that Bakker received in the wake of the board's approval of bonuses.

Dash confirmed that Bakker received a wire transfer of a bonus in March 1984, which the board of directors had apparently approved. The gross amount of that bonus was $390,000, and the net amount received by Bakker, after taxes, was $195,000. A wire transfer was made on May 18, 1984, to transfer those funds to Jim and Tammy Bakker's personal bank account. Of significance, Dash testified that the $195,000 wired to the Bakkers' personal account came from the Grand Hotel deposit account and was apparently used by Jim and Tammy Bakker to purchase a $449,000 home in Palm Desert, California, on or about May 24, 1984. Specifically, approximately $145,700 was used out of the $195,000 wire transfer to make the down payment on that home, according to Inspector Dash's testimony.

In July 1986, Jim and Tammy Bakker received gross bonuses of $300,000 and $100,000, respectively. The net amount received by Jim Bakker was $150,000, and Mrs. Bakker netted $50,000 from her bonus. Checks were issued reflecting those amounts on July 16, 1986. The Bakkers then closed on a home in Gatlinburg, Tennessee, on August 16, 1986. At the time of closing, they paid $155,000 cash for the property. Inspector Dash testified that, once again, the funds used to purchase the Gatlinburg home came out of the account into which they had deposited their bonus checks. Prior to the deposit of those bonus checks, there had been insufficient funds in that account to cover the purchase price.

Where did PTL obtain the net amount of $200,000 that it paid to the Bakkers from these gross bonuses totaling $400,000? Dash testified that the money came from the Victory Warriors account. The money was then transferred to the Towers account and ultimately transferred to the Special Payroll account, on which the Bakkers' bonus checks were drawn.

Finally, Agent Dash testified that the Bakkers bought a $600,000 home in Palm Springs, California, on or about February 20, 1987, with a $350,000 down payment. He also affirmed that Bakker received a $150,000 PTL check on February 13, 1987; according to a review of the board's minutes, it had never been authorized by the board.

That check for $150,000, along with two previously authorized bonus checks, were deposited in Bakker's account and used by Jim Bakker to make the down payment on the Palm Springs home.

Prosecutor Deborah Smith asked Dash, "Were you able to trace the source of funds of the $150,000 payment that Mr. Bakker received February 13, 1987?" Dash responded, "Yes." Smith asked, "What was the source of that money?" He answered, "That money came from the Bunkhouse deposit account. . . . [and] [i]t was subsequently transferred to the Executive Payroll account," from which the $150,000 check was written to help purchase the Bakkers' Palm Springs home.

This testimony of Robert Dash corroborates Dortch and Taggart's assertions concerning the Bakkers' bonuses. Furthermore, it clearly indicates that the funds used to provide the Bakkers with several of their bonuses came directly from the various lifetime partnership programs.

Jim Bakker disputed Dortch's testimony and the mechanics of how he received bonuses. He testified at the bankruptcy proceedings that he never asked the board of directors for a bonus. That assertion, however, disputes the testimony of not only Dortch and David Taggart but also Don Hardister, Jim Bakker's personal bodyguard, who overheard Bakker discuss his need for bonuses with David Taggart.

The issue that is still unresolved concerns how much bonus money Bakker received. There is a wide discrepancy between the addendums to the minutes of the board of directors and what the various board members themselves have to say in this regard. (At Richard Dortch's instructions, the bonus amounts were included in one-page addenda; however, they were never shown to the board.)

Exhibit A-27 is a copy of the November 3, 1986, minutes of the board, which reflect that "Reverend Don George brought before the board the tradition of Christmas bonuses for Reverend Bakker, Tammy Bakker, and Richard Dortch." Conspicuously missing from this document are the amounts of the bonuses; the addendum to these minutes of the board shows that Jim Bakker got $500,000, Tammy Bakker got $100,000, and Richard Dortch got $100,000. (Exhibit A-28.)

The minutes from December 16, 1986, reflect that "the Board discussed the prospect of a Christmas gift being given to Reverend Jim Bakker, Tammy Bakker, and Reverend Dortch. A motion was made that the gifts be given as a token of appreciation by the Board of Directors. It was seconded and passed with Reverend Bakker absent from the room and Reverend Dortch abstaining from the voting." Just six weeks after having given the Bakkers and Dortch a Christmas bonus, the board had now authorized a Christmas "gift." Consistent with all board meetings held after December 1982, the bonus amounts were included not in the minutes themselves but on a one-page addendum that was never seen by the board, which reflected that Jim Bakker, Richard Dortch, and Tammy Bakker were to receive Christmas gifts of $50,000, $25,000, and $25,000, respectively. These were the net amounts; that is, many of the addenda reflected the bonus amount in "after tax dollars." Because the Bakkers and Dortch were in the 50 percent tax bracket, Jim Bakker received a gross sum of $100,000, whereas Richard Dortch and Tammy Bakker each received $50,000. This process of paying bonuses and making certain that all taxes were paid on them became known at PTL as "grossing up."

Board members Cookman, Cortese, Franzone, George, Lawing, Spencer, and Zimbalist are in agreement on at least three different areas. First, none of the board members were ever made aware by Bakker or Dortch of the oversale of lifetime partnerships. Second, none of the board members felt that they had been fully advised of the true financial condition of PTL. Third, none of the board members recall awarding bonuses of the magnitude reflected in the addenda to the board minutes. There is, however, a disagreement among the board members concerning their recollections of the largest bonus ever voted for Jim or Tammy Bakker.

Charles Cookman testified that as the district superintendent for the North Carolina District of the Assemblies of God, he had been the supervisor of Jim Bakker and Richard Dortch while they worked at PTL. Cookman responded to questions asked by Deborah Smith concerning bonuses for Jim and Tammy Bakker as follows:

Q: So according to your memory, the largest bonus you recall voting for was a total amount of $100,000?
A: Yes, ma'am.
Q: You recall doing that twice?
A: On two occasions.
Q: Now, more than two times during various meetings through 84, 85, 86, bonuses for Mr. Bakker. Based upon your memory, what was your memory or impression of the size of those other bonuses that were voted, beyond the two you've mentioned, that you recall being $100,000.
A: Well, I don't recall any particular number.
Q: What was your understanding of the size of those bonuses at the time of your voting?
A: Well, earlier, we had given bonuses in the range of five, [to] ten thousand dollars, and my assumption was that anything that was unspecified would be in that range.

Cookman also disputed a statement found in the December 17, 1982, minutes of the board that indicated Cookman had made a motion that Jim Bakker's salary be raised by 91.2 percent, and that Tammy Bakker's salary be increased by 53.8 percent. Not only did he not recall making such a motion, but his testimony also reflected that he could not imagine any circumstance under which he would make a motion for a salary increase of 91.2 percent for Jim Bakker.

Aimee Cortese testified that after much reluctance, she had joined the board of directors after being told by Richard Dortch that "[her] calling to PTL would be of a spiritual value, [and] . . . [her] expertise would lie in the field of the spiritual part."

Both Cortese and Cookman testified that they were aware of the size of Jim Bakker's salary. Cookman was told by Richard Dortch that Bakker had an annual salary of $250,000. Aimee Cortese had a vague recollection of raising Jim Bakker's salary from $95,000 to $250,000. Although Cortese testified that she never recalled giving Jim and Tammy Bakker bonuses in excess of $100,000 and $50,000 before tax, respectively, she did indicate that Richard Dortch came in and told the board that Jim Bakker needed money. "As a matter of fact, I don't recall them explaining the need. . . . We just trusted that he knew what was going on," she testified. She also made the following assertions concerning her understanding as to how bonuses were awarded:

Q: What was the reason that was, that you saw for granting a bonus to Reverend Dortch at the time he got one?
A: The same reasons we gave it to Tammy.
Q: What was that?
A: Mainly that we were told to.

Aimee Cortese then elaborated on her answer: "I wouldn't know anything about [Jim Bakker's] needs. I would just understand what Reverend Dortch would come and tell us, and he seemed to be emphatic, he seemed to have understood their need and in that way we would comply with whatever he would ask us to do."

Cortese was asked whether or not she recalled a $500,000 bonus being given to Jim Bakker and a $100,000 bonus being given to Tammy Bakker. Cortese answered emphatically, "Never."

Aimee Cortese was also asked about the November 12, 1985, minutes of the PTL board of directors, which reflect that the board authorized obtaining loans for PTL in the amounts of $500,000 and $300,000 from two different banks or lending institutions. Cortese acknowledged that at that time board members questioned why bonuses were being authorized if in fact PTL was having to borrow money. According to Cortese's testimony, "[t]he answer that Reverend Dortch gave us was that our problem was just a cash flow problem, a problem most big organizations had, and that it would just take a week or two to settle or to be taken care of, and that as soon as everything was in order and as soon as the cash flow of whatever had to be in order—would be in order, then at that time he would see to it that they got their bonuses."

Aimee Cortese also testified that she was familiar with the Bakkers' lifestyle. For example, she knew about the Bakker's homes in Gatlinburg, Palm Desert, and Tega Cay, South Carolina.

Aimee Cortese affirmed in court that Richard Dortch had spoken to attorneys concerning whether Jim Bakker's compensation, bonuses, and benefits were legal. According to Cortese, Dortch told the board that the attorneys had made a comparison study that proved Bakker was being legally compensated by the board.

Concerning her service on the audit committee of the PTL board of directors, Cortese's statements were particularly interesting. According to Cortese, she thought the letter from Jim Bakker stating that "we have added your name to serve on [the audit] committee" to be a joke. "I do not have expertise in numbers and financial reports and anything, for this, the letter was a joke and the situation was a joke, and I was just waiting, [to resign since the letter] says we will let you know when the committee meets. It never met." Because the audit committee never met Cortese never formally resigned from the audit committee.

Cortese also testified that Richard Dortch had informed her of Jim Bakker's sexual encounter with Jessica Hahn in Florida and that Hahn had been calling PTL on a regular basis. At Dortch's instruction, Cortese delivered $2,000 and later $10,000 to Jessica Hahn; the second payment was given on the condition that Hahn sign a statement releasing Jim Bakker and PTL of any legal liability or responsibility. Cortese swore that she had no knowledge of the $265,000 that was ultimately paid to Jessica Hahn by way of Roe Mesner and that she did not advise any other board members concerning the Jessica Hahn affair.

Ernie Franzone testified that he recalled one occasion when Jim Bakker received a $100,000 bonus, whereas Tammy Bakker's bonuses usually ran around $25,000. Richard Dortch sometimes received $25,000 or $50,000 bonuses. Furthermore, he testified that the board "voted for bonuses approximately three times a year to four times a year." "Richard Dortch made this statement to the board that the bonuses included taxes." That was the first time that Franzone realized that the bonuses he was voting for did not include taxes.

Prior to Pastor Don George joining the PTL board of directors, Jim Bakker gave $100,000 from PTL to George's church, Calvary Temple Church of Dallas, Texas, for landscaping purposes. George testified that although he did not know Bakker's salary at the time, the largest bonus he recalled voting for was $150,000 plus taxes. George's attention was called to the board minutes of April 2, 1986, the addenda to which reflected that Bakker received a bonus of $100,000 plus taxes and that $50,000 plus taxes was voted for Tammy Bakker. George testified that "those are the specific figures that I recall. It is my recollection that something was stated in the board meeting that day to the effect that this was actually a Christmas bonus for the year just past, [and] that Christmas bonuses were not given in 1985 because of the [poor] financial condition of the ministry. So it would be an appropriate thing at this time to award Christmas bonuses retroactively to 1985 because the ministry at the time of this meeting was in such financial condition that those bonuses could now be given, and I specifically recall that the information that I gathered came, basically, from Richard Dortch."

Prosecutor Deborah Smith then directed Don George's attention to the minutes of the board meeting of November 12, 1985, which indicated, in fact, that Bakker had received a Christmas bonus in the amount of $200,000. George testified that he was not aware of Bakker's salary; it had been his feeling that Jim Bakker "lived on a rather meager salary." George also testified that he had no recollection of voting the Bakkers a second Christmas bonus in 1986.

On February 18, 1987, George resigned from the board of directors because he "was concerned about the endless fundraising projects. It was a concern of mine that there never seemed to be a balanced period in the ministry when a large amount of funds were not raised on the television program. I was also concerned about the fund raising of Farm Land, U.S.A. I knew that a considerable amount of money had been raised for Farm Land, U.S.A., and I had concern that money was not being spent in that area but was, in fact, being spent to complete the Towers project. I had no evidence of that. It was simply a concern that I had from observation."

A.T. Lawing, the charter member of the board of directors, testified it was his understanding that Jim Bakker's salary had been approximately $200,000 a year. Lawing's recollection of the largest bonus ever awarded to Jim Bakker was $100,000 plus taxes. Lawing was a member of the board until March 1987.

Dr. Evelyn Carter Spencer testified that the largest bonus she recalled approving for Jim Bakker amounted to $150,000 plus taxes. Her testimony was that the board clearly knew the amount of the bonus at the time it was awarded.

Board member Efrem Zimbalist, Jr., who had previously starred in the television series, "The FBI," as FBI Inspector Lewis Erskin, testified that he was, in his words, "abusing" his profession as an actor in Madrid, Spain, where he was playing the part of the father in the series, "Zorro," and returned to Charlotte to testify in the Bakker criminal trial.

Zimbalist testified that he had attended only six or seven board meetings and ultimately resigned in April 1985. He affirmed that the PTL board of directors "at no time functioned as a board of directors normally does, which is a regulatory body or a body that controls the financial—the budget and the disbursement of funds and programs and so forth. It was not that kind of board. It was a board you might say of approval or a board of affirmation, something like that. . . . I never assumed that I was responsible for anything, because I wasn't, because the board didn't do that." Zimbalist apparently viewed his role on the PTL board of directors differently than other board members.

Concerning the bonuses, Richard Dortch testified as follows:

Q: I believe you testified earlier today—but correct me if I'm wrong—that the bonuses which you were paid and which Reverend Bakker and Tammy Bakker were paid, were authorized by the board of directors; is that your testimony?
A: Yes, Sir.

□ □ □

Q: At those meetings which you attended, was there on every occasion a discussion as to the specific amount of the bonus which was being considered?
A: Yes.
Q: Are you aware of any occasion where the board of directors of PTL authorized a bonus for you or for the Bakkers without knowledge of the amount of that bonus?
A: No.

□ □ □

Q: On the times you saw those addenda, did the amounts recorded on those addenda correspond with the amounts which had been authorized during the board of directors meetings?

A: I never noticed any difference from what I had remembered happened in the board meeting.

Dortch also testified that he informed the board members several times that the bonuses included the net amount plus the applicable tax. Consistent with Dortch's testimony was a statement signed by Shirley Fulbright and mailed to all members of the U.S. Congress. Shirley Fulbright had been Jim Bakker's personal secretary and had also served as assistant secretary to the corporation. The minutes and the addenda of board meetings had all been signed by her. Fulbright stated in her correspondence: "On every occasion where bonuses were given, the board recommended and authorized a specific amount. During the meeting, there was discussion of a specific amount and that was stated and set forth. There was clear approval and authorization by the board of directors of amounts of bonuses received by Jim and Tammy Bakker."

Interestingly, John Yorke testified that while he served as outside counsel for PTL, Shirley Fulbright called him on one occasion to tell him that Reverend Dortch wanted her to change the minutes of a board meeting. Furthermore, according to Yorke, Dortch told her that if she didn't do what he said, she was going to be fired. Yorke warned Fulbright that if she changed the minutes, the consequences could be even worse.

It should also be noted that Fulbright testified at the Taggart criminal trial that, at the direction of David Taggart, she signed Bakker's signature on a memo that gave her a $90,000 bonus, $45,000 of which was used to pay off a loan she had obtained from PTL. Fulbright also testified that she had signed Bakker's name to several documents authorizing payment to both Taggart brothers without Bakker's knowledge. One of these memoranda authorized PTL to pay James Taggart's interior design firm a monthly retainer fee of $10,000, whereas another memo authorized a $100,000 payment to James Taggart's design firm. "I assumed I could sign everything . . . if it were necessary," Fulbright testified.

Shirley Fulbright's total compensation in 1986 amounted to roughly $160,000. In January through March of 1987 she received approximately $50,000. The IRS "Report of Examination" noted that Shirley Fulbright was paid $174,051 in bonuses paid out of the executive checking account from December 1983 until March 1987.

Fulbright also told the court that she had received expensive gifts and gone on trips paid for by David Taggart. For example, he gave her clothing and a $4,000 fur coat during the time that they worked together.

It is impossible to reconcile Fulbright's statement and Dortch's testimony with the sworn testimony of the other PTL board members. Dortch and Fulbright contend that the board members approved all bonuses reflected in the addendum to the minutes. The board members testified such was not the case. It is also difficult to reconcile the testimony of the board members among themselves concerning the amount of the bonuses to the Bakkers and Dortch. Exhibit A-29 does, however, reflect the chronology of events related to the bonuses; these documents were used by the government at Jim Bakker's resentencing. Closely related to these documents is Exhibit A-30, which represents a chronology of events relating to the sale of lifetime partnerships.

It is difficult to reach a definitive conclusion concerning the actions of the board of directors of PTL. Clearly, they relied, in good faith, on the positive representations made by Jim Bakker and Richard Dortch, and what they saw at Heritage USA supported these representations. Furthermore, the financial data presented to the board was always positive, and no one ever brought the gross irregularities that we now know transpired at PTL to the board's attention. As will be discussed in the next chapter, board member Aimee Cortese was charged in a civil case with breaching her fiduciary duties as a member of the board of directors. She was found not guilty by a federal jury.

It may very well be that the board of directors of PTL was completely unaware of the irregularities and frauds that were occurring all around them. Probably the worst that can be said is that there were signals during their tenure that, in hindsight, should have made them begin to ask questions.

As stated earlier, the board members were unanimous in attesting that they never knew of the gloom-and-doom memos of Peter Bailey and that had they been aware of that information, they would have acted more skeptically and cautiously. They never received any contrary information concerning PTL's finances from its auditors or lawyers; instead, any negative information was fed to Richard Dortch and then to Jim Bakker, never to the outside board members.

PTL's Last Hours

On March 17, 1987, PTL's board members were called to an emergency meeting. They were not informed of the subject matter of the meeting, but the urgency of the meeting was stressed. It was not until 9:00 P.M. on March 18 that the board was able to convene at the executive offices of PTL, with Richard Dortch serving as chair of the meeting.

It became clear that the purpose of the meeting was to accept Jim Bakker's resignation and to appoint Jerry Falwell as president and chairman of the board. It also became apparent that the board of directors would have to "resign," or as one board member later said, "be fired" at that particular meeting. As the meeting progressed, Bakker tendered his resignation by telephone, effective immediately, and Jerry Falwell was unanimously elected chair of the board. Each board member resigned "effective upon the adjournment of the meeting," and a new board was nominated and elected.

The meeting was adjourned, and the board members were standing by the door about to exit the room. At that moment, Richard Dortch suddenly remembered that he had forgotten to have the board annul the 1980 board of directors resolution, which provided that the Assemblies of God could take control of PTL if Reverend Bakker was unable to serve as president as provided by PTL's bylaws.

Dortch asked for a "show of hands" by the former board members to annul the resolution. It passed unanimously.

Clearly, former board members have no authority in relation to the corporation with which they were previously associated. It is unclear why the official minutes of the PTL board of directors indicated that the vote for annulment of the resolution was taken prior to the resignation of the board members.

CHAPTER EIGHT

□ □ □

Insights into the Civil Trial

For which of you intending to build a tower, does not first sit
down and count the cost, whether he has enough to complete
it? Otherwise, when he has laid the foundation, and is not
able to finish, all that see it begin to mock him.

Luke 14:28-29, quoted by Deborah Smith,
Criminal Fraud Section, Department of Justice
in *United States v. Bakker*

JIM BAKKER, RICHARD DORTCH, AND THE TAGGART BROTHERS were
indicted in December 1988; their subsequent convictions in the summer and fall of 1989 represented society's judgment of the various
frauds and acts of income tax evasion in which they engaged. If society
as a whole was vindicated by the criminal process embodied in the
trials of Bakker, Dortch and the Taggarts, then who would vindicate
the specific rights that arose from those people who gave to PTL?

As already stated, there were 152,903 fully paid lodging partnerships at PTL, and those lodging partnerships produced at least
$158 million for the PTL coffers. What rights did those people have?
Did the people who contributed to PTL under the auspices of the
lifetime partnership program have any legal rights that allowed them
to get their money back? Did the lifetime partners have rights different
from society as a whole such that the criminal prosecution of certain
defendants may have vindicated society's rights, but did not vindicate
the rights of those individuals who gave to the lifetime partnership
program?

In a large federal courtroom in Charlotte, North Carolina, an
attempt was made to vindicate the rights of the PTL lifetime partners.

A class action lawsuit was filed seeking $758 million in damages from Jim Bakker, David Taggart, PTL's outside independent auditors, and other defendants who, according to the plaintiffs, aided and abetted Jim Bakker in perpetrating many massive frauds. This lawsuit was filed in November 1987, before any indictments had been handed down to PTL participants and long before any public criminal litigation concerning the PTL scandal.

Before going any further, however, it should be noted that the plaintiffs were only partially successful in their attempts to recover damages from the defendants. On December 14, 1990, after a seven-week civil trial, a jury of six men and two women found that only Jim Bakker was guilty of fraud and "outrageous or malicious" conduct. They awarded the lifetime partners $129,618,000 in actual damages and $129,618 in punitive damages. All other defendants were found not guilty.

The judgment against Jim Bakker was probably more symbolic than meaningful. "The only asset Mr. Bakker has that I know of is a 45 year lease on a five by seven foot room at a federal prison in Minnesota," said Gene Carr, one of Jim Bakker's civil attorneys. "It's going to be an uphill battle for the plaintiffs to collect any money." Carr was referring to Bakker's 45-year prison sentence that had been handed down by Judge Potter; it had not yet been reduced by Judge Graham Mullen. Although Jim and Tammy Bakker had received millions in salaries, bonuses, and other payments from PTL, Jim Bakker was now only earning 11 to 12 cents an hour working as an orderly at the federal prison hospital in a medium-security facility in Rochester, Minnesota.

The jury, which deliberated for close to 28 hours over a five-day period, found that David Taggart had not conspired with Bakker to perpetrate a fraud and that former PTL board member Aimee Cortese had not been grossly negligent in the performance of her duties as a member of the board of directors. Furthermore, the jury found that PTL's accounting firm, Deloitte, Haskins and Sells (hereafter referred to as "Deloitte") had not conspired with Bakker or helped him defraud the lifetime partners.

"My client's integrity has been vindicated," said Jim Williams, one of Deloitte's attorneys. "This has been a tough three years for them."

PTL's other accounting firm, Laventhol and Horwath (hereafter referred to as "Laventhol") declared bankruptcy during the proceedings, and no verdict was rendered in regard to any alleged misconduct by Laventhol.

The significance of this litigation is that it primarily focused on the business aspects of PTL, specifically the role played by PTL's outside auditing firms. This litigation resulted in voluminous PTL documents and audit work papers being made public. It provided an opportunity to examine, from a business perspective, what was transpiring at PTL as recorded by its outside auditors.

Prior to discussing the issues and significant points addressed in this litigation, it is important to understand exactly who was involved and why.

The Plaintiffs

The plaintiffs were represented by Thomas T. Anderson, an attorney from Indio, California. Considered by many to be the lawyer's lawyer, he had served a stint as president of the California Trial Lawyers Association. Anderson had a national reputation and was cited in 1985 by *Town and Country Magazine* as one of the 100 best trial lawyers in the United States. Anderson had worked on a wide variety of cases, including lawsuits involving personal injury losses and corporate fraud. He won many lawsuits involving cases where the jury awarded verdicts in excess of $1 million.

Anderson, a born-again Christian, said at the time of filing this class action lawsuit, "[t]o take money for the cause of Christ fraudulently and defer it to your own selfish purposes is beyond comprehension." Working with Anderson was Wendell Bird, an attorney from Atlanta, Georgia, who was quoted as having said, "Frankly, we do feel a sort of mission in what we are doing."

At the conclusion of the trial, Anderson stated that he had spent more than $2 million of his own money to finance the lifetime partners' litigation. As expected, he expressed extreme disappointment with the jury's verdict and indicated that the decision would be appealed. (The case is currently on appeal before the Fourth U.S. Circuit Court of Appeals, and no decision has yet been rendered.)

Although the case brought by the plaintiffs was cited *Teague et al. v. Bakker et al.*, WDNC CC-87-514-M, this was a class action lawsuit. A *class action* is a procedure that permits a limited number of persons to represent a large group of persons who purport to have similar claims. Joseph Teague, Helen Teague, Stephen Barker, Rita Strahowski, Swannee Beck, and Karen Tucker were the so-called named plaintiffs who were representatives of a "nationwide class consisting of 160,904 lifetime partners and of 29,805 persons who have partially paid for a lifetime partnership." There has always been a dispute concerning the total number of actual lifetime partners. Although there is no dispute concerning the number of fully and partially paid lodging partnerships, many people purchased multiple partnerships; therefore, it is generally accepted that approximately 114,000 people had bought one or more lifetime lodging partnerships offered by PTL.

According to the complaint, the Teagues "are residents of the state of South Carolina, where they received PTL solicitations from Charlotte, North Carolina, and from where they sent their investment for two regular lifetime partnerships, a Silver 7000 Club lifetime partnership, and an 1100 Club lifetime partnership, as well as their contributions to PTL at Charlotte, North Carolina. They were and are committed supporters of PTL, but shifted from their earlier favorable attitude toward Bakker and to their opposition as they learned of improper activities in using lifetime partners investments." Each of the named plaintiffs were cited as having purchased lifetime partnerships; their support for the PTL organization later shifted because they learned of "improper activities in using lifetime partners investments." Karen Tucker, a named plaintiff, represented those lifetime partners who were suing all defendants except for the former PTL officers.

The class action lawsuit allows for efficient use of limited judicial resources. Rather than each lifetime partner bringing a cause of action against Bakker and others, all lifetime partners who desired to participate in this one lawsuit could "opt in" and become plaintiffs. The class action, therefore, also allows the plaintiffs to pool their potentially limited resources and present a case against the defendants with resources from all plaintiffs. The court goes through a process whereby it "certifies" the class, making the litigation final and binding on any participants of the class action lawsuit.

The plaintiffs testified that they mailed to 157,519 potential class members during the period December 18 through December 20, 1989, a notice that would allow these individuals to either become a member of the class or to "opt out" of the lawsuit. A total of 10,444 members of the class chose the latter option and were excluded from this lawsuit.

The Defendants

At the time of the trial, the defendants in this class action lawsuit were Jim Bakker; David Taggart; Aimee Cortese; Deloitte; Laventhol;

and William J. Spears, the partner in charge of the Laventhol audit of PTL. When this lawsuit was originally filed, many more defendants had been named; however, because of negotiated settlements and amending the cause of action, many defendants were omitted from the lawsuit by the time the case actually went to trial.

Some of the original defendants who never went to trial were Steve Nelson; William Robinson, who had been the bankruptcy examiner; Roe Messner, who had declared bankruptcy prior to the trial; and the Rock Hill National Bank, which had helped finance a large portion of the Silver 7000 Club memberships.

Deloitte had served as outside auditor to PTL from 1977 to 1984, and Laventhol had been PTL's auditor for the fiscal years 1985 and 1986. Laventhol was, at one time, the seventh-largest accounting firm in the country, with 425 partners and 51 different offices, and many once considered Laventhol to be one of the premier hotel auditing firms in the country. Deloitte subsequently merged with Touche Ross to form the firm Deloitte Touche, which is now the third-largest accounting firm in the country. In a recent full page ad in the *Wall Street Journal*, Deloitte Touche advertised that it was "the auditor's auditor."

The duties of the outside auditor included ensuring that financial statements were presented in conformity with generally accepted accounting principles. Both Deloitte and Laventhol played a key role not only in reporting the current financial status of PTL but also in maintaining the executive payroll which, as previously discussed, disbursed millions of dollars to top PTL executives in the form of salaries and bonuses.

As discussed in more detail later, the lifetime partners' lawsuit was not premised on alleged negligent conduct on the part of each of the accounting firms; rather, the plaintiffs contended that each accounting firm had "participated in, conspired in, and aided and abetted wrong doing[s] by . . . [engaging in certain wrongful] acts," which included "covering up" the oversale of lifetime partnerships, insolvency, "secret bank account management," diversion of funds, private inurement/officer embezzlement, tax-exemption loss, construction embezzlement, time share violations, and securities law violations. In addition, the allegations against Laventhol included a contention made by the plaintiffs that Laventhol "manipulated PTL's income by $46 million by wrong accounting methods and then engaged in a concealment and misleading description of that change in the accounting method."

What Was Litigated?

The issues arising out of the *Teague v. Bakker* litigation were substantial and complex. The initial issue was whether or not Bakker committed a violation of the Racketeering Influenced Corrupt Organizations Act (RICO) and, if so, whether or not Taggart or Deloitte knowingly and substantially aided and abetted Bakker in doing so. The same question was asked in regard to the North Carolina Racketeering Influenced and Corrupt Organizations Act (NC-RICO).

Next, the jury was asked to return findings as to whether or not Bakker had committed a common law fraud and, if so, whether or not Deloitte had knowingly and substantially aided and abetted Bakker's fraud or conspired with Bakker to commit common law fraud.

The final statute that the jury examined was whether or not there was sufficient evidence to show that the lifetime partnerships were time shares within the meaning of the South Carolina Time Share Act, and if so, whether or not Bakker or Deloitte violated that act.

As to defendants Aimee Cortese and David Taggart, the issues the jury was asked to decide were whether or not either defendant was grossly negligent in the performance of his or her duties, and if so, whether or not the defendant's negligence was the proximate cause of the plaintiff's damages.

When the jury returned, U.S. Federal District Judge James B. McMillan published the jury's findings: Jim Bakker had committed a common law fraud, and Bakker's fraud caused injury to the plaintiffs. The jury found that the plaintiffs had failed to prove all other allegations made against the other defendants.

In order to understand and appreciate the litigation in *Teague v. Bakker*, several points need to be made. First, neither Deloitte nor Laventhol were tried under a theory of negligence. This is very significant. Negligence is much easier for a plaintiff to prove than fraud. That is, if the plaintiffs had chosen to sue each of the accounting firms under a theory of negligence, then the plaintiffs would have had to prove that each accounting firm violated the duty of care that it owed to the plaintiffs and that the plaintiffs relied on the audited financial statements.

Instead, the plaintiffs alleged that the accounting firms knowingly and substantially aided and abetted Bakker's fraudulent activities and that the firms knowingly and willfully conspired with Bakker to commit fraudulent activities. In a press release prior to trial, the plaintiffs "alleged that the accounting firm helped Bakker conceal the [PTL] fraud[s] for over three years by issuing false and misleading financial statements and by secretly issuing the checks which paid Bakker's illegal million dollar a year salary. Without the assistance of the two accounting firms, the lifetime partners claimed, the fraud[s] at PTL could never have happened."

The judge's 140 pages of instructions to the jury illustrated the relative difficulty of proving fraud as compared to proving negligence. The jury was instructed that in order to find Deloitte guilty of aiding and abetting the commission of a fraud by Bakker, the plaintiffs had to prove "that Deloitte had actual knowledge of the fraud and of [Deloitte's] alleged role in furthering that fraud." Furthermore, the plaintiffs had to prove that Deloitte "knowingly and intentionally gave substantial assistance to the fraud" and "that Deloitte's alleged aiding and abetting of the fraud actually and proximately caused harm to the plaintiffs." Clearly, this is much more difficult to prove than mere negligence.

Given the difficulty of proving fraud, why did the plaintiffs pursue a fraud charge as opposed to a negligence charge? Not being a party to the litigation, one can only speculate concerning the plaintiffs' strategy. One reason might be that the plaintiffs recognized that they would have difficulty in proving the lifetime partners actually relied on the audited financial statements prior to purchasing their partnerships. That is, when charges of negligence are brought against auditors, the plaintiffs generally must show that they relied on the (negligently) audited financial statements. However, the plaintiffs cited court cases, over the defendants' objections, that RICO and fraud do not require proof of reliance. Although the plaintiffs contended that they had relied on the work of the auditors, reliance would not be as critical to the plaintiffs in proving a fraud charge as it would be in proving a charge of negligence. Second, if the plaintiffs had been able to prove fraud, securities fraud, time share law violations, and the other elements relating to RICO causes of action, the plaintiffs would have received triple damages and all of the plaintiffs' attorneys' fees would be paid by the defendant.

Jim Williams, the attorney for Deloitte, seemed to recognize that the plaintiffs were really alleging negligence on the part of Deloitte as opposed to intentionally fraudulent misconduct. In speaking to Judge McMillan on April 18, 1990, Williams said, "[t]his is an accounting negligence case, and they're trying to squeeze it into the form of a securities or RICO case. If they had just accused us of some negligence and if this were an accounting negligence case in State Court, I wouldn't be standing here, because there are issues of fact that we would have to try out. But there are not issues of fact with respect to fraud and RICO because they haven't shown we knew of any fraud.''

The point that Williams seemed to be making was that there may be litigable questions of fact for the jury to decide as to whether or not Deloitte exercised proper care and whether or not Deloitte was negligent in its work for PTL. However, because the plaintiffs never sued Deloitte (or Laventhol) based on negligence, no determination was made concerning whether Deloitte committed any negligence or professional malpractice. Instead, the jury in this lawsuit found Deloitte not guilty of knowingly and substantially aiding and abetting Bakker's common law fraud or of knowingly and willfully conspiring with Bakker to commit a common law fraud.

As stated earlier, Laventhol declared bankruptcy just days before it was to present its defense, and none of the plaintiff's allegations concerning Laventhol were resolved. Technically, the proceeding was actually "stayed" as to Laventhol, as is required by the bankruptcy code; should the firm come out of bankruptcy, the charges could be revived. It should also be noted that it is conceivable that the 266 partners and 52 principals of Laventhol could be required to litigate the charges asserted by the plaintiffs in a different forum. It should also be noted that when Laventhol declared bankruptcy in New York, only the case of *Teague v. Bakker* was actually discussed in the complaint.

Another crucial tactical decision was made by the plaintiffs concerning Aimee Cortese. Cortese had knowledge of Jim Bakker's affair with Jessica Hahn. She had, pursuant to instructions from Richard Dortch, delivered money to Hahn in an attempt to silence her, and got her to sign a document releasing PTL from any potential liability. Cortese never shared these critical matters with other board members, matters which could have forced Jim Bakker's resignation according to PTL's own bylaws. These matters were also never presented to the jury in the civil class action litigation. Again, why didn't the jury hear what was arguably devastating evidence against Cortese?

Not having been a party to the litigation, only a courtroom observer, my speculation is that the plaintiffs feared that Cortese's contacts with Hahn and her failure to disclose these matters to other board members could be found by the jury to be *intentional* wrongdoing on the part of Cortese as opposed to simply *negligent* wrongdoing. Cortese's actions as a member of the board of directors were covered by a directors' and officers' insurance policy, which contained provisions covering negligent actions by board members but not intentional wrongdoings. The plaintiffs did not inform the jury of Cortese's involvement in the Hahn matter, possibly because they feared that the insurance company might contend that she engaged in intentional misconduct and would not be covered by the insurance policy. Ultimately, the jury found Cortese not guilty of gross negligence.

Clearly, the "deep pockets" in this litigation were the accounting firms, and they seemed to be the focus of the plaintiffs' case. The challenge facing the plaintiffs' counsel in any accounting case is to present the case in an understandable, credible, and interesting fashion; this was the challenge faced by Anderson and Bird.

The central issue in this case was examining the extent to which the accountants knew of improprieties in the presentation of PTL's financial statements. The initial focus in any plaintiffs' case should be to show that the financial statements are false and misleading and then turn the focus on the defendants to expose what they knew or should have known concerning such improprieties.

In my opinion, this trial should have focused around one issue: "What new evidence came out at the Bakker criminal trial that the auditors didn't already know at the time that they conducted their audit?" If no new evidence was gleaned from the Bakker criminal trial, then how could Deloitte have rendered an unqualified or clean opinion, and how could Laventhol have rendered a qualified opinion, but only in reference to an on-going IRS examination, during the very time the massive wire and mail fraud was occurring at PTL? In other words, if the auditors had all the facts as outlined in the Bakker criminal trial, how could they have failed to detect and note the fraud?

On the other hand, if new evidence came out during the Bakker criminal trial of which the auditors had not previously been aware, then the question has to be asked, "Why were the auditors not aware of that particular evidence?"

I had over 80 of my students attend the civil case on various days. Their unanimous conclusion, which was mine as well, was that the plaintiffs were not persuasive in presenting the voluminous exhibits that were relevant to their case in a logical and orderly fashion.

Issues Not Litigated

As discussed in the next chapter, a wide variety of issues, primarily relating to the auditors' activities at PTL, were litigated in the *Teague v. Bakker* case. However, other, extremely fascinating issues were not fully litigated or explored.

Some of these had to do with PTL's primary contractor, Roe Messner, and his corporation, Commercial Builders of Kansas, Inc., which declared bankruptcy prior to the trial; therefore, the proceeding was stayed as to Roe Messner and his corporation.

Although these issues were never resolved, it should be noted that the plaintiffs charged that Messner and his corporation "participated in, conspired in and aided and abetted wrong doings by [committing] these and other knowing acts: 1) Messner and company's participation in officer embezzlement through laundering the Jessica Hahn payoff and Bakker home improvements; 2) Messner and company's construction embezzlement through massive overcharges and false invoices; 3) Messner and company's donor fraud through Kevin's House; 4) Messner and company's lifetime partnership fraud through televised misleading omissions and misrepresentations."

Roe Messner was more than just the primary builder at PTL. According to the custodian of the videotape, "Roe Messner appeared on the PTL program no less than 87 times between February 22, 1984, and March 7, 1987." On many of those programs Jim Bakker discussed how the lifetime partnership program would operate, including the limitations on the number of lifetime partners and how the funds raised by the program would be used.

Although the entire case against Roe Messner was stayed because of his bankruptcy, nevertheless the "plaintiffs' brief and opposition to defendant Messner" raises numerous questions concerning the business propriety of Messner, and the audit environment in which Deloitte and thereafter Laventhol was working.

The plaintiffs' restated amended complaint, dated August 17, 1990, states that Messner's company "has been paid approximately $70 million by PTL for construction in connection with Heritage USA, and Messner claims that another $14,897,457 is owed him by PTL. Nearly all of that $70 million in construction was done on a no contract basis and without competitive bids until late 1986, and receipts or invoices allegedly do not exist on most of that work; and thereafter the remaining $14,897,457 of construction was done on a cost plus 10% basis."

According to the plaintiffs, the Grand Hotel and Towers Hotel were built without a contract. Starting on January 17, 1984, Jim Bakker made at least three televised statements to the effect that the Grand Hotel was being built without a contract. There was, however, a contract for the building of the Grand Hotel dated December 1, 1983, which, according to the plaintiffs, had been backdated. Likewise, the contract for the Towers Hotel had allegedly been backdated to make it appear as though it had been signed on May 14, 1985. According to the plaintiffs, approximately $27 million of unsupported construction costs had been charged to PTL.

Another construction project that received little, if any, attention during either the Bakker criminal trial or *Teague v. Bakker* was "Kevin's House," which was to have been built for Kevin Whittum, who suffered from brittle bone disease. Although 18 years old at the time the project was being considered, he weighed 20 pounds and measured 28 inches in length. He used a motorized wheelchair to get around.

On April 17, 1986, Jim Bakker described to the PTL television audience how he intended to build Kevin Whittum a house at Heritage USA where he and other handicapped children could live. Bakker made several gut-wrenching appeals concerning Kevin's House; during the May 6, 1986, telecast, he told viewers that PTL was finalizing the blueprints that day, that all the money being raised for Kevin's House was being put into a special bank account, and that construction of the house would continue day and night until it was completed. Bakker wanted to build the house in 30 days.

Kevin Whittum became a frequent guest on the PTL program as Jim Bakker, Richard Dortch, and Doug Oldham kept up their efforts to raise money for what seemed to be a noble undertaking. Over 40,000 people contributed a total of $3,027,856 toward construction of Kevin's House.

On one PTL program in 1986, Doug Oldham, the chair of Kevin's Club, the fundraising effort to build Kevin's House, was told by Richard Dortch that the Bakkers, the Dortchs, and others had each given $1,000 to Kevin's Club. Oldham then said that he and his wife would give $1,000 next payday. It is unclear why Oldham was soliciting others to give when he had not yet given $1,000, given his role as chair of Kevin's Club. As previously noted, Doug Oldham's W-2 form for 1986 reflected that he received total wages of more than $189,000 from PTL.

Although Kevin's House was finally built for approximately $1,554,000, it was never functional as a home for handicapped children because it failed to meet design and building code specifications. Consequently, Kevin Whittum, his adopted sister, and his mother and father were the only ones ever to live there. The plaintiffs (i.e., in *Teague v. Bakker*) alleged that Messner knew that Kevin's House was being represented to the public as a home for handicapped children.

However, the building permit, apparently signed by Roe Messner, stated that the home was to be a "single family dwelling," not a group home for the handicapped as it had been promoted in mailed and televised solicitations. In fact, the plaintiffs cited a terse letter dated May 28, 1986, from Richard Dortch to the York County building inspector, in which he states: "[t]his letter is to certify that the amended plans for Kevin's House are for his residence. This home will be occupied by Kevin, his parents and family members. Cordially, Richard W. Dortch." The plaintiffs further alleged that even while the house was under construction, the defendants were notified by York County authorities that the home did not meet fire safety codes for use as a home for handicapped children because it lacked such requirements for group care as enclosed stairwells, 44-inch wide fire-resistant doors, and the requirement to have fire hydrants nearby.

In the "Jim and Tammy Newsletter" from the summer of 1988, Jim Bakker addressed this apparent inconsistency found in Richard Dortch's memo: "This letter was written to allow Kevin in before the other children because of fears he would die before the house that was named for him could be licensed and occupied as a children's home."

Although the facts and circumstances surrounding the design and construction of Kevin's House may never be fully explored because of Roe Messner's bankruptcy, this project seems to be yet another example of a PTL project that was, at minimum, poorly planned and poorly managed.

On August 18, 1992, Kevin Whittum died at his Michigan home at age 23. Kevin and his family had voluntarily vacated Kevin's House after Jerry Falwell's administration had begun proceedings to remove Kevin from the Victorian-style mansion built by Jim Bakker. The Falwell administration had made plans to allow Kevin to remain at Heritage USA, but in a more modest house.

Kevin's death prompted Jim Bakker to give his first and only interview from prison. "Kevin Whittum was an inspiration to all he came in contact with," Bakker said. "I am deeply grieved by his death, but I know he is in a better place and his tiny body that was racked with pain is made perfect and whole as he walks with his God."

CHAPTER NINE

□□□

Where Were the Auditors?

By certifying the public reports that collectively depict a corporation's financial status, the independent auditor assumes a public responsibility transcending any employment relationship with the client. The independent public accountant performing this special function owes ultimate allegiance to the corporation's creditors and stockholders, as well as to the investing public. The "public watchdog" function demands that the accountant maintain total independence from the client at all times and requires complete fidelity to the public trust.

U.S. Supreme Court discussing the role of the independent auditor
in the case *United States v. Arthur Young*,
465 U.S. 805, 817–18 (1984)

IN ORDER TO APPRECIATE the significance of the role played by Deloitte and then Laventhol as PTL's independent auditors, it is essential to understand exactly what an auditor does. After discussing the duties of an auditor, in particular the auditor's duty to remain independent and whether or not an auditor has a duty to detect fraud, this chapter examines some of the issues that arose from the *Teague* litigation and ends by drawing a disturbing parallel between the PTL audits and the savings and loan crisis.

What Do Auditors Do?

Auditors and accountants offer and provide a wide array of services to their clients, including tax and business planning, management advisory services, compilation and review services, and financial audits. The accountant may also be engaged to perform specialized procedures to meet a client's specific needs including procedures designed to uncover theft or other illegal acts. The responsibilities of both client and auditor are spelled out for their mutual understanding in an engagement letter.

Of all the many services offered by accountants, the financial audit is the most commonly requested (and important). Approximately 50 percent of the Big Six firms' revenue comes from performing audits; the remainder comes from consulting work and tax work.

The independent audit is generally defined as being a professional evaluation of corporate financial statements by an outside or independent auditor and is designed to provide the financial statement user with reasonable assurances that management has not unfairly biased the economic information in its favor. The financial statements generally consist of a balance sheet, which lists the corporation's assets and liabilities; an income statement, which reflects the corporation's operating results through its revenues and expenditures; and a cash flow statement, which reflects the flow of cash into and out of the corporation.

The objective of an audit is to determine whether a given corporation's financial statements, as prepared by its management, fairly present the corporation's financial position and operating results. To make this determination, the information contained in the corporation's financial statements is verified by examining underlying accounting records and other such evidence. Auditors are required to prepare and maintain work papers that reflect the overall plan for the audit and the specific procedures that the audit team is to perform; in addition, auditors also prepare more detailed papers that reflect work on internal controls and the substantive test of the financial statements.

Auditors work with a pyramid-style management structure to complete their assigned tasks; the number of auditors assigned to an engagement depends on its size. At the top of the pyramid is the person ultimately responsible for the audit, the *partner-in-charge,* below whom are the audit manager, the audit senior, and a few (or possibly a platoon of) staff auditors. Accountants who perform audits are generally well compensated for their professional services. An article in the *New York Times* cited "company documents" in estimating that the average earnings per partner at Deloitte, Haskins and Sells for fiscal year 1989 were $240,000; the same article estimated that the average earnings per partner for fiscal year 1989 were

$245,000 at Touche and Ross, $228,100 at Ernst and Whinney, and $156,100 at Arthur Young.

The American Institute of Certified Public Accountants (AICPA), the professional association of CPA's, has promulgated principles and standards to guide accountants in their profession. For example, all auditors follow procedures commonly referred to as Generally Accepted Auditing Standards (GAAS), which include examining tangible assets and inventory; confirming the corporation's account balances; tracing recorded transactions; and speaking with management, creditors, purchasers, and other business associates.

The GAAS, therefore, constitute the basic professional standards for conducting an audit; they range from broadly stated guidelines (for example, "[d]ue professional care is to be exercised in the performance of the examination and the preparation of the report") to more precise procedural directives that amplify and expand on the general provisions.

GAAS procedures are utilized to ensure that the corporation's financial statements present its financial position fairly and in accordance with another set of accounting rules, Generally Accepted Accounting Principles (GAAP), which govern methods of quantifying and recording assets, liabilities, revenues, and expenditures. The goal of GAAP is to attempt to ensure some degree of uniformity in the reporting of financial data from various companies.

The actual audit process can be divided into five stages. The auditor first plans the audit by gathering information about the corporation's internal business and accounting systems. Next, the auditor uses this knowledge to evaluate the client's own internal controls. During the third stage, the auditor ensures the proper control in the execution and recording of corporate transactions. In the fourth stage, the auditor examines documentation and verifies account balances in order to test the audit system and in particular to determine if the client's own internal controls are reliable. Finally, the auditor issues a report, usually one page in length, stating that the audit was conducted in accordance with GAAS and offering an opinion as to whether the corporation's financial statements present its financial position fairly and in accordance with GAAP.

There are four types of reports, the most common (and most desired) of which is the *unqualified report,* which documents that the auditor believes that the financial statements have been fairly presented. However, auditors do not consider an unqualified opinion to be an absolute "clean bill of health."

A *qualified opinion* may be necessitated by a material uncertainty within the financial statements or deviations from the GAAP, whereas an *adverse opinion* results from financial statements that do not fairly present the firm's financial position in conformance with GAAP. Finally, the auditor may issue a *disclaimer of opinion,* which is issued when the auditor lacks sufficient information to form an opinion; this is often the result of inadequate recordkeeping on the part of the client.

It should be noted that every audit is subject to certain constraints. Because the auditor does not examine each available piece of evidence but only samples various entries and transactions using a statistical methodology designed to arrive at a reasonably accurate judgment, there is always some room for error.

Compliance with GAAP and GAAS can substantially reduce the likelihood that an auditor will be subjected to liability but is not in itself a complete defense. For example, in *United States v. Simon,* 425 F. 2d 796 (1970), the Second Circuit U.S. Court of Appeals ruled as follows:

> Generally Accepted Accounting Principles [GAAP] instruct an accountant what to do in the usual case where he has no reason to doubt that the affairs of the corporation are being honestly conducted. Once he has reason to believe that this basic assumption is false, an entirely different situation confronts him.

Consistent with this ruling, an Oregon Court of Appeals held that the GAAP and GAAS standards "may be useful to a jury in determining the standard of care for an auditor, but . . . are not controlling."

Therefore, in critiquing and evaluating an auditor's work, one should certainly consider GAAP and GAAS as starting points for proper evaluation, not as absolute standards. The question that remains is, What are the auditor's duties and responsibilities concerning the detection and reporting of fraud? Shouldn't this be one of the most important objectives of an audit?

There is a wide discrepancy between what auditors themselves and what the public (and the courts) perceive an audit to entail, especially in relation to the amount of assurance that an audit provides. This disparity is commonly referred to as "the expectation gap."

Many people believe that auditors act as corporate detectives possessing cool logic, a skeptical air, and an independent voice, that they ferret out fraud, dig out aberrations, and blow the whistle at even the slightest hint of corporate wrongdoing. Many people see a clean audit opinion as similar to a "Good Housekeeping Seal of Approval," grudgingly given by auditors after painstakingly combing through the records, tracking down every lead, and finding no wrong or impropriety.

The Supreme Court, in *United States v. Arthur Young and Company*, found that auditors, although selected and compensated by their clients, have duties that may extend beyond the client to certain third parties and public investors. Indeed, the court ruled that "the independent auditor assumes a public responsibility transcending any employment relationship with the client" and serves as a "public watchdog." Watchdogs should be willing to "bite" and certainly to "bark" when they see irregularities within a company. What type of watchdog did PTL have?

The auditors themselves, however, generally believe that their work entails expressing an "opinion on the fairness with which [the financial statements] present the [company's] financial position in conformity with Generally Accepted Accounting Principles."[1]

Historically, auditors have considered fraud detection to be a primary function of auditing. In fact, auditing textbooks from the early 1900s listed the threefold objectives of the audit as "the detection of fraud, the detection of technical errors, and the detection of errors of principle."[2] By the late 1930s, however, there seemed to be a consensus among auditors that they should not be primarily concerned with the detection of fraud.

In 1977, the pendulum swung slightly, and auditors, according to their "statement on auditing standards," required that the auditor "search for" errors and irregularities as opposed to stating affirmatively that the auditor had a duty to detect fraud. From a practical point of view, the auditor could assume that management was honest and that supporting documentation was genuine. Given this level of presumption as opposed to a negative presumption, it was unwarranted to rely on auditors to detect management fraud. In reality, auditors remained unwilling to acknowledge any substantial responsibility for detecting fraud beyond assuring that the financial statements complied with GAAP.

While the standards for auditors' detection of fraud changed in 1989, and the accounting profession has taken affirmative steps in an attempt to "close" the expectation gap, it may be that the accounting profession has done too little, too late. Given this standard of responsibility for detecting fraud, "where were the auditors at PTL during the time of the massive wire and mail fraud?"

The PTL Audits and Oversale of Lifetime Partnerships

Issues Relating to Deloitte

Although numerous issues (and very serious allegations) were raised and discussed in the *Teague* litigation, by far the most critical of these concerned the actions and inactions of PTL's independent auditors regarding the oversale of lifetime partnerships. How is it that neither Deloitte nor Laventhol detected the wire and mail frauds?

Deloitte served as PTL's independent accountant and auditor from 1977 until May 1985, when Laventhol took the post. For the fiscal year ending May 31, 1984, PTL's financial statements received an unqualified opinion in an audit report by Deloitte that was dual-dated August 31, 1984, and October 24, 1984.

The Deloitte audit team spent approximately 1,350 hours on its 1984 audit of PTL; they worked on-site at Heritage USA for approximately two to three months and charged at least $165,000 for their services.

On January 18, 1984, Bob Brown, partner-in-charge of Deloitte's audit of PTL, and Guy Forcucci, one of Deloitte's tax partners, met with Richard Dortch, Peter Bailey, and two attorneys for PTL, John Yorke and Don Etheridge. It was at this meeting that Deloitte first became aware of the Grand Hotel lifetime partnership concept. The next day, Etheridge prepared a memo that reflected his thoughts concerning the solicitation. Etheridge stated that the PTL brochure soliciting Grand Hotel lifetime partners "is somewhat misleading in that it appears to be for a charitable type purpose." His memo also noted that the "obvious legal issues involved" included: "application of South Carolina timesharing law to the offering" and "[t]he possibility of a securities offering . . . ." It is not clear if Etheridge expressed these concerns at the January 18, 1984, meeting, but clearly he and Yorke had discussed them.

In addition to these "obvious legal issues," Deloitte was fully aware of the limited number of lifetime partnerships for the Grand Hotel. The manager of the Deloitte audit team testified "[t]hat limitation was based on discussions with people at PTL, I believe it is also based on the brochure that went out to the lifetime partners." Significantly, the 25,000-member limit was also reflected in a commitment and contingencies note to PTL's interim financial statements that were prepared for the six-month period ending November 30, 1983. That note stated in part: "The total amount of one time partner gifts has been limited to $25 million. As of March 20, 1984, approximately $17 million in pledges had been received, of which, approximately $9 million had been collected." Testimony received in the *Teague* case indicated that the note was probably drafted by a member of the Deloitte audit team. The year-end audited financial statements did not contain any reference to the limit that had been placed on the number of Grand Hotel lifetime partnerships.

There was a sharp conflict in testimony during the *Teague* litigation concerning whether or not the Grand Hotel lifetime partnership program's membership limit should have been included in the year-end financial statements. The plaintiffs contended that the professional accounting standards required such disclosure, and disclosing the 25,000-member limitation of the Grand Hotel and lifetime partnerships was useful information to financial statement readers. Deloitte argued that such disclosure might be interesting but was not necessary or required by the professional accounting standards.

The financial statements for fiscal year 1984 contained $16,816,117 of deferred revenue collected from lifetime partnership contributions. No mention was made in the notes to these financial statements or in the auditor's report that the Grand Hotel lifetime partnerships had been oversold or that the number of lifetime partnerships for the Grand had been limited to 25,000.

The amount of deferred revenue listed on the financial statements was correct. However, what had been omitted from the financial statements and from the auditor's report was the fact that the number of lifetime partnerships for the Grand had exceeded 25,000 on July 7, 1984. But did Deloitte have an obligation to examine the number of lifetime partnerships sold after May 31, 1984, PTL's fiscal year-end date? The plaintiffs in the *Teague* case said that not only did Deloitte have an obligation to determine the number of lifetime partnerships sold for the Grand prior to signing the auditor's report but that Deloitte must have known of the oversale.

Deloitte contended that its audit team had been well aware of the limits that had been placed on the Grand Hotel and the Towers Hotel lifetime partnership programs. However, Deloitte strongly asserted that while its team was doing the audit, PTL never exceeded those stated limits. In fact, the last audit that Deloitte provided for PTL was for the fiscal year ending May 31, 1984. The Towers Hotel had not even been introduced as of that date, and the Grand Hotel was not oversold until July 7, 1984. But Deloitte's unqualified audit report on PTL's financial statements was signed after that date. Were there certain checking procedures that Deloitte should have followed that would have detected the oversale of lifetime partnerships?

Bob Brown, the partner-in-charge of the PTL audit, testified that not only did he not inquire concerning PTL's sales of lifetime partnerships after May 31, 1984, but also did not think the number of partnerships sold by PTL as of August 31, 1984, was available. When Brown was asked to "[t]ell us every reason you know of, sir, that on August 31, '84, the number of sales weren't available to you," he responded, "I don't think that their system provided adequate information that would give you a reliable number." Brown's testimony was confirmed by PTL's Jeff Eggen.

It is unclear how Deloitte intended to proceed with any degree of technical confidence with the audit given this sworn testimony by Brown. PTL's inability to provide adequate information and give a reliable number of lifetime partnership sales wasn't the only flaw in their system of internal accounting controls.

Deloitte prepared a 23-page document designed to evaluate PTL's "system of internal controls" as required by GAAS. According to Deloitte, the "study and evaluation disclosed no condition that [Deloitte] believe[d was] a material weakness." However, the next 22 pages disclose "conditions that, although not considered by [Deloitte] to be material weaknesses, are weaknesses in internal control for which corrective action might be taken." Deloitte proceeded to list specific findings and backgrounds and then provided a recommendation to PTL concerning these "weaknesses in internal accounting control[s]," some of which are listed here:

1. Mail receipts, which can exceed $1 million per day, are picked up at the post office by unarmed couriers. The couriers do go in pairs, but partners are not rotated on a regular basis.
2. Cash receipts are handled several times by individuals in the cashier's department before initial recording.
3. Advances to employees are sometimes made for as much as $10,000. (Deloitte went on to recommend that PTL should "[e]stablish a maximum employee advance amount. Advances in excess of this amount should be made only when specific documentation for the purpose of the advance is provided and approved ahead of time.")
4. Many outstanding employee advances are over six months old. (For background, Deloitte acknowledged that "[t]he age of these advances indicates a lack of effective follow-up on the part of the Ministry once an advance is made.")

5. Adequate documentation of travel and meal charges made on American Express cards is frequently not received or maintained by the ministry.

6. Journal entries may be made without sufficient documentation attached to support the entry.

7. There is no formal system to inventory and identify property items or to compare such items in the property records.

8. There is no system for recording donated assets retained for use by the Ministry in the property records.

9. The Ministry pays $12 per check for payroll checks returned for not sufficient funds (NSF). Charges amounted to approximately $20,000 in May 1984 alone.

10. There are 23 bank accounts for PTL and 12 for the Campgrounds.

11. No formal system exists for capital budgets. (Deloitte recommended that PTL "[i]mplement and maintain a formal system for capital budgeting which would be submitted for approval by the Board of Directors.")

12. Numerous adjusting journal entries (over 150) were made during the 1984 examination as a result of our audit procedures. (Of significance, Deloitte stated that "[t]he excessive number of entries required indicate that the accounting department has been unable to perform some important functions, such as periodic review of the general ledger, investigation and correction of errors, and analysis of specific accounts. An increase in the qualified staff of the accounting department and reassignment of duties among existing staff is critically needed to help alleviate this problem.")

13. The Ministry does not currently provide functional reporting of expenses in the statements of revenues and expenses.

Given all of these weaknesses in PTL's internal accounting control, how could Deloitte have been reasonably certain about anything during its audit? Furthermore, did PTL intentionally or unintentionally have a control environment that was conducive to fraud?

For example, PTL wasn't bouncing just its payroll checks; many checks to parties with whom PTL did business were also bouncing. On April 12, 1984, PTL's check written to their building contractor,

Roe Messner, was returned for "insufficient funds." The amount of the check was $1,000,000.

Carl Dean, senior vice-president for Security Bank and Trust Company of Charlotte, North Carolina, testified that PTL had between 15 and 20 checking accounts with his bank in 1985 (when Laventhol was PTL's auditor) and that he had to talk to Peter Bailey about PTL's chronic bounced-check problem as often as twice a month. The bank charged PTL $15 for every check that bounced, and as many as 250 checks bounced on any given day. The situation was so bad that the bank was concerned whether or not PTL would be able to repay its loan, which had been secured by the TV station, one of the chapels at PTL, the Children and Youth Rec Center, and several pieces of property within the PTL complex. The bank demanded payment of the loan, and PTL had to go to another bank to acquire the money to pay off the loan to Security Bank.

Although PTL always covered the bounced checks, funds had to be continually transferred from the various accounts; on occasion, money was wired in to cover checks from the previous day. Dean testified that he would "spend maybe an hour [or] two hours a day looking after [the PTL] account."

While major checks to PTL's builders and employee payroll checks may have been bouncing, there were some checks that never bounced. Dean's testimony was particularly interesting concerning problems he had with the general payroll account versus the executive payroll account, from which Bakker and another corporate officers were paid:

> Q: And was there a problem with non-sufficient funds checks on [the general] payroll account from time to time?
> A: Oh, yes, on many times in the month. It was a matter that, you know, I would tell Peter Bailey, I said Peter, you had money in the other account, why did you move it in the payroll account instead of having all those bad checks out of that account, and I never did get a satisfactory answer.

□ □ □

> Q: Was there ever a problem with non-sufficient funds checks on the account that Mr. Bakker's check was paid from?
> A: Not to my knowledge.

This was the business and audit environment Deloitte found itself working in while doing the audit of PTL. Given this environment, should Deloitte have been skeptical of PTL's representations concerning total sales of lifetime partnerships?

Auditors are to disclose information when such is necessary to keep the financial statements from being misleading. This obligation applies not only to the period of the audit but extends to the date of the auditor's report. Thus, in addition to the period of time covered by the audit, the auditors must also examine anything relevant to their work during the subsequent events period, which "is considered to extend from the balance sheet date [in this case, May 31, 1984] to the date of the auditor's report," in this case, August 31, 1984. This is why the plaintiffs contended that Deloitte should have disclosed the fact that the lifetime partnerships had been oversold as of July 7, 1984.

Auditors are supposed to perform certain checking procedures upon completion of the field work. If any subsequent event is deemed important, "the auditor may wish to include in his [sic] report an explanatory paragraph directing the reader's attention to the event and its effects."

The auditing standards (specifically AU Section 560) outlines specific procedures that auditors are to follow during the subsequent events period. Deloitte apparently complied with all such requirements. Specifically, Deloitte had discussions with management regarding possible contingencies and received assurances from management that everything was fine. Deloitte also inquired of PTL's legal counsel concerning litigations, plans, and assessments. Be all this as it may, AU Section 560.12f requires the auditor to "[m]ake such additional inquiries or perform such procedures as he [sic] considers necessary and appropriate to dispose of questions that arise in carrying out the foregoing procedures, inquiries, and discussions." The *Teague* plaintiffs contended that this provision specifically required Deloitte to check on the number of sales for the Grand Hotel lifetime partnership program during the subsequent events period.

Mary K. Cline, an auditor for Deloitte who served as audit senior during the PTL audit, testified that she was personally and totally responsible for doing the "subsequent events" work, and signed off as having performed the steps comprising Deloitte's procedures in auditing PTL. Cline, who at the time had four and a half years of auditing experience, explained that she determined the amount of lifetime partnership contributions as recorded in PTL's general ledger as of May 31, 1984. She testified that the number and amount of contributions made after that date was never an issue in her mind "because we were auditing as of May 31, 1984." Other Deloitte auditors who were a part of the PTL engagement confirmed that they were never aware that more than 25,000 lifetime partnerships had been exceeded by PTL. "Well, we make a lot of judgements in the course of the audit, and we were auditing the balance sheets as of May 31, and there was no reason in my judgment to look at this number after May 31," attested Cline.

Testimony from the Deloitte auditors indicated that in early May 1984, and while planning the 1984 audit, Deloitte was informed by Bailey that $22 million had been pledged to date for the Grand. This $22 million was an "unaudited number," and Deloitte was correct in not recognizing pledges as income. However, this number is important in another regard; PTL was getting close to reaching its proclaimed $25 million cap on the Grand solicitations and would reach that amount sometime in the summer of 1984 if the rate of contributions stayed the same.

The following testimony given by Cline, in response to Tom Anderson's questions, neatly summarizes Deloitte's stance regarding the oversale question:

Q: Tell us all the information you have that as of August 31, 1984, that the sales, cash, had not exceeded $25 million?
A: I don't have any information on that.
Q: And that is basically because nobody asked?
A: Correct, that's what we have gone through.

The audit manager, Ted Leinbach, was asked the same questions and responded this way:

Q: My question to you, sir, did you determine as of August 31, 1984, please, the amount of sales of the Grand?
A: No, sir, I don't recall we did.
Q: So, you can't tell us as of that date how many sales had been made?
A: No, sir, I cannot.

Also, Deloitte was putting in large amounts of audit and tax time during the very time the overselling of lifetime partnerships was occurring. Exhibit 9-1 represents PTL's bills for hundreds of hours Deloitte was spending at Heritage USA doing audit and tax work. Yet, they failed to detect the oversale of Grand Hotel lifetime partnerships.

Auditors are not only required to inquire about illegal acts but are, of course, also required to disclose them when material amounts of revenue have been derived from transactions involving illegal acts.

Deloitte contends that it was never aware that the Grand Hotel had been oversold and furthermore that there had been no reason to

AUDIT

6/22/84	$ 3,400.00
6/22/84	2,100.00
7/19/84	12,500.00
7/27/84	11,750.00
8/15/84	10,500.00
8/29/84	8,000.00
9/7/84	9,700.00
9/14/84	10,000.00
9/20/84	18,500.00
10/24/84	4,700.00
11/14/84	8,500.00
TOTAL	99,650.00

TAX

6/2/84 ....$	3,700.00
6/28/84	6,900.00
8/24/84	19,000.00
9/20/84	18,000.00
11/1/84	21,000.00
11/14/84	5,420.00
11/30/84	6,000.00
12/12/84	5,000.00
1/10/85	7,800.00
TOTAL	$ 92,820.00
GRAND TOTAL	$192,470.00

Exhibit 9-1   Invoices Sent by Deloitte to PTL

even suspect such might be the case. It is also important to note that PTL's top management never indicated to Deloitte (or to Laventhol) that there were illegal acts transpiring at PTL. Furthermore, Archie Mangum, a member of the Public Oversight Board, testified for Deloitte. Mangum stated that Deloitte "did an excellent audit and that is my firm belief."

The Public Oversight Board is an autonomous body consisting of five prominent individuals who have an extensive background in finance and business. According to Mangum's testimony, the Public Oversight Board "is to be the public watchdog or the representative of the public to ensure or to monitor the quality control procedures that are instituted by the various accounting firms."

Before considering Mangum's testimony concerning Deloitte's audit of PTL, it is important to put his testimony in proper context of what he considered an auditor's functions to be. When questioned by Anderson, Mangum testified under oath as follows:

Q: Would you agree, sir, that an auditor also performs a function of a public watchdog?
A: No, sir, they do not.

□ □ □

Q: Do you ever remember reading a United States Supreme Court case that used the phrase public watchdog?
A: They may have used that word in that particular case, . . . but that does not assign to an auditor any responsibility as being a public watchdog.

□ □ □

Q: And certainly they [Deloitte] didn't owe a public watchdog function to the people who purchased the lifetime partnerships. Correct?
A: . . . the only obligation they had in connection with those financial statements is to make an audit in accordance with general accepted accounting principles and to report accordingly.

Deloitte took the position that it had not been required to determine, as a part of the subsequent events review procedures, the amount of money or the number of lifetime partners received from the lifetime partnership program after May 31, 1984. As explained by Mangum in his testimony:

[Deloitte was] auditing the year end May 31, 1984, and just as you don't go to determine . . . what the sales are for any business after the year that you are auditing . . . [Deloitte] had no obligation or no reason to check on the other contributions . . . so they had no reason for, quite honestly, wasting the client's money by spending time on something that did not affect the May 31 numbers.

Later in his testimony, Mangum returned to the issue of whether or not Deloitte had an obligation to inquire as to the number of lifetime partnerships sold after May 31, 1984. He testified "that you are not concerned with the revenue that is collected after year end, whether it be recorded as current year revenue or deferred revenue. . . . What you are concerned with is this number that is in the financial statement. . . . not what they did after year end."

Archie Mangum noted that it was appropriate to disclose in the notes to PTL's interim financial statements that PTL had received $17 million in pledges and of that amount, had collected $9 million, because doing so provided an explanation of "where they were going to get the money to pay for the building. . . ." Also, according to the Deloitte audit senior, Mary K. Cline, "we had looked at the pledge issue during the course of the audit and decided that they were not going to be recorded on the financial statements, so they are not in the financial statements." The pledges were not legally enforceable, and not all the pledges made were collected.

The plaintiffs argued that Deloitte was well aware of the fact that PTL was about to reach the 25,000-member cap on the Grand Hotel lifetime partnership program. At the rate that PTL was receiving subscriptions for the Grand Hotel lifetime partnership program, the plaintiffs contended that PTL would have raised $26.9 million by August 31, 1984, and that pledge subscriptions would have amounted to $31 million by August 31, 1984.

Deloitte was also aware of the tremendous cash crisis PTL was facing, as evinced by the memos that Peter Bailey wrote to Jim Bakker on September 13, 1984: "The main concern expressed in [Deloitte's] report is whether PTL will be able to continue as a 'going concern' based on current assets of only $8.6 million against $28.5 million in current liabilities. There is a concern whether PTL will have the ability to meet its debt obligations during the coming year." (Exhibit A-31.) The prospective sale of Towers Hotel lifetime partnerships was one reason why Deloitte did not deliver a qualified opinion. It is difficult to understand how Deloitte could understand PTL's future financial plans but yet not evaluate the current sales status of the Grand Hotel lifetime partnerships.

Ultimately, Deloitte was able to alleviate their concern and not issue a qualified opinion based on representations made by management concerning funds to be received from the Towers Hotel lifetime partnerships. That concern was not satisfied until October 24, 1984, which was the date of the auditor's report regarding Note 7 of the financial statements concerning subsequent events.

Of course, as previously noted and discussed, Peter Bailey was writing voluminous memos painting a rather gloom-and-doom picture of the cash flow crisis that existed at PTL. Although the auditors never saw the Bailey memos, it is puzzling that Peter Bailey and the auditors apparently came to two different conclusions concerning the financial status of PTL. (Bailey did testify that he never thought PTL would go bankrupt.)

According to Deloitte's witness, Archie Mangum, Deloitte complied with all of the provisions of GAAP and GAAS. Mangum also testified that Deloitte conducted a "darn good audit." But was it really? Might there have been more that Deloitte could have or should have done? Obviously, it is easy enough using today's 20/20 hindsight to say what else Deloitte should have done. But shouldn't GAAP and GAAS and the entire audit function be premised on professional skepticism? That is, don't auditing standards presume that auditors will not merely follow the technical standards outlined in GAAP and GAAS but also apply them as appropriate to the audit environment? Neither GAAP nor GAAS can be expected to address every conceivable contingency that may arise during the audit process. However, a mature level of professional skepticism must and is presumed to be a part of each audit activity and must undergird each of the standards promulgated by the accounting profession. Isn't this what the investing public expects, and isn't this what the expectation gap is really all about?

The American Institute of Certified Public Accountants (AICPA) has adopted generally accepted auditing standards, three of which apply to every phase of the audit engagement:

A. The audit is to be performed by a person or persons having adequate training and proficiency as an auditor.
B. In all matters relating to the assignment, an independence in mental attitude is to be maintained by the auditor or auditors.
C. Due professional care is to be exercised in the performance of the audit and the preparation of the report.

It seems to me that this standard requires auditors to exercise professional skepticism as part of their work.

But exactly how skeptical should an auditor be? In making that determination, auditors should examine the environment in which they are working. Just as certain conditions must be present in order to grow cultures within a biology laboratory, generally certain conditions must be present in order to "grow" corporate fraud. Auditors need to be aware of this and look for internal controls that would not only detect but also discourage fraud. The auditor should have a "show me" attitude; that is, auditors should demand a high degree of verification and documentation rather than simply accept management's contentions.

Was there evidence of matters transpiring at PTL that should have alerted the auditors to the possibility of fraud? Such would clearly appear to be the case.

During my days at the SEC, when a corporation under our investigation was strapped for cash, we knew to be especially inquisitive. Not only Peter Bailey's memos but also PTL's financial statements show that PTL was in constant and dire need of massive infusions of cash. Even to a casual observer, this might have suggested that PTL might be trying to cut corners in order to sustain corporate existence. If this makes sense to the casual observer, shouldn't it have been even more readily apparent to paid professionals?

Because PTL's principal income-producing projects were the lifetime partnership programs, it would seem that outside professionals would have had a clear and firm understanding of the program, how it was supposed to work, and how it was actually being implemented. As previously discussed, PTL was receiving huge sums of money (and in its later years, the majority of its money) from the lifetime partnership programs. Where were the auditors and the attorneys when all of this was going on?

Ted Leinbach, Deloitte's audit manager for the PTL engagement, took notes concerning a meeting he had with PTL attorneys; these were introduced in evidence in the *Teague* litigation. Some of the statements found in Leinbach's note are very interesting, especially in relation to the topic of professional skepticism (or lack thereof). For example, Leinbach writes: "Tax counsel considering withdrawing from PTL; Accountants and Attorneys aren't allowed to talk to Board of Directors; [and] IRS exam will find private inurement and it'll go to court, we'll lose."(Exhibit A-32.) Leinbach explained in court that his statement concerning private inurement reflects what one of PTL's attorneys said would happen to PTL in an absolute worst-case scenario and that neither he nor the attorneys believed that anything like that would ever happen.

Issues Relating to Laventhol

Although Deloitte's position was that its audit team had known of the limits placed on the Grand Hotel but not that PTL had exceeded them, Laventhol took an opposite but somewhat consistent position. Laventhol's position was that its audit team had known the total number of lifetime partnerships that had been sold but had been unaware of any promised limitations on the lodging facilities at Heritage USA.

During 1985 and 1986, a number of Laventhol auditors spent more than 4000 hours obtaining necessary information and written representations from PTL's attorneys and from PTL's top-level management. Based on this information, Laventhol believed they had a reasonable basis to opine on PTL's 1985 and 1986 financial statements.

According to the government exhibits that were introduced into evidence at Jim Bakker's criminal trial, over 1.3 million brochures were mailed by PTL expressing some type of limitation on either the Grand Hotel or the Towers Hotel partnership programs. This, of course, is in addition to the numerous statements to that effect made by Jim Bakker on television.

Laventhol's auditors testified that they never saw these brochures or knew of any limitations. Specifically, the audit manager, Samuel Long III, testified as follows:

> Q: Did you ever run across any document in any place that indicated there was a limitation for 25,000 or 30,000 [partnerships for the Grand or the Towers]?
> A: No.

□ □ □

> Q: Now, sir, did you ever ask anybody what it was that PTL sent to the lifetime partners in writing?
> A: We asked, when we were trying to get information concerning the lifetime partnership program, whether or not there was a written contract, and we were told that there was not. And then we asked, you know, various questions, trying to get information about the terms and the details of the, you know, the lifetime partnership program. And at that point in time we were, you know, we were given copies of letters that were sent out to the partners after they had, you know, had signed, had sent their money in and become partners. What I referred to as welcome letters.

□ □ □

> Q: Well, what did you think it was, sir, that lifetime partners responded to?
> A: Well, promotional materials or appeals on the air.
> Q: What did you think those promotional materials were, sir?
> A: I don't know what they were.

Furthermore, Long did not ask Peter Bailey what the promotional materials were because, as Long testified, "[t]hose were promotional materials and are not financial documents. . . ."

Bill Spears, the partner-in-charge of Laventhol's PTL audit, testified he was unaware of the 25,000-member cap on the Grand Hotel partnership program until Laventhol was named a defendant in the *Teague* litigation.

A Laventhol work paper used by the plaintiffs in the *Teague* litigation to defeat the defendant's motion for summary judgment states that "Crystal Towers is to be started in '87. Towers w/b first construction moved up because overbooked on HG Towers. Commitments to be disclosed at 5/31/86." It is unclear exactly what the writer of this work paper meant by the phrase "construction moved up because overbooked on H[eritage] G[rand] Towers." (Exhibit A-33.)

The initial Grand Hotel lifetime partnership brochure was developed and mailed while Deloitte was PTL's independent auditor. As mentioned earlier, that brochure was mailed to 140,282 individuals and clearly indicated that only 25,000 lifetime partnerships for the Grand Hotel were available.

When Bill Spears was asked under oath about that brochure, he testified as follows:

Q: Did you see the brochure in the work papers of Deloitte?
A: No.
Q: Do you know now that they were there, do you now know that a brochure was in fact in the work papers of Deloitte?
A: Based on testimony I've heard in this trial, it apparently was.
Q: Can you explain why it was, sir, that you didn't see the brochure?
A: The brochure was not in the May 31, 1984 audit working papers. It was somewhere else. I don't know where it was. It probably was in a permanent file that was not given to us.

It should be noted that Peter Bailey, PTL's chief financial officer, testified that he did not recall having seen the brochure until 1987, after he had left PTL, and that he never discussed the Grand Hotel limits with anyone from Laventhol.

Auditors from Laventhol also testified that they had not seen the Deloitte review report for PTL's interim financial statements for the period ending November 30, 1983, the notes to which reflected the limitation on the Grand Hotel and specifically stated that "the total amount of one time partner gifts has been limited to $25 million."

Like Deloitte, Laventhol was apparently not privy to the Bailey memos. Like Deloitte, Laventhol never issued a going concern qualification, and never detected any fraud. However, it should be noted that the Laventhol work papers stated that, "PTL's televised broadcast was viewed periodically by staff throughout the engagement."

Laventhol responded to the Bakker fraud by contending that even though its audit team had not known of the limitations placed on the Grand and Towers Hotels, the notes to PTL's financial statements disclosed, rather than "covered up," the number of lifetime partnerships as of the end of each audited fiscal year. Specifically, Note 5 to PTL's 1985 audited financial statements reflected that PTL had received the following sums from lifetime partners as of May 31, 1985: $16,827,547 prior to June 1, 1984, and $30,485,303 during fiscal year 1985 with respect to the Grand Hotel lifetime partnerships, and $19,001,159 during fiscal year 1985 with respect to the Towers lifetime partnerships.

Note 5 to PTL's 1986 financial statements reflect that PTL had received the following sums from lifetime partners as May 31, 1986: [i] $16,827,547 prior to June 1, 1984, and $30,485,303 during fiscal year 1985, and $18,516,703 during fiscal year 1986 with respect to the Grand Hotel lifetime partnerships; (ii) $19,001,159 during fiscal 1985 and $20,319,006 during fiscal 1986 with respect to the Towers lifetime partnerships.

Because lifetime partnerships cost $1,000 each, it would have been easy enough to simply divide each of the cumulative numbers by 1,000 to determine the number of lifetime partnerships that had actually been sold. Using this method, Note 5 to PTL's 1985 audited financial statements would indicate that approximately 47,000 lifetime partnerships had been sold for the Grand Hotel and about 19,000 had been sold for the Towers Hotel. As well, the 1986 audited financial statements would indicate that over 65,000 memberships had been sold for the Grand Hotel lifetime partnership program and over 39,000 Towers lifetime partnerships had been sold.

Also, in compliance with GAAS, Laventhol solicited and obtained information from PTL's attorneys concerning their knowledge of asserted and unasserted claims against PTL during its 1985 and 1986 audits. Deloitte obtained the same information during its audit of PTL's financial statements.

Even if Laventhol had not known of the promised limits on the hotels and had not received evidence of managerial irregularities from PTL's officers and legal representatives, then what about the practical limits of the hotels at PTL? At the time Laventhol completed the 1986 audit, the plaintiffs contended that there were 68,041 fully paid Grand Hotel lifetime partners and 53,691 fully paid Towers lifetime partnerships. It would have been impossible to fulfill the promise of four days and three nights of lodging for each of the lifetime partners in the 250 rooms available in the Grand Hotel—in fact, the promises could not have been fulfilled even if *all* the rooms in the Grand were made available to lifetime partners. In short, the promised lodging, given the total sales, was a physical impossibility. That is why Jim Bakker is in jail.

In summary, Laventhol knew the total number of lifetime partnerships not only from having access to the computer runs giving cumulative totals of lifetime partners but also by simply having divided the total dollars received for each program by 1,000. However, Laventhol testified that they were unaware of any limitations on the number of lifetime partnerships that could be offered.

PTL and Issues Relating to Solvency

In the *Teague* case, both accounting firms maintained that their decisions not to issue a so-called going concern, or qualified, auditor's opinion was a reasonable judgment consistent with the facts and all relevant professional standards. In fact, PTL was a going concern even until May 31, 1987. Laventhol pointed out that PTL's balance sheets for May 31, 1985, and May 31, 1986, clearly reflected that PTL's current assets were less than its current liabilities as of those dates. However, PTL's total assets exceeded its total liabilities on both May 31, 1985, and May 31, 1986.

PTL's bounced check problem continued during Laventhol's tenure as PTL's independent auditor. Laventhol noted in its work papers that "NSF fees are ridiculous each month" and that checking accounts were being closed "with insufficient funds to cover any outstanding checks." In addition, Laventhol had the unusal entry, on the 1985 and 1986 financial statements of "checks issued against future deposits." This is what Peter Bailey had discussed in his January 1985 memo as a "float."

Deloitte's expert witness, Archie Mangum, testified that although PTL may have had a cash flow or liquidity problem, the corporation clearly was not a candidate for receiving going concern qualification.

Auditor Independence

While the issues surrounding the oversale of lifetime partnerships and the auditors' responsibilities for detecting and reporting fraud were key issues in the *Teague* litigation, the issue of auditor independence was at the bottom of many of the other claims asserted by the plaintiffs. The independence issue was explicitly articulated in terms of the role that Deloitte and then Laventhol played in "maintaining the executive payroll at PTL."

The concept of independence represents the most basic tenet of the auditing profession. Were it not for the fact that independence undergirds all audit functions, the auditor's work would be meaningless. An auditor must be objective in making decisions.

The public expects auditors and accountants to exhibit integrity and the highest of ethical standards. When auditors compromise their independence, they undermine investor confidence in the reliability of financial statements and threaten the integrity of securities markets. Independence is, therefore, perhaps the most important auditing standard in existence today. It is not surprising that this critical issue has been extensively discussed in accounting journals as well as by the U.S. Supreme Court, according to which "the accountant [must] maintain total independence from the client at all times and . . . complete fidelity to the public trust."

GAAS requires, among other things, that an auditor be independent. Consequently, if the auditor is not independent, the auditor is precluded from issuing an opinion (AU 504.08-.10). Specifically, GAAS states that

> it is of utmost importance to the profession that the general public maintain confidence in the independence of independent auditors. Public confidence would be impaired by evidence that independence was actually lacking, and it might also be impaired by the existence of circumstances which reasonable people might believe likely to influence independence. To be independent, the auditor must be intellectually honest; to be recognized as independent, he must be free from any obligation to or interest in the client, its management or its owners. . . . Independent auditors must not only be independent in fact; they should avoid situations that may lead outsiders to doubt their independence.

GAAS states that the precepts concerning independence that are codified in the AICPA Code of Professional Conduct "have the force of professional law for the independent auditor." Article IV of the AICPA Code of Professional Conduct requires the auditor to be independent not only in fact but also in appearance in providing auditing and attestation services.

Independence in fact entails "intellectual honesty" in the absence of any obligation to potential users of financial statements. On the other hand, independence in appearance is "the perception of the auditor's independence by parties interested in the audit reports."

The distinction between these two different types of independence is that independence in fact questions the auditor's state of mind, whereas independence in appearance considers the state of mind of persons other than the auditor. The appearance that an auditor attempts to convey may not be that which is perceived by an observer. Finally the AICPA Code also provides that in providing "all other services," a member should maintain objectivity and avoid conflicts of interest. The rhetorical question that must be asked concerning PTL's independent auditors (as well as all others) is whether or not auditors can maintain their independence in fact and in appearance when they are responsible for handling the corporation's executive payroll.

PTL's executives were paid from the executive payroll account, which was administered by Deloitte and subsequently Laventhol. While serving as independent audit firms for PTL, they maintained the check register and prepared payroll, bonus, and other checks for 20 to 30 PTL executives—all under the direction of PTL's management. PTL sometimes prepared compensation and bonus checks on its own. Neither accounting firm exercised any discretion with respect to the disbursement of funds from the executive payroll accounts, and neither firm signed any of the checks written on the accounts.

In documents filed with the U.S. Federal District Court in North Carolina, Deloitte stated the following concerning its involvement with the PTL executive payroll account:

> The sum total of Deloitte's activities were that Deloitte would fill in the date, payee and amount of the check and record information for PTL's tax records. The checks would then be forwarded either to PTL's attorneys or to PTL for signature. This limited role in connection with the account resulted from Deloitte's careful investigation of its professional responsibilities. When Dortch requested that Deloitte administer the account, Deloitte went to the books and investigated the impact on its audit services of performing that task. It determined that it could do so long as it did not sign any of the checks or set compensation for any of the employees to be paid through the account. As a result, Deloitte never signed any of the checks or possessed a PTL signature stamp.

In documents filed with the same federal court, Laventhol stated the following concerning its involvement with the PTL executive payroll account:

> No Laventhol partner or employee decided who was to be paid from the Executive Payroll account. No Laventhol partner or employee

determined the amount of compensation which was to be paid to any PTL employee. Such managerial, discretionary decisions were made by PTL's officers and directors, who then communicated them to Laventhol personnel for a mechanical and clerical execution. No Laventhol employee or partner had any check-signing authority on the Executive Payroll Account at any time, and no Laventhol employee or partner ever had possession of any PTL facsimile signature stamp.

The audit manager of Laventhol testified that from reviewing the minutes of the PTL board of directors, he was aware of the bonuses that certain executives at PTL received, but that he became aware of Bakker's salary from reading about it in the newspaper. He also testified that neither he nor (to his knowledge) anyone else at Laventhol had ever spoken with the board of directors (excepting Bakker and Dortch) to confirm salaries or bonuses mentioned in the addenda to the PTL minutes. Likewise, the compensation and bonus checks prepared by Deloitte were never discussed with the full PTL board of directors. Instead, the checks prepared by the firms were sent by courier to PTL's lawyers or to PTL for signature.

However, PTL's outside counsel refused to sign the checks even on behalf of PTL, reasoning that his signing the checks might be taken as an act of affirming or approving the compensation being received by PTL executives.

While Deloitte and then Laventhol had no problem with performing ministerial functions like writing payroll checks and doing Bakker's tax returns while being aware that tax-exempt organizations should be concerned about private inurement, one person did have a problem with the checks that were being issued out of the executive payroll account maintained by the outside auditors. That was Ann Foxe, who was John Yorke's secretary at his law firm. In addition to her secretarial duties, she was responsible for stamping or providing the signature on the PTL checks that were prepared by Deloitte. "I believe [Deloitte] discovered an auditor couldn't audit an account if they were a signatory on the account," testified John Yorke. "So they needed somebody else to actually put a stamp in the signature line and they called and asked if we would put the stamp in the signature line. . . . My secretary, Ann Foxe, was the one who put the stamps on the checks, [after] she would receive a package from Deloitte and she would stamp them. . . ." A courier from PTL would then pick up the checks and deliver them to the appropriate parties.

Ann Foxe started stamping PTL checks in December 1983, but by February 1984, just three months later, she brought one batch of checks to John Yorke and commented that they were coming in more frequently than the law firm had originally thought. She said that Yorke . . . "need[ed] to look at the size of the checks that are coming." He looked at the checks and then went to two senior partners in the law firm "and decided that PTL might consider our stamping those checks to be acquiescing in the amount[s] that were being paid and we decided we wouldn't want to do that." "It was contrary to the advice that we had been giving them about payroll and salaries. . . . The amounts were larger than [what] we thought was appropriate," testified Yorke.

The maintenance of PTL's executive payroll by Deloitte and then by Laventhol may very well be considered to be proper, according to current accounting literature. Deloitte and Laventhol's position is bolstered by the fact that the minutes and the related addenda reflect apparent approval by the board of directors of bonuses that were being awarded. Furthermore, there is no evidence from any source that either accounting firm was notified that the compensation to Bakker and other executives had not been approved by the PTL board of directors. Accounting firms are not there to attempt to manage otherwise mismanaged organizations.

However, given the magnitude of the compensation paid to certain key executives of this tax-exempt organization and the requirement to ensure independence in appearance, both firms should have verified that compensation with the entire PTL board of directors. Such verification, although not specifically required by the accounting literature, but rather as an act of professional skepticism, might have prevented one of the overt acts of fraud or resulted in the firm's withdrawing from the audit engagement.

Related to the matter of maintaining the executive payroll was the question of private inurement. The compensation received by the Bakkers, Dortch, and the Taggart brothers raised the issue of whether or not PTL, as a tax-exempt entity, was in violation of Section 501(c)(3) of the IRS Code, which requires that a tax-exempt organization operate for the benefit of the public rather than for the benefit of select individuals. Officers, directors and other employees of tax-exempt organizations cannot receive excessive or unreasonable compensation. If the IRS determines that individuals are receiving excessive compensation, the organization's tax-exempt status may be revoked.

The plaintiffs claimed that both the auditor's report and PTL's financial statements failed to reflect the tax problems that PTL was having not only concerning the issue of private inurement but also relating to income being raised for unrelated businesses.

Deloitte claimed that the IRS never conclusively found any tax problems to exist at PTL while Deloitte was conducting its audit. PTL's attorneys never brought any IRS tax problem to their attention and, in any case, Deloitte claimed that the notes to PTL's financial statements disclosed all that it knew was proper to disclose concerning the IRS.

Specifically, the notes to the May 31, 1984, PTL audited financial statements reflect:

> *Internal Revenue Service Examination*—During the year ended, May 31, 1984, the Internal Revenue Service (IRS) began an examination of the Ministry's records for the fiscal years ended May 31, 1980, 1981 and 1982. No report with respect to the examination has been received; further, the Ministry has not been advised of any assertion of tax liability or of any other matters concerning its tax status. Adjustments, if any, which might be required as a result of the examination, are not presently determinable.

Attorney Don Etheridge, along with David Hardee and Lloyd Caudle, had power of attorney in connection with the IRS audit and initially handled PTL's tax problems with the IRS. Deloitte never had power of attorney to speak with the IRS. Etheridge's testimony was very clear. He never told anyone from Deloitte that the IRS had raised private inurement as an issue and, in fact, while PTL was his client, the IRS never raised any such issues at all. Etheridge testified that the notes to PTL's financial statements accurately portrayed his knowledge of the IRS investigation of PTL and that there had been adequate disclosure in connection with the IRS audit in the notes to PTL's financial statements. Deloitte's expert, Archie Mangum, also agreed that disclosure was adequate, and former commissioner of the IRS, Donald Alexander, testified that he thought the IRS would have worked with PTL in keeping its tax-exempt status and would not have revoked it.

As previously discussed, Deloitte was certainly aware of the level of compensation that Bakker was receiving and of the expenditures and internal controls that existed at PTL. In addition, Guy Forcucci, a tax partner at Deloitte, prepared the Bakkers' personal tax returns for calendar years 1982 and 1983. Forcucci testified at the Bakker criminal trial that he recalled Bakker's salary in 1982 to have been approximately $290,000, whereas his salary in 1983 had been approximately $461,000. Forcucci attested that he had met with Bakker and gone through some of his tax return "page by page," and that in 1982, he had "[i]ndicated to Mr. Bakker that the salary [he] had [received] increased from the prior year and that it's something that should be monitored." Forcucci also testified that he reminded Jim Bakker about a previous conversation concerning private inurement and that his salary should be "monitored in light of reasonableness."

Laventhol became aware that the IRS Agent Report that was issued on November 13, 1985, related to PTL's fiscal years 1981 through 1983. The IRS had proposed revocation of PTL's tax-exempt status based on private inurement and unrelated business income. As a result of this investigation, Laventhol issued a qualified auditor's report on PTL's financial statements for fiscal years 1985 and 1986. In addition, the notes to the 1985 and 1986 audited financial statements disclosed the nature of PTL's contingent liability with respect to the IRS examination.

When Laventhol became PTL's auditor, Bakker, Dortch, and Taggart's levels of compensation only increased. Laventhol knew this because they prepared not only the executive payroll but, like Deloitte, Bakker's personal tax return as well. Bakker's 1986 return shows gross income of 1.4 million. It is interesting to note that Bakker listed his occupation as "minister"; Tammy's occupation is listed as "co-host." It is also interesting to note the "additional statement" and the disclosures showing Laventhol's knowledge of accusations against PTL. (Exhibit A-34.)

Richard Dortch testified that during a 1985 meeting between himself, Bakker, and auditor Bill Spears, Bakker complained about a note in the financial statements that referred to the IRS investigation. Dortch said that Bakker was worried that contributions would decrease when partners read of the investigation.

"Did Laventhol modify the language?" Wendell Bird, the plaintiff's attorney, asked Dortch. "I remember the language being changed," Dortch testified. "It was modified so it would be more palatable, in Mr. Bakker's estimation, to the public."

Although a note to PTL's financial statements may have been changed, during cross-examination it became clear that the auditor's report had not been changed. Laventhol continued with its qualified opinion of the financial statements. The plaintiffs contended that Laventhol didn't go far enough and didn't disclose enough information so that anyone reading the financial statements could glean what the IRS problems really were.

PTL's Attorneys and Their Relationship with PTL's Auditors and Corporate Officers

PTL not only changed its auditors during the time of the oversale of lifetime partnerships but also frequently changed its attorneys. Although PTL had, for a period of time, an in-house attorney, most of its legal work was performed by outside counsel. The first firm to serve in this capacity was the Charlotte firm of Wardlow, Knox, Knox and Freeman. Eddie Knox, a senior partner, acted as general counsel, and the day-to-day responsibilities of dealing with PTL's legal problems were generally left to John Yorke. Yorke assumed primary responsibilities for PTL as a client in 1982. In its role as general counsel, the firm secured the services of tax lawyers, labor lawyers, and other specialists. They also gave general advice from time to time concerning a myriad of legal issues.

In late 1979 or early 1980, the firm of Caudle and Spears was hired by Eddie Knox to respond to tax problems and specific IRS matters concerning PTL. Don Etheridge, Bob Gunst, and Lloyd Caudle, occasionally handled tax matters for PTL. The IRS issued its report in November 1985 recommending revocation of PTL's tax-exempt status for the years 1981, 1982, and 1983. Dortch indicated that he wanted another attorney, Mike Wigton, to represent PTL concerning those tax problems. At that point, Caudle and his firm indicated their desire to simply let Wigton handle the matter as opposed to working with Wigton and his firm. By this time, the relationship between PTL and Eddie Knox's law firm had also begun to cool. On November 26, 1985, Knox wrote a letter in which he told Bakker the following:

> Years ago I agreed to be your general counsel in exchange for your agreement that I would be totally in charge of the legal representations and totally informed of what was going on. For years, this system worked quite well, and we acted as a sort of clearinghouse for all of the PTL legal representation. . . . For years, the understood system at PTL was that nothing was signed or sent out until we had reviewed it first. Often we would feel the need to call on some of the other lawyers working on your behalf in order to get their opinion on the subject, but we always gave you an opinion, and hopefully, made you aware of the benefits and consequences of taking or not taking a particular act. At some point, the procedure was changed, and the prevailing attitude was suddenly that no one could call the lawyers. . . . The purpose of this letter is not only to point out what I think are urgent needs in regard to your legal representation, but also to ask you for a better understanding of what our role is to be. As I've said, for years we coordinated the legal representation and

now we find ourselves in a position of not knowing what is going on. Even worse, as far as we can tell, no one has a grasp of the total picture anymore. I need to know whether we are, in fact, to continue as general counsel for the ministry. . . . Our role has been changed already and we are, for the most part, uninformed and uninvolved. We would gladly resume our former role of being your general counsel. Some decisions need to be made as to who is in control of your legal representation, and this is a good time to make it. . . .

In early 1985, Eddie Knox's law firm ceased to be general counsel. Caudle and Spears also ceased to be PTL's tax attorneys and were replaced by Mike Wigton.

Wigton retained the services of Charles Chapel in March 1986 to assist in the preparation of a response to the IRS Agent's Report concerning possible revocation of PTL's tax exempt status for the years 1981 through 1983. By September 9, 1986, Chapel was writing to Jim Bakker indicating that his firm was resigning as counsel to the PTL ministry. Although Chapel had been engaged to do the response to the initial IRS report, the IRS had since issued a notice of its desire to audit the years 1984 and 1985. According to Caudle's testimony, "We didn't want to let the IRS audit '84 and '85 until the '81 through '83 audit issues had been resolved, and we got into a dispute with Mr. Dortch concerning that strategy, and the organization, therefore, employed new counsel to handle the years 1984 and '85, leaving us with '81 through '83. I didn't believe that would work, and I did not want to continue in the case under those circumstances."

In their letter to Bakker, Chapel and Wigton raised not only the issue of multiple law firms representing PTL on related matters but also others, some of which are mentioned here:

Further it was and is especially now our intent to encourage change in Heritage Village Church's administrative control. We had argued in the submission [to the IRS] that the Board rather than a few officers or individuals controlled Heritage Village Church, but in our subsequent dealing, it appears that Reverend Dortch is making all the decisions without consulting the Board with the representation that he is receiving input from you and other responsible fiduciary. My calls to you have gone unreturned and I have no indication that the Board is aware of the specifics of what is going on. One of the arguments is that the three of you are not in control, rather that the broad public board is and yet how can we sustain that argument before the [IRS] under these circumstances?

□ □ □

The Church's policy of hiring lawyers to handle isolated, specific narrow problems is certainly its prerogative. However, any competent lawyer is going to call to your attention problems he [sic] observes even outside the sphere of his concern. My associates and I had done so, and our observations made in the spirit of helpfulness have been met with inaction, so far as we can determine, and even hostility. An example of this is the Church's sale of memberships in the hotel. In the context of our tax work, we observed this action and recognized numerous potential state and federal legal issues. We made a few verbal inquiries and determined that, basically, no legal research or consideration had been given these issues. Our verbal inquiries indicated a lack of concern. Therefore, we felt constrained to put our concerns in a letter. The Church's reaction was, basically, that the matter was not our business, and since then we note that the Church is offering similar memberships in a bunkhouse. Now, we have not concluded that there are, in fact, legal prohibitions against these programs. We have concluded only that there are serious and substantial legal issues involved in these programs, which should be researched by competent counsel (not necessarily us, but independent counsel). And to our knowledge, no legal opinion has been sought on these issues. The Church is, of course, free to ignore our advice on such matters. However, we do not desire to continue our representation under such circumstances.

I have repeatedly attempted to convince you all of the seriousness of the tax problems. I do not believe I have succeeded. My belief is based on lack of responsiveness to request for assistance and resistance to our advice. Let me reiterate what I have told you before. You have very serious problems in 1981 through 1983, and based on what we have seen, even more serious problems in '84 '85. . . . I have always emphasized the absolute necessity of the organization committing itself to strict compliance with the law in the future. The organization's past problems are indicative of a lack of understanding of what is required of a tax exempt organization. You need advice and counsel not only as to 1981, '82, '83, '84, and '85, but also 1986, '87 and years in the future. You have been entrusted with the care, custody and control of hundreds of millions of dollars. You have an extremely high responsibility, and we have not seen the kind of commitment required for us to continue to represent the Church.

In a rather prophetic statement, Chapel and Wigton warned, "You have got to take charge and get your business under control, otherwise your Church will be lost."

On cross-examination, Chapel outlined differences that he had with Richard Dortch concerning fees and mentioned Dortch's desire to make Chapel's legal briefs read "more like a preacher" and include quotes from the Bible. Dortch had also questioned the professional fees that were being charged in the case.

Although Dortch may or may not have had valid complaints against Chapel, Wigton, and other attorneys, it would certainly appear that the advice given by Chapel and Wigton in their letter was sound and prudent.

After Caudle and Wigton resigned, PTL hired the Washington, D.C., law firm of Baker and McKenzie. Burt Harding, an attorney with the firm, testified that the firm had 45 offices around the world and over 1,500 lawyers; as of the date of his testimony, it was the "largest law firm in the world."

Harding and other attorneys at Baker and McKenzie were responsible for preparing a 100-page brief outlining PTL's response to the IRS's "Proposed Audit Adjustments for the Years 1981, 1982 and 1983." Harding testified that PTL had been billed between $150,000 to $200,000 by his firm for professional work concerning the IRS's proposed revocation of PTL's tax-exempt status for 1981 through 1983 as well as the IRS examination into PTL's finances during 1984 and 1985. Harding testified that he thought PTL could have settled the case with the IRS because the IRS' legal positions had been "very weak" and that the IRS would have been willing to work with PTL to resolve this matter. Harding added that was his experience, having previously worked at the IRS.

Concerning private inurement, it was Harding's position "that because the Church had an independent Board of Directors that had actual and legal control over the organization . . . as a matter of law, you could not have private inurement in this type situation. . . ." A second argument was that the items the IRS had contested were in fact not items of private inurement.

Harding wrote in his brief for PTL:

> Finally, the Board's good faith in setting Reverend Bakker's compensation is demonstrated by the fact the Board retained a highly qualified and expert certified public accounting firm to review the Church's books to insure that the Church was operating within the scope of section 501(c)(3). In this regard, these auditors also reviewed the amounts of compensation that the Board determined to pay to Reverend Bakker. These auditors, however, *never* advised the Board that the amount of Reverend Bakker's compensation could cause a problem with the Church's Section 501(c)(3) status. Thus the Board took every possible step and precaution to insure that it was operating within the intent of the statute.

When Harding was asked under oath where he got those facts, he responded, "[f]rom Reverend Dortch."

On cross-examination, Harding acknowledged that he had referred to the Bakker's daily TV show as a daily worship service. He testified that his characterization of the PTL program as a worship service was based "on the videotapes I watched and . . . the manner in which they were characterized by the organization." Harding also testified that Bakker should have been compensated at whatever level the Board had authorized. "So, if they would authorize $10 million a year, you would not have had an objection to that as being private inurement, something improper for a nonprofit organization like PTL?" asked Wendell Bird. "Under the law as we read it, no," testified Harding.

"If they had authorized $20 million a year, you would not have had an objection to Jim Bakker being paid that under the law?" continued Bird on his cross-examination. "Not as the term private inurement is defined, no," testified Harding. Harding also indicated that for fiscal years 1984 and 1985, they had made a tentative decision that there was no private inurement at PTL.

These frequent changes in attorneys combined with PTL's seeming inattention to serious legal problems, would seem to have triggered suspicions in any auditor. However, as Deloitte and Laventhol pointed out in their *Teague* litigation briefs, the information that they had been receiving from corporate counsel never indicated the enormity of the problems that some attorneys had noticed. First, the oversale of lifetime partnerships had apparently never been detected by attorneys or auditors. John Yorke testified at the Bakker criminal trial that he was asked by a PTL employee, whose name he could not recall, about the effect of "hypothetically" oversubscribing the Grand Hotel lifetime partnership program. Yorke had responded that if the program were oversubscribed, the original 25,000 lifetime partners would have to be advised as to the charge in partnership limits and their partners must be given "an opportunity to get their money back if they wanted it."

Evidently, this was never communicated to Deloitte or Laventhol.

In fact, in compliance with GAAS, Deloitte had inquired of PTL's general counsel and other PTL lawyers as to whether there were matters of legal substance that should have been considered in Deloitte's 1984 audit. Their responses had made no mention of such matters and the IRS, according to Etheridge, had never identified any specific issues to him.

Laventhol had solicited and obtained information from PTL's attorneys concerning their knowledge of asserted and unasserted claims against PTL. Laventhol had also obtained a client representation letter from PTL, which had been signed by PTL's chief executive officer, chief operating officer, and chief financial officer; these individuals had attested that they had made available to Laventhol all financial records and related data, including minutes of all the meetings of

PTL's board of directors. They had further represented that no material irregularities or material unasserted claims had needed to be disclosed in the financial statements.

The Change in PTL's Auditors

On May 15, 1985, Peter Bailey contacted Bob Brown and advised him that PTL's board of directors had decided to change auditing firms for the upcoming audit. He advised Brown that PTL's new auditor would be Laventhol but that he wanted Deloitte to continue to "handle our Executive Payroll" until further notice. Peter Bailey's action prompted a letter signed by Bob Brown that explained the loss of PTL as a Deloitte client. (See Exhibit 9-2.)

This document certainly gives the impression that Deloitte was happy to bid a fond farewell to PTL as an auditing client. It is especially worthy to note that Brown wrote that PTL was an ". . . audit risk and related exposure to the firm appears to be increasing" and that "exposure is at an all-time high." Brown also noted that carrying PTL as a client had resulted in "negative community reaction as well as some adverse sentiment to our involvement from within the profession and also within the firm."

Although Brown wrote this "good riddance" memo on May 16, 1985, J. Cary Findlay of Deloitte wrote a letter to Dortch on April 11, 1985, in which he actively and aggressively sought to keep PTL as an audit client. Findlay acknowledged that PTL still owed Deloitte "$195,000 of which over $167,000 is in excess of 90 days" past due and represents billing for virtually all of Deloitte's services to PTL "for this past year." (See Exhibit 9-3.) It is unclear what, if anything, happened between the Findlay memo of April 11 and Bob Brown's memo of May 16 that could have caused such a radical shift in attitude.

Now it was Laventhol's turn to serve as independent auditors for PTL. In a memo reflecting a conversation that occurred on or about July 1, 1985, Jim Thyer, an accountant for Laventhol who had been assigned to the PTL engagement, had a meeting with Guy Forcucci of Deloitte. This memo, shown in Exhibit 9-4, possibly tells as much about Deloitte as it does about Laventhol's knowledge of their newly acquired client, PTL.

Concerning travel and entertainment, how is it possible that "PTL lost or threw out all their records"? If an auditor has a mindset of professional skepticism and sees him- or herself as a public watchdog, could it be that the destruction of records was not only the result of mere oversight or negligence, but also of fraud?

Explanation for the Loss of Client:

The loss of Heritage Village Church (PTL) as an audit and tax client is attributed to the following factors:

(1) According to Mr. Peter Bailey, Vice President and Controller, PTL sought proposals from other firms and decided to make a change in auditors for the 1985 examination in order to obtain a "fresh look". Based on our discussions with Mr. Bailey our fee proposal of $120,000 for 1985 was not a deciding factor. The decision was one of establishing a "rotation policy" and therefore to make a change. We had been the auditors since 1977.

(2) Also checked is "Voluntary withdrawal – Difficulty in Collecting Fees", a secondary factor which has been of considerable concern to us. The client is unusually slow to pay. As of May 16, 1985, $67,000 of our 1984 examination is still outstanding together with a substantial amount of tax billings. Our billings were consistently in the past due column.

(3) Further, the client has been the subject of unfavorable publicity at various times since its inception, based on the nature of its fund raising and the purposes for which it spends money. We have been aware for sometime of negative community reaction as well as some adverse sentiment to our involvement from within the profession and also within the firm. At the completion of each examination we reevaluated the desirability of continuing as auditors in view of the pressures, and each year the decision to go forward was less conclusive.

The Client has advised us that Laventhol & Horwath will succeed us as auditors, although we have not been contacted by that firm at this time. The Laventhol firm was contacted since they were brought in by the Hotel management firm handling the "GRAND HOTEL" operations on the property of Heritage Village.

(4) The audit risk and related exposure to the firm appears to be increasing because of over-extension of capital projects in the past year built largely on faith. While we have been reluctant to view a church in the same light as a business as it relates to the "going concern" concept, this particular entity probably does qualify for concern because of the foregoing facts, and a "subject to" qualification is a strong possibility for 1985. In this scenario, with ever-increasing outstanding debt, the possible challenge to its non-exempt status by the IRS and the other factors described above, together with the fact that it is a "one-man show", the exposure is at an all-time high.

Signed ~~R.B.Brown~~   Date 5/16/85

PLAINTIFF'S
EXHIBIT

B00154

Exhibit 9-2   Bob Brown's Letter Concerning Deloitte's "Loss" of PTL as a Client (May 16, 1985)

Reverend Richard W. Dortch   April 11, 1985
Senior Executive Vice President
Heritage U.S.A.
Post Office Box 21
Ft. Mill, South Carolina 29715

Dear Reverend Dortch:

We regret to learn that the Board of Directors of Heritage Village
Church and Missionary Fellowship is considering requesting proposal
for audit services from other firms for the fiscal year ending
May 31, 1985.

I would like very much to meet with you prior to your requesting
any proposals for services as we believe there are a number of
factors which could influence your decision.

Initially, I also would appreciate the opportunity for you to
share with me the reasons for your considering a change of
independent auditors. In view of our long-term relationship with
PTL since its beginning and our commitment through some very
trying and difficult times, I am taken back at this action with
no discussion as to any possible dissatisfaction. We are prepared
to deal with any dissatisfaction on your part. For instance,
if you consider the quality or timeliness of our services to be
less than your expectations, then we are prepared to make the
necessary changes to accomplish the job in a more satisfactory
manner.

Further, if your concern relates to billings for services, then
I will be pleased to provide and review with you the details of
our charges which I believe will bear out our sincere interest
in providing PTL quality service over the years at reasonable
rates.

As you know, our charges are based on the time requirements of
our personnel and such factors at Heritage Village Church and
Missionary Fellowship have mushroomed in the past several years,
much like your organization has grown. We firmly believe we can
favorably respond to any concerns you may have in this area. This
belief applies also to our involvement in your tax examination,
the restructuring of your organization, assistance in the payroll
area, preparation of tax returns, and advice and consultation
with respect to various other tax matters.

Exhibit 9-3   J. Cary Findlay's Letter on Behalf of Deloitte (April 11,
1985)

Reverend Richard W. Dortch   April 11, 1985   2

As your current auditors, we are the most knowledgeable with
respect to your organization, and for that reason we can best
quantify the costs which must be incurred to provide you with
quality service to meet your needs. While we recognize that
another firm will, over a period of years, gain a working
knowledge of your records and procedures, there will necessarily
be a learning process which must be endured by your organization.
With your present staff already stretched relatively thin, we
believe that the change will be very difficult, particularly this
late into the fiscal year.

Another matter which should not go unnoticed is our proven
willingness to work with PTL regarding the amount and payment
of our fees. We have never insisted on "payment-up front" for
our services, but have recognized that you are subject to "peaks
and valleys" with respect to revenues. Accordingly, we have
consistently relied on your integrity to meet your obligations
as an organization. We have also been sensitive to the amount
of our bills in view of PTL's financial situation. To put this
into proper focus, as of April 4, 1985 we have outstanding billings
to you of $195,000 of which over $167,000 is in excess of ninety
days from billing date which represents billings for substantially
all of our accounting, audit, payroll and tax services for this
past year. This amount was significantly effected by the tax
matters with the I.R.S.

In the interest of continuing our long relationship which began
in 1977 and has weathered with you during your many trials and
tribulations, we are willing to work with your accounting personnel
in establishing an audit plan for 1985, and quantifying our estimates
of costs. We will also work closely with your people in the other
areas of tax and related matters on a pre-established basis which
will allow you to know in advance the charges to expect. We have
worked with you in this manner in earlier years, and would like
to continue this relationship.

I look forward to meeting with you to discuss this matter further.

Yours very truly,

J. Cary Findlay
Partner-in-Charge

cc: Reverend James O. Bakker
    Peter G. Bailey ✓

Exhibit 9-3   *Continued*

[LH] Laventhol & Horwath / Charlotte
Certified Public Accountants

Subject	CONVERSATION WITH *Guy* FORCUCCI	Date	7/1/85

From   Jim Thyer   Copies

To   Files of PTL

Guy Forcucci is a tax partner at Deloitte Haskins & Sells who ~~is~~ *was* responsible for the tax affairs of the PTL prior to our engagement. We discussed the following items:

IRS Examination

DH&S was not listed on the power of attorney and had no direct involvement in the tax examination. Robert C. Gunst of Caudle & Spears, P.A. is tax counsel for the PTL. The issues involved may be summarized as follows:

Travel and Entertainment

For one year the PTL lost or threw out all of their records. Guy Forcucci had no idea if this was the result of a mere oversight or negligence.

Private Inurement

Because of the salaries etc., for Jim and Tammy Bakker, the question of private inurement was raised. This issue goes to the exempt status of the organization. Mr. Forcucci advised that they have written letters to the PTL in the past on this issue but he was of the opinion that they did not want to listen to his advice. He said that he feels that this perhaps is a reason why their relationship with the PTL deteriorated.

Exempt Activities

According to Mr. Forcucci the PTL views their entire activities related to running a modern day religious campground. Accordingly they feel that all activities should be exempt from tax.

LH000881

COMMITTED TO PROFESSIONAL EXCELLENCE

Confidential Subject
To Court Order

Exhibit 9-4   Jim Thyer's Memo to PTL

DH&S Study

DH&S did a study and issued a 20 ~~cross~~ page memo to the PTL that included a full organization chart identifying entities and tax status. Also enclosed was a proposed organization chart and discussion of various tax issues such as Parsonage allowances, etc.

Tax Differed Annuity

DH&S has discussed with the PTL the correctness of the calculation of tax deferred annuities, and ~~it is~~ documented in letters to the PTL. *these discussions are*

Tax Return Filing

The most recent years tax returns apparently have not been filed. Apparently DH&S was engaged to prepare the tax returns but before they got involved with the actual preparation they spent time with the PTL discussing the previously mentioned 20 page memo. They were disengaged before any tax returns were prepared. Mr. Forcucci has written to Mr. Bailey advising him that he should file returns, even for the shell companies to avoid the state of South Carolina and or the IRS issuing assessment notices and seizure activities.

Additional Information

Mr. Forcucci recommended that we contact Peter Bailey to get copies of their prior correspondence. However, he offered to be of any assistance that he could provided that Peter Bailey first contact him to authorize him to share information with us.

Jim Tyson

Exhibit 9-4   *Continued*

One would think that the information in this document would have indicated to Laventhol that PTL's system of controls, checks, and balances may have been less than adequate. Was this a client that an auditor would have wanted to keep, let alone acquire?

Certainly the paragraph concerning private inurement could be interpreted to imply that if an auditor wanted to maintain PTL as a client, the auditor should avoid raising the issue of private inurement.

In Laventhol's audit plan, dated May 31, 1985, the firm discussed the "overall audit risk"—specifically the "[r]isk relating to management's attitude, confidence and credibility with respect to matters affecting the financial statements." The following excerpt very circumspectly expresses Laventhol's misgivings:

> Overall, management projects a conservative attitude toward reported earnings and decision-making concerning major matters. . . . The Ministry's operations are basically controlled and all decisions made through the senior executive, Jim Bakker. His overall integrity and that of the top executives who report to and work with him appear to be higher than average. However, the public is concerned with his and the Ministry's interest in the manner in which he spends the Ministry's money. Therefore, we have to consider the risk of errors and irregularities that could occur that would result in the understatement or misappropriation of cash receipts.

Laventhol went on to note that "the organizational structure of the ministry is not well defined and is extremely complex due to the diversified operations. . . . Generally, there appears to be a lack of coordination of all of the functions in accounting and financial departments and between the various entities. . . ."

Laventhol's evaluation of overall audit risk based on examining the two factors just discussed, and seven other factors, concluded that: "overall risk for the audit as a whole is normal. (Higher than normal for certain assertions within some cycles.)"

One could certainly question Laventhol's conclusion that the overall audit risk for PTL engagement was "normal" given what they had learned from discussions with Deloitte as well as the unfavorable press PTL had been receiving.

It is also interesting to note in the Laventhol audit plans concerning "audit approach by cycle" that Laventhol noted, "there were no key controls in this cycle which would substantially reduce substantive testing" for the following cycles: (1) Revenue Cycle; (2) Conversion Cycle; (3) Expenditure Cycle; (4) Payroll Cycle; (5) Productive Asset Cycle; (6) Financial Management Cycle; (7) Prepayments and Accrual Cycle.

Obviously, an abundance of audit-related issues that go far beyond the scope of this chapter were discussed during the six-week civil trial. Although I have not discussed the procedures used by Laventhol to recognize lifetime partner revenue, the Federal Bankruptcy Court found that Laventhol's treatment of lifetime partner revenue in 1986 had increased PTL's income by almost $25 million. "If the same method used for 1985 had been used in 1986, expenses would have exceeded income by $5,102,011," the court stated. It noted that "[n]either method of amortizing the lifetime partner revenue, either as reflected in the audits for the fiscal year ending May 31, 1985, or in the audit for the fiscal year ending May 31, 1986, was in accordance with generally acceptable accounting practices. . . . The effect of failing to amortize this revenue over the life expectancy of the donors was to reflect an artificial increase in income for 1985 and 1986 in the year-end audits, and convey to bankers and other outside parties a false sense of financial solvency."

What the Lifetime Partners Saw

While the auditors, the attorneys, and the senior management at PTL were getting one impression of the organization, the contributing public was seeing something totally different. Bakker would frequently complain about the *Charlotte Observer* and the unfair treatment that he and his ministry had received not only from that newspaper but also from the press in general. Bakker hosted one program, entitled "PTL Reports," that was designed to respond to various allegations and accusations made about him and his ministry by the press.

On at least three television programs, Bakker sought to comfort viewers by telling them that PTL had been audited.

On January 31, 1986, Jim Bakker sat on the couch with Tammy at his side and said the following to the television audience:

> We are accountable. We have been audited by Deloitte, Haskins and Sells for many years, and now, by Laventhol and Horwitz [sic], and here is the audit for 1977. How many ministries can say this? 1978, complete audit. 1979, 1980, 1981, 1982, 1983, 1984, and 1985. We are also a member of ECF&A, and we are people who want you to know the truth, and we want to reveal it to you. Please write us. They say a man is known by his friends. I think he is also known by his enemies.

As Bakker spoke, the covers of the audited financial statements were shown to the viewing audience.

On April 18, 1986, during his "Enough Is Enough" telethon, Jim Bakker had this to say:

> We answer to God. We answer to our partners. We answer to ECF&A. We answer to our denomination. We answer to our Board of Directors. We answer to everybody. And so we are going to talk to the people who are important, the ones who are important, and we don't mind telling you what we do. We don't mind letting you know that we print audits of this ministry. We have done it for, what, ten years now, and we go through an audit almost a hundred percent of the time.
>
> An outside auditing firm, one of the big audit firms of America, is in here at all times auditing this ministry at our own expense, thousands of dollars, tens of thousands of dollars, to be responsible. And we are going to go forward, but it's time God's people say enough is enough.
>
> Some of you haven't renewed your pledge, yet, and we are waiting for you. We have been here—let's see, this is our tenth hour of this telethon. So come on.

Finally, on February 6, 1986, Jim Bakker, Richard Dortch, and Tammy Bakker directly responded to allegations of misuse of PTL funds. Jim Bakker said: "In fact, I'm having an audit firm now—an outside audit firm come in to audit that because they don't want to take any of our word, even though they can see the checks, they can see the statements, they are still going to go through this audit and have someone outside of PTL come in and look at it that knows bookkeeping and can—and can say, yes this is exactly how it was done." At that point, Tammy Bakker interrupted Jim, saying, "It has already been audited once anyway, Jim." "We have audits every year," he responded.

As previously discussed, there was much dispute between the plaintiffs and the defendants concerning the need to show actual reliance on audited financial statements in order for the plaintiffs to proceed with their case. While that matter was hotly disputed before the federal judge, it is clear that Jim Bakker did make references on the television program concerning the fact that PTL was audited, and he tried to use that fact to alleviate viewers' concerns regarding PTL's use of contributors' funds.

It should also be noted that some people did write to PTL and ask for copies of the audited financial statements, and PTL provided them in accordance with ECFA rules. For example, a woman from Lawrence, Kansas, wrote that her husband was questioning how much of their contributions were actually being used for missionary work. Peter Bailey responded, in a letter dated May 10, 1984, with a copy of the audited financial statements for the year ending May 31, 1983.

Many of the letters sent to "Jim and Tammy" bore witness to the sacrifices that many of the PTL faithful made for the cause. A woman from Ontario wrote:

> we are sorry that we have not been able to send in our donation on a regular basis, but now that I am only working at the odd job, it is no longer possible to promise a monthly support on a regular basis. . . . on top of this, the old devil caused someone to tell my husband that the money sent to PTL is not always used for what it is designated for, but is put to other use. What he means by this I do not know as I do not believe this for one minute or I would not have supported the work for the past few years. I believe that Jim and Tammy Bakker are doing a wonderful work for the Lord and even though it seems as though funds are always needed to build something else, we realize that the Lord is using Jim for His Glory and that His one desire is to build larger accommodation[s], etc., in order to take care of the people who long to go to Heritage Village to get closer to God or, in some cases, in order to have their marriage restored. We are one-hundred percent behind Jim and his work, but if there is someway that you could send us a copy of a financial report or something showing where this money goes, perhaps I could prove to my husband that everything at PTL is on the level.

Accompanying this letter was a gift of $10.

Other viewers wrote to PTL concerning what they perceived to be apparent irregularities. One PTL viewer from Belleville, Illinois, wrote a letter dated June 19, 1987, in which she made this complaint: "I have donated a total of $13,000, plus gave a $2,100 diamond necklace inscribed with Praise The Lord on it for an auction last year, and one day while watching the television, I actually saw Tammy Bakker wearing it on the program!!! To this day, I'd love to know how she ended up with it."

Where Do We Go from Here?

Other lifetime partners might be asking how the frauds at PTL could have gone undetected for so long by highly paid professionals. Clearly, an auditor is not a guarantor of the absolute accuracy of every detail of a client's financial statements.

If auditors find that their client's corporate environment is conducive to fraud, however, then they should reevaluate their testing procedures or else refuse to accept the corporation as a client. Auditors should test transactions more frequently, or, in high-risk areas, test every transaction. Although this would be more expensive for the client, such testing would provide greater assurances for the investing and contributing public and would help to decrease the expectation gap.

An auditor's signature on a corporation's financial statement is not the equivalent of a "Good Housekeeping Seal of Approval." Clearly, corporate failure does not always point to audit failure. An auditor should have a responsibility and a duty to detect fraud. This obligation is probably best captured in the following quote: "The first object of an audit is to say that the accounts can be relied on, that they are 'alright'; it is absurd to say that they are alright subject of course to the possibility that undetected frauds may have made them all wrong."[3] Of course, auditors must exercise a higher level of professional skepticism than that.

U.S. Congressman Ron Wyden of Oregon has said: "They are called certified public accountants because they are accountable to the public. Accountants are not living up to their public duty. If they find wrongdoing, they have an obligation to come forward."

Today's accounting firms bring in approximately $46 billion in revenues; the "Big Six" firms account for up to 25 percent of that amount. However, the accounting profession is currently in a crisis. U.S. accountants face approximately 4,000 liability suits and more than $15 billion in damages. The six largest accounting firms have paid more than $300 million in just the past year to settle pending lawsuits. Roughly two-thirds of this litigation comes from the savings and loan scandals.

Unfortunately for the investing (and contributing) public, there is at present a plethora of cases that seem likely only to widen the expectation gap. Miniscribe Corporation shipped boxes of bricks labeled as disk drives and counted them as sales. Although investigators blamed corporate executives for the company's "cooked books," reflecting bogus and inflated transactions, a jury found its auditors, Cooper and Lybrand, liable for damages of $200 million. The accounting firm settled the case for $95 million. Ernst and Young agreed to pay $63 million to settle claims that its negligence helped Charles Keating, Jr., defraud some 23,000 investors in the Lincoln Savings and Loan; Arthur Andersen paid $22 million for fraud claims arising from the same savings and loan collapse. In fact, "28 of 30 savings-and-loans that failed in California in 1985 and 1986 . . . received clean audits the year before they went belly up."[4] Ernst and Whinney gave a clean review report to ZZZZ Best, a California carpet-cleaning corporation run by a 20-year-old entrepreneur whose major contracts turned out to be nonexistent.

On November 23, 1992, Ernst and Young agreed to a $400 million settlement after the Government claimed that it improperly audited federally insured banks and savings and loans that failed.

The rhetorical questions that now must be asked concerning the audits of PTL are: Did the audits of PTL increase or decrease the expectation gap? Did these audits bring credit to the accounting profession and the critical role that auditors play in providing an objective and independent report of a corporation's financial statements? Were the audits that were conducted at PTL by two national accounting firms indicative of the way that audits are being conducted by accounting firms of publicly held companies, or were the audits of PTL an aberration? What actions should the accounting profession take to ensure that frauds of the magnitude committed at PTL will not go undetected by outside independent auditors?

Notes

1. *Codification of Accounting Standards*, Statement on Auditing Standards No. 1, Section 110.01 (American Institute of Certified Public Accountants, 1972).
2. D. Carmichael and J. Willingham, *Perspectives in Auditing: Readings and Analysis Situations* (1971).
3. The Commission on Auditors' Responsibilities, Report, Conclusions, and Recommendations (1978 at page 32 [(Quoting A.N.C. Morrison, *The Role of Reporting Accountants Today*, Accountancy (England) March 1971, at 122).
4. Stermberg, William, "Cooked Books," *The Atlantic*, January 1992, p. 20.

CHAPTER TEN

□□□

Where Was the ECFA?

> In summary, in view of what appears to be a continual cash flow problem, I do not think we should be overly surprised if certain of PTL's operating companies are forced into bankruptcy by its creditors in the near future.
>
> Memo written to ECFA standards board members by Bill Altman more than one year before PTL did go bankrupt.

As estimated by the American Association of Fund-Raising Counsel, contributions to religious organizations in the United States totaled $67.59 billion in 1991, up 6.76% from the previous year. Given the magnitude of this sum, should the government take steps to ensure proper and ethical use of these tax-exempt funds? Because each charitable organization serves as a public trust, it seems logical that certain standards of accountability are in order.

However, some would contend that governmental interference would violate the First Amendment of the U.S. Constitution concerning freedom of religion. Specifically, critics of such governmental control of religious charities point to the Establishment Clause, which has been interpreted by the U.S. Supreme Court to mean that a wall of separation must exist between Church and State.

If the government is to be discouraged from involving itself in policing religious organizations, then shouldn't religious organizations find a way to police themselves?

A strong, independent, self-regulating organization, modeled after the National Association of Securities Dealers (NASD), for example, would help to promote fiscal integrity and increase the public's confidence in all charitable organizations.

Many would contend that the Evangelical Council for Financial Accountability (ECFA) is a kind of "Better Business Bureau" for evangelists. Art Borden, then president of the ECFA, testified at the Bakker criminal trial that the ECFA is "an accrediting agency for Christian Ministries . . . we have a set of standards concerning governance of the organization, Board of Directors, composition function(s), audits and disclosure of financial reports, fundraising practice(s), ethical practices [and] conflict of interests." It may be surprising to learn that PTL was a member of the ECFA from April 1981 until December 1986. Testimony and exhibits produced during *Teague v. Bakker* seemed to raise questions concerning the ECFA's own review of the PTL organization and the actions (or lack thereof) that the ECFA took as a result. PTL's association with the ECFA is also of interest because the ECFA was relying on PTL's audited financial statements in deciding whether or not to allow PTL to join and remain a member of ECFA.

Background of the ECFA

The ECFA was founded in 1979 after Christian leaders were challenged by Senator Mark Hatfield to police their own mission agencies or face the possibility of government intervention. The ECFA, according to its own literature, is "an association with 660 Evangelical, non-profit organizations requiring the highest standards of financial accountability and disclosure to donors, government, and other interested persons. ECFA issues a seal of membership to each qualifying organization, and provides continuing services, consultation, and information to its members. The ECFA seeks to interpret its causes before the public as well as the federal and state governments. The combined annual income of the ECFA members exceed $2.7 billion."

The ECFA's mission is to increase the public's confidence in the business affairs of evangelical organizations by establishing standards, helping organizations meet the standards, certifying compliance with those standards, and communicating with the public.

Art Borden testified that there are several advantages to belonging to the ECFA. "One, it means that an organization is subscribing to a set of published standards which are recognized as good business practices, and it helps the donor have confidence that good business practices are being followed. And in the more recent years, I think that many people have testified that it helps them raise additional funds because it helps some donors make up their mind whether they want to support an organization or not."

The ECFA has six standards of what it terms "responsible stewardship." At the time PTL was a member of the ECFA, these included the following:

1. Every member organization shall be governed by a responsible board, a majority of whose members shall not be employees/staff and/or related by blood or marriage to such, which shall meet at least semi-annually to establish policy and review its accomplishment.
2. Every member organization shall obtain an annual audit performed by an independent public accounting firm in accordance with Generally Accepted Accounting Standards (GAAS) with financial statements prepared in accordance with Generally Accepted Accounting Principals (GAAP).
3. Every member organization shall have a functioning Audit Review Committee appointed by the board [of directors]. . . .
4. Every member organization shall provide a copy of its current audited financial statement upon written request.
5. Every member organization shall conduct its activities with the highest standard of integrity and avoid conflicts of interest.
6. Every member organization shall insure that its fundraising clearly identifies the purposes and programs to which the donations will be applied and shall ensure that these donations are used for the purpose for which they were raised.

Responsibility for enforcement of and compliance with ECFA's standards lies with ECFA's president and its standards committee. Minor violations of the standards are usually resolved by corrective action and a report to the standards committee, whereas more serious violations may result in termination of the entity's membership in the ECFA.

The ECFA certainly seems to be a step in the right direction. Its standards, as well as its requirement of having audited financial statements from member organizations on file, should be a source of comfort to the contributing public. But how could PTL have remained a member of the ECFA while it was engaged in extravagant spending and overselling of lifetime partnerships?

PTL and the ECFA

PTL was a problem for the ECFA almost from the very beginning. PTL's application for membership with the ECFA was accepted in April 1981, but by May 1983, Art Borden was writing to Jim Bakker asking him to provide information concerning the purchase of the now infamous Florida condominium. In his letter to Bakker, Borden made the following statements: "Mr. Bakker, we need your full response and help in this matter. The initial [PTL] response was brief and rather disappointing. ECFA is here to help its members and the entire cause of Christ by promoting, maintaining and enforcing high standards. Our role is not that of an adversary, but that of a friend and fellow sojourner. . . . At present, the Standards Committee has a number of newspaper articles and a one page press release. We do not feel that this is an adequate basis upon which to resolve the issues. However, we can only work with the information that is available to us."

In an attempt to justify this seemingly inappropriate purchase (the costs involved amounted to more than $600,000), PTL called on Charles Cookman. In his roles as board member for PTL and superintendent of the Assemblies of God for North Carolina, Cookman wrote to the Standards Committee of the ECFA in July 1983 that PTL's board of directors had "charged Jim Bakker with awesome responsibilities" and that the "physical pressures [on Bakker] are nearly beyond comprehension." Cookman then expressed how Bakker's need for rest was critical; unfortunately, "the opportunity for rest in Charlotte is almost non-existent. The Bakkers are recognized wherever they go and [are] often ridiculed or treated in less than a pleasant way, or [else are] swarmed by well-wishers." Also, according to Cookman, the board's "desire was to free [the Bakker Family] from their 'confinement' in Charlotte and the proposed retreat was to accomplish this goal." In addition to Cookman, Bakker later arranged for Porter Speakman, who was Peter Bailey's predecessor, and John Yorke to meet with Art Borden and present PTL's case.

On October 12, 1983, Art Borden wrote the first of many letters to Jim Bakker concerning the ECFA standards. His letter stated that the purchase of the Florida condominium was not necessarily a violation of the ECFA standards. He also noted that "it is not the duty of the [Standards] Committee to second guess the management of an organization concerning their decisions. We recognize that different executives and boards could easily arrive at different decisions and different courses of action, even when placed in similar circumstances."

In the same letter, Borden mentioned what the ECFA Standards Committee considered to be "the real concern" regarding the "fulfillment of the fiduciary responsibility of the Board of Directors." The ECFA specifically inquired: "Could not and should not more responsibility be delegated?" Other specific questions raised in Borden's letter to Bakker included these: "Has the PTL Board adopted policies regarding budgetary controls for major projects? Are these policies clearly stated and do they apply to everyone in the organization?" and

"What assurances can PTL give the ECFA or anyone else [that] such an organization was being well managed and was using the financial resources in a responsible manner?"

In addition to these concerns, the ECFA recommended that, among other things, the board of directors be enlarged to include the expertise of many different kinds of people and that "Senior Staff members meet with the Board and the Committee."

If Jim Bakker had relayed all of the ECFA's concerns to the PTL board of directors and if they had acted on them, the tragedies that occurred within PTL might very well have been avoided. Unfortunately, he did not. Just two weeks later, on October 26, 1983, Borden was again writing to PTL. This time, the focus of his letter concerned an article appearing in *Christianity Today* alleging that Bakker had spent four days in a $1,000-a-day hotel suite in Buena Vista, Florida. The next month Bakker responded to Borden indicating that the suite was in a secure area and was able to accomodate his staff of 14 people. Bakker also indicated that no donor gifts were used to fund the trip; instead, the trip had been paid for with funds from "for-profit" corporations located at PTL.

On April 5, 1984, the ECFA Standards Committee, via Art Borden, notified Jim Bakker that PTL's 1984 renewal membership had been deferred until the ECFA had received "accurate, complete and current information [from PTL]. . . ." The letter went on to say: "Because your application of membership renewal for 1984 has not yet been approved, and since the ECFA credentials and the ECFA seal remain property of the ECFA and may be used only in the event of an organization's good faith compliance with the ECFA Standards and the organization's current membership in the ECFA, PTL shall not be authorized to use the ECFA seal on any literature, films, correspondence or other fund raising material. In the event of public request for information as to the membership standards of PTL in the ECFA, both PTL and the ECFA shall respond that the renewal application is being considered by the ECFA." PTL's renewal application with the ECFA was eventually approved on August 20, 1984.

Apparently without the knowledge of the ECFA (and directly contrary to Borden's letter of April 1984), PTL did continue to display the ECFA logo at the end of its TV broadcasts.

Should the ECFA have known that PTL might continue to display the ECFA logo to the viewing public even after being instructed not to use it? Had there been previous instances of PTL engaging in questionable activities that were brought to the attention of the ECFA but were ultimately found not to be in violation of its standards?

Unfortunately, such was the case. For example, the ECFA allowed PTL to continue to be a member in good standing despite its knowledge that the PTL ministry had purchased a seaside condominium that was believed to be worth $375,000. The ECFA was also aware that PTL had purchased a $935,000 jet aircraft. After PTL's renewal of membership was approved in August 1984, the ECFA became aware that Jim Bakker had purchased a $449,000 house in Palm Springs, California, and spent $93,000 on antique cars.

Art Borden testified in the *Teague* litigation that he was aware of each of these activities, that they had been examined by the ECFA, and that the ECFA found they were not in violation of any of its standards.

On June 12, 1984, Jim Bakker wrote to Borden outlining how PTL was spending its funds. Bakker's letter was especially of interest in relation to his satisfaction with Deloitte:

> Our accountants, the firm of Deloitte, Haskins and Sells, have not, as yet, implemented this program [to indicate PTL's goals for the use of contributions and fundraising activities in amounts and percentages] which has distressed us. Quite frankly, as part of our displeasure, we are now getting bids from the accounting firm of Price Waterhouse, as to the possibility of them doing our audit for us.
>
> Our tax attorneys have advised us that this is something they should have been doing for us all along. I am aware of the fact that the audit firm cannot give us our goals, but they should have been doing a better job seeing to it that the information that we need is available to us.

The very next year, on March 25, 1985, Borden again wrote to Bakker, Dortch, and Bailey, advising them that their application for renewed membership was "to be held in abeyance pending compliance review of your organization." (This letter sounds remarkably similar to Borden's 1984 letter to PTL.) He went on to tell the three PTL executives that the "decision to initiate this compliance review was based on the Standards Committee's concern about your organization's compliance with the ECFA standard about certain weaknesses with respect to budgetary and financial controls . . . . The [ECFA] Board and Standards Committee have frequently heard from PTL that financial accountability and integrity are important issues, yet little real substantive progress appears to have been made in the areas enumerated below."

The March 1985 ECFA correspondence specifically concerned the percentages of donated income being allocated to fundraising and management costs compared to the percentage of total income that was allocated to the ministry or to program services. Borden stated in his letter that the Standards Committee was troubled by the fact that PTL had indicated that it spent approximately 50 percent of its total income on program services. As Borden stated in his letter, "These concerns have been brought to your attention a number of times over the past several years."

The same letter also noted that there was "an apparent inconsistency" between the information that had been relayed to the ECFA and PTL's audited financial statements for 1984. Specifically, PTL had indicated in its 1985 application to the ECFA that it had adopted a policy designed to ensure that funds raised for specific purposes were properly applied; PTL claimed that "all designated contributions are stored in our computer with monthly reports generated on a quarterly basis [to] make sure the designations have been fulfilled." However, the notes to PTL's 1984 audited financial statements reflected the opposite: "It is management's opinion that it is not practicable to allocate broadcast time charges and production and other costs of such projects as would be required if separate accounting were employed for such purposes." While PTL was assuring the ECFA that funds raised for a specific purpose were being spent only for that purpose, the notes to PTL's financial statements reflected that management did not believe it was practical to segregate funds.

The ECFA was also continuing its complaint regarding the small size and the amount of independence exercised by the PTL board of directors. The ECFA recommended "that PTL enlarge its [board of directors] to eleven members in 1985, as had been suggested by Mr. Dortch to the ECFA."

This letter, unlike the 1984 letter, stated that PTL could use the ECFA seal and represent itself as a member of the ECFA until a decision was made concerning PTL's membership renewal.

PTL provided several written responses to the questions raised by the ECFA. Many of these responses seemed incomplete and lacked sufficient supporting documentation to substantiate PTL's claims. For example, Peter Bailey wrote Art Borden on April 12, 1985, stating that he had gone through PTL's expenses for fiscal year 1984, "in order to see if we could adjust the percentages for program services. After doing so, we arrived at these adjusted percentages for the fiscal year ending May 31, 1984: Fundraising—8.52%; General and Administration—28.22%; Program Services—63.26%." Bailey did not indicate how he had arrived at those numbers or what the basis was for "adjusting the percentages."

Finally, on October 23, 1985, Art Borden wrote a letter to Jim Bakker and Richard Dortch that seemed to indicate that the ECFA had finally bitten the bullet and taken action to terminate PTL's ECFA membership. However, before final action was taken by the ECFA, Bakker and Dortch advised the ECFA that they had responded to the ECFA's most recent concerns in a letter but that one of Dortch's assistants had failed to mail it. PTL had dodged the bullet.

On October 24, 1985, Jim Bakker wrote to Art Borden in an attempt to minimize the negative press PTL was now receiving. In attempting to alleviate the ECFA's continuing concerns, Bakker claimed that PTL's budget director, Mark Burgund, was now responsible for overseeing the budget of the ministry each month. He also reported that "Peter Bailey, along with our financial team, has come up with updated figures for program services," which were listed as follows: fundraising—1.64 percent, general and administrative expenses—11.42 percent, and program services—89.86 percent.

Bakker also stated that he had "asked William J. Spears of Laventhol and Horwath to audit our designated funds and their accountability. To quote from [Spears'] internal report, 'The system presently in effect as we understand it, is adequate, assuming satisfactory compliance, to give reasonable assurance that designated contributions are expended in the manner and for the purposes for which they were intended.' Mr. Spears assures me that he will be more than happy to work closely with the ECFA to give you any additional information to assure you of PTL's accountability in the designated funds area."

Borden's letter back to Bakker on November 11, 1985, had an air of skepticism: "Based upon the previous financial information that PTL provided, it appeared that insufficient funds were allocated to program services. The percentages in your letter of October 24, seem to go to another extreme, especially as regards to fundraising. ECFA needs an explanation for the wide disparity between the two sets of figures."

Borden's concerns were well founded. Even if Mark Burgund really had been a part of the "financial team" that provided updated figures, this would have been the same Mark Burgund who calculated that a Silver 7000 Club membership was worth over $1 million. Borden did not, however, question why Bakker's figures totaled more than 100 percent.

On January 27, 1986, Art Borden and various representatives of the ECFA had one of seven face-to-face meetings with PTL over the years. Prior to coming to Heritage USA, Art Borden had sent Bakker a letter outlining seven areas about which the ECFA would be seeking information. Borden first questioned the fact that only two of the eight members of the PTL Audit Committee were not staff or family. The fifth question was particularly significant. "Is it correct to assume that the deferred income relative to the Hotel and Towers is not less than projected expenses to provide future services, including depreciation of facilities?" The ECFA therefore knew that it should inquire as to whether or not PTL had set aside sufficient funds to cover the future costs incurred by lifetime partners. Concerning that particular point, Art Borden testified in the *Teague* case that William Spears had assured the ECFA "that significant funds had been set aside to handle the obligations for the lifetime partners" during its meeting with PTL's staff, board members, legal counsel, and auditors.

Details of the meeting between PTL officials and Laventhol auditor Bill Spears are candidly reflected in a memo from Bill Altman, who was then a partner in the accounting firm of Ernst and Whinney, and was attending the meeting with PTL on behalf of the ECFA. This memo is shown as Exhibit 10-1.

Altman's "personal comments," found at the end of his memo, are particularly interesting. After describing a litany of financial problems, he also seems to question the integrity of what was represented to be the "financial condition of Heritage" USA. He concludes his memo by saying he would not be surprised if PTL went into bankruptcy. If Altman made these findings after only a one-day visit to PTL, what findings and conclusions were being reached by PTL's outside professionals?

PTL's ultimate financial demise and subsequent filing for bankruptcy in June 1987 was clearly no surprise to the ECFA. However, in a letter written by Art Borden to PTL on February 28, 1986, less than three weeks after the on-site review conducted by Altman and others, he advised them that PTL had "taken adequate corrective actions to restore itself to compliance with the ECFA's standards." However, in the same letter, he stated the following: "PTL's current liabilities are significantly in excess of liquid assets. In terms of non-fixed assets and liabilities from a strict accounting standpoint, the organization is technically bankrupt. In other words, the organization's continued financial viability is largely dependent on the forbearance of its lenders. . . ." PTL's membership in the ECFA was continued.

PTL's "technical bankruptcy" of February 28, 1986, became fact on June 12, 1987. However, PTL had remained a member of the ECFA until it voluntarily resigned on December 23, 1986.

February 11, 1986

CONFIDENTIAL

To: ECFA Standards Board Members

From: Bill Altman

Subj: Visit to Heritage Village Church (PTL)

SUMMARY

On Monday, January 27, 1986, Arthur Borden, Gerald Bridges, Richard Capin and I visited Heritage Village Church (PTL) near Fort Mill, South Carolina. Messrs. Borden, Bridges and Capin arrived the night before and I joined them on Monday at approximately 9:00 a.m.

To summarize the visit, the PTL people, as expected, were most hospitable. I do not believe that we found evidence that they were in violation of ECFA's seven standards of responsible stewardship, particularly those in question, Standard No. 6 and No. 7. Standard No. 6 relates to integrity and Standard No. 7 relates to fund raising appeals and the requirement that donations are used for the purposes for which they are raised. However, please see my personal comments at the end of this memo.

DAY'S ACTIVITIES

Richard Dortch, Associate Minister, was with us during the entire day. The day's agenda was as follows:

        9:00 - 10:30AM   Tour of Heritage USA facilities by Messrs. Jim
                         Bakker and Richard Dortch. This included visits
                         to the Billy Graham Home, the Home for Unwed
                         Mothers, Fort Hope (in construction), the Upper
                         Room, Passion Play Amphitheater, Food and Clothes
                         for Needy facility, and shipping and office areas

        10:30 - 12:00   Visit to television studio and viewing of "Jim
                         and Tammy Show".

        12:00 - 1:00PM Lunch with Richard Dortch and Ernest Franzone,
                         Board Member, at Heritage Grand Hotel.

        1:30 - 3:30   Meeting with Messrs. Dortch, Franzone, Peter
                         Bailey (Chief Financial Officer), William Spears,
                         (Partner, Laventhol & Horvath, PTL's auditors),
                         Ralph McMillan (Attorney) and several others.

        4:00   Departure for airport.

Exhibit 10-1   Bill Altman's Memo

Besides visiting the facilities on the morning tour, Messrs. Bakker and
Dortch described the PTL ministry and spoke of the substantial negative
press coverage given PTL by the <u>Charlotte Observer</u>, particularly the
January 26 and 27, 1986, editions. Mr. Bakker acknowledged that the
ministry had made a number of mistakes over the years during its rapid
growth period. However, he felt that the ministry's accomplishments
substantially outweighed any financial and other mistakes they have
made during that period.

ACCOUNTABILITY AND TAX PROBLEMS

At lunch, Mr. Dortch discussed PTL's attempt to get things under
control financially and felt that this has been accomplished. He said
all operations are now budgeted and accounted for on a
project-by-project basis. When asked about the status of the tax
issues discussed in its May 31, 1985, audited financial statements
(completed December 1985) he stated that he expected these matters to
be resolved favorably in the near future.

MEETING WITH PTL MANAGEMENT

During the afternoon meeting, the six questions previously submitted to
Mr. Dortch (see copy of letter attached), in addition to the tax
question, were discussed as well as other matters. The PTL
representatives reiterated that the organization was now under tight
budget control and that their financial condition had improved
substantially.

ALLEVIATING THE FINANCIAL PROBLEMS

Mr. Dortch mentioned two potential projects which he felt would raise
substantial revenue for the ministry:

1.   Possible sale of satellite "dishes" to Partners (members). Sales
      price $1,000, cost approximately $325, estimated 100,000 units
      sales will net at least $60 million.

2.   Potential venture with Bank One, whereby a "Heritage Card" would
      be offered to Partners. The card would be a Visa card. PTL
      would get one half of a $60 annual membership fee plus 1 1/2% of
      all sales. Potential is for 500,000 cards to be issued, which
      would bring in $30 million from membership fees alone.

Mr. Dortch also indicated that the ministry was in the process of
consolidating its debts into a $40 million bank loan.

AUDIT COMMITTEE

Mr. Dortch indicated PTL's audit committee consists of Ernest Franzone,
Aimee Cortese, Arthur Lawing, and Messrs. Bakker and Dortch, thus
meeting ECFA Standard No. 4.

-2-

Exhibit 10-1 *Continued*

FUNDRAISING AND G&A ALLOCATIONS

When the question of the rather "broad brush" approach to calculation of fund raising and general administrative expenses was raised, Mr. Spears became somewhat belligerent and felt that a more sophisticated approach was a waste of time. I pointed out that a number of organizations, far less sophisticated than PTL, had been able to develop a more refined approach without creating a "monster" (as described by Mr. Spears) in the process.

DESIGNATED FUNDS

In response to the question relating to L&H's letter, Mr. Bailey stated that PTL was using designated (restricted) funds for the purposes designated.

HOTEL OPERATIONS

Management indicated that the deferred revenue recorded for the Heritage Grand Hotel was not less than estimated expenses to fund the commitment to Partners for free lodging. We did not discuss any accounting ramifications relating the "Silver Club" memberships, whereby lifetime free admissions are provided to workshops, water park, non-food events, etc.

A statement was made that the hotel was at 80% occupancy in January (which would be expected to be the slowest part of the year). Of the 80%, 43% were Partners (free lodging). The hotel had shown a profit of $19,000 after depreciation for the year to date. We were reminded that the hotel had been funded by Partners contributions and therefore no debt service was needed.

TAX STATUS OF PARTNER GIFTS

PTL indicated it does not consider any portion of the gifts from Partners for Hotel and Tower accommodations as a charitable contribution and so informs the donor. Review of PTL literature supports this statement.

ECFA FUND RAISING GUIDELINES - PREMIUM VALUATIONS

A discussion then took place regarding the proposed fund raising guidelines as tentatively approved by ECFA's Board of Directors, particularly the requirement that the cost of any premiums be disclosed at the time that the premiums are offered to the public. The PTL people were less than enthused about this provision and raised several questions regarding the IRS' position in this area and whether this disclosure requirement would cause more problems than it resolved. The matter was left open for further discussion at a later date. Based on my subsequent review of some of PTL's mailings, I can see where this would be a sensitive area.

Exhibit 10-1 *Continued*

MEMBERSHIP DECISION

At the close of the meeting, Mr. Dortch inquired as to the timing of
the decision by ECFA regarding PTL's continuing membership in that
organization. Mr. Bridges responded that the Standards Board as well
as the Board of Directors was meeting toward the end of February and a
decision would be rendered at that time.

＊   ＊   ＊   ＊   ＊   ＊   ＊

PERSONAL COMMENTS

As stated previously, I do not believe that our visit to Heritage
Village Church showed evidence of violations of ECFA standards.
However, I offer the following comments as an outside observer with
some financial background.

We were furnished the November 30, 1985 financial statements prior to
our visit to Heritage. The financial statement appeared to be very
poorly prepared, probably on a cash basis rather than an accrual basis,
and gave no effect to income which must be set aside for the commitment
to Partners for Hotel lodging and other future services. Further, the
income and expense has no breakdown at all by project. It is not
possible to determine whether PTL is operating at a profit or loss
either on a project basis or overall. It seems strange that a
financial statement would be prepared in this matter in view of PTL's
insistence that it now is able to account for expenditures and income
on a project by project basis.

I believe that the financial condition of Heritage is much more
critical than was represented to us during our visit. As evidence of
this, the November 30, 1985 financial statements indicate a cash
position of $178,000 at that date. There appeared to be no other
liquid assets on the balance sheet. As of that date, unpaid payroll
approximated $1 million, accrued payroll taxes were approximately
$400,000, and total accounts payable was $18 million. PTL must be
under tremendous pressure from its creditors.

The completion of the Heritage Towers appears to be completely
dependent on future donations, unless financing is obtained.

Although there may be no debt against the hotel and towers, PTL has
substantial other debt totalling approximately $38 million, some of
which appears to be at a relatively high interest rate.

Although I certainly claim no expertise in hotel accounting, I find it
hard to believe that the hotel can show a profit at a 37% occupancy
rate (the rate after deducting the PTL Partners' free lodging),
particularly since it serves no alcoholic beverages nor does it cater
to business meetings, both of which are substantial profit makers for
most hotels.

-4-

Exhibit 10-1 *Continued*

I suspect that the tax situation will not be resolved as easily as Mr.
Dortch indicated to us. When I questioned him about state
accommodations tax relative to the Partners' contributions, he said
this was never an issue, however there is disclosure to the contrary in
PTL's financial statements published only one month previously.

The financial condition of PTL has been discussed by Mr. Bakker on
several subsequent "Jim and Tammy" shows, specifically the February
10th and 11th shows in which he indicated that the financial condition
was critical.

In summary, in view of what appears to be a continual cash flow
problem, I do not think we should be overly surprised if certain of
PTL's operating companies are forced in bankruptcy by its creditors in
the near future. Although this would be a disaster for any ministry, I
feel it would be particularly catastrophic for PTL in view of its
commitment to provide future services (lodging and other facilities)
for a substantial number of people. I do not believe, though, that a
rapidly deteriorating financial condition, including substantial
delinquencies to creditors, in itself is a violation of either Standard
No. 6 or 7. However, consideration should be given to the effect on
ECFA if my prediction of financial disaster comes true (I hope it does
not) and PTL is a member of ECFA at that time.

Exhibit 10-1 *Continued*

The ECFA's Response to PTL's Demise

The ECFA issued a press release reflecting its report on PTL. Although
the ECFA was never furnished with PTL's audited financial statements
for 1986, it did have the financial statements for 1984 and 1985. The
ECFA represented that they had "relied heavily" on the auditor's
opinion of PTL's financial statements and noted that neither auditing
firm, in issuing their opinions from 1978 until 1985, "gave any indication whatsoever of the serious problems we now know existed."

The ECFA knew of the IRS inquiry that was reflected in the notes
to the 1984 financial statements and also resulted in the 1985 auditor's report being qualified. As was noted in Altman's memo, this
was one of the matters about which the ECFA made an inquiry while
at Heritage USA, but Richard Dortch gave assurances that all would
turn out favorably for PTL.

As discussed in the previous chapter, the 1984 financial statement
did not note any overselling of partnerships. However, the 1985 financial statements reflected that over 47,000 lifetime partnerships
had been sold for the Grand Hotel, which was, of course, 22,000 more
than the promised limit.

The ECFA knew that there was a promised limit of 25,000 memberships in the Grand Hotel and that PTL's audited financial statements filed with the ECFA reflected sales in excess of 47,000 for the

year ending May 31, 1985. Borden was questioned under oath concerning his knowledge that sales for the Grand Hotel were in excess of the 25,000-member limit:

Q: You didn't tell anybody about that?
A: No.
Q: You didn't raise any questions with PTL about that?
A: No, we did not, it is not our policy to manage the organization. If they decided to change the number of partners, that would be a management decision. ECFA is not second guessing management for their decisions.
Q: Did they ever tell you they were changing the numbers?
A: No.
Q: You never raised any concerns about this?
A: No.

No evidence was presented in the *Teague* case that anyone from the ECFA had attempted to determine if there had in fact been a change in the number of promised partnership limits or whether this was the inception of the largest consumer fraud in U.S. history.

It should also be restated that the ECFA was not the only entity that received PTL's audited financial statements for 1985. As previously discussed, the PTL board of directors also received them on January 28, 1986. The board minutes reflect that "the 1985 annual audit by Laventhol and Horwath, Certified Public Accountants, was presented to the Board for review. A motion was made, seconded, and passed unanimously that the audit be accepted."

Neither the ECFA's knowledge of the oversale of the Grand Hotel nor the board of director's approval of PTL's financial statements for fiscal year 1985 were ever directly addressed in the Bakker criminal trial. Certainly Jim Bakker might have been able to argue that he had no intent to defraud, because the excessive sale of the Grand Hotel partnerships had not only been implicitly approved by PTL's board of directors but had also been made public by filing its 1985 financial statement with the ECFA.

One can only speculate as to what might have happened had the ECFA vigorously pursued all of these and other matters. At a minimum, the ECFA could have proved itself to be a viable, self-regulating organization; had it done so, the great tragedy that occurred to PTL's lifetime partners might have been avoided. In a Gannet News Service article dated May 1, 1987, Art Borden was quoted as having said the following: "It's obvious we didn't ask enough questions or all the right ones or the answers we got weren't full answers." This response appears to accurately reflect the ECFA's actions and inactions concerning PTL.

□□□

CHAPTER ELEVEN

The Purchase of PTL: Reverend Morris Cerullo and Arthur Andersen

I believe that there will be someone that God will speak to, to give $10,000. You obey the spirit. If you don't have it in your checkbook, postdate the check so that you can take it out of your saving, put it into your checking account—perfectly alright. Postdate it—for a few days on into next week.

Dr. Morris Cerullo, in his taped message, "The Crisis!"

AT A 9 P.M. MEETING on April 18, 1987, Jim Bakker and the entire PTL board of directors resigned en masse. Jerry Falwell was named the new chair of the board, and the new board members had all been hand picked by him. Bakker later contended that he had been tricked into giving his ministry over to Falwell; he claimed that Falwell had secretly approached him with news that the Jessica Hahn affair would be made public and that another minister might be making a bid for a "hostile takeover" of the PTL ministry. Jerry Falwell maintained that he was simply confronting Bakker with allegations of Bakker's indiscretions as required by the Bible. There are many such conflicts in the public statements made by both men and their associates concerning the events surrounding Falwell's takeover of and involvement in the PTL corporation. In any case, little did both men know that over the next three and a half years they, along with at least four other individuals, would be making their own attempts to either gain control of, or regain control of the Heritage USA property.

Although Jerry Falwell was successful in raising funds for PTL, he simply could not hold a candle to Jim Bakker in this regard. Then again, Jerry Falwell refused to sell any more lifetime partnerships.

Richard Dortch, the only executive held over from the Bakker era, was terminated at the second official meeting of the new board of directors. Also gone were David Taggart, Peter Bailey, and Shirley Fulbright. Fulbright filed a claim alleging that PTL owed her $20,835 plus related payroll taxes based on eight weeks of severance pay and four weeks of vacation pay. She claimed that this arrangement had been agreed to by Harry Hargrove, the person whom Jerry Falwell named as president of PTL.

Despite Falwell's best efforts, including his "May Miracle" fund-raising effort that raised over $7 million in May of 1987 alone and resulted in Falwell taking a plunge down the gigantic PTL waterslide, PTL was simply not able to make it. The bickering, or "holy war," that had developed between Falwell and Bakker simply was too much for PTL to overcome. Consequently, PTL filed for bankruptcy under Chapter 11 on June 12, 1987. Eventually, Heritage USA was sold for $45 million on December 14, 1990, which marked the end of three and a half years of attempting to dig PTL out of bankruptcy and then find a suitable buyer. The former lifetime partners, the people who had contributed more than enough money to purchase and build Heritage USA, never saw—and probably never will see—any of the funds received from its sale. The only people involved with PTL who were not deprived of funds were the scores of lawyers, accountants, and advisors. As a group, these professionals received, as of September 1992, $6,487,487 from the sale of the PTL property.

As of September 1992, the law firm of Allman, Spry, Humphreys of Winston-Salem, North Carolina, had been paid $2,442,631 in their role as attorneys for the bankrupt PTL. Norman Roy Grutman, who represented PTL and Falwell for an eight-month period after Bakker's departure, was paid $315,000. The accounting firm of Arthur Andersen was hired by Falwell and was paid $415,360 for fees and expenses. Dennis Shedd, who was the court-appointed trustee, sold the property and was paid $493,891.17 for his nine months' employment.

Who purchased the PTL property? It was Morris Cerullo *and* others.

Who Is Morris Cerullo?

Among Christians in the United States, Morris Cerullo's name received very little recognition until the 1980s. Cerullo, a half-Jewish orphan who grew up to build an international Christian ministry, began his "Morris Cerullo World Evangelism" (MCWE) in 1960 by converting his garage into a mailing room for literature.

After his Jewish mother died when he was two years old, Cerullo's alcoholic father was unable to care for the family's five children. Morris Cerullo was eventually placed in an Orthodox Jewish orphanage in Clifton, New Jersey. Although he received religious instruction in the orphanage, he converted to Christianity.

As Cerullo explained: "My spirit was taken out of this world. Then I had an experience similar to that which Moses had when the Lord appeared to him in the burning bush. The Lord appeared to me in the same type of manifestation, a ball of fire that was about . . . six feet tall, two or three times as broad, no physical features whatsoever; just a ball of flaming brightness like a million moons and suns and stars all rolled together."

Like Jim Bakker before him, Cerullo claimed his actions were based on God's instructions. Cerullo said God told him, "Build me an army," when he was touring Brazil in 1962. Since then, Cerullo has traveled to numerous foreign countries to hold religious meetings that typically feature healings (with on-the-spot testimonials of their validity), clapping, exuberant worshiping, and frequent "speaking in tongues."

Cerullo, a short, barrel-chested man with a raspy, high-pitched voice, was eventually ordained by the Assemblies of God—the same denomination that once counted Jim Bakker among its pastors. He was to receive other instructions from God. "[The Lord] asked me in my spirit: 'Morris, will you be an instrument in My hands to take back what the devil tried to steal?' " Cerullo said in his news conference concerning his involvement in the purchase of Heritage USA.

According to a letter that he sent to his followers, Cerullo's involvement in the purchase of the PTL assets begin in early 1989. "I began to feel the Lord speak to me about Heritage U.S.A. Would I be willing to be used by God as his instrument to take back from the devil what he tried to steal from the Body of Christ?" wrote Cerullo.

According to Cerullo, he first visited the PTL property and began a series of dialogues with Dennis Shedd, the court-appointed trustee, concerning Cerullo's desire to purchase it. After months of intensive negotiations, the trustee, the creditors, and the bankruptcy court accepted Morris Cerullo's offer.

Morris Cerullo's purchase was accomplished in two phases. First, he bought the Inspirational Network, which was, of course, the PTL satellite system. The court approved his offer to purchase the satellite/

television network on May 31, 1990, for $7 million. Cerullo asserted in his correspondence to faithful followers that the $7 million used to purchase the network "was borrowed from our MCWE Endowment and Scholarship fund." "Paying for the network in full in addition to making the initial deposit on Heritage, took virtually every penny we had," Cerullo added. In any case, Cerullo's ministry, MCWE, became the sole owner of the renamed "New Inspirational Network," the satellite and cable system that reached 6.5 million homes in the United States and parts of Britain. Phase two of the purchase consisted of acquiring the balance of the assets of Heritage USA at a purchase price of $45 million; this included 2,200 acres, all of the buildings, and everything else not associated with the television network. That offer was accepted by the Bankruptcy Court on August 2, 1990.

Cerullo penned a letter to his followers dated March 28, 1991, in which he said that he had previously commissioned a major international consulting and accounting firm, Pannell Kerr Forster, to do an economic and marketing feasibility study on the Heritage assets. A positive business plan was drafted as a result of this feasibility study. According to Cerullo, "We were able to obtain from a financial institution a letter of financial commitment. This letter indicated that they would loan us the money necessary to fund the purchase of Heritage as well as the needed funds for repairs, for completion of construction that had been previously halted, and for some new construction as well, if we could meet the terms and conditions."

Again, according to Cerullo, "It was this letter that gave the bankruptcy trustee and the court confidence to accept our offer [to purchase the remaining assets]."

With the total MCWE bid of $52 million for the Heritage USA assets, consisting of $7 million for the satellite network and $45 million for everything else, the MCWE organization began a massive, intensive fundraising effort that included using not only mailed solicitations but also the New Inspirational Network in an attempt to raise the $52 million.

The "Take It Back from the Devil" Telethon and Arthur Andersen

"God, God, God," Cerullo would shout to the studio audience at Heritage USA during his telethons that often lasted as long as two hours a night. David Cerullo, Morris Cerullo's son, told the studio audience that "we are here to get the devil off your finances, to get the devil off your bodies . . . to get the devil off your family relationships, to get the devil out of your life."

Supposed healings occurred in the studio audience and in viewers' homes as well. These healings were reported by Cerullo, his son, and his wife, Theresa, in televised broadcasts. Periodically throughout the telethons, (and always at their conclusions), a board was displayed that reflected how much money had been raised that night towards the $52 million goal of the "Take It Back from the Devil" campaign. Morris Cerullo's pitch was that he was attempting to wrest PTL from the claws of Satan.

Night after night, Cerullo revealed how much money had been raised to date in the telethon. Of course, Cerullo had already paid $7 million to purchase the satellite network, so what was really needed was $45 million to purchase the remaining assets, but he also wanted to be reimbursed.

Cerullo claimed on his television program in November 1990 that he "wanted to be able to come before the cameras with absolute integrity." Consequently, he indicated on the "Take It Back" Telethon that he had hired an accounting firm "by the name of Arthur Andersen" to take the funds, on a daily basis, that were being raised by the Take It Back Telethon and put them into a separate escrow savings account. At the appropriate time, all funds were to be transferred to the trustees for the purpose of purchasing the remaining PTL assets. However, Cerullo said he had a "written contract" with Arthur Andersen whereby the firm was "legally obligated" to return to the contributor 100 percent of all funds sent in if MCWE did not close on the property.

Later, Morris Cerullo was to write this boast to his followers: "Arthur Andersen and Company, one of the largest public accounting firms in the world, is retained by MCWE (since 1983) to do an annual audit which includes full testing of our procedures and the handling of all monies received in the ministry. Based on their report, Morris Cerullo World Evangelism has received the highest rating that an auditing firm is allowed to issue for the past five years."

These representations are extremely significant. According to Cerullo's statements on national TV, Arthur Andersen had now taken responsibility for returning 100 percent of all monies sent in if MCWE did not close on the PTL property. Contributors received comfort from knowing that if MCWE did not close on the property, their funds would be returned, according to Cerullo, "under the auspices" of Arthur Andersen, which was "legally obligated" to do so.

Several of my students and I have attempted to contact both Morris Cerullo World Evangelism and Arthur Andersen in order to obtain a copy of MCWE's contract with Arthur Andersen. Neither Arthur Andersen nor Morris Cerullo have responded to our requests.

Through mailings and telethons, Morris Cerullo contended that it had been his "intention from the beginning to raise as much money as we could through fundraising. We knew we were facing what seemed to be insurmountable hurdles. The challenge for a ministry like ours to raise $52 million within a matter of weeks would truly be one of the greatest financial miracles in history."

Cerullo communicated that "based on the commitment letter we had received from the financial institution . . . we felt confident that what monies we weren't able to raise we could borrow."

According to Cerullo, MCWE was not able to meet all of the "technical conditions" of the agreement with the financial institution; consequently, this left MCWE far short of the total sum needed to buy Heritage USA. According to Cerullo, "All [of] this happened just weeks before the deadline to close escrow." This aspect of his attempt to purchase the PTL assets will be explored later in this chapter.

The Acquisition of PTL Assets

Ultimately, in October 1990, Morris Cerullo and MCWE approached a Malaysian business conglomerate, the MUI Group, and proposed that it join MCWE in purchasing the PTL complex.

Cerullo's consummation of the purchase of the PTL property was announced by bankruptcy trustee Dennis Shedd and Cerullo's attorney, Timothy Treadwell, at about 7 P.M. on December 14, 1990. Ironically, earlier that day the federal civil court jury had found Bakker liable for fraud.

Initially, Cerullo did not disclose any details concerning the financial arrangements surrounding his purchase of the PTL assets; neither did he discuss any other party's involvement in purchasing the assets. For example, *Charisma Magazine*, a Christian magazine based in Florida, mentioned in its March 1991 issue that Heritage USA had a new owner; the Morris Cerullo World Evangelism Association had been able to come up with the $52 million sale price. The magazine article merely stated that "Cerullo purchased the entire spread, including the hotel, television studios, waterpark and satellite television network. . . . A management firm from Malaysia [will] help oversee the opening of the Heritage Grand Hotel and other lodgings."

Those statements are not accurate. The acquisition of the PTL assets was completed with funds that had been provided by MUI Hong Kong, Limited; MUI International, Limited; and Seraphim Investments, Limited. The MUI firms are part of the 37 holding companies of the parent corporation, Malayan United Industries Berhad. MUI's subsidiary companies are incorporated not only in Malaysia but also in Hong Kong, Singapore, Canada, and the United States. The principal activities of the subsidiary companies include trading and investments, hotel and catering, commercial banking, and real estate investments.

These three companies became the majority investors in the newly formed New Heritage USA (NHUSA) by contributing $23,501,200, which gave them a 51 percent controlling interest. They also provided, through their affiliates, an $8.4 million loan to MCWE to enable it to complete the acquisition of its 49 percent ownership in NHUSA. In addition, MCWE was allowed to claim a $2 million credit at the time of closing due to an environmental problem that had been noted on the property by both MCWE and the trustee. Consequently, the total cash amount provided by Morris Cerullo at closing was only $11,100,980. Finally, an affiliate of the two MUI companies provided a working capital loan of $5 million to the newly formed corporation.

Clearly, Cerullo's Malaysian business partners had a more substantial stake than just being "a management firm from Malaysia [helping to] oversee the opening of the Heritage Grand Hotel and other lodging." Cerullo and *Charisma Magazine* also failed to indicate that Cerullo was only a minority shareholder of NHUSA. Yet-King Loy, the President of NHUSA, immediately wrote to *Charisma Magazine* to correct the magazine's inaccuracies.

The board of directors of New Heritage was controlled by the majority shareholders, represented by Yet-King Loy, Lawrence Chai, and Kok Yin Khet. Morris Cerullo and his son, David Cerullo, represented MCWE, the minority shareholders. Initially, Morris Cerullo was chairman of the board, and Yet-King Loy served as president.

The Malaysians were not only professionally very astute businessmen, but they were also very devout Christians. However, they may not have been prepared to deal with the U.S. televangelist, Morris Cerullo.

Yet-King Loy, who is a member of the board of directors of MUI in addition to being a board member and president of New Heritage USA, was quoted in the *San Diego Business Journal* as having said the following concerning his first meeting with Morris Cerullo: "He was very eloquent. . . . I think he presented his facts very well, I'm sure he has a very sharp mind." Loy reluctantly added, "I think some of his practices need to be reviewed."

The Gold and Platinum Card Programs

One of the practices to which Loy may have been referring was Morris Cerullo's Gold Card program. In a letter dated August 31, 1990, and mailed to over 158,000 people, Morris Cerullo announced the "Heritage Gold Club." According to his letter: "I have established the Heritage Gold Club in honor of all those who will help me raise the $52 million that I must have by October 31 to take back what the devil tried to steal and redeem Heritage USA debt-free for the Kingdom of God. You can join the Heritage Gold Club with a one-time gift of $300 or more. And when you join the Heritage Gold Club, you will become part of a very special and exclusive group of charter members who will have brought about a world wide healing in the Body of Christ."

The Heritage Gold Club, just like the Grand Hotel partnerships, offered "these wonderful benefits":

1. A 50 percent discount on published room rates at the Heritage Grand Hotel and the new Heritage Towers. Gold card holders also got a 50 percent discount on fees for the RV Park, all camp sights, and all other attractions at New Heritage USA
2. A 20 percent discount on all records, books, and video- and audiotapes at the New Heritage bookstores
3. A 10 percent discount on all meals at New Heritage USA
4. Special discount airfares to any MCWE event
5. Group discounts resulting in savings of hundreds of dollars on airfares to New Heritage USA
6. An invitation to "an all expense paid, exclusive pre-opening weekend for one person at New Heritage U.S.A. . . . Friday, Saturday through Sunday noon"; "all expenses" included lodging and two meals each day

In addition, Morris Cerullo also instituted a Platinum Card program. According to written promotional materials disseminated by Cerullo, the cost of a Platinum Card membership was $1,000 or more, and members could enjoy all of the benefits of the Gold Club membership plus exclusive 24-hour access to the Platinum lounge in the New Heritage Grand Hotel.

These "wonderful benefits" seemed strikingly similar to those offered by Jim Bakker's Grand Hotel lifetime partnership program. And Morris Cerullo's pleas for financial support sounded much like the pleas that Jim Bakker had made years before: "And you can be a member of the Heritage Gold Club for as little as $300. What is even more amazing is . . . if you, and my other partners like you, will join me and give a one time gift of $300 or more, we will be able to redeem Heritage USA and literally stop Satan from trying to steal this ministry. We will be able to restore this marvelous 2300 acre facility for the Kingdom of God."

Despite these striking resemblances between Cerullo's Gold Card program and Bakker's lifetime partnership program, there were also some significant differences. For example, Jim Bakker at least limited the use of the lifetime partnership to four days and three nights each year for the duration of each partner's life. In Cerullo's promotional literature, however, the discounts on hotel room rates under the Gold Card program were touted as being for an "unlimited number of days . . . as often as the cardholder likes . . . each year for the rest of the cardholder's life." The Gold Card program also applied to all members of the immediate family who stayed in the same room.

Although Bakker's lifetime partnership program had very clearly stated terms and limits, the Cerullo Gold Card memberships were much less clear concerning the 50 percent discount on the published room rate at the Grand and Towers Hotels. Was this 50 percent off the standard room rate or 50 percent off the price for a room after seasonal or other promotional discounts had been figured in? In any case, this statement was vague, nebulous, and open to numerous interpretations.

In addition to soliciting laypeople for Gold and Platinum Club memberships, Cerullo also solicited ministers. Approximately 18,909 letters were sent to ministers in October 1990, requesting that they become a Gold or Platinum Club member. The same solicitation was made again in the January/February issue of Morris Cerullo's *Victory* tabloid, which promised that for $300, not only could a minister receive the previously discussed discounts, but also that if he or she brought a congregation, they, too, could use the minister's benefits. The tabloid specified, however, that the congregation could be no larger than 3,000! With 18,000 letters offering this special benefit to ministers, which was also being promoted to the 200,000 or so readers of *Victory,* this meant that tens of millions of people could have received the benefits of the card programs.

To receive a Gold Card membership, a person had to pay a fee, described in the promotional literature as "your gift of $300 or more," payable to MCWE. The Platinum Club membership cost $1,000, also payable to MCWE. Additionally, while Morris Cerullo never stated publicly what the membership limit was for the Gold Card program, he did indicate in his promotional material that "limited charter gift memberships [are] now open."

According to Bill Salinas-Jones, the senior vice-president of operations and finance for MCWE, "There were a total of 1,750,733 mailings and telemarketing solicitations made in connection with the Card Club Program promotional efforts," which were sent to a basic core group consisting of less than 200,000 individuals.

Salinas-Jones, who stated in a declaration that he was "very familiar with the overall fundraising activities of MCWE" and "was directly involved in the operation of the New Heritage Gold Card Club and the New Heritage Platinum Card Club," stated the following: "A total of 13,761 persons subscribed to the Gold Card program and 561 persons subscribed to the Platinum Card program, for an overall total of 14,322." The statistical data that Salinas-Jones compiled reflect that approximately $4.5 million was raised through the card programs.

At first glance, the Gold and Platinum Card programs would appear to have been very ill-conceived. Sending out over 1.75 million solicitations to under 200,000 people promising such deep discounts was not a very prudent business decision. The indeterminable long-term NHUSA corporate commitments and the ambiguities in exactly what is being discounted, together with no specified limitations on the use of the discounts would seem to have made the actual implementation of the Gold and Platinum Card programs nothing short of corporate suicide.

According to the majority shareholders, there was, however, one other problem with the Gold and Platinum Card programs: Cerullo never told them of the existence of either program.

Yet-King Loy stated in his affidavit dated March 11, 1991: "On January 25, 1991, I attended a meeting in Fort Mill, South Carolina, with Morris Cerullo to discuss a hotel management contract for the hotel facilities at New Heritage USA. At the meeting, Morris Cerullo offhandedly mentioned to me that MCWE had issued thousands of 'Gold Cards' to individuals which would permit 50% discounts on hotel room rates at New Heritage USA."

Loy contacted Hal Tysinger, chief operating officer of NHUSA, to provide him with the facts on the Gold Card program referred to by Cerullo. Tysinger stated that he had previously received telephone inquiries concerning the Gold Card program and had referred all such inquiries to MCWE's corporate headquarters in San Diego, California.

According to Loy's affidavit, he learned from the promotional brochures "dated January 25, 1991, that Morris Cerullo and MCWE intended to use the proceeds from the card club sales to pay off the $8.4 million loan that Morris Cerullo and MCWE had borrowed to finance MCWE's equity participation in NHUSA."

After reviewing the promotional brochures that had been sent to date and determining that the Gold Card program could have a potentially serious economic impact on the corporation, Loy contacted the other two majority shareholders, Kok Yin Khet and Lawrence Chai, concerning the details of the newly discovered card club programs.

What happened next was a classic example of how a board of directors ought to function. Loy, Khet, and Chai each faxed correspondence to Morris Cerullo reflecting their disapproval of the Gold Card solicitations and their demand that he "cease and desist" issuing or promoting any such cards. As Lawrence Chai stated in his correspondence: "Dr. Cerullo, I am shocked to learn that you have initiated this action without the prior approval of the Board of Directors of the New Heritage USA Corporation and the Executive Committee. In my opinion, this action of yours has not only serious financial implications, but also other legal consequences." Board Director Kok Yin Khet was even more direct in his fax to Cerullo:

> I am not aware that the Board of Directors of New Heritage U.S.A. Corporation has discussed, let alone, approved the issuance of such Gold Club cards with the accompanying benefits and concessions as outlined in the brochure. Since such Gold Club cards may well impose punishing liabilities and severe financial commitments on the part of the corporation, the extent of which cannot be ascertained at this moment, I write to advise you that as a director of New Heritage USA Corporation, the issuance of such Gold Club cards unilaterally, without prior discussion and the approval by the Board is a serious matter and I would urge you to cease issuing such Gold Club cards and other similar cards forthwith. I would point out that quite apart from the negative impact on the viability of the business of the corporation, your action may well give rise to some unpleasant consequences which may affect the Corporation.

This prompt and immediate action by the New Heritage USA majority shareholders illustrates how a board of directors should function from not only an ethical basis but also a legal standpoint. In my opinion, they acted in a timely and professional manner.

Morris Cerullo called Loy on January 29, 1991, and confirmed that he (Cerullo) had taken "all immediate steps to stop and cancel further solicitations and issuance of any Gold Card, Platinum Card and any other arrangements purportedly from New Heritage USA and/or its corporations."

Loy confirmed that telephone conversation in correspondence that he sent to Cerullo by fax and Federal Express on the very next day. Again, the procedure followed by Loy illustrates exactly how a member of a board of directors should function, both legally and ethically.

Not to be outdone, Cerullo sent a confidential memorandum back to Loy, dated January 31, 1991, in which he indicated that "we have a mailing, already in the mails, on this subject. It cannot be held . . . it is gone."

Loy sent a note to Cerullo the very same day, thanking him for his memorandum and asking him to elaborate on his statement that "we have a mailing already in the mails." Loy reiterated that "the mailings, etc., including the issuance of the cards, were to be ceased and discontinued immediately. . . ." Loy again asked Cerullo to "cease and desist" all activities relative to the Gold and Platinum Card Programs.

Cerullo had apparently become quite irked at the correspondence that he had been receiving from the majority shareholders. As chair of the board of the New Heritage USA, he sent Yet-King Loy, president of the corporation, a copy of his latest fax with several handwritten notations. These notations include, as shown in Exhibit A-35, circling the phrase, already in the mails. Cerullo writes, "means exactly what it says too late to stop it—. . ." At the bottom of the same page, Cerullo wrote this note: "Dear Loy—it is apparent that letters and notes back and forth from your associates and *Et al* reveal a total lack of comprehension—it is best to wait until next week's [Board of Directors] meeting that I called." Cerullo signed his note to Loy, "As Ever Your Partner Morris Cerullo."

Cerullo was apparently just as perturbed with the correspondence that he had received from board member Khet, to whom he sent the following note: "Dear Khet—I find your fax of January 31 very *offending*, and in extremely poor taste, as *my* director—you have overstepped the bounds of your position in issuing directives to the Chairman of the Board of New Heritage USA. Who do you think is calling this meeting to discuss this issue—not Mr. Loy—I did—an apology is in order!" Cerullo ends his correspondence with the remark, "God Bless You. Dr. Morris Cerullo." (Exhibit A-36.)

According to Loy's affidavit, Morris Cerullo had initially "advised [him] that there were only 8,000 cards issued." Loy's affidavit also reflects that at the board meeting held February 6–8, 1991, Morris Cerullo said that there were 10,000 cardholders; it also reveals that neither Morris Cerullo nor MCWE had undertaken any feasibility studies or investigations to determine the financial soundness of the card program. Furthermore, MCWE had already used approximately $3 million in proceeds collected from the card club programs to pay for MCWE Investments' subscription of shares in NHUSA. (It should be noted that this $3 million is separate from the $8.4 million that had been previously borrowed by MCWE from the majority shareholders.)

As reflected in the minutes of the board of directors from this meeting, Cerullo agreed to discontinue and withdraw MCWE's card club program, take prompt steps to inform all MCWE cardholders of the discontinuance of the program and offer refunds, and execute an appropriate indemnification agreement to hold NHUSA harmless from any and all claims. An agreement was also reached that Morris Cerullo was to submit this agreement for ratification by the board of directors of MCWE immediately.

Yet-King Loy was advised by William Lund, the chair of the asset management team of New Heritage USA (a select group of professional individuals responsible for advising on the reopening and the development of the former PTL assets), that Morris Cerullo had indicated on February 16, 1991, that there were 12,000 card club subscribers. Loy believed the memberships were apparently increasing, and no steps were being taken to discontinue the program as had been promised by Cerullo.

Cerullo had not honored any of the agreements promised at the February board meeting as of the next board meeting held on March 6, 1991. Instead, David Cerullo, MCWE, and he continued to try to justify the continuance of the Gold and Platinum Card programs.

At the March 6, 1991, executive session of the board of directors, Morris Cerullo, according to Loy's affidavit, "admitted that he had not disclosed the Gold and Platinum Card program to NHUSA, NHC, or the majority shareholders. He also admitted that he had made 'six other obligations before closing' that were not disclosed." The minutes of the board meeting held on March 6 reaffirm Cerullo's earlier promise to withdraw the Gold/Platinum cards. However, at the March board meeting Morris Cerullo and his son, David, "expressed full support for the Gold and Platinum card program."

Also at this meeting, the board authorized Yet-King Loy to take all action necessary, including legal action, to resolve the matter of the card programs.

The Litigation

On March 18, 1991, NHUSA filed a lawsuit in the South Carolina Federal District Court against MCWE and Morris and David Cerullo. The complaint was based on an alleged conspiracy among the defendants to defraud NHUSA and thousands of unsuspecting members of the public by making an improper and unauthorized offering of Gold and Platinum Cards that were claimed to provide benefits with respect to property owned by NHUSA and the defendants. The complaint also alleged that the defendants had used the proceeds from this card sale for their own personal benefit.

Morris Cerullo's version of the facts concerning the Gold and Platinum Card programs were remarkably different. In an affidavit from Morris Cerullo dated September 30, 1991, he acknowledged that after acquiring the (former) Inspirational Network for $7 million, he immediately proceeded attempting to raise $45 million for the purpose of purchasing the remaining assets of the former PTL ministry. The closing for these assets was originally scheduled for October 31, 1990, but was subsequently delayed until December 14, 1990.

Cerullo admitted that his fundraising campaign included the Gold and Platinum Card programs: "The card programs were developed by MCWE in July 1990, following a business planning meeting (a charette) held in Charlotte in June. At that meeting and in their feasibility study, Pannell Kerr Forster recommended that a discount card program be developed to attract people back to New Heritage in the wake of the Jim Bakker/PTL scandal. The card programs were developed by MCWE in response to this recommendation."

Cerullo also made this statement in his affidavit: "In designing the programs, MCWE attempted to ensure that the economic benefits to New Heritage would more than offset the discounts offered, so that the program would realize a net economic benefit from the programs."

Cerullo went on to dispute the majority shareholders' claim that they had been unaware of the Gold Card program. He cited two occasions during which he allegedly informed Mr. Tan Sri Khoo, the chief executive officer at Malayan United Industries, that MCWE had instituted a Gold Card program as part of its fundraising efforts for New Heritage. "Although Mr. Khoo and myself did not discuss the details of the card programs at these meetings because of other more pressing matters on the agenda, I am confident that Mr. Khoo was aware before the [purchase of the New Heritage property] of the existence of the card programs and that such programs were designed to provide benefit at New Heritage to the holders of such cards." Cerullo also contended that he had spoken to Yet-King Loy about the Gold Card program.

According to Cerullo, the first time that he became aware "that the Malaysian Directors of New Heritage claimed not to have known of the card program before the [purchase of the New Heritage property] was when [he] received a telecopied letter from Mr. Loy on January 29, 1991." Cerullo contended that he had immediately discontinued the Gold Card solicitations—with the exception of the "February Donor," a monthly MCWE direct mailing that had already been sent out.

When it became apparent that Cerullo did not have the votes to persuade the NHUSA board of directors to adopt the card program, Cerullo contended that he agreed to withdraw the program and, subject to approval of his own board of directors, agreed to indemnify and hold NHUSA harmless for any losses arising from the card programs.

Cerullo's affidavit indicated that he had met with the asset management team on February 16, 1991, and "[a]t the conclusion of the meeting, the consensus of the [asset management team] was that the card program should not be terminated, or that, at a minimum, there should be further discussion of this issue before a final decision was made. The [asset management team] asked Bill Lund, Chairman . . . to approach Mr. Loy on its behalf and to request that further consideration be given to the matter."

Cerullo stated that because Loy acquiesced, another NHUSA board meeting was scheduled on March 6, 1991, to again consider the card programs. In addition to the legal counsel being present, Cerullo "also requested Arthur Andersen and Company to prepare an economic impact study of the card programs on New Heritage in anticipation of the March 6 meeting."

As will be discussed in detail later, Cerullo's affidavit reflected that he had presented the directors with copies of the economic impact study prepared by Arthur Andersen and Company which concluded that the card programs would have "no material adverse impact on New Heritage." Cerullo also stated in his affidavit that at the same board meeting, the representatives of the asset management team (Lund, Peterson, and Clark) "also expressed the view that the card programs would not have an adverse economic impact on New Heritage."

Thinking that the card program dispute could be resolved, Cerullo stated that he was surprised that the majority shareholders had instituted legal proceedings against him. If he was surprised concerning the first lawsuit, he was probably even more surprised when they filed a second lawsuit. This one claimed that in the January/February addition of *Victory*, Cerullo had asked people to send contributions to restore the Upper Room Prayer Center, reduce New Heritage's debt, and complete $15 million worth of renovations to New Heritage USA. According to Cerullo, that issue of *Victory* had been prepared at a time when MCWE was not expecting to have any partners, and the funds were to have been used as promised. In any case, even though he solicited donations, NHUSA ended up paying the $15,000 that was required to renovate the Upper Room without receiving any money from Cerullo.

Cerullo's attorneys alleged in court that the majority shareholders were simply trying to "oust" him. However, Cerullo had already tendered his resignation as chairman on February 8, 1991; that resignation was effective as of May 9, 1991, and had been accepted by the board of NHUSA. As Yet-King Loy noted, Cerullo could be removed as chair by a majority vote of the board of NHUSA; a lawsuit (let alone two lawsuits) was not necessary.

According to a press release issued by Yet-King Loy: "The crux of the complaint by New Heritage against Morris Cerullo and MCWE is that MCWE is, by way of the Gold/Platinum Card program, collecting money for itself at the expense of New Heritage. In essence, MCWE is offering, through such cards, huge discounts on the products and services of New Heritage in consideration of cardholders donating specified sums to MCWE, an organization entirely separate and distinct from New Heritage. Thus, while the contributions for the Gold/Platinum Cards have gone to MCWE, the burden of paying for such benefits is, under Morris Cerullo's scheme, to be borne by New Heritage. This form of 'creative' financing is, in the judgement of the directors representing the majority investors of New Heritage, fraudulent."

In essence, Loy was saying that Morris Cerullo was, through his "wonderful benefits," giving away the "family farm." The problem was, of course, that the family farm was not Cerullo's to give away.

Loy concluded his press release by stating, "New Heritage will continue to manage its affairs in accordance with the highest standards of integrity and accountability based on Christian principles."

The litigation between the majority shareholders and Morris Cerullo provided an opportunity to examine some of the behind-the-scenes business aspects of the Gold Card program. The litigation exposed some matters that otherwise would not have been made public and that raised serious questions concerning the business practices of the MCWE organization.

As mentioned previously, Morris Cerullo had stated in his affidavit that "in designing the programs, MCWE attempted to ensure that the economic benefits to New Heritage would more than offset the discounts offered so that the project would realize a net economic benefit from the programs." The facts brought to light by this litigation seemed to indicate that such an analysis had never occurred.

MCWE had apparently gone directly from vague, introductory conceptual discussions right into making promises to hundreds of thousands of people. Billy Salinas-Jones stated in his declaration that as vice-president of operations and finance for Morris Cerullo World Evangelism, he had been "very familiar with the overall fundraising activities of MCWE. [He] was directly involved in the operation of the New Heritage Gold Card Club and the New Heritage Platinum Card Club." In his deposition, conducted by attorneys for the plaintiffs, Salinas-Jones admitted that he was unaware of any economic analysis being conducted prior to the initiation of the card programs:

Q: . . . You don't know how the concept evolved from the general discussion to the precise terms and conditions of the Gold Card when it was mailed out?
A: No, Sir.

□ □ □

Q: At the meetings you were at, was there any specific analysis as to how that would work at Heritage USA? Any economic or financial analysis of the costs, the actual costs, the value of the program, the differential?
A: No.
Q: Did there ever come a time when MCWE had data on those points before the gold card program was initiated?
A: I was not aware of any.

Three other MCWE agents who had been directly involved in the Gold Card solicitations admitted that there had been little, if any, discussion concerning the cost or benefit of the card programs and certainly no conclusion that the benefits would be worth the cost.

Jack Sheline, an agent for MCWE, testified as follows:

Q: Was there any discussion—did you hear any discussion at any time prior to the closing [December 14, 1990] about the cost of the card program?
A: No.

Later in his deposition, the following colloquy occurred:

Q: How was it decided that $300 would be the price for a Gold Card and $1,000 would be the price for a Platinum Card?
A: That recommendation came from Dr. Cerullo.
Q: Was there any discussion or was it just adopted?
A: It was adopted. There was very little discussion.
Q: Do you know from where he got those numbers?
A: I assume it was from the input that he was receiving from his business side of the charette, but, no, I don't know where it came from.
Q: He didn't tell you?
A: No.
Q: Did you see any documents recommending that $300 would be the price for the Gold Card and $1,000 would be the price for the Platinum Card?
A: No.

Kirt Salsbury, another agent and employee of MCWE, was asked:

Q: And there was no discussion, I take it, that you recall about how much this effort [the card programs] would cost the facility, New Heritage?
A: I don't recall that.

Likewise, MCWE Agent Ronald J. Collins testified that he had never heard of any discussion concerning the economic impact that the card program might have on Heritage USA.

After MCWE was questioned concerning the Gold Card program by the majority stockholders, Collins attempted to justify the program by explaining that it had been recommended in a report done by Pannell Kerr Forster (PKF), an accounting and management consulting firm. However, the PKF report was written for MCWE's use in securing primary mortgage financing in Cerullo's attempt to acquire Heritage USA; there are only four sentences in the 200-page report making reference to a "recreation club" to be directed at former PTL lifetime partners.

MCWE was asked during the litigation to produce its taped transcripts of all "creative committee meetings" in which the card programs had been discussed. These transcripts record the frantic brainstorming of ideas among Morris Cerullo, David Cerullo, Kirk Salisbury, Jack Sheline, and Billy Salinas-Jones.

The following are selected segments of transcripts that were produced by Cerullo and attached to plaintiff's exhibits in the civil litigation. They provide rare insights into the ethical standards of the participants, who were identified by initials only.

1. "(KS) And I think we've got to keep in mind . . . the story that we tell the financial people is a different story than we tell the Christians, because you've got two different objectives in mind . . . " (Transcript from 6–12–90 meeting, pp. 12–13)

2. "(MC) [L]et's make it bigger than life, and let's hit the $52 million, and then let's go for it. And then let's give people . . . a club, a membership club, a charter membership . . . if you'll give $1,000 right now . . . let's make them Gold Card members . . . it won't be a credit card, but it will be a Gold Card membership card, which will entitle you to 50% off of the room rate, which will entitle you to a package . . . what do you call that? A script . . . you know, when you get all those nice goodies. . . ." (Id., p. 17)

3. "(DC) I guess my concern here is . . . like I expressed when I thought this idea up originally a couple of weeks ago, and that is, we're offering people things that aren't in existence yet." (Id., p. 18)

4. "(DC) Well, the important thing I'm trying to communicate is that we're not building on the another man's vision, as this was a vision God gave you 20 years ago, and if the truth be known, it's probably something Bakker stole from us in the first place." (Id., p. 19)

5. "(DC) The biggest thing I'm turned off on for the Gold Card Club . . . maybe it's only a figment of my mental inability, but I hate to try to sell out of an empty wagon. I hate to pretend that we've got this value here." (Transcript from 6-14-90 meeting, p. 14)

6. "(DC) We could even fake our own headline in the newspaper with out typesetting in here and fake our own article. Bankruptcy court . . . Judge Bishop awards Heritage

USA to Morris Cerullo World Evangelism for $45 million,
or whatever. We can create our own headline." (Id., p.
10)

7. "(DC) . . . but if we could get permission, if we could get
this property . . . if we could come up with the money
. . . I would do a live satellite feed from Bakker's cell . . .
Jim live on satellite watching, and two way communication, with the tears on his face. . . ." (Id., p. 20)

8. "(DC) Okay, but aren't people going to be asking, if you
don't get the $52 million have you lost the network, too?"
"(JS) Let them think it, Yeah, let them think that."
"(DC) You think so?"
"(JS) Yeah."
"(KS) As far as response, that would be good."
"(JS) Let them think it . . . all or nothing." (Id., p. 24)

9. "(DC) Ok, let's be ridiculous here. Let's say . . . now, I'm
just throwing out examples that happen to fit what I'm
trying to get to. Let's say we only raise $8 million and
we don't do the deal and all those people are wondering
where's my money? We're not going to send back $8
million. It went to buy the satellite network."
"(JS) All of that is going to be far too complicated for
that. If you can't say it simply, then we just can't say it."
"(DC) Well, let's figure out a way of saying it simply, but
let's also figure out a way not to have to give $8 million
back." (Id., p. 38)

10. "(KS) I'm just being objective. It's not in existence so
we're selling 50 percent of something that doesn't exist."
(Transcript from 6-28/29-90 meeting, p. 1)

Morris Cerullo and MCWE showed not only a lack of business
sophistication but also a recalcitrant attitude in their failure to cease
and desist offering and promoting the card programs. The minutes of
the February 6, 1991, meeting of the board of directors clearly reflect
that Morris Cerullo had advised the board that he would discontinue
and withdraw card programs, offer refunds to all cardholders, and
execute an appropriate indemnification agreement to hold NHUSA
harmless from any and all claims and actions that might arise from
the card programs. Morris Cerullo did not implement that which he
had promised on February 6 and apparently attempted to take steps
only to justify the decisions that he had made and implemented several months earlier.

Billy Salinas-Jones did a feasibility study that was ultimately used by Arthur Andersen and Company, which was hired to do an "economic impact study." The Arthur Andersen impact study was almost identical to the earlier study done by Billy Salinas-Jones. For example, the Arthur Andersen study noted that "additionally, MCWE has historically experienced *less than a 1% response* to its invitations to those meetings despite the TREMENDOUS rates offered to our partners. . . ." Obviously, if Arthur Anderson and Company had written that sentence, it would have read, "offered to its partners."

In any event, the Arthur Andersen report is highly qualified and relies solely on information provided by MCWE. Arthur Andersen made no attempt at independent clarification. Despite the fact that the report had been marked "Tentative and Preliminary—Subject to Change," Arthur Andersen's summary was "that the Gold Card plan will not have a material adverse economic impact on the operation of New Heritage Carolina Corporation."

In a certification by Harold W. Perry, Jr., an expert for the majority shareholders, the extensive shortcomings and fallacies of the Arthur Andersen report were noted in detail. (Exhibit A-37.) Despite the qualifications Arthur Andersen had placed on its report, (and the flaws outlined by Perry), the report was used by Cerullo and others in an attempt to justify the card programs.

Despite Cerullo's assertion to the contrary, the New Heritage Asset Management Committee did not support the card programs. William S. Lund, chair of the asset management team, made this statement in an affidavit that "in my opinion, the Gold and Platinum Card program instituted by Morris Cerullo was ill advised and poorly structured. Although in concept, a discount card program was a good promotional technique, I believe there are serious deficiencies in the MCWE Gold and Platinum Card program that can negatively impact the operation and profitability of New Heritage USA." In the same affidavit, as well as in a letter to Yet-King Loy, Lund disputed Cerullo's claim concerning the alleged support that the Asset Management Team had given to the card club programs. Lund also stated in his affidavit that Cerullo had told him that he (Cerullo) "had not notified the majority shareholders of the sale of the Gold cards."

Lund wasn't the only one contradicting and questioning the assertions that had been made by Morris Cerullo. Harold Tysinger, chief operations officer at New Heritage, gave an affidavit prior to his untimely death. In that affidavit, Tysinger said: "When I began serving as Chief Operations Officer of NHCC, Dr. Cerullo restricted me from speaking to any of the other directors of NHCC without his approval. I was specifically told not to speak with Mr. Loy regarding any matters without the pre-approval of Dr. Cerullo. On December 21, 1990, Dr. Cerullo reminded me that I worked only for him after I had responded to a question of Mr. Loy's regarding several New Heritage contracts without Dr. Cerullo's pre-approval. . . . On approximately January 6 or 7, 1991, Dr. Cerullo told me to accommodate Mr. Loy, who was now working on the New Heritage premises. However, Dr. Cerullo reinforced that I still worked only for Morris Cerullo. While I was to answer Mr. Loy's questions, I was not to openly discuss or divulge any NHCC information without Dr. Cerullo's pre-approval." Tysinger indicated that he had a general knowledge of the Gold Card program as of October 1990, but the first time that he had heard the Gold Card program mentioned in Loy's presence was on January 25, 1991. This is consistent with Loy's statement.

Finally, two weeks after the majority shareholders filed a civil case in federal district court, Morris Cerullo terminated the card program and told cardholders that they could request refunds.

Unfortunately, that was not the end of the story. Rather than sending each cardholder a refund check, MCWE held onto the money until the cardholder wrote in to ask for a refund. Moreover, cardholders had only a limited period of time in which to do so. At the end of an eight-page, single-spaced letter, dated March 28, 1991, Morris Cerullo gave each cardholder four options. First, the cardholder could write back to Morris Cerullo and request a refund. Second, the cardholder could donate $300 to the MCWE ministry and deduct that $300 from their taxes. Third, the cardholder could obtain a premier card, which would offer discounts to MCWE events only and had nothing to do with NHUSA. Fourth, if MCWE did not hear from the cardholder by May 14, 1991, it would assume that the cardholder wanted the contributed funds to be counted as a tax deduction, and no refund would be given.

It would seem that if MCWE had really wanted to abide by its agreement to offer refunds, then it would have simply included checks with the termination letter instead of burying the refund information and cutoff date on the last page.

The frustration and aggravation that MCWE's actions caused cardholders was probably best expressed by this former cardholder:

> . . . To add to my distress of this action, a clause in this letter indicated
> that if I did not respond by a specified date that this money would

be automatically transferred to other activities within your organization.

□ □ □

If, for some reason, this letter had not reached me or had I failed to read the entire letter to the very last page where you informed that I would have to respond by a specified date . . . the money would not be returned. I wonder if this might not be the underlying effort, hoping that many would not see the necessity to respond and therefore, the monies would not be returned. It is hard to believe that a Christian organization would not honor an agreement to refund all monies. . . . I also do not believe this action to be legal.

For those cardholders who did request a refund, the tribulation was still not over. Once MCWE received refund requests, cardholders were admonished, through the mail or telephone, to "reconsider" their request. The telephone campaign was conducted by a special management corporation and was apparently very short-lived due to the extremely negative reactions received from cardholders who simply wanted their money back.

In a particularly touching letter, one of the cardholders wrote that rather than giving $500, she had given $5,000 to MCWE for the purpose of securing a Gold Card. After learning of the litigation concerning the Gold Cards and because of pressing medical needs, the cardholder requested a total refund. In a response signed by Bill Salinas-Jones, she was told that ". . . we had to use all funds raised from the acquisition of Heritage USA, of which the $5,000 you gave was a part. Those funds were spent for the purpose we intended and are no longer available." Salinas-Jones then went on to indicate that MCWE "may be able to borrow" $2,000 and send that to the particular cardholder "as a love gift from this ministry. . . ." However, the $2,000 love gift could only be sent if the cardholder were to substantiate her need by submitting the following: "1. A doctor's statement regarding the test you are currently undergoing, as well as a statement as to your overall health; 2. A document reflecting the debt you referred to in your phone call to the Inspirational Network; 3. A copy of your savings account."

Even after the deadline for requesting refunds had come and gone, MCWE started a new campaign to raise $8.4 million to repay the loan that had been previously taken out by MCWE from the majority shareholders. In letter after letter, Morris Cerullo recounted the story of how he had been sued by his "Malaysian partners" and how he could lose his prized "Mission Control Center," the heart of the administrative operation of MCWE, if he did not have $8.4 million by December 15, 1991.

On December 17, 1991, U.S. Federal District Judge Joseph F. Anderson, Jr., entered an order granting Morris Cerullo's motion for summary judgment and adopted a consent indemnity order and stock pledge agreement. In effect, the attorneys for the majority shareholders had failed to show that they were entitled to any recoverable damages. The court also rejected an argument made by the plaintiffs that MCWE did not have a funding commitment from the "First California Capital Markets Group." That funding commitment was previously presented to the Bankruptcy Court and to the trustee reflecting a funding commitment to MCWE for the acquisition of NHUSA. The federal judge found that Morris Cerullo had offered the plaintiffs the equitable relief that they had requested and, furthermore, that the plaintiffs "failed to show reckless, willful, wanton or malicious conduct on behalf of the defendants." The court noted, "there is no evidence in the record that defendants actively concealed the existence of the card programs from the plaintiffs." The lawsuit concerning the Gold and Platinum Card programs was over. Only the second lawsuit remained.

In the meantime, Morris Cerullo and the majority shareholders were able to work out an agreement whereby Cerullo surrendered his ownership of NHUSA to the majority shareholders. The details of that agreement were not made public.

The New Heritage USA properties opened on June 23, 1992, as a for-profit corporation with a pledge by the corporation never to take or solicit donations and always to have in place a management team that would be above reproach. All of the evidence from the civil litigation clearly indicates that these Christian entrepreneurs from Malaysia will keep their promise and their commitment.

Morris Cerullo still owns the New Inspirational Television Network and continues to minister from his Mission Control Center in San Diego, California, from which he broadcasts his program, "Victory With Morris Cerullo."

It is not known whether or not the woman who requested the refund of her $5,000 ever complied with Salinas-Jones' request to provide the necessary documents that would allow her to obtain a $2,000 "love gift."

CHAPTER TWELVE

□□□

Epilogue

The government went on to tell the witnesses, including the
PTL Board of Directors, that the Ministry was collapsing financially. Why didn't the PTL audits show this?

James O. Bakker, in his 1990 "New Years Letter to PTL Partners,"
written from his prison cell in Rochester, Minnesota

AS OF THIS DATE, Jim Bakker is still serving his prison sentence for
wire and mail fraud in Rochester, Minnesota. On December 22, 1992,
U.S. Federal District Judge Graham Mullen reduced Bakker's sentence to eight years. Saying that his previously imposed sentence of
18 years was "unduly harsh," Mullen's decision makes Bakker immediately eligible for parole, especially since, from every indication,
Bakker is a model prisoner.

The Taggart brothers are serving their time at a minimum security
prison in Montgomery, Alabama.

Richard Dortch served his time at the minimum security federal
prison at Eglin Air Force Base on the Florida coast. He is currently
president and founder of Life Challenge, Inc., an agency caring for
professionals in crisis, located in Clearwater, Florida.

When I teach the course "Ethics and Evangelism: A Case Study
of PTL," my students and I generally come to the conclusion that if
you were to ask the parties responsible for the financial downfall of
PTL to stand, there would be a room full of standing people, not just
Bakker, Dortch, and the Taggarts.

Many professionals involved with PTL had the opportunity to "do
the right thing" but, for one reason or another, they didn't.

What is the answer to Jim Bakker's question? Why didn't the PTL audits show that the ministry was "collapsing financially" or that there had been an oversale of lifetime partnerships? Jim Bakker may be asking the same questions that U.S. Federal District Judge Stanley Sporkin was asking in the case concerning Charles Keating and the failed Lincoln Savings and Loan Association.

Judge Sporkin said:

> There are other unanswered questions presented by this case. Keating testified that he was so bent on doing the "right thing" that he surrounded himself with literally scores of accountants and lawyers to make sure all the transactions were legal. The questions that must be asked are:
>> —Where were these professionals, a number of whom are now asserting their rights under the Fifth Amendment when these clearly improper transactions were being consummated?
>> —Why didn't any of them speak up or disassociate themselves from the transaction?
>> —Where also were the outside accountants and attorneys when these transactions were effectuated?
>
> What is difficult to understand is that with all the professional talent involved (both accounting and legal), why at least one professional would not have blown the whistle to stop the overreaching that took place in this case.

□ □ □

> One of the great attributes of this nation is it learns from its mistakes. It is clear that this case should provide all of us with a very valuable learning experience. If the lessons are learned well, we will have gone a long way in preventing these abusive activities from recurring in the future.

Although these comments by Judge Sporkin clearly applied only to the case he was hearing, one might ask whether or not these same questions and principles apply not only to the PTL situation, but to the vast number of other business failures. Needless to say, business professionals have ethical responsibilities that they owe not only to their firm and their clients but also to the public at large.

Finally, when I was at the SEC, we were always very quick to point out the very crucial role that accountants, and in particular auditors, play in helping to maintain the integrity of our capitalistic system. I remember my first accounting fraud case, during which I was given some very good advice by a senior member of the enforcement division concerning accounting fraud cases:

1. Keep your eye on the fraud

2. Beware of financial statements that have numbers that check in but don't check out
3. Beware of financial statements that bear notes telling the truth, but only half of it—usually it's the good half

I think that is good advice not only for new attorneys at the SEC but also for accountants, attorneys, and all those who have fiduciary responsibilities to their employer or corporation and in whom the public places their trust and reliance.

APPENDIX

Use of Mail, Telephone and Television

Mail Fraud

Count 1
July 4, 1985
From Rebecca Rabon, Salisbury, NC to PTL, Charlotte, NC

Count 2
Oct. 9, 1985
From John Bernard, Merrillville, IN to PTL, Charlotte, NC

Count 3
Nov. 3, 1985
From Floyd Hines, Stanley, NC to PTL, Charlotte, NC

Count 4
June 26, 1986
From PTL, Charlotte, NC to Dana Angel, Atlantic Beach, FL

Count 5
March 19, 1987
From Lamar Kerstetter, Shamokin, PA to PTL, Charlotte, NC

Count 6
Sept. 22, 1986
From Barbara Schmidt, Rotunda West, FL to PTL, Charlotte, NC

Count 7
Jan. 7, 1987
From PTL, Charlotte, NC to Western, NC and Other States

Count 8
Dec. 11, 1986
From Carl Elliott, Asheboro, NC to PTL, Charlotte, NC

Telephone

Count 9
May 27, 1986
From George Dudley, Alexander, AR to PTL Operators, Pineville, NC

Count 10
June 18, 1985
From Alan Kent Foor Beavertown, PA to PTL Operators, Pineville, NC

Count 11
Sept. 16, 1986
From Gabrielle Betzer, Dearborn Heights, MI to PTL Operators, Pineville, NC

Wire Fraud

Television

Count 12
July 25, 1984
PTL TV Transmissions to All Prospective Partners in NC and Other States

Count 13
April 16, 1985
PTL TV Transmissions to All Prospective Partners in NC and Other States

Count 14
Sept. 17, 1984
PTL TV Transmissions to All Prospective Partners in NC and Other States

Count 15
May 6, 1986
PTL TV Transmissions to All Prospective Partners in NC and Other States

Count 16
Nov. 19, 1985
PTL TV Transmissions to All Prospective Partners in NC and Other States

Count 17
June 9, 1986
PTL TV Transmissions to All Prospective Partners in NC and Other States

Count 18
June 16, 1986
PTL TV Transmissions to All Prospective Partners in NC and Other States

Count 19
April 12, 1987
PTL TV Transmissions to All Prospective Partners in NC and Other States

Count 20
March 7, 1987
PTL TV Transmissions to All Prospective Partners in NC and Other States; Received by Irvin Gaddie, Louisville, KY

Count 21
Aug. 7, 1986
PTL TV Transmissions to All Prospective Partners in NC and Other States

Count 22
Nov. 24, 1986
PTL TV Transmissions to All Prospective Partners in NC and Other States

Count 23
Feb. 10, 1987
PTL TV Transmissions to All Prospective Partners in NC and Other States; Received by Phillip & Edith Murray, Fuquay-Verina, NC

Conspiracy

Count 24
Conspiracy to Commit Mail Fraud and Wire Fraud

Exhibit A-1   List of Counts of Mail and Wire Fraud Against Jim Bakker

Promotional Brochure for the Grand Hotel Partnerships

Mailed to 140,282 Individuals on January 7, 1984

Once every lifetime an idea is born so filled with potential for good that it must be shared immediately....

• • • • • •

A maximum of 50% of Heritage Grand Hotel rooms will be available at any given time for Lifetime Partners, allowing for proper hotel maintenance and operation.

There has never been a better value for your investment in the ministry of PTL. For a one-time gift of $1,000 you will be able to stay free for 4 days and 3 nights, every year, for the rest of your life, in the Heritage Grand Hotel!

Think of the thousands of dollars you will save during your lifetime!

According to the current rate of inflation, if you use your PTL Lifetime Partner membership for 40 years, the gift value of your room at the Heritage Grand Hotel could be worth almost $20,000!* You will not be able to find a better investment opportunity anywhere!

• • • • •

After we hear from 25,000 Lifetime Partners and receive their investment of $1,000, Lifetime Membership in the PTL Partner Center will be closed!

Exhibit A-2

293

Promotional Brochure for the Grand Hotel Partnerships

Mailed to 570,874 Individuals in March 1984

Lifetime PTL Partnerships will be limited to 25,000 memberships, with only one Lifetime Partnership available per family.....

Because of the value being invested in exchange for your payment of $1,000, no part of this $1,000 is a charitable contribution and should not be claimed as a tax-deduction.

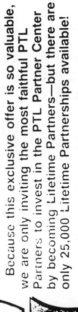

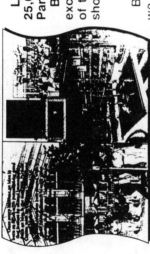

Because this exclusive offer is so valuable, we are only inviting the most faithful PTL Partners to invest in the PTL Partner Center by becoming Lifetime Partners—but there are only 25,000 Lifetime Partnerships available!

* * * * * *

Become a Lifetime Partner now—invest in the PTL ministry today, and save thousands of dollars in the years to come!

Exhibit A-3

294

Promotional Letter *Reopening* the Grand Hotel Partnerships

Mailed to 594,794 Individuals From April 29 - May 3, 1985

A couple of weeks ago, I received a final tabulation on the Lifetime Partnerships and was shocked to discover that because of checks and credit card payments that did not go through, over 900 Lifetime Partnerships were still needed to meet our goal.

The Memberships in the Towers are now $2,000 and will go up to $3,000 shortly . . . but, for those who help me finish this miracle, the remaining original Lifetime Partnerships are available for a $1,000 gift! This Lifetime Partnership gives you 4 days and 3 nights at the Heritage Grand Hotel every year for the rest of your life. This is not a Towers Membership . . . you may use this Lifetime Partnership in the Heritage Grand Hotel this year.

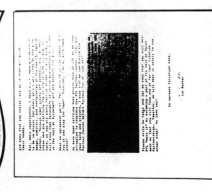

Exhibit A-4

Grand Hotel

Total Lifetime Partnership Funds Received — $66,938,820

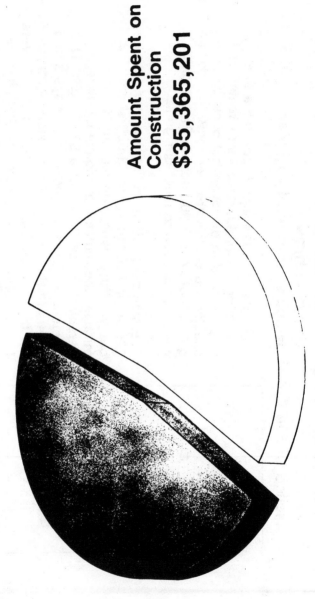

Amount Spent on Construction $35,365,201

Exhibit A-5

WARDLOW, KNOX, KNOX, FREEMAN & SCOFIELD
ATTORNEYS AT LAW
1490 BB&T CENTER
CHARLOTTE, NORTH CAROLINA 28202-3281

CHARLES E. KNOX
H. EDWARD KNOX
JOHN B. FREEMAN
MICHAEL B. SCOFIELD
JOHN B. YORKE
— CHARLES W. BARKLEY
LISA G. CADDELL
MARK T. SUMWALT

RICHARD E. WARDLOW
OF COUNSEL

AREA CODE 704
372-1360

January 6, 1984

Reverend Richard Dortch
Senior Executive Vice President
Heritage Village Church and·
 Missionary Fellowship, Inc.
P. O. Box 11871
Charlotte, North Carolina 28220

Re: Heritage Grand Hotel

Dear Richard:

Let me take this opportunity to further clarify my position on the Heritage Grand· Hotel fund-raising packet.

As you know, I received the color brochure on Wednesday afternoon from you with a request that I review it. Obviously, I cannot give a legal opinion in this short amount of time as to whether this is regulated by any of the securities laws. As I indicated to you in your office today, it is my opinion that this offering comes within the purview of the South Carolina Time Share Statute and requires a registration with the South Carolina Real Estate Commission. However, it is my understanding from our conversation that because of financial pressures, the mailing is to go out today notwithstanding our opinion. Since a decision has been made to go ahead with the mailing, I will not delve any further into the matter unless you request that I do so.

If you have any questions, do not hesitate to call.

Very truly yours,

John B. Yorke

JBY:af

Exhibit A-6 Letter from PTL's Attorney Regarding the Heritage Grand Hotel Fundraising Packet

Promotional Letter for the Towers Hotel Partnerships
Mailed to 596,865 Individuals From October 15-19, 1984

...25,000 people have joined with PTL as Lifetime Partners and have helped make that vision a reality!...

But as I watched the construction of the PTL Partner Center, and walked through the sites every day, I became aware of two very serious problems:

First, the Lifetime Partnerships went so quickly that many of our PTL partners couldn't be part of the 25,000....

Secondly, reservations for the Heritage Grand Hotel have been pouring in. As I looked at our reports, I realized that we turned away more people for lack of lodging last year than would fill the Heritage Grand Hotel for one entire year!

* * * * * *

Help us complete the miracle today. Write and join as a Heritage Grand Tower Partner, and become part of the Hall of Agreement as well....

* * * * * *

P.S. There can only be 30,000 Heritage Grand Tower Partners, so please be sure to write today!

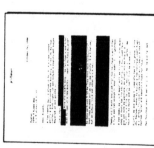

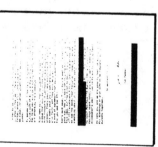

Exhibit A -7

CONFIDENTIAL

PREPARED BY HGG 8-1-24 DATE
REVIEWED BY [illegible] DATE

HVCHF, Inc.
HERITAGE GRAND HOTEL
5-31-84

$9/5/84

17-3

AUDIT NOTE EXPLANATIONS FOR 17-2

①   Amount includes expense for 25000 David &
Goliath statues at $10 each. Examined
invoices and other supporting documents.
(Expensed 25000 based on expected 25000
lifetime partners). Remaining expense relates
to some mailing expenses in addition to
those at ② below. Expense appears
reasonable. HGG

②   Expenses are for various mailing supplies
for statues and lifetime partner items.
Examined invoices and other supporting
documents. Expense appears reasonable HGG

③   Expense relates to printing of lifetime
partnership cards, brochures, etc. Examined
invoices and other supporting documents.
Expense appears reasonable. HGG

④   Relates to service charge for American
Express, MC and VISA. Examined statements
for March, April and May w/ charges
totaling $60435. Expense appears
reasonable. HGG → the notes at 17-3-5, $11,014.74 are
amounts that were recorded twice in May. Remaining
balance of $91,865.99 should be transferred
to P&L books. jma

⑤   As noted at ④ at 17-1-4, $91,970 represents fees
paid to Morrisons & is reclassified to Morrison
mgmt fee by AJE ⑪ Remaining $39,585.62 relates
to feasibility studies for the H&H which
should be capitalized. jma

Exhibit A-8   Deloitte, Haskins and Sells Work Paper

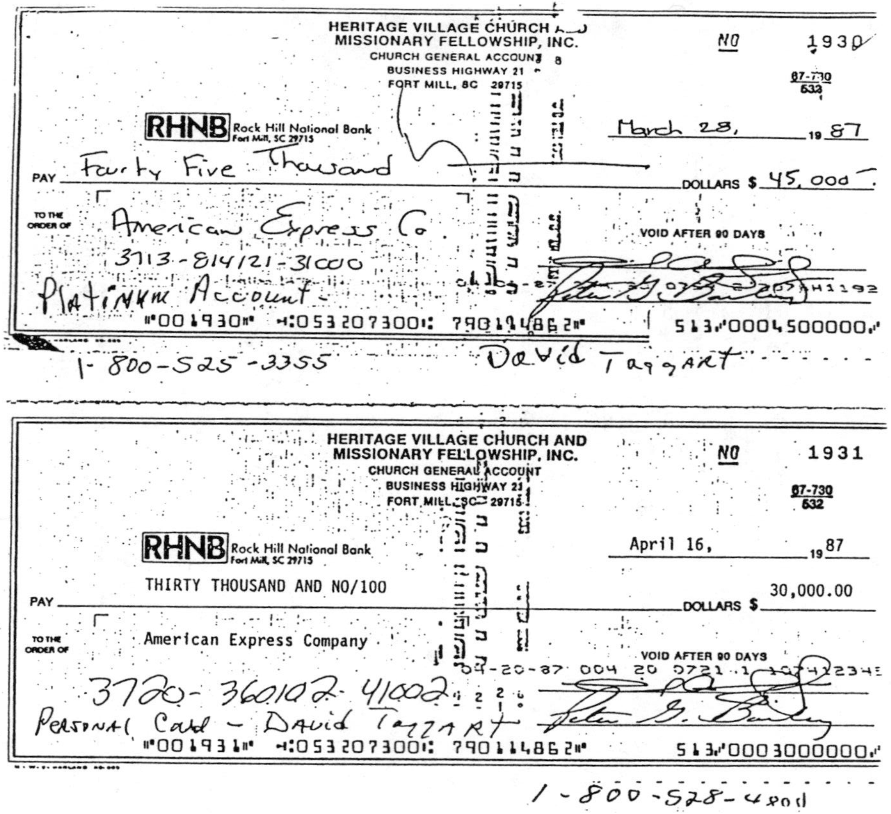

HERITAGE VILLAGE CHURCH AND
MISSIONARY FELLOWSHIP, INC.
CHURCH GENERAL ACCOUNT
BUSINESS HIGHWAY 21
FORT MILL, SC 29715

NO 1930

87-730
532

RHNB Rock Hill National Bank
Fort Mill, SC 29715

March 28, 19 87

PAY Forty Five Thousand DOLLARS $ 45,000

TO THE ORDER OF American Express Co.
3713-814121-31000
Platinum Account

VOID AFTER 90 DAYS

⑈001930⑈ ⑆053207300⑆ 790114862⑈ 513⑈0004500000⑈

1-800-525-3355 David Taggart

HERITAGE VILLAGE CHURCH AND
MISSIONARY FELLOWSHIP, INC.
CHURCH GENERAL ACCOUNT
BUSINESS HIGHWAY 21
FORT MILL, SC 29715

NO 1931

87-730
532

RHNB Rock Hill National Bank
Fort Mill, SC 29715

April 16, 19 87

PAY THIRTY THOUSAND AND NO/100 DOLLARS $ 30,000.00

TO THE ORDER OF American Express Company

VOID AFTER 90 DAYS

3720-360102-41002
Personal Card - David Taggart

⑈001931⑈ ⑆053207300⑆ 790114862⑈ 513⑈0003000000⑈

1-800-528-4800

Exhibit A-9 Cancelled Checks Made Payable to American Express for David Taggart's Personal American Express Account Drawn from the PTL Ministries' Account

REPORT R11D- *-*-*-* MEMBERSHIP SUMMARY FOR ALL PARTNERS PLEDGING OR CONTRIBUTING--

LIFETIME MEMBERSHIP DESCRIPTION	*-*-*-*-*-* NUMBER OF MEMBERSHIPS -*-*-*-*-*									*-*-*- DOLLARS -*-*-*	
	FULLY PAID	51-99% PAID	1-50% PAID	TOT WITH DOLLARS	PLEDGED NOT PAID	MONEY REFUNDED	BAD CHECK INVAL CHG	LOAN DEFAULT	TRANS-FERRED	TOTAL PAID	BALANCE DUE
HERITAGE GRAND (GH)	66,663	255	1,524	68,462	-16,969	1,908	935	9	1,467	66,938,820	1,569,733
HERITAGE TOWERS (TH)	26,981	171	734	27,886	-5,057	633	561	309	10	27,079,069	907,027
HERITAGE TOWERS (ZT)	91	1	29	121	-48	5	3	0	1	187,657	62,342
PENTHOUSE (PH)	5	0	4	9	0	0	0	0	0	53,200	36,800
DIAMOND (DL)	4	0	0	4	-1	0	1	0	0	39,995	10,005
GOLD (GL)	230	0	25	255	-66	5	1	0	1	464,505	47,495
SILVER (SL)	7,630	48	134	7,812	-883	83	60	214	0	7,501,739	330,732
BUNKHOUSE (BL)	9,682	1,756	15,282	26,720	-24,629	67	165	0	0	6,681,961	6,696,336
SILVER 7000 (TX)	2,344	49	135	2,528	-1,385	80	44	414	1	7,176,779	467,156
VICTORY WARRIOR (TY)	35,957	89	379	36,425	-3	591	353	5	0	36,075,160	385,070
VW STAFF (TZ)	27	163	150	340	-1	15	0	0	0	160,135	179,864
1100 CLUB (EL)	7,783	651	6,608	15,442	-11,059	110	118	0	0	10,700,267	6,310,132
FAMILY FUN (FF)	1,626	52	1,135	2,813	-1,452	31	47	0	0	1,857,663	959,336
FAMILY FUN SPEC.(FS)	1,056	14	33	1,103	-263	28	26	0	0	1,075,100	28,900
FAMILY FUN 500 (FD)	668	17	68	753	-240	4	1	0	0	622,968	54,731
* * TOTALS FOR COLUMNS-----	160,767	3,466	26,440	190,673	-62,076	3,760	2,315	951	1,480	166,620,035	18,045,661

* *

ALL PARTNERS LISTED ON THIS SHEET HAVE CONTRIBUTED TO LIFETIME MEMBERSHIPS EXCEPT THOSE WITH UNPAID PLEDGES.
CCUNT UNDER -PLEDGED NOT PAID- IS THE NUMBER THAT HAVE MADE NO PAYMENT AT ALL ON THE PLEDGE TO THAT SPECIFIC LIFETIME APPEAL.

Exhibit A-10   Summary of Lifetime Partnership Accounts as of May 31, 1987

1. Jim Bakker constantly talked to me about all the money he could raised from Lifetime Partnerships. He told me had a plan to raise much more out of the present Lifetime program we had.

   He stated, "I struck gold when I got this idea. There's no limit to what we can get!" "There's no end to the money we can raise."

   He told me it was the easiest money that could be raised. He constantly said, "I have a plan. There's a lot more that can be raised." When I asked him what it was, he said, "I can handle the partners, I can keep them away or get them here as I wish.' "I can control it so that we can offer as many as we would like."

   "No one understands this idea but me, I can raise all the money I want on this plan."

   I never understood that. I believe now that he actually meant that he could offer many more and keep the people away not to use the lifetime partnerships if he told them not to come. **** (See last page.)

2. It was normal the past year and a half to two years for David Taggart to tell me prior to a Board meeting that Jim needed a certain amount of money as a bonus from the Board. Examples were, $100,000, or $200,000, or however much he wanted. There were occasions where I mentioned this to Board members, to let them know that Jim was requesting those amounts. At different times, I spoke to Evelyn Carter Spencer, Ernest Franzone, and Aimee Cortese.

Exhibit A-11 Notes Prepared by Richard Dortch and Used as He Testified Against Jim Bakker

3. Jim Bakker constantly told us not to keep records, memos or documents of anything unless we just absolutely had to. He told us that, "someday they will be in here snooping around and I don't want them to find anything".

4. Jim Bakker told me, in the presence of David Taggart, to do whatever I had to do to pay off Jessica Hahn....that I had to "do it". He said he "hated to do it", but that he knew we had to, so,"Do what you have to do".

5. Jim Bakker did not want me to know what he paid a number of people.

--- I never knew what David Taggart was paid. He would not tell me. I was never told about any bonus that David received. I read it in the paper the first time I knew it.

--- I never knew what Shirley Fulbright was paid. I was never told of bonus for her. I read it in the paper the first time I knew it.

--- I tried to find out what James Taggart was paid. I asked Jim once and he told me he had taken care of it. That's all I knew.

--- I tried to know and find out what it was that Pat Harrison did. I asked about seeing her accounts. I was told they knew about it. (Pat Harrison was the bookkeeper of the executive accounts on the third floor -- executive floor.)

Exhibit A-11 *Continued*

--- The copy of executive payroll that I saw on about three occasions was not the same as what I saw when I actually saw the payroll sheets from Laventhol and Horwath when Jim had resigned. Jim was paying more that I knew, and to people I did not know about.

--- Jim told me once, "As long as I pay the income tax, I can take what I want."

David Taggart would clam up when I began to inquire about the executive accounts, cash advances, and third floor expenses. He told me that Jim was directing him and Jim knew what he was doing.

David Taggart was constantly preparing envelopes of large sums of cash for Jim. He commented often, "Well, I have to get this $50,000 (or whatever the amount) for Jim. David would frequently say, "How can they spend this much money?"

David Taggart mentioned to me once that Jim had to have the money he was requesting. David said he told Jim that he had taken his bonus money. David said that Jim replied, "I must have it anyway".

On a number of occasions, I discussed with Jim about our incurring debt we could not pay back. I mentioned that Mildred and I always paid our bills on time, that I had heard that he and Tammy did, too. I felt it was wrong for us to be making debts we could not pay, and that we must not spend money we did not have.

Exhibit A-11 *Continued*

***** (1. continued)

Jim stated that he is the only one that got the numbers
from Steve Nelson, and that even Steve did not understand
the Lifetime plan.

The times I would ask about the number or discuss with Jim
about the issue, he would tell me he had it worked out.

Exhibit A-11 *Continued*

You can see that our chart shows where we started from (left to right) with the building of the Heritage Grand and continued our expansion program with the Expanded Heritage Grand, then the Heritage Grand Towers, the Expanded Heritage Grand Towers, and all the way to the right you will see Farmland, USA. At the completion of that phase we would have had over 211,00 Units. This was <u>more than 50,000 Units over</u> what was need to fulfill the memberships!

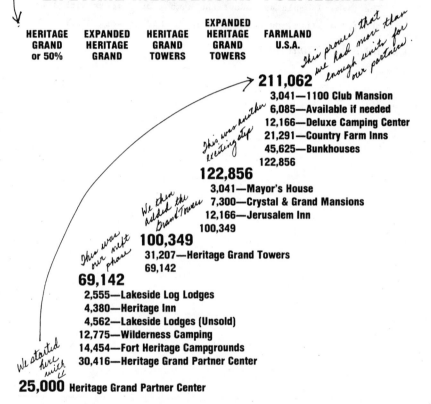

LIFETIME MEMBERSHIP FULFILLMENT

HERITAGE GRAND or 50%	EXPANDED HERITAGE GRAND	HERITAGE GRAND TOWERS	EXPANDED HERITAGE GRAND TOWERS	FARMLAND U.S.A.

This proved that we had more than enough units for our partners.

211,062

3,041—1100 Club Mansion
6,085—Available if needed
12,166—Deluxe Camping Center
21,291—Country Farm Inns
45,625—Bunkhouses
122,856

This was another exciting step

122,856

3,041—Mayor's House
7,300—Crystal & Grand Mansions
12,166—Jerusalem Inn
100,349

We then added the Grand Towers

100,349

31,207—Heritage Grand Towers
69,142

This was our next phase

69,142

2,555—Lakeside Log Lodges
4,380—Heritage Inn
4,562—Lakeside Lodges (Unsold)
12,775—Wilderness Camping
14,454—Fort Heritage Campgrounds
30,416—Heritage Grand Partner Center

We started here with

25,000 Heritage Grand Partner Center

If at anytime a lifetime member, for any reason, was dissatisfied with their lifetime membership—a refund was granted upon request!

Exhibit A-12   Lifetime Membership Fulfillment Chart Used by Bakker but Not Admitted into Evidence

BASIC LODGING AND CAMPING
BUILT, BEING BUILT, or ON DRAWING BOARD
(*) LIFETIME MEMBERS USING 50%

	Nights	Units	Annual Memberships
*Heritage Grand Partner Center	3	500 Rooms	30,416
*Heritage Grand Towers	3	513 Rooms	31,207
*Heritage Inn	4	96 Rooms	4,380
Fort Heritage Campgrounds	10	396 Sites	14,454
Wilderness	10	350 Sites	12,775
Deluxe Camping Center —1100 Club—	6	200 Sites	12,166
(Additional Available If Needed)	6	100 Sites	6,083
*Bunkhouses	2	500 Rooms	45,625
Crystal & Grand Mansions	3	60 Rooms	7,300
Mayor's House	3	25 Rooms	3,041
1100 Club Mansion	3	25 Rooms	3,041
*Jerusalem Inn	3	200 Rooms	12,166
*Country Farm House Inns	3	350 Rooms	21,291
Lakeside Log Lodges	3	21 Rooms	2,555
Lakeside Lodges	2	(Unsold)	4,562
		TOTAL	211,062

NOTE: These figures <u>do not include</u> the Hotel planned at Heritage International Golf Course, Crystal Palace Towers, or long-range plan of Crystal Palace Hotel.

Also, these figures do not include Phase II of Farm Village (Farmland USA) or lodging planned around the new lake area.

Exhibit A-13 Lodging Accommodations Chart Used by Bakker but Not Admitted into Evidence

DEVELOPERS/BUILDERS

August 28, 1989

SUMMARY OF CONSTRUCTION on the residences of James O. Bakker
and Tammy Faye Bakker, and Richard Dortch. Records pertaining
to these construction projects have previously been reviewed
by PTL Auditors and the IRS. To the best of my knowledge and
ability to reconstruct from our records, the following information represents the amounts spent on four projects as noted:

> GARAGE/ATRIUM EXPANSION
> Bakker - 8022 Kittridge Bay Lane, Tega Cay
> 11/82 thru 1/83
> Total Cost: $25,592.
> Paid by Heritage Village Church & Missionary Fellowship
>
> KITCHEN/DINING ROOM/LIVING ROOM REMODELING
> Bakker - 8022 Kittridge Bay Lane, Tega Cay
> 12/82 thru 8/83
> Total Cost: $139,900.
> Paid by Heritage Village Church & Missionary Fellowship
>
> BEDROOM ADDITION/CLOSET ADDITION/OFFICE REMODELED
> Bakker - 8022 Kittridge Bay Lane, Tega Cay
> 8/85 thru 2/86
> Total Cost: $92,278.
> Payment not received
>
> LAKE HOUSE REMODELED
> Dortch - 17737 Langston Drive
> 10/83 thru 12/83
> Total Cost: $48,591.
> Paid by Heritage Village Church & Missionary Fellowship

Haines A. Maxwell, Sr.

HAM:cr

Exhibit A-14   List of Construction/Remodeling Services Performed
by the Maxwell Company for the Bakkers and Dortchs and Paid for
by PTL

MEMO

To: Jim Bakker

From: Peter Bailey

Date: March 12, 1984

RE: Financial Situation

CC: Richard Dortch

Prior to the telethon, we projected a $6.5 million income for March, April and May of this year. Income for January and February has been between $3 million to $3.5 million per month.

Based on our present spending, loan payment commitments and construction projects (not including the Partner Center, which is funded separately), we need $7 to $7.5 million per month for March, April and May. At present, income for March will end up being approximately $3.3 million.

Our payroll is far too high and cannot be sustained by general funds any longer, as we have many other bills that we need to pay now. We have negotiated with vendors for months and felt that the telethon would provide the necessary funds. Our payroll is now running at an annual rate of $17 million.

American Express has to be paid very soon, as we are cut off until we pay $85,000. Mark IV will stop delivery of our video tapes if we do not pay $60,000 this week. We are behind on our gift payments of about $350,000. This is because we have been required to prepay gift items such as David and Goliath and the United Kingdom leather Bible. Blue Cross is behind and will not pay claims if not paid immediately. We have been able to pay only $25,000 a day on time charges. We need to pay $50,000 to stay even.

We are pushing Security Bank to increase our line of credit by at least $500,000. We are also negotiating on financing the telecommunications system and the water park as well as a finance package on the hotel from three different companies. But, as you know, this will increase our overhead (interest) and loan payment commitments for the future. This will mean a need for an even larger income for our general fund.

This is just factual information, and we need to do something about it. I am not discouraged. Who said it would be easy? But I think we must either raise more money or cut expenses quickly.

Jesus is never late, and He is coming soon!

PGB

Exhibit A-15   Memo to Jim Bakker Regarding PTL's Financial Situation

PTL Television Network

Memo

To: Jim Bakker

From: Peter G. Bailey

Date: November 16, 1984

RE: Weekly Report

CC: Richard Dortch

We still owe $296,463 on the payroll paid on November 9, 1984. With contributions averaging $130,000 per day the past several weeks, payroll is using $65,000 per day. This leaves $65,000 per day for T.V. ($50,000) and partners expense ($15,000). This leaves nothing for Christmas City, utility bills, honorariums, employee medical insurance, taxes, travel and daily necessary expenses. This means we must continue using hotel funds until we either raise contributions to our spending level or cut our level of operations and projects. We are in a very serious cash flow position.

But we do have much for which to be thankful. During next week, it will be necessary to cut out spending for Thursday and Friday so that the overdraft in the checking accounts can be alleviated.

Jesus is coming soon!

                                             PGB

  ✓
/plg

Exhibit A-16   Memo to Jim Bakker Regarding PTL Spending

PTL Television Network

Memo

To: Richard Dortch

From: Peter G. Bailey

Date: June 30, 1985

RE: Heritage Village Church and Missionary Fellowship, Inc.
Financial Statement

CC: Jim Bakker

Attached, find the Balance Sheet and Income and Expense Statements for Heritage Village Church and Missionary Fellowship, Inc. for the 12 month period ended May 31, 1985. These figures will be adjusted when the final audit comes out. In particular, there are no real estate figures from Haines Maxwell for the year ended 5/31/85.

Heritage Village Church and Missionary Fellowship, Inc. shows a year-to-date loss of ($20 million). This is because contributions this year were $40 million against $52 million last year due to the emphasis on Lifetime Partners. The balance of deferred income for Lifetime Partners is $65 million. This amount will be realized in income over the next several years.

Our payroll cost is now running at $30 million a year, gift expense is up $1.5 million, roads, ground maintenance and repairs are up $1.2 million, utilities and telephone expense are up $600,000, and interest on debt is up $1.8 million to $4.2 million. Food service shows a loss of ($1.3 million), and special activities lost ($1.3 million) also.

Above are the major areas that have caused our ($20 million) loss this year.

I know Jesus will see PTL through and with a commitment to expand our partner base and better contract agreements for our real estate development, we will make it. Jesus is coming soon!

PGB

/plg

Attachment

Exhibit A-17   Memo to Richard Dortch Regarding Heritage Village Church Financial Statements

PTL Television Network

Memo

To: Jim Bakker

From: Peter G. Bailey ✓

Date: April 16, 1986

RE: Emergencies

CC:

The following is a list of real emergencies:

1. Finalco - Lease of telephone switches $312,692.54. Payments for January, February, March and April - In process of suing us.

2. National City Bank - Trustee for bonds. Owe $627,229.21 for January, February, March & April payment. Coupons due May 1, 1986.

3. Trinity Tapes - $200,000 - represents agreement to pay balance due him.

4. Fairfax Savings & Loan - $165,000 - April payment. They are very demanding and can put us in default.

5. Beacon Knolls - settlement of pending lawsuit $275,000.

6. Balance owed on payroll $408,312.23

7. HBO for March - $200,000

8. Water Park - ?

The total of the above is $2,188,233.98, not including water park.

I do not see how the above can be paid unless - a) We close the loan quickly b) Stop paying Roe and make some partial payments or c) a miracle happens with partner contributions.

We are continuing to operate far in excess of what is coming in. The contributions are flat. We can have all the financial controls in the world but if we don't live within our means it doesn't mean anything.

Jesus is still coming soon!

                                        PGB

/plg

Exhibit A-18

PTL Television Network

Memo

To: Jim Bakker

From: Peter G. Bailey

Date: July 10, 1986

RE: Victory Warrior Update

CC: Richard Dortch

Our Victory Warrior income and expenditures are as follows:

INCOME: THROUGH 7/9/86 $ 34,908,076

EXPENDITURES:

Trinity Tapes	$ 140,000
General Council Assemblies of God	294,140
Marsh Mclennan-Insurance	604,026
Samaritans Purse	100,000
HBO	400,000
Special Projects	819,382
Television	2,890,792
Commercial Builders	6,000,000
Church & HUSA past due bills-120-90-60 days	1,288,408
Retail past due bills-120-90-60- Days	363,212
Creative Ser. and TV past due bills-120-90	497,477
Savings	11,617,460
Real Estate settlements	347,500
Float covered-Payroll & operations Church and HUSA	5,963,209
Mike Wigton	111,273
HUSA-Grounds project	1,057,100
Water Park	919,264
Harris Corp.	340,000
Sioux Valley S&L	475,000
Furniture & Fixtures-Panche	100,000
South Carolina tax audit	125,194
Installments for June	454,639

TOTAL EXPENDITURES: $ 34,908,076

BALANCE LEFT IN VICTORY WARRIOR   -0-

There are still $2.9 million in checks written by the Church & HUSA Finance Divisions that have not cleared the bank.

Exhibit A-19   Memo to Jim Bakker Regarding the Victory Warriors Promotion

PTL Television Network

Memo

To: Jim Bakker

From: Peter G. Bailey

Date: June 2, 1986

RE: Victory Warriors

CC:

Here is a day by day breakdown of Victory Warriors receipts:

	Date	Checks	Charges	Total
Monday-Thurs.	May 19-22	196,070.76	72,150.00	268,220.76
Friday	May 23	124,480.66	11,700.00	136,180.66
Monday	May 26	301,475.00	955,350.00	256,825.00
Tuesday	May 27	669,820.00	1,182,215.00	1,852,035.00
Wednesday	May 28	77,200.00	307,515.00	384,715.00
Thursday	May 29		451,000.00	451,000.00
Friday	May 30	3,774,034.00	2,219,900.00	5,993,934.00
Saturday	May 31	3,807,362.04	1,440,000.00	5,247,362.04
TOTAL-------		$ 8,950,442.42	7,639,830.00	16,590,272.46

Exhibit A-20   Memo to Jim Bakker Regarding the Victory Warriors Receipts

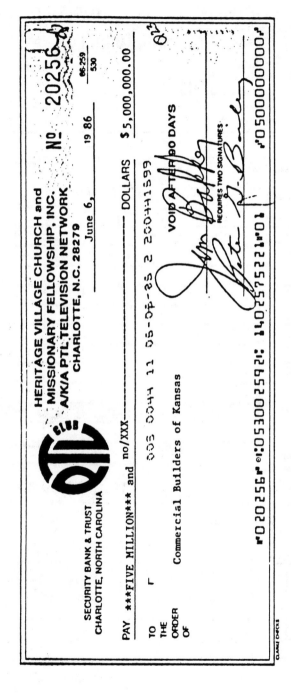

Exhibit A-21 PTL check that included a $265,000 payment to Jessica Hahn

315

STATEMENT COPY

A. Sulka & Company

PARK AT 55
(430 PARK AVENUE)
NEW YORK, NY 10022

(212) 980-5200

CHARGE TO

3713 (814121 31330

12/85 THRU 11/87 79 AX

DAVID A TAGGART

ACCOUNT NUMBER

DATE 7/10/87

7204- 9

METHOD OF PAYMENT: CASH ☐ CHECK ☐ N. CHG. ☐ AMEX ☒ MC ☐ VISA ☐ D.C. ☐

SALESPERSON 10

AMOUNT RECEIVED

QTY	CLASS	DESCRIPTION	UNIT	AMOUNT
1		SMOKING JACKET		3500 —
			SUB TOTAL	3500 —
			TAX	288 75
			SHIPPING & HANDLING CHARGE	
			TOTAL	3788 15

WILL CALL | SEND | GIFT

MERCHANDISE ACCEPTABLE FOR EXCHANGE WITHIN 30 DAYS. NO CASH REFUNDS WITHOUT SALES CHECK.

CUSTOMER'S SIGNATURE

A. Sulka & Company Inc.

PARK AT 55
(430 PARK AVENUE)
NEW YORK, NY 10022

INSURED 1728

SEND TO

M Trump Tower

ADDRESS APT.

CITY STATE ZIP

5th

Exhibit A-22 Invoice for David Taggart's Smoking Jacket

PTL Television Network

Memo

To: Steve Nelson

From: Hollis Rule

Date: September 3, 1985

RE: Lifetime Member Counts

CC:

Steve,

Here are the lifetime counts as of the update of Thursday, August 29.

IBM PARTNER FILE	MEMBERSHIPS	$	% OCCUPANCY
Grand	63,341	63,671,958	104.1%
Towers	19,100	19,327,898	31.3%
	82,441	82,999,856	67.7%

ULTIMATE LIFETIME FILE	MEMBERSHIPS
Grand	64,298
Towers	19,938

The counts are actually beginning to drop slightly now, as we are in the last stages of file clean up.

Again, the Ultimate counts should not be higher than the IBM counts. I will make an extra effort to pinpoint the problem in the next couple of days. The IBM counts are right, and reflect the true membership. I expect to have an answer tomorrow.

Exhibit A-23   Memo to Steve Nelson Reflecting Lifetime Partnership Counts

REPORT R11D-- #-#-#-# MEMBERSHIP SUMMARY FOR ALL PARTNERS PLEDGING OR CONTRIBUTING--

LIFETIME MEMBERSHIP DESCRIPTION	NUMBER OF MEMBERSHIPS #-#-#-#-#				#-#-#-#-#-#				#-#-# DOLLARS #-#-#		
	FULLY PAID	$51-99% PAID	$1-50% PAID	TOT WITH DOLLARS	PLEDGED NOT PAID	MONEY REFUNDED	BAD CHECK INVAL CHG	LOAN DEFAULT	TRANS-FERRED	TOTAL PAID	BALANCE DUE
HERITAGE GRAND (GH)	25,303	494	1,074	26,871	-13,102	499	372	0	11	25,930,763	947,873
HERITAGE TOWERS (TH)	3	0	12	15	0	3	0	0	1	2,875	15,125
HERITAGE TOWERS (ZT)	0	0	0	0	0	0	0	0	0	0	0
PENTHOUSE (PH)	0	0	0	0	0	0	0	0	0	0	0
DIAMOND (DL)	0	0	0	0	0	0	0	0	0	0	0
GOLD (GL)	0	0	0	0	0	0	0	0	0	0	0
SILVER (SL)	3	0	0	3	0	0	0	0	0	3,000	0
BUNKHOUSE (BL)	0	0	0	0	0	0	0	0	0	0	0
SILVER 7000 (TX)	0	1	14	15	0	0	0	0	0	15,000	29,200
VICTORY WARRIOR (TT)	0	0	0	0	0	0	0	0	0	0	0
VH STAFF (TZ)	0	0	0	0	0	0	0	0	0	0	0
1100 CLUB (EL)	0	0	0	0	0	0	0	0	0	0	0
FAMILY FUN (FF)	0	0	0	0	0	0	0	0	0	0	0
FAMILY FUN SPEC. (FS)	0	0	0	0	0	0	0	0	0	0	0
FAMILY FUN 900 (FD)	0	0	0	0	0	0	0	0	0	0	0
#-# TOTALS FOR COLUMNS	25,309	495	1,100	26,904	-13,102	502	372	0	12	25,952,430	992,190

ALL PARTNERS LISTED C: THIS SHEET HAVE CONTRIBUTED TO LIFETIME MEMBERSHIPS EXCEPT THOSE WITH UNPAID PLEDGES.
COUNT UNDER --PLEDGED NOT PAID-- IS THE NUMBER THAT HAVE MADE NO PAYMENT AT ALL ON THE PLEDGE TO THAT SPECIFIC LIFETIME APPEAL.

Exhibit A-24   Membership Summary for the Heritage Grand Hotel as of July 7, 1984

Memo

To: Peter Bailey
From: Jeff Eggen
Date: June 18, 1987
Subject: Lifetime Memberships
CC:

PTL Television Network

Membership Name	1984	1985	1986	1987	TOTALS
(GH) Heritage Grand	3,137	61,335	2,570	734	67,776
(TH) Towers	11,511	7,319	8,401	226	27,457
(TX) Silver 7000	1	1,696	645	29	2,371
(SL) Silver	6	1,579	5,997	142	7,724
(GL) Gold		198	34	1	233
(DL) Diamond		3	1		4
(TY) Victory Warrior		18	36,027	278	36,323
(TZ) Staff/Victory Warrior			341	9	350
(BL) Bunkhouse			7,184	1,898	9,082
(EL) 1100 Club			3,782	3,832	7,614
(FF) Family Fun			2	1,598	1,600
(FS) Family Fun Special				1,108	1,108
(FD) Family Fun Discount			1	664	665
YEARLY TOTALS	14,655	72,148	64,985	10,519	162,307

Exhibit A-25 Memo to Peter Bailey Reflecting Lifetime Partnerships

MEMO

TO: HEK

FROM: JBY

DATE: January 11, 1983

RE: Office conference with Lloyd Caudle, Don Etheridge, Bob Brown and
    Evan Webster

As you remember, we asked Deloitte, Haskins & Sells to look into the books
at PTL and identify any expenditures that might be considered suspect by
the IRS and which might give us a problem if the threatened audit materializes.
They reported the following:

There are 60 divisions at PTL which are designated in the General Ledger.
Division 100 is the expenses for Jim Bakker's office and 101 would be the
expenses for Tammy Bakker's office. These figures that they presented us
all deal with only these two accounts, i.e. if a personal expense was run
through John Franklin's American Express, it would not show up in any of
these figures. Jim and Tammy rarely sign any charge accounts or charge
card statements. They are all signed by either David Taggart or Joyce
Caudle.
Summary sheet is attached to this memo.
On the line for general ledger postings, and under the column designated for
wardrobe, you will see the figure $8,397.02. All of these are expenses that
have been designated as clothes for host or clothes for hostess. $1,083.58
is for magazines that were charged to the two accounts and that were either
sent to their offices or to their home. These range from religious magazines
to Gentlemen's Quarterly to magazines on clothes. (I think you could certainly
argue to the IRS that talk show hosts must stay abreast of current happenings
whether it be current news events or current fashion.) The next column is
designated personal errand gas reimbursement and has the amount of $825.00.
This is all reimbursement to Joyce Caudle for running errands for Tammy.
The next figure under Campground charges is for $6,482.07. This is for charges
at the various stores at Heritage USA made by Jim, Tammy, and the kids. The
next column shows $1,931.30 for dry cleaning. (This would go along with
wardrobe and if the wardrobe is thrown out this would be too; if the wardrobe
is kept in this would be, I would think, preservation of Company assets.) We
are not sure what the figure under the column designated for children is for.
The next column is for miscellaneous expenses. $1,200.00 of this is labled
"pictures for Tammy". $2,100.00 of this is for moving Tammy's parents, Mr.
and Mrs. Grover, to Charlotte. $396.00 of the $2,100.00 was paid to Tammy's
brother for moving his own parents down here.

In the line for petty cash, the full $1,500.00 is probably wardrobe, although
$1,200.00 is identified as wardrobe and $300.00 is identified as miscellaneous.

Exhibit A-26 Memo from John Yorke Regarding Meeting with Tax
Attorneys and Auditors

The parsonage account is particularly interesting. The offering from the Church services goes into the parsonage account so that they can say on the air that Jim and Tammy's salary is paid by the Church members who attend services out there. Out of this account comes their salaries, note payments on the house and other things, expenses for the house, withholdings, telephone, power, Tega Cay Homeowners fee, etc. (It is really a secondary payroll account, for all practical purposes). Jim and Tammy also get $1,000.00 each per month that they do not have to account for and which is designated as living expenses. This was included on their last return as income to them. The miscellaneous expenses for the parsonage included a payment to the maid of $600.00 for food, payment for the Charlotte Observer, property additions, a vibrator massage apparatus, and lots of nik naks for the parsonage. Everything in the parsonage is paid for by the Church. Evan Webster commented that if Jim and Tammy ever leave the Ministry they would have to walk out with nothing but the clothes on their back. I am not sure why he thinks they could walk out with the clothes since they are paid for out of Church funds too!

Employee advances is also interesting. They regularly advance money to ~~different~~ Jim + ~~Tammy that are going for~~ travel. Apparently, they get a cash advance for the trip and then they pay for all their expenses on American Express and other charge cards and use the cash advances to go shopping. Over $23,000.00 was for wardrobe (all of which was signed for by either David or Joyce Caudle). Another $22,000.00 was just not accounted for. It was written off rather than charged to any account. (The $23,000.00 for wardrobe was charged to Jim and Tammy's accounts since it was all signed for by David or Joyce). The $22,000.00 was not charged to any account but was just not accounted for. All but $1,000.00 of that amount went to David. $300.00 went to Tammy and $700.00 went to Jim. This should have either been charged to some account or it should appear on someone's W2 Form.

Under the American Express line you can see that $59,000.00 was charged for Jim and Tammy under either clothes, magazines, or miscellaneous. David would have signed most of these and would have designated them for Jim and Tammy's wardrobe, magazines, or their miscellaneous expenses. The Visa and Mastercharge are much the same.

The checks payable (3941.02) were all to Tammy for reimbursement for wardrobe. Evan pointed out that under all these wardrobe expenses, there are certain things that aren't even arguably used on the show. As an example, he pointed out that Tammy charged a camisole to the Church! Down at the bottom of the sheet you will notice the figure $28,755.83 in unlocated amounts of American Express, Mastercharge and Visa expenses. Th~~is is~~ are additional amount paid to these companies for charges made on the cards charged to Jim and Tammy's account and for which there is no receipt at all. In all probability, this is more wardrobe or similar expenses.

The next area that we discussed was the family inurement. Seven relatives are on the payroll, including: Donna Puckett (Jim's sister), Don LaValley (Tammy's brother), Debbie Johnson (Tammy's sister), Norman Bakker (Jim's brother), Norman Bakker, Jr. (Jim's nephew), Lynn LaValley (Tammy's sister), Mrs. Grover (Tammy's mother). Both Tammy's parents and Jim's parents live in a house that is owned by the Church and each have company cars.

Jim says he + Tammy no longer buy personal clothes

2

3088 002

Exhibit A-26 *Continued*

The following are checks that were found to be suspect, and which are not included in the figures that are on the summary sheet:

1. A check for $9,800.00 advanced to Roger Flessing that was journalled off to Tammy's travel and entertainment (probably Roger cashed the check and gave the money to Tammy).

2. A $2,500.00 check made out to cash that ended up in the parsonage account but no record to show what it was for.

3. A check for $3,250.00 made payable to cash that was charged to the parsonage account but no record of what it was for.

4. A $2,000.00 check made out to cash and given to James Taggart. It was charged to Jim Bakker's miscellaneous account.

5. A check for $2,100.00 made out to cash and given to David Taggart and not charged to any account and no record of what it was for.

6. A check for $3,000.00 which was labeled a personal advance to Jim Bakker.

In addition, there are $9,000.00 in additional American Express expenses on Roger Flessing's card that are very suspect.

It was decided that I should try to get David to sit down with the DH&S representative and try to figure out where some of these amounts went. He was supposed to respond earlier but has not done so. There may be some explanation but the fact that there is no journal entry and the checks are made out to cash and that no supporting documents are present is certainly going to be a red flag to an IRS agent that comes in.

After Lloyd and Don left, Evan and Bob Brown and I had a further discussion about this. I told them that the alarming thing to me is that the suspect expenses are growing exponentially. Bob Brown said that he thought Richard Dortch was part of the problem. It was interesting to me that he recognized that. I really didn't have time to go into it in any depth with him but it seems everyone is thinking the same on that point.

I have not received the minutes from the December Board Meeting for review, as of yet, but I did talk to A.T. Lawing when he was in the office to see CEK. He said, if I remember correctly, that they voted to give Jim a $75,000.00 bonus and Tammy a $40,000.00 in December. They also raised Jim's salary from $102,000.00 to $193,000.00 and raised Tammy's substantially but I cannot remember the figures on her salary.

The conclusions that were drawn from the meeting were the following:

1. A definite policy needs to be established on the wardrobe. This is consistently the largest problem. Also, tax strategy needs to be developed on how to treat the wardrobe. Lloyd suggested an inventory of wardrobe be kept and that when something

3088 003

3

Exhibit A-26 *Continued*

is contributed or done away with otherwise, that it be taken out of the inventory. Obviously, better records need to be kept on all the expenses and the expenses need to be better justified. After the rest of the information is gathered, Lloyd thinks we need to have another strategy session.

Exhibit A-26 *Continued*

MINUTES OF A MEETING OF THE BOARD OF DIRECTORS OF
HERITAGE VILLAGE CHURCH AND MISSIONARY FELLOWSHIP, INC.

A meeting of the Board of Directors of Heritage Village Church and Missionary
Fellowship, Inc., was held on Monday, November 3, 1986, at 2:00 p.m., in the
Board Room of the World Outreach Center at Heritage USA, Fort Mill, South
Carolina.

Those present at the meeting included the following Board Members: Reverend
Jim Bakker, Reverend Aimee Cortese, Reverend Richard Dortch, Ernest Franzone,
Reverend Don George, A. T. Lawing, Jr., and Reverend Evelyn Carter Spencer.
Also present was Shirley Fulbright, Assistant Secretary and Treasurer of the
Corporation.

The meeting was called to order by Reverend Bakker and Reverend Dortch led in
prayer. The Minutes of the Board of Directors' meeting of July 3, 1986, were
adopted as printed.

Reverend Bakker gave the Board an overview of the current status of the
Corporation.

It was reported that the response by December 1, 1986, to the Atlanta Office
on the IRS audit is proceeding on schedule, and that there is every reason to
be encouraged in this matter.

Reverend Bakker updated the Board on the recent sale of Heritage Village to
Forest Hill Presbyterian Church and that the Editing and Satellite Control
Center will be out by December 1, 1986. Mr. Bakker wanted the Board to know
that the new facility will be the finest in the world. Mr. Bakker stated that
the operation of the entire ministry will all be in one place, which will drastically improve our systems.

A copy of The Inspirational Network Program Selection Guidelines was presented
to the Board for consideration. A discussion ensued on the requirement of all
Broadcasters on The Inspirational Network to follow these guidelines for programming. A motion was made that these guidelines be adopted. It was seconded
and passed unanimously.

The Board was asked to consider a line of credit with Rock Hill National Bank.
A motion was made that this line of credit be obtained. The motion was seconded
and passed unanimously.

Reverend Dortch presented to the Board the necessity of establishing a maintenan
and beautification fee on all financial transactions at Heritage USA by the mer-
chants at Heritage USA. The Board was asked to consider a 1.5 percent fee for
every financial transaction for beautification and maintenance and a 1 percent
fee on all real estate transactions, with an additional fee for maintenance of
the grounds to be assessed each month, as well as a $25 a month fee for the
Homeowners Association. A motion was made, seconded, and passed unanimously.

A preliminary audit was presented to the Board for its consideration.

Reverend Bakker brought the Board up-to-date on the first phase of Farmland,
stating that the opening would be Thanksgiving week.

Exhibit A-27

The sale of Safari Campground was brought before the Board for consideration, stating that it is in the best interest of the Corporation that this property be sold to Tracy Trigg Camping Resorts, Inc. A motion was made, seconded, and passed unanimously.

Reverend Bakker asked the Board to consider the new National Religious Broadcasters financial accountability organization, to be joined by Oral Roberts, Pat Robertson, Jerry Falwell, Jimmy Swaggart, and others. Reverend Cookman made a motion that the Church submit itself to this organization for accounting ethics and integrity because of our long standing with NRB and because of the peculiar need of religious broadcasters. It was further stated that it would be in the best interest of the Church to be administered by its peers. The moti was made, seconded, and passed unanimously.

Reverend Dortch reported that the absence of adequate security at Reverend Bakkers' home, recently purchased, in Gatlinburg, Tennessee, and the similar absence of security during the many trips that he and his family are required to take on behalf of the Church have raised serious concerns regarding the personal safety of Reverend Bakker and his family. In addition, the absence of adequate security has created a situation in which it is virtually impossible for Reverend Bakker to obtain the rest that he needs to escape the pressure of his duties at the Church. Therefore, the Board authorized that the Church pay for the costs of constructing and maintaining a security fence around Reverend Bakker's home in Gatlinburg, Tennessee, and that, as part of the security arrangement, there be a security gate installed at the Gatlinburg home which will be maintained on a 24-hour basis by security guards. In addition, the Board authorized that the Church pay the costs of providing personal security for Reverend Bakker and his family while traveling away from Church premises.

Discussion ensued on the Church's responsibility to its Pastor to provide the needs for seclusion and rest. Reverend Cookman made a motion that a bonus be given to pay for the addition on the home in Gatlinburg, Tennessee, to equal the costs. It was seconded, and passed unanimously, with the exception of Reverend Bakker, who was absent from the room at the time.

Reverend Don George brought before the Board the tradition of Christmas Bonuses for Reverend Bakker, Tammy Bakker, and Reverend Dortch. A motion was made that bonuses be given. It was seconded and passed unanimously, with the exception of Reverend Bakker, who was absent from the room during the discussion, and Reverend Dortch, who abstained from the voting.

A date of December 16, 1986, was set for the next Board Meeting.

A motion was made that the meeting be adjourned. It was seconded and passed unanimously.

Respectfully submitted.

Shirley A. Fulbright
Assistant Secretary
Heritage Village Church and
Missionary Fellowship, Inc.

Exhibit A-27 *Continued*

PTL Television Network, Charlotte, NC 28279

Office Of The President

Jim Bakker

ACTION TAKEN BY THE BOARD OF DIRECTORS OF HERITAGE VILLAGE
CHURCH AND MISSIONARY FELLOWSHIP, INC., AT A MEETING ON
NOVEMBER 3, 1986:

BONUSES TO BE PAID TO:

Jim Bakker	500,000
Tammy Bakker	100,000
Richard Dortch	100,000

Shirley J. Fulbright
Assistant Secretary
Heritage Village Church and
Missionary Fellowship, Inc.

Exhibit A-28

Chronology of Events Related to Bonuses
1982

December 17, 1982 Dortch requests Attorney Yorke leave board meeting and that amount of bonuses no longer be reflected in minutes.

December 17, 1982 *Board Meeting.* Dortch moves that PTL obtain Florida condo and car for Bakker's use and that PTL increase contributions to Bakker's retirement fund to 50% of his salary. Board increases Bakker's salary 91%.

1982

Bonuses and Benefits Obtained   Management Actions

Gov. Ex. D Page 1

Exhibit A-29

327

Chronology of Events Related to Bonuses
1983

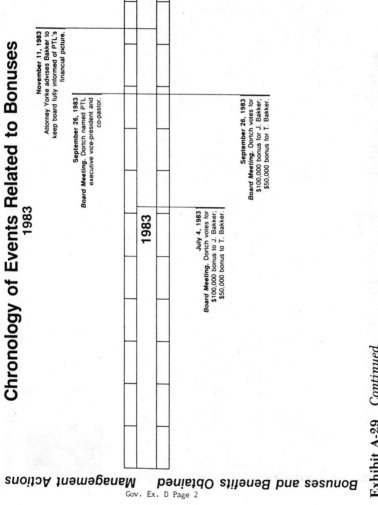

November 11, 1983 Attorney Yorke advises Bakker to keep board fully informed of PTL's financial picture.

September 26, 1983 *Board Meeting.* Dortch named PTL executive vice-president and co-pastor.

July 4, 1983 *Board Meeting.* Dortch votes for $100,000 bonus to J. Bakker; $50,000 bonus to T. Bakker.

September 26, 1983 *Board Meeting.* Dortch votes for $100,000 bonus for J. Bakker; $50,000 bonus for T. Bakker.

1983

Management Actions

Bonuses and Benefits Obtained

Exhibit A-29 *Continued*

Chronology of Events Related to Bonuses
1984

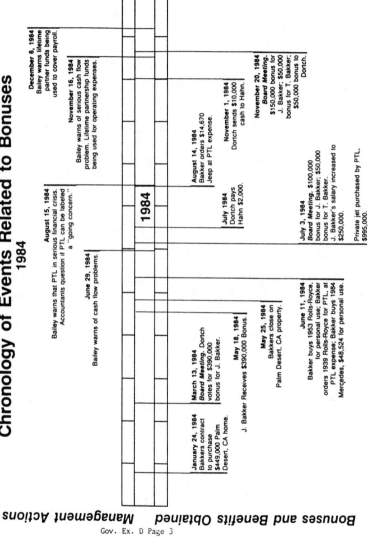

January 24, 1984 Bakkers contract to purchase $449,000 Palm Desert, CA home.

March 13, 1984 *Board Meeting.* Dortch votes for $390,000 bonus for J. Bakker.

May 18, 1984 J. Bakker Receives $390,000 Bonus.

May 25, 1984 Bakkers close on Palm Desert, CA property.

June 11, 1984 Bakker buys 1953 Rolls-Royce, for personal use; Bakker orders 1939 Rolls-Royce for PTL, at PTL expense; Bakker buys 1984 Mercedes, $48,524 for personal use.

June 29, 1984 Bailey warns of cash flow problems.

July 3, 1984 *Board Meeting.* $100,000 bonus for J. Bakker; $50,000 bonus for T. Bakker. J. Bakker's salary increased to $250,000.

Private jet purchased by PTL, $995,000.

July 1984 Dortch pays Hahn $2,000.

August 14, 1984 Bakker orders $14,670 Jeep at PTL expense.

August 15, 1984 Bailey warns that PTL in serious financial crisis. Accountants question if PTL can be labeled a "going concern."

November 1, 1984 Dortch sends $10,000 cash to Hahn.

November 16, 1984 Bailey warns of serious cash flow problem. Lifetime partnership funds being used for operating expenses.

November 20, 1984 *Board Meeting.* $150,000 bonus for J. Bakker; $50,000 bonus for T. Bakker; $50,000 bonus to Dortch.

December 6, 1984 Bailey warns lifetime partner funds being used to cover payroll.

Management Actions   Bonuses and Benefits Obtained

Gov. Ex. D Page 3

Exhibit A-29 *Continued*

329

Chronology of Events Related to Bonuses
1985

February 7, 1985
Bailey warns Tower Account balance down to $78,000.

April 18, 1985
Bailey warns that PTL loss for March was $1.6 million.

June 30, 1985
Bailey warns that PTL loss to date in 1985 is $20 million.

August 19, 1985
Bailey warns that PTL is spending double its income.

December 11, 1985
Steve Nelson warns that $400,000 of PTL bills to vendors are 90 days past due.

November 13, 1985
IRS proposes revocation of PTL's tax exempt status.

November 12, 1985
$500,000 check to Messner bounces.

Management Actions

1985

Bonuses and Benefits Obtained

February 26, 1985
Dortch agrees to pay Hahn $265,000.

March 28, 1985
Board Meeting. $200,000 bonus for J. Bakker; $50,000 bonus for T. Bakker.

April 1, 1985
Dortch authorizes increase of $265,000 to invoices from Commercial Builders for payment to Hahn.

April 16, 1985
Board Meeting. $20,000 bonus for T. Bakker.

July 5, 1985
Board Meeting. $200,000 bonus for J. Bakker; $50,000 bonus for T. Bakker; $50,000 bonus for Dortch.

November 12, 1985
Board Meeting. $200,000 bonus for J. Bakker; $100,000 bonus for T. Bakker; $100,000 bonus for Dortch.

November 30, 1985
Dortch authorizes increase of $64,000.82 to invoices from Commercial Builders for improvements to Parsonage.

December 31, 1985
Dortch authorizes increase of $70,144.37 to invoices from Commercial Builders for improvements to Parsonage.

Exhibit A-29 *Continued*

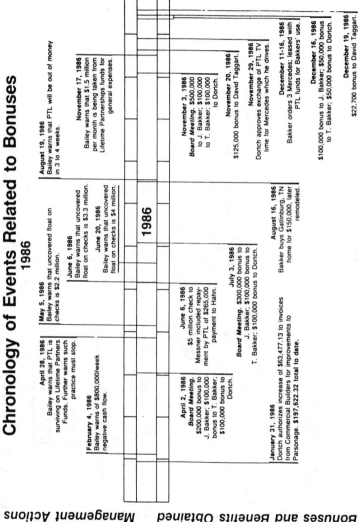

Chronology of Events Related to Bonuses
1986

April 28, 1986
Bailey warns that PTL is surviving on Lifetime Partners Funds. Further warns such practice must stop.

February 4, 1986
Bailey warns of $800,000/week negative cash flow.

May 5, 1986
Bailey warns that uncovered float on checks is $2.2 million.

June 6, 1986
Bailey warns that uncovered float on checks is $3.3 million.

June 20, 1986
Bailey warns that uncovered float on checks is $4 million.

August 19, 1986
Bailey warns that PTL will be out of money in 3 to 4 weeks.

November 17, 1986
Bailey warns that $1.5 million per month is being taken from Lifetime Partnerships funds for general expenses.

1986

April 2, 1986
Board Meeting.
$200,000 bonus to J. Bakker; $100,000 bonus to T. Bakker; $100,000 bonus to Dortch.

June 6, 1986
$5 million check to Messner included repayment by PTL of $265,000 payment to Hahn.

July 3, 1986
Board Meeting. $300,000 bonus to J. Bakker; $100,000 bonus to T. Bakker; $100,000 bonus to Dortch.

November 3, 1986
Board Meeting. $500,000 to J. Bakker; $100,000 to T. Bakker; $100,000 to Dortch.

November 20, 1986
$125,000 bonus to David Taggart.

January 31, 1986
Dortch authorizes increase of $63,477.13 to invoices from Commercial Builders for improvements to Parsonage. **$197,622.32 total to date.**

August 16, 1986
Bakker buys Gatlinburg, TN home for $150,000, later remodeled.

November 29, 1986
Dortch approves exchange of PTL TV time for Mercedes which he drives.

December 11-16, 1986
Bakker orders 3 Mercedes; leased with PTL funds for Bakkers' use.

December 16, 1986
$100,000 bonus to J. Bakker; $50,000 bonus to T. Bakker; $50,000 bonus to Dortch.

December 19, 1986
$22,700 bonus to David Taggart.

Bonuses and Benefits Obtained — Management Actions

Gov. Ex. D Page 5

Exhibit A-29 *Continued*

331

Chronology of Events Related to Bonuses
1987

Management Actions

January 1987
$10 million owed Messner for Towers construction.

April 28, 1987
Dortch Terminated.

1987

Bonuses and Benefits Obtained

April 2, 1987
$56,000 of PTL funds provided to Tammy Sue Bakker for record royalties, at Taggart's direction.

March 19, 1987
Bakker Resigns.

February 20, 1987
Bakkers purchase Palm Springs, CA home for $600,000.

February 16, 1987
$225,000 bonus to David Taggart.

February 13, 1987
Bakker obtains $150,000 payment, not authorized by board.

Gov. Ex. D Page 6

Exhibit A-29 *Continued*

332

Chronology of Partnership Events
1984

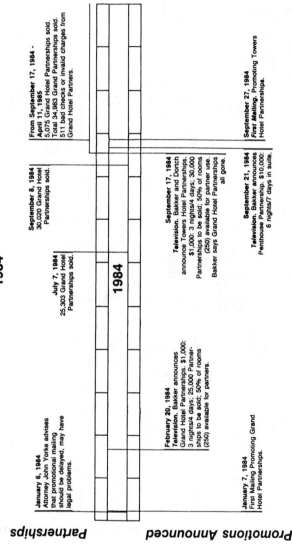

Partnerships

January 6, 1984
Attorney John Yorke advises that promotional mailing should be delayed, may have legal problems.

July 7, 1984
25,303 Grand Hotel Partnerships sold.

September 8, 1984
30,020 Grand Hotel Partnerships sold.

From September 17, 1984 - April 11, 1985
5,075 Grand Hotel Partnerships sold. Total 34,983 Grand Partnerships sold. 511 bad checks or invalid charges from Grand Hotel Partners.

1984

Promotions Announced

January 7, 1984
First Mailing Promoting Grand Hotel Partnerships.

February 20, 1984
Television. Bakker announces Grand Hotel Partnerships. $1,000: 3 nights/4 days; 25,000 Partnerships to be sold; 50% of rooms (250) available for partners.

September 17, 1984
Television. Bakker and Dortch announce Towers Hotel Partnerships. $1,000: 3 nights/4 days; 30,000 Partnerships to be sold; 50% of rooms (250) available for partner use. Bakker says Grand Hotel Partnerships all gone.

September 21, 1984
Television. Bakker announces Penthouse Partnership. $10,000: 6 nights/7 days in suite.

September 27, 1984
First Mailing. Promoting Towers Hotel Partnerships.

Exhibit A-30

333

Chronology of Partnership Events
1985

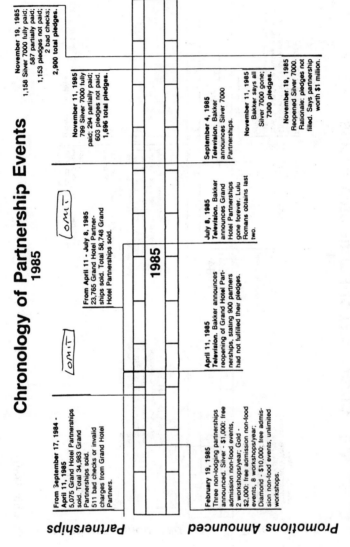

Partnerships

From September 17, 1984 - April 11, 1985
5,075 Grand Hotel Partnerships sold. Total 34,983 Grand Partnerships sold.
511 bad checks or invalid charges from Grand Hotel Partners.

OMIT

From April 11 - July 8, 1985
23,765 Grand Hotel Partnerships sold. Total 58,748 Grand Hotel Partnerships sold.

OMIT

November 11, 1985
799 Silver 7000 fully paid; 294 partially paid; 603 pledges not paid. **1,696 total pledges.**

November 19, 1985
1,158 Silver 7000 fully paid; 587 partially paid; 1,153 pledges not paid; 2 bad checks; **2,900 total pledges.**

1985

Promotions Announced

February 19, 1985
Three non-lodging partnerships announced. Silver - $1,000: free admission non-food events, 2 workshops/year; Gold - $2,000: free admission non-food events, 8 workshops/year; Diamond - $10,000: free admission non-food events, unlimited workshops.

April 11, 1985
Television. Bakker announces reopening of Grand Hotel Partnerships, stating 900 partners had not fulfilled their pledges.

July 8, 1985
Television. Bakker announces Grand Hotel Partnerships gone forever. Lulu Romans obtains last two.

September 4, 1985
Television. Bakker announces Silver 7000 Partnerships.

November 11, 1985
Bakker says all Silver 7000 gone; 7300 pledges.

November 19, 1985
Reopened Silver 7000. Rationale: pledges not filled. Says partnership worth $1 million.

Exhibit A-30 *Continued*

334

Chronology of Partnership Events
1986

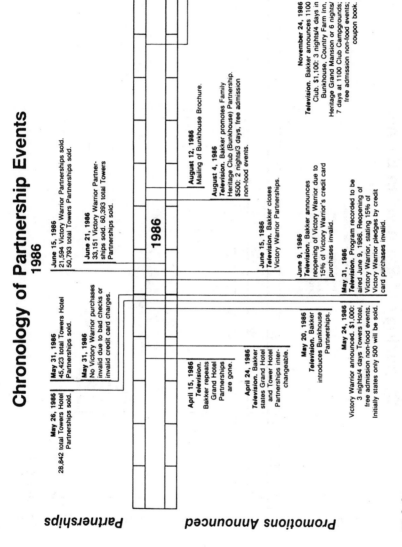

Partnerships

May 26, 1986
28,842 total Towers Hotel Partnerships sold.

May 31, 1986
45,423 total Towers Hotel Partnerships sold.

May 31, 1986
No Victory Warrior purchases invalid due to bad checks or invalid credit card charges.

June 15, 1986
21,594 Victory Warrior Partnerships sold. 50,793 total Towers Partnerships sold.

June 21, 1986
33,151 Victory Warrior Partnerships sold. 60,393 total Towers Partnerships sold.

Promotions Announced

April 15, 1986
Television. Bakker repeats Grand Hotel Partnerships are gone.

April 24, 1986
Television. Bakker states Grand Hotel and Tower Hotel Partnerships interchangeable.

May 20, 1986
Television. Bakker introduces Bunkhouse Partnerships.

May 24, 1986
Victory Warrior announced. $1,000: 3 nights/4 days Towers Hotel, free admission non-food events. Initially states only 500 will be sold.

May 31, 1986
Television. Program recorded to be aired June 9, 1986. Reopening of Victory Warrior, stating 15% of Victory Warrior pledges by credit card purchases invalid.

June 9, 1986
Television. Bakker announces reopening of Victory Warrior due to 15% of Victory Warrior's credit card purchases invalid.

June 15, 1986
Television. Bakker closes Victory Warrior Partnerships.

August 4, 1986
Television. Bakker promotes Family Heritage Club (Bunkhouse) Partnership. $500: 2 nights/3 days, free admission non-food events.

August 12, 1986
Mailing of Bunkhouse Brochure.

November 24, 1986
Television. Bakker announces 1100 Club. $1,100: 3 nights/4 days in Bunkhouse, Country Farm Inn, Heritage Grand Mansion or 6 nights/ 7 days at 1100 Club Campgrounds; free admission non-food events; coupon book.

1986

Exhibit A-30 *Continued*

335

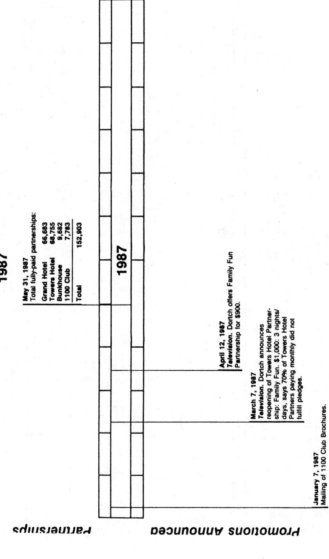

Chronology of Partnership Events
1987

May 31, 1987
Total fully-paid partnerships:

Grand Hotel 66,683
Towers Hotel 68,755
Bunkhouse 9,682
1100 Club 7,783

Total 152,903

April 12, 1987
Television. Dortch offers Family Fun
Partnership for $900.

March 7, 1987
Television. Dortch announces
reopening of Towers Hotel Partnership: Family Fun, $1,000: 3 nights/
days, says 70% of Towers Hotel
Partners paying monthly did not
fulfill pledges.

January 7, 1987
Mailing of 1100 Club Brochures.

1987

Partnerships

Promotions Announced

Exhibit A-30 *Continued*

336

PTL Television Network

Memo

To: Jim Bakker

From: Peter G. Bailey

Date: September 13, 1984

RE: DH & S Audit

CC: Richard Dortch

I met with Bob Brown of DH & S today to review the audit report for the year ended May 31, 1984. The main concern expressed in the report is whether PTL will be able to continue as "a going concern" based on current assets of only 8.6 million against 28.5 million in current liabilities. There is a concern whether PTL will have the ability to meet its debt obligations during the coming year.

I went over PTL's plan to raise funds to meet the above need as outlined below:

1.	Telethon beginning 9/17		$	30,000,000
	Construction of Tower			15,000,000
				15,000,000
	Pay off accounts payable			10,000,000
				5,000,000
	Construction of Studio Auditorium			5,000,000

2.	Hall of Agreement			10,000,000
3.	Hotel Mortgage	21,000,000		21,000,000
	Complete HGH	10,000,000		
		11,000,000		
	Invest-6 Mos CD	11,000,000		

	In 6 mos – pay on mortgage			11,000,000
	Balance of Mortgage		$	10,000,000

Mr. Brown was pleased to see this and wants to discuss with myself and Richard Dortch the wording in the audit report about their concern.

0334 004

PGB

Exhibit A-31 Memo to Jim Bakker Regarding DH&S Audit

*→ • $1,000 life time S/B going into Ministry

• Jim solicits on behalf of the Church = cannot be
   CG

• Church will own Hotel?

CSC • Need application for School's tax exempt
     status

Dortch wife & daughter on payroll — never seen

Sales tax on deferred revenue use at "Motel"

Tax counsel considering w/D from PTL

acc'ts & attorney's even't allowed to talk to B of D

contract for mgmt of HGH who audits, if PTL
→ get a   pays even DH should do
copy

ruling needed to address HGH lifetime partners

stock to be issued for PTL Enterprises as sub of CG

sub need to be independent w/a separate Bd. Now it is
Jim as sole Director

Who are officers of subs? Or are they just to be
run by Church & charged through intercompany a/cs.

Need common paymaster

ICS will find private enurement & it'll go to court, we'll lose

They're doing things & asking us later for tax or other
acctg matters need a mtg w/ them

FTC Review — HGH — Water Buck

Exhibit A-32   Notes Taken by Ted Leinbach

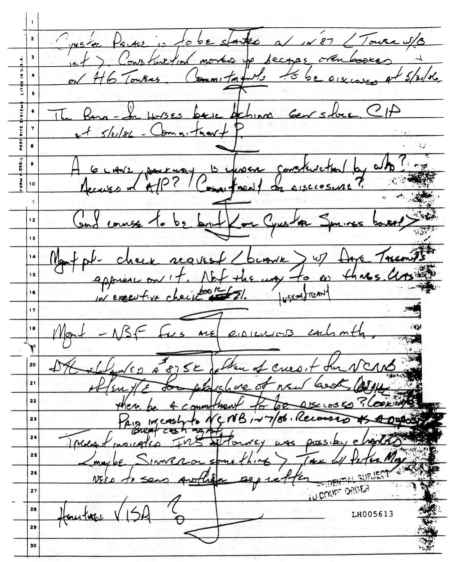

Exhibit A-33 Laventhol and Horwath Work Paper

```
6A1210   •01   00004    790279-3632
  •     10/08/87
   1040  Department of the Treasury–Internal Revenue Service    1986     0721128313416
         U.S. Individual Income Tax Return
```

For the year January 1 – December 31, 1986, or other tax year beginning				ending	OMB No. 1545-0074

JAMES O. & TAMARA F. BAKKER

Your social security number: 371-36-6827

P. O. BOX 1208

Spouse's social security number: 476-44-8570

FORT MILL,, SOUTH CAROLINA 29715

If this address is different from the one shown on your 1985 return, check here ▶ [X]

Presidential Election Campaign — Do you want $1 to go to this fund? ... Yes [X] No [ ] If joint return, does your spouse want $1 to go to this fund? Yes [X] No [ ] Note: Checking "Yes" will not change your tax or reduce your refund.

Filing Status (Check only one box.)
1 [ ] Single
2 [X] Married filing joint return (even if only one had income)
3 [ ] Married filing separate return. Enter spouse's social security no. above and full name here.
4 [ ] Head of household (with qualifying person). (See page 6 of Instructions.) If the qualifying person is your unmarried child but not your dependent, enter child's name here.
5 [ ] Qualifying widow(er) with dependent child (year spouse died ▶ 19   ) (See page 6 of Instructions.)

Exemptions (Always check the box labeled Yourself. Check other boxes if they apply.)
6a [X] Yourself   [ ] 65 or over   [ ] Blind
b [X] Spouse   [ ] 65 or over   [ ] Blind
c First names of your dependent children who lived with you TAMMY, JAMIE
Enter number of boxes checked on 6a and 6b ▶ 2
Enter number of children listed on 6c ▶ 2
d First names of your dependent children who did not live with you (see page 5)
e Other dependents:
(1) Name | (2) Relationship | (3) Number of months lived in your home | (4) Did dependent have income of $1,080 or more? | (5) Did you provide more than one-half of dependent's support?
Enter number of other dependents
Add numbers entered in boxes above ▶ 4
7 Total number of exemptions claimed (also complete line 36)

Income (Please attach Copy B of your Forms W-2, W-2G, and W-2P here. If you do not have a W-2, see page 4 of Instructions.)

7	Wages, salaries, tips, etc. (attach Form(s) W-2) ... SEE STATEMENT	7	1,467,318.
8	Interest income (also attach Schedule B if over $400)	8	292.
9a	Dividends (also attach Schedule B if over $400) 9b Exclusion		
c	Subtract line 9b from line 9a and enter the result	9c	
10	Taxable refunds of state and local income taxes, if any, from the worksheet on page 9 of Instructions	10	106.
11	Alimony received	11	
12	Business income or (loss) (attach Schedule C)	12	
13	Capital gain or (loss) (attach Schedule D)	13	
14	40% of capital gain distributions not reported on line 13 (see page 9 of Instructions)	14	
15	Other gains or (losses) (attach Form 4797)	15	
16	Fully taxable pensions, IRA distributions, and annuities not reported on line 17 (see page 9)	16	
17a	Other pensions and annuities, including rollovers	17a	
b	Taxable amount, if any, from the worksheet on page 10 of Instructions	17b	
18	Rents, royalties, partnerships, estates, trusts, etc. (attach Schedule E)	18	(-21,214.)
19	Farm income or (loss) (attach Schedule F)	19	
20a	Unemployment compensation (insurance). Total received	20a	
b	Taxable amount, if any, from the worksheet on page 11 of Instructions	20b	
21a	Social security benefits (see page 10)	21a	
b	Taxable amount, if any, from worksheet on page 11, (tax-exempt interest)	21b	
22	Other income (list type and amount—see page 11 of Instructions) SEE STATEMENT 1	22	1,359.
23	Add the amounts shown in the far right column for lines 7 through 22. This is your total income ▶	23	1,447,861.

(stamped: RECEIVED OCT ... ATS / IRS #605)

Adjustments to Income (See Instructions on page 11)

24	Moving expenses (attach Form 3903 or 3903F)	24	
25	Employee business expenses (attach Form 2106)	25	
26	IRA deduction, from the worksheet on page 12	26	
27	Keogh retirement plan and self-employed SEP deduction	27	
28	Penalty on early withdrawal of savings	28	
29	Alimony paid (recipient's last name and social security no.)	29	
30	Deduction for a married couple when both work (attach Schedule W)	30	3,000.
31	Add lines 24 through 30. These are your total adjustments ▶	31	3,000.

Adjusted Gross Income
32 Subtract line 31 from line 23. This is your adjusted gross income. If this line is less than $11,000 and a child lived with you, see "Earned Income Credit" (line 58) on page 16 of Instructions. If you want IRS to figure your tax, see page 13 of Instructions ▶ | 32 | 1,444,861.

6A1210 3.000

0006 001

Exhibit A-34 Portions of Jim and Tammy Bakker's Tax Return for 1986

6A1220   10/08/87

form 1040 (1986) JAMES O. & TAMARA F. BAKKER   371-36-6827 Page 2

Tax Computation	33 Amount from line 32 (adjusted gross income)	33	1,444,861.
	34a If you itemize, attach Schedule A (Form 1040) and enter the amount from Schedule A, line 26	34a	173,223.
(See instructions on page 13)	Caution: If you have unearned income and can be claimed as a dependent on your parents' return, see page 13 of Instructions and check here ▶ ☐ Also see page 13 if you are married filing a separate return and your spouse itemizes deductions, or you are a dual-status alien.		
	b If you do not itemize but you made charitable contributions, enter your cash contributions here. (If you gave $3,000 or more to any one organization, see page 14) ... 34b		
	c Enter your noncash contributions (you must attach Form 8283 if over $500) 34c		
	d Add lines 34b and 34c. Enter the total	34d	
	35 Subtract line 34a or line 34d, whichever applies, from line 33 ...	35	1,271,638.
	36 Multiply $1,080 by the total number of exemptions claimed on line 6f (see page 14)	36	4,320.
	37 Taxable income. Subtract line 36 from line 35. Enter the result (but not less than zero)	37	1,267,318.
	38 Enter tax here. Check if from ☐ Tax Table, ☒ Tax Rate Schedule X, Y, or Z, or ☐ Schedule G.	38	613,588.
	39 Additional taxes. (See page 14 of Instructions) Enter here and check if from ☐ Form 4970, ☐ Form 4972, or ☐ Form 5544	39	
	40 Add lines 38 and 39. Enter the total ▶	40	613,588.
Credits (See instructions on page 14)	41 Credit for child and dependent care expenses (attach Form 2441) 41		
	42 Credit for the elderly or for the permanently and totally disabled (attach Schedule R) 42		
	43 Partial credit for political contributions for which you have receipts 43		
	44 Add lines 41 through 43. Enter the total	44	
	45 Subtract line 44 from line 40. Enter the result (but not less than zero)	45	613,588.
	46 Foreign tax credit (attach Form 1116) 46		
	47 General business credit. Check if from ☐ Form 3800, ☐ Form 3468, ☐ Form 5884, ☐ Form 6478, ☐ Form 6765 47		
	48 Add lines 46 and 47. Enter the total	48	
	49 Subtract line 48 from line 45. Enter the result (but not less than zero) ▶	49	613,588.
Other Taxes (Including Advance EIC Payments)	50 Self-employment tax (attach Schedule SE)	50	
	51 Alternative minimum tax (attach Form 6251)	51	
	52 Tax from recapture of investment credit (attach Form 4255)	52	
	53 Social security tax on tip income not reported to employer (attach Form 4137)	53	
	54 Tax on an IRA (attach Form 5329)	54	
	55 Add lines 49 through 54. This is your total tax ▶	55	613,588.
Payments Attach Forms W-2, W-2G, and W-2P to front.	56 Federal income tax withheld 56	614,083.	
	57 1986 estimated tax payments and amount applied from 1985 return 57		
	58 Earned income credit (see page 16) 58		
	59 Amount paid with Form 4868 59	NONE	
	60 Excess social security tax and RRTA tax withheld (two or more employers) 60		
	61 Credit for federal tax on gasoline and special fuels (attach Form 4136) 61		
	62 Regulated Investment Company credit (attach Form 2439) 62		
	63 Add lines 56 through 62. These are your total payments ▶	63	614,083.
Refund or Amount You Owe	64 If line 63 is larger than line 55, enter amount OVERPAID ▶	64	495.
	65 Amount of line 64 to be REFUNDED TO YOU ▶	65	495.
	66 Amount of line 64 to be applied to your 1987 estimated tax ▶ 66		
	67 If line 55 is larger than line 63, enter AMOUNT YOU OWE. Attach check or money order for full amount payable to "Internal Revenue Service." Write your social security number, daytime phone number and "1986 Form 1040" on it ▶ Check ▶ ☐ if Form 2210 (2210F) is attached. See page 17. Penalty:	67	

Please Sign Here

Under penalties of perjury, I declare that I have examined this return and accompanying schedules and statements, and to the best of my knowledge and belief, they are true, correct, and complete. Declaration of preparer (other than taxpayer) is based on all information of which preparer has any knowledge.

signature *Jim Bakker*	Date Oct 10/87	Your occupation MINISTER
Spouse's signature (if joint return, BOTH must sign) *Tamara F. Bakker*	Date Oct 10/87	Spouse's occupation PTL-HOST

	Preparer's signature *William A. Spears CPA* ✱	Date 10/9/87	Check if self-employed ☐	Preparer's social security no. 266-62-4943
Paid Preparer's Use Only	Firm's name (or yours, if self-employed) and address ▶ LAVENTHOL & HORWATH ONE NCNB PLAZA - SUITE 3500 CHARLOTTE, N. C.		E.I. No. 23-1416947 ZIP code 28280	

6A1220 2.000   ✱ SEE ADDITIONAL Statement by PREPARER

Exhibit A-34   *Continued*

JAMES & TAMMY BAKKER
FORM 1040 - 1986

Additional Statement By Tax Return Preparer

This tax return was prepared on the basis of the taxpayers'
Forms W-2, check stubs, cancelled checks, Forms 1099 and other
information submitted by the taxpayers. It includes all items
of taxable income of which the preparer has any knowledge. The
taxpayers and their former employer, Heritage Village Church and
Missionary Fellowship, Inc. ("PTL"), have been the object of extensive media attention and both the taxpayers' and PTL's prior years
tax returns are presently under examination and investigation by
the IRS and the U. S. Justice Department.

The following items which may eventually be determined to
effect the taxable income of the taxpayers for 1986 have not been
included in this return.

1. The media has reported accusations of Jim and Tammy Bakker
   using PTL funds, credit cards, and other assets for personal purposes without reimbursing PTL. The tax return
   preparer has no information to support such a claim and
   has been advised by a representative of the taxpayer that
   such claims are inaccurate.

2. The taxpayers made a claim that they are be entitled to
   keep the parsonage owned by PTL that was their residence
   while they were employed by PTL. This claim was rejected
   by PTL and to the best of the knowledge of the tax return
   preparer this rejected claim would not be the basis for
   creating taxable income.

The taxpayers donated their Rolls Royce automobile but no deduction was claimed on this return because it was not possible to get
the Certification of Appraiser as required by IRS Form 8283 completed
by the extended tax return due date.

William J. Spears ID# 266-62-4943

William J. Spears, CPA
LAVENTHOL & HORWATH, CPA'S
ID# 23-1416 947
One NCNB Plaza, Suite 3500
Charlotte, North Carolina 28280

Exhibit A-34 *Continued*

January 31, 1991   VIA FAX # 619-459-0779
& Federal Express

Dr. Morris Cerullo
Morris Cerullo World Evangelism
3545 Aero Court
San Diego, CA 92123

Dear Dr. Cerullo:

I thank you for your note this morning and I have difficulty in comprehending your statement:

"We have a mailing, already in the mails."

Kindly elaborate.

The understanding was the the mailings, etc., including the issuance of the cards, were to be ceased and discontinued immediately and the Board of Directors of the New Heritage USA Corporation and the New Heritage Carolina Corporation shall consider and determine the matter and its various ramifications.

If I may, I shall earnestly request and advise you that MCWE should cease and desist all activities whatsoever, including telemarketing relating to the invitations and issuance of the cards by MCWE. Please and kindly treat this matter of utmost importance and consequence.

Yours sincerely,
New Heritage USA Corporation

Tet-Kim Loy
President

TKL:vs

Exhibit A-35

MORRIS CERULLO WORLD EVANGELISM

RECEIVED
- 2 FEB 1991
OFFICE OF THE
SR EXECUTIVE
DIRECTOR

** FAX COVER SHEET **

DATE: __________

TO: __________

FROM: __________

Return FAX Number - (619)459-0779

Number of Pages (Including cover sheet) __________

IF THERE IS A PROBLEM WITH THIS TRANSMISSION, PLEASE FAX ME AT THE ABOVE NUMBER - (619) 459-0779

OPERATOR: PLEASE Submit Copy to TAN SRI P.400

COMMENTS:

DEAR KHET-

I FIND YOUR FAX of JAN. 31 Very offending, and in extremely POOR taste.

As MY DIRECTOR - you have over stepped the Bound's of your position in issuing Directives to the Chairman of the Board of New Heritage USA.

Who Do you think is calling this meeting to Discuss this issue - NOT MR COY - I DID - An Apology is in ORDER!

GOD Bless You. Dr Morris Cerullo

3545 AERO CO... SAN DIEGO, CALIFORNIA ... • POST OFFICE BOX 700 • SAN DIEGO, CALIFORNIA 9...
(619) 277-2200 • FAX (619) 277-5111 • TELEX: 62005354

TOTAL P.0...

Exhibit A-36 Fax to Khet from Cerullo

4.   Based upon my review of the PKF study and the
Arthur Andersen report, I find these reports to be deficient
in analyzing the economic impact of the MCWE Gold/Platinum
Card Program in the following ways:

(a)   The PKF study is solely a market feasibility
study on the reopening of Heritage USA. It is not an
economic feasibility analysis of the Project and does not
consider the economic impact of the MCWE Gold/Platinum Card
Program. In the study, PKF outlines one option for "Lifetime
Partners" that is very different from the MCWE Gold/Platinum
Card Program:

> Form a nonprofit corporation which will be a
> recreation club called the Heritage Club
> (Club). Each Lifetime Partner can join the
> newly formed Club for a $200 one-time fee. All
> Club members would be entitled to a 50 percent
> discount on lodging only. We estimate that 15
> percent of the 114,000 Lifetime Partners
> (17,100) will elect this option.

Although recommending this option, PKF provides no basis for
the assumption underlying this option. Further, PKF does not
attempt to evaluate the economic impact of this option. In
addition, PKF fails to clearly limit or restrict the usage of
the suggested Gold Card which makes the economic impact of
this card unquantifiable.

(b)   In my opinion, the Arthur Andersen report is not
reliable because it does not provide adequate analysis,
support or documentation for their findings. The Arthur
Andersen report is a highly qualified report which relies

- 3 -

Exhibit A-37   Certification by Harold W. Perry, Jr.

solely on information provided by MCWE. Arthur Andersen made no attempt at independent verification.

5.   With regard to the Arthur Andersen report, in my opinion, the reliability and accuracy of the economic impact estimate is questionable. In addition, I point out that the Arthur Andersen report is technically not an economic impact analysis of the MCWE Gold/Platinum Card Program because it does not factor into its findings the fixed and variable expense projections for the Project.

6.   The Arthur Andersen report is based on a number of faulty assumptions:

(a)   Several categories of possible discounts/benefits were not analyzed as part of the Arthur Andersen report. These discount categories include: RV park and campsite rentals; costs for the pre-opening event for platinum card holders; construction, furnishing and operation costs for the Platinum Lounge; discounts/benefits received by all members of card-holding minister-led church groups; and the cost of admissions other than the water park and the passion play, such as special events (Christmas City, July 4th, festivals, concerts, etc.), recreational village amenities (skating rink, carousel, bikes, boats, giraffe, putt-putt golf, swim, tennis);

(b)   Arthur Andersen assumes that the cardholders would visit the New Heritage USA theme park once for a three-day visit. Arthur Andersen provides no foundation for this assumption. This assumption totally disregards the fact that a cardholder is entitled to visit the theme park for an unlimited number of times over his/her lifetime.

(c)   There is no discussion in Arthur Andersen's report as to how discounted rate cardholders would displace full rate paying visitors during full booking nights if the cardholders made reservations prior to a full rate visitor. This

- 4 -

Exhibit A-37 *Continued*

is a factor in analyzing the impact of the MCWE
Gold/Platinum Card Program on New Heritage USA.

(d)   Arthur Andersen ignored costs which would have
        been incurred in additional staff time needed to
        handle the discount program including:
        additional visitor volume; benefit program
        administration time; group travel
        administration.

(e)   Arthur Andersen did not allow for the usage of
        the discounts/benefits by all immediate family
        members of the cardholders or by all members of
        a church where the pastor is a cardholder.
        According to an offering letter issued by MCWE,
        all immediate family members of a cardholder and
        up to 3,000 members of a congregation where a
        pastor or minister is a cardholder are entitled
        to the discounts/benefits as stated on the card
        Obviously, this usage would increase the dollar
        impact on the New Heritage Companies.

7.   Arthur Andersen's estimate of an average of $120

published rate for the hotels at New Heritage USA is too

high. Arthur Anderson's estimate of that rate is incorrect

because:

        (a)   Arthur Andersen incorrectly assumes the hotels

have reached a stabilized operation in its analysis. This

assumption totally disregards PKF's five-year stabilization

period for the New Heritage USA resort. The PKF stabiliza-

tion period estimate appears reasonable but I have not

independently evaluated it. As a result, Arthur Andersen's

$120 rate is skewed upwards.

        (b)   Arthur Andersen uses only the higher double

occupancy rates in their calculation of the $120 published

rate. Based upon my experience in the hotel industry, this

assumption is not valid. In fact, Arthur Andersen disregards

- 5 -

Exhibit A-37   *Continued*

the estimated market demand mix for the hotels at New Heritage USA to be 25% group business as stated in the PKF study. The group segment has a much lower double occupancy factor. As a result, the $120 published rate estimated by Arthur Andersen is overstated.

(c)   Arthur Andersen improperly includes Guest Quarters hotel as a comparable hotel to those at Hew Heritage USA. Guest Quarters provides all-suite hotel accommodations and therefore is not a comparable hotel. Given that Guest Quarters had the highest published rate (approximately $20 higher) of all other comparable hotels, the range of published rates in the Arthur Andersen analysis is therefore artificially skewed upward.

8.   This Certification does not attempt to quantify the economic impact of the MCWE Gold/Platinum Card Program because I did not have sufficient data or time to perform that analysis.

I certify under penalty of perjury that the foregoing is true and correct.

Executed on: _April 14, 1991_
Washington, D.C.   Harold W. Perry, Jr.

- 6 -

Exhibit A-37   _Continued_

Index

700 Club, 18–19
1100 Club, 69, 71–73, 75–76, 301, 306–7, 318–19, 335–36

Alexander, Donald, 229
Allman, Spry, Humphreys, 264
Altman, Bill, 248, 256–61
American Association of Fund-Raising Counsel, 248
American Institute of Certified Public Accountants, 128, 206, 219, 225–26
Anderson, Joseph F., Jr., 286
Anderson, Thomas T., 194, 200, 215, 217
Angel, Dana, 292
Arthur Andersen and Company, 137, 246
   and Morris Cerullo's purchase of PTL, 267–68
   PTL fees paid to, 264
   and the Gold and Platinum Club programs, 277–78, 283, 344–47
Arthur Young and Company, 206, 208
Assemblies of God Church, Illinois District, 137, 140–41
Auditors
   and accounting fraud cases, 288–89
   general duties of, 204–8, 219–20, 245–46

Bailey, Peter G., 251
   accounting career of, 114
   and bankruptcy of PTL, 133, 135
   and change in PTL's outside auditors, 236–37, 241, 244–45, 337
   dismissed from PTL, 264
   and memos concerning the financial status of PTL, 98, 100, 111–12, 113, 116, 119–34, 136–37, 309–14, 329–31
   on his relationship with Richard Dortch, 143–44

on relationship between David Taggart and Jim Bakker, 147
   and overselling of PTL lifetime partnerships, 44, 102, 133–34, 149, 153, 155, 161, 209, 215, 218–22, 319
   and PTL board of directors, 175, 181, 190
   PTL bonuses of, 136, 153
   and PTL check bouncing, 213
   and PTL checks and cash advances for David Taggart, 87, 89, 92
   and PTL credit cards, 119, 122
   and PTL executive bonuses, 120, 121, 122, 124, 128
   and PTL involvement in world missions, 169
   and PTL's deferred revenue, 128–29
   and PTL's floating of funds, 122, 127, 130–32, 224
   and the Evangelical Council for Financial Accountability (ECFA), 253–55, 259
   and the PTL executive payroll account, 117–19
   and travel receipts of David Taggart, 150–52
Baker and McKenzie, 234
Bakker, Bob, 9
Bakker, Donna
   See Puckett, Donnna
Bakker, Furn, 8–9, 10, 12
Bakker, James Charles (Jamie), 11, 168
Bakker, Jim (James O.)
   and assessment of Deloitte, Haskins and Sells, 253
   automobiles of, 140
   and Peter Bailey's memos concerning PTL funds, 98, 100, 111–12, 113, 116, 119–34, 136–37, 309–14
   bonuses for from PTL, 69, 80, 97, 98, 111, 120, 121, 122, 124, 128, 138, 167, 170, 171, 179–90, 302, 325–31

career as traveling revivalist, 14–16
and changes in operating procedures of
    PTL board of directors, 143
childhood of, 8–12, 13–14
and Christian Broadcasting Network,
    16–19, 22, 23
civil verdict against, 268
class action lawsuit against, 193–200
compensation of from PTL, 1–2, 9, 17,
    38, 42, 99, 117–18, 136, 142, 166–67,
    168, 170, 185, 187–88, 198, 227–28,
    229–30, 234–35, 240, 242, 321–22
and construction contracts for the Grand
    Hotel, 201
and corporate financial structure of PTL,
    115–17
and crisis fundraising, 15–16, 18
and David and Goliath statues, 74, 76,
    110–11
and destruction of PTL lifetime partner-
    ship reports, 110
relationship with Richard Dortch,
    111–12, 138–39, 167–71
and Evangelical Council for Financial Ac-
    countability (ECFA), 250–53, 255–58,
    261
and facilitators to provide perks for,
    139–40, 147–49, 151–52
and Jerry Falwell's takeover of PTL,
    263–64
and founding of Heritage USA, 24–27
and founding of PTL, 22–25
general overselling of lifetime partner-
    ships by, 2–5, 29–30, 76, 96–98,
    100–104, 107–10, 149, 153–55,
    157–61, 162–63, 179, 181–82, 201,
    302, 305, 333–36
and Gold and Platinum Club programs,
    281–82
and Jessica Hahn, 4, 28, 29, 144–47, 186,
    199, 303
health problems of, 19
indictment of, 192
Internal Revenue Service investigates his
    PTL compensation, 176–78, 186
Internal Revenue Service investigates
    PTL, 230, 320–21
and Kevin's House, 202–3
and letters from PTL contributors, 245
and marriage to Tammy Faye Bakker,
    12–15
media coverage of, 258
and hiring of Roe Messner, 33
and misrepresentations to the PTL board
    of directors, 172–73, 174–75, 178–79
misuses PTL corporate funds, 80–82,
    85–86

and *Move That Mountain*, 8
office of, 137
on PTL's outside auditors, 243–44,
    287–88
oversells 1100 Club lifetime partner-
    ships, 69, 71–73, 75–76
oversells Bunkhouse Partnerships, 67,
    69–73, 75–76
oversells Grand Hotel lifetime partner-
    ships, 31–46, 48–49, 51–52, 56, 218,
    221, 224, 271, 295, 298
oversellings Towers Hotel lifetime part-
    nerships, 45–69, 75–76
personal tax returns of, 227, 229–30,
    340–42
and prosperity theology, 15, 18
and PTL parsonage account, 119
and PTL audits by Deloitte, Haskins and
    Sells, 337
and PTL bankruptcy trial, 78–89
and PTL board of directors' minutes,
    324–26
and PTL building construction funds,
    24–25
and PTL check bouncing, 213
and PTL credit cards, 119, 149, 176–77
PTL-funded building construction for,
    308
PTL-funded real estate holdings of, 1,
    17–18, 120, 142, 148, 171, 182–83,
    186, 250–51, 253, 325, 327, 329,
    331–32, 342
PTL leadership style of, 11
and PTL's executive payroll, 303–4
religious calling of, 12
resignation of, 7, 29, 66, 95, 179, 191,
    263, 332
sentencing of, 1, 2, 193, 287
and hiring of David Taggart, 92–93
and treatment by the media, 243
and Trinity Broadcasting Systems,
    21–22, 23
wire and mail fraud charges against, 292
wire and mail fraud trial of, 2, 4, 77–78,
    94–112, 262
Bakker, Norman, 9, 321
Bakker, Norman, Jr., 321
Bakker, Raleigh, 8–9, 10, 11, 12
Bakker, Tammy Faye, 304
automobiles of, 140
bonuses for from PTL, 80, 82, 84–85,
    120, 121, 122, 124, 128, 138, 167,
    179–90, 325–26, 328–31
compensation for from PTL, 1–2, 9, 38,
    42, 99, 117–18, 142, 171, 185, 240,
    321–22
and career as traveling revivalist, 14–16

and David and Goliath statues, 74, 76
health problems of, 19
Internal Revenue Service investigates PTL compensation, 176–77
and Internal Revenue Service investigations of PTL, 320–21
and Jessica Hahn affair, 146
joins the Christian Broadcasting Network, 16–17
and letters from PTL contributors, 245
and marriage to Jim Bakker, 12–15
office of, 115
and overselling of Grand Hotel lifetime partnerships, 31–33, 38–39, 40
and overselling of Towers Hotel lifetime partnerships, 45, 47, 49, 59, 60, 62
and perks granted by the PTL board of directors, 168
personal tax returns of, 230, 340–42
and prosperity theology, 15
and PTL bankruptcy trial, 78–89
and PTL credit cards, 176–77
PTL-funded building construction for, 308
and PTL's outside auditors, 243–44
puppet ministry of, 16, 17
and right to succeed Jim Bakker, 168–69, 170
t-shirts depicting, 94
and wire and mail fraud trial of Jim Bakker, 95, 105, 109
Bakker, Tammy Sue, 19, 95, 168, 332
Ball, Richard, 76, 104, 153–54, 157, 161
Barker, Stephen, 194
Barton, Forbes M., Jr., 166
Beck, Swannee, 194
Bender, Harold, 96, 102
Benton v. Bakker, 5
Bernard, John, 292
Betzer, Gabrielle, 105, 292
Bird, Wendell, 194, 200, 230, 235
Blue Cross, 122
Board of Directors, PTL
   attorneys banned from meetings of, 171
   and outside auditors, 227–28, 236, 287
   and bonuses for executives, 167, 179–90
   and bonuses for Jim Bakker, 302
   and contact with PTL accountants and attorneys, 220
   and control of the PTL organization, 232
   and executive compensation, 234–35
   and Evangelical Council for Financial Accountability (ECFA), 251–52, 254
   and financial information from auditors, 173–74
   and hiring of Richard Dortch, 138–39
   and Internal Revenue Service, 175–78, 186

minutes of, 166, 171–73, 189, 324–25
   and misrepresentations by Jim Bakker and Richard Dortch, 172–73, 174–75, 178–79
   and overselling of lifetime partnerships, 262
   and perks for Jim Bakker, 167–71
   resignation of, 179, 191, 263
   Richard Dortch implements changes in operating procedures of, 141–43
   role of, 4–5
   suggested expansion of, 139
Borden, Art, 249–57, 262
Brennecke, Connie Jenkins, 160–61
Bridges, Gerald, 257, 260
Brock Hotel Corporation, 35, 106–7, 172
Brown, Bob, 176–77, 209, 211, 236–37, 320, 322, 337
Brown, David, 92
Bunkhouse Partnerships, 67, 69–73, 75–76, 105, 132, 135, 162, 183, 301, 306–7, 318–19, 335–36
Burgund, Mark
   on Richard Dortch's personal finances, 140–41
   and Richard Dortch's handling of the executive payroll, 139, 149
   and Evangelical Council for Financial Accountability (ECFA), 255
   hired by PTL, 138
   and overselling of PTL lifetime partnerships, 102, 153
   and perks for Jim Bakker, 139–40
   salary of from PTL, 140
   and selling of Silver 7000 Club lifetime partnerships, 56–58
Burgund, Wanda, 102, 131, 138, 153

Capin, Richard, 257
Carr, Gene, 193
Carson, Johnny, 17
Caudle, Joyce, 320–21
Caudle, Lloyd, 176–77, 229, 231–34, 320, 322–23
Caudle and Spears, 231–32, 240
Cerullo, David, 266–67, 269, 275–76, 281–82
Cerullo, Morris
   evangelical career of, 264–65
   and Gold and Platinum Club programs, 270–86
   Gold Card program of, 6
   and Heritage USA telethons, 266–67
   and Morris Cerullo World Evangelism (MCWE), 265–70, 272–73, 275–86, 343–47
   and New Heritage USA board of directors, 343

New Heritage USA lawsuit against,
    276–86
and purchase of PTL assets, 264–69, 273,
    275–76, 280, 286
Yet-King Loy on, 269–70
Cerullo, Theresa, 267
Chai, Lawrence, 269, 273
Chapel, Charles, 232–33
Chapman, Tammy Sue
    See Bakker, Tammy Sue
Christian Broadcasting Network (CBN),
    16–19, 22, 23
Christian Retreat Center, 114
Cline, Mary K., 214–15, 218
Collins, Ronald J., 280
Combs, Elizabeth, 105
Cookman, Charles A., 172
    and bonuses for Jim Bakker, 184–85, 325
    and bonuses for Tammy Faye Bakker,
        184–85
    and changes in operating procedures of
        PTL board of directors, 142
    elected to PTL board of directors, 169
    and Evangelical Council for Financial Ac-
        countability (ECFA), 251
    and long-range loans for PTL, 170
    and misrepresentations of PTL's financial
        status, 175, 184
    on relationship between David Taggart
        and Jim Bakker, 147
    and PTL finance committee, 174
Cooper and Lybrand, 246
Cortese, Aimee, 172, 324
    and audit committee of PTL, 186, 258
    and bonuses for Jim Bakker, 185–86, 302
    and bonuses for Tammy Faye Bakker,
        185–86
    civil case against, 190
    class action lawsuit against, 193–200
    elected to PTL board of directors, 169,
        185
    and hiring of Richard Dortch, 138
    and Jim Bakker's PTL-funded real estate
        holdings, 142
    and long-range loans for PTL, 170
    and misrepresentations of PTL's financial
        status, 175, 184
    and payments to Jessica Hahn, 145, 186,
        199–200
Cotton, Ben, 92
Cronkite, Walter, 167
Crouch, Jan, 22, 23
Crouch, Paul, 22, 23

Dash, Robert, 181–83
David and Goliath Statues, 74, 76, 110–11,
    123, 299, 309

Davis, George T., 96, 97, 101
Dean, Carl, 213
Deloitte, Haskins and Sells, 166
    and assessment by Jim Bakker, 253
    average earnings per partner at, 205
    and change in PTL's outside auditors,
        236–42
    class action lawsuit against, 193–200
    and David and Goliath statues, 76
    as PTL's auditors, 4, 170, 173, 209, 214,
        337
    and Internal Revenue Service investi-
        gates PTL, 175–77, 228–30, 320, 322
    and overselling of PTL lifetime partner-
        ships, 209–11, 213–20, 222–24, 299
    and PTL's executive payroll account,
        117–18, 224–28
    PTL's pastdue account with, 121, 127
    and weaknesses in PTL's internal ac-
        counting controls, 211–12
Deloitte Touche, 4, 196
Dortch, Mildred, 304
Dortch, Richard
    and auditors of PTL, 174, 236, 238–39,
        337
    and Peter Bailey's memos concerning
        PTL funds, 113, 116, 119, 121–34, 311
    and board of directors of PTL, 141–43,
        169, 189, 191, 324–26
    and bonuses from PTL for Jim Bakker,
        181, 183, 185–87, 190, 302, 327–28
    bonuses for from PTL, 69, 80, 167, 179,
        183–85, 188, 190, 325–26, 329–31
    and building construction funded by PTL,
        308
    and distribution of PTL bonuses, 85
    compensation of at PTL, 94, 117–18,
        176–78, 228, 230
    corporate duties at PTL, 137–47
    and credit cards of PTL, 119
    and destruction of PTL lifetime partner-
        ship reports, 101
    and Evangelical Council for Financial Ac-
        countability (ECFA), 253–55, 257,
        260–61
    and executive payroll of PTL, 117–18,
        139, 141, 144, 149, 303–4
    and financial structure of corporate PTL,
        115–17
    firing of, 139, 264, 332
    general overselling of lifetime partner-
        ships by, 29–30, 76, 97–98, 100–104,
        107, 153, 155, 157, 159–61, 162–63,
        302, 305, 333, 336
    and payments to Jessica Hahn, 144–47,
        186, 199, 303, 329–31
    Internal Revenue Service investigates his
        PTL compensation, 176–78

and Internal Revenue Service investigations of PTL, 230–34, 322
and Kevin's House, 202–3
and Life Challenge, Inc., 287
and Mark Burgund's handling of his personal finances, 140–41
and misrepresentations to the PTL board of directors, 172–73, 174–75, 178–79
and overselling of 1100 Club lifetime partnerships, 71
and overselling of Bunkhouse Partnerships, 69
and overselling of Grand Hotel lifetime partnerships by, 35, 37, 39–40, 42, 44, 209, 297
and overselling of Towers Hotel lifetime partnerships, 5, 45–46, 50, 52, 54–55
and parsonage account of PTL, 119
and relationship with Jim Bakker, 111–12, 141, 143, 144
resigns from PTL board of directors, 191
role of in securing PTL perks for Jim Bakker, 167–71
and transfer of funds between PTL accounts, 128
trial and conviction of, 4, 192, 287
wire and mail fraud charges against, 77, 94–95, 97
and wire and mail fraud trial of Jim Bakker, 94–95, 100, 102–4, 107
Dudley, George, 292

Egert, Philip D., 168
Egert, Ruth, 168
Eggen, Jeff, 154–55, 156, 211, 319
Elliott, Carl, 292
Ernst and Whinney, 206, 246, 256
Ernst and Young, 246, 247
Etheridge, Don, 231, 320, 322
and Internal Revenue Service investigations of PTL, 175–77, 229, 235
and overselling of Grand Hotel lifetime partnerships, 209
Evangelical Council for Financial Accountability (ECFA), 243–44
and audit and finance committees of PTL, 174
and bankruptcy of PTL, 248, 256, 261
description of, 249–50
and overselling of PTL lifetime partnerships, 256, 261–62
PTL membership in, 5, 249–62
and PTL's outside auditors, 261

Fairfax Savings and Loan, 45, 60, 130, 131, 132, 312
Falwell, Jerry, 135, 136, 137, 325

and Kevin's House, 203
as president of PTL, 191, 263–64
Family Fun Special, 53, 66–67, 75, 301, 336
Federal Communications Commission, 166
Finalco, 129–30, 312
Findlay, J. Cary, 236, 238–39
Flessing, Roger, 322
Foor, Alan Kent, 105–6, 292
Forcucci, Guy, 177, 209, 229–30, 236, 240–41
Foxe, Ann, 227–28
Franklin, John, 320
Franzone, Ernest, 257, 258, 324
and bonuses for Jim Bakker, 302
elected to PTL board of directors, 172
and executive bonuses, 186–87
and misrepresentations of PTL's financial status, 175, 184
Fringe Benefit Corporation, 122
Frost, Robert, 91
Fulbright, Shirley, 11, 150
and board of directors of PTL, 189, 324–26
bonuses from PTL, 189–90
compensation of from PTL, 118, 303
and corporate structure of PTL, 138
and credit cards of PTL, 119
dismissed from PTL, 264
and gifts from David and James Taggart, 149
and misuse of PTL funds, 152–53
office of, 115, 137
Fundraising Strategy, 15–16, 18

Gaddis, Irvin, 292
Galaxy Network, 129
Generally Accepted Accounting Principles (GAAP), 206–8, 219, 250
Generally Accepted Auditing Standards (GAAS), 2, 206–7, 211, 219, 223
George, Don
elected to PTL board of directors, 172
resigns from PTL board of directors, 187
and bonuses for Jim Bakker, 183, 187
and executive bonuses, 324–25
and Internal Revenue Service investigations of PTL, 178
and misrepresentations of PTL's financial status, 175, 184
Gibbs, J'Tanya Adams, 158–60
Givens, Thomas, 44, 45
Gold Card Club, 6, 270–86, 344–47
Grand Hotel, 27–28
description of, 164
funds for construction of, 3, 42, 45, 46–47, 49, 52, 54–5, 127, 135, 201–2, 296, 337

management of, 106–7
overselling of lifetime partnerships in, 3, 31–46, 48–49, 51–52, 56, 108, 133–34, 154–55, 157–60, 162–63, 173, 218, 221–24, 235, 259–62, 295, 298, 301, 306–7, 317–19, 333–36, 338
promotional brochures for, 293–94, 297
and the Gold and Platinum Club programs, 270–71
Gross, Fred, 45, 52, 54, 62–64
Grutman, Norman Roy, 264
Gunst, Robert C., 92, 231, 240

Hahn, Jessica, 1, 2, 4, 45, 52, 54, 62–64
and affair with Jim Bakker, 28, 29
and Jerry Falwell's takeover of PTL, 263
PTL payments to, 81, 144–47, 186, 199–200, 201, 303, 315, 329–31
Haines Maxwell Company, 308, 311
Hardee, David, 229
Harding, Burt, 234–35
Hardister, Don, 148, 183
Hargrove, Harry, 264
Harrison, Henry, 46
Harrison, Patricia, 148
office of, 115–16, 137
and PTL corporate structure, 138
PTL duties of, 303
and travel receipts of David Taggart, 150
Hatfield, Mark, 249
Heller, Jacob, 74, 110–11
Heritage Grand Hotel
See Grand Hotel
Heritage USA
building construction funds used for, 25
description of, 163–64
founding of, 24–27
and Kevin's House, 202–3
maintenance and beautification fees for, 324
Roe Messner's construction costs for building, 201
sale of, 264–69
selling of lifetime partnerships at, 2–5, 29–76, 96–98, 100–104, 107–10, 133–34, 149, 153–55, 157–61, 162–63, 179, 181–82, 201, 209, 218, 221–24, 259–62, 295, 298, 301, 306–7, 317–19, 333–36
See also Grand Hotel; PTL; Towers Hotel
Heritage Village Church and Missionary Fellowship, Inc. (HVCMF)
See PTL
Hines, Floyd, 292

Internal Revenue Service, 37

and Jim Bakker's PTL–funded real estate holdings, 142
and destruction of PTL lifetime partnership reports, 101
investigates PTL, 42, 82, 83, 117, 122, 173, 200, 220, 228–30, 235, 240–41, 259, 261, 320, 322, 324, 338
and David Taggart's use of PTL funds, 148
and tax evasion trial of David and James Taggart, 89–94
and tax-exempt status of PTL, 4, 22, 26, 108, 129, 163, 171, 175–78, 231–34, 330
and Trinity Broadcasting Systems, 21–22

Johnson, Debbie, 321
Johnson, James E., 166–67, 168

Keating, Charles, Jr., 246, 288
Kerstetter, Lamar (Larry), 105, 292
Kevin's House, 201, 202–3
Khet, Kok Yin, 269, 273–75, 343
Khoo, Tan Sri, 276–77, 343
King, Paul, 102, 153
Knox, Eddie, 138–39, 177, 231–32

LaValley, Don, 321
LaValley, Lynn, 321
Laventhol and Horwath, 339, 341–42
and auditing procedures of PTL, 4, 173, 221
and change in PTL's outside auditors, 236, 240–42
class action lawsuit against, 193–200
and executive payroll of PTL, 117–18, 224–28, 304
and Evangelical Council for Financial Accountability (ECFA), 255–57, 259
and Internal Revenue Service investigations of PTL, 228–30
and overselling of PTL lifetime partnerships, 134, 209, 216, 220–24, 235, 243, 262
Lawing, A. T., Jr., 171, 172, 324
and audit and finance committees of PTL, 174, 258
and bonuses for Jim Bakker, 187–88
and executive compensation of PTL, 322
and hiring of Richard Dortch, 138
and misrepresentations of PTL's financial status, 175, 184
and perks granted by the PTL board of directors, 168
Leinbach, Ted, 177, 215, 220, 338
Life Challenge, Inc., 287
Long, Samuel, III, 221

Loy, Yet-King, 343
  on Morris Cerullo, 269–70
  and purchase of PTL assets, 269
  and the Gold and Platinum Club programs, 272–79, 283–84
Lund, Peterson, and Clark, 278
Lund, William S., 275, 277–78, 283

Mabrey, William, 106–7
McKinney and Givens, 44
McMahon, Ed, 46
McMillan, James B., 197, 198–99
McMillan, Ralph, 257
Malayan United Industries (MUI), 268–69, 277
Mangum, Archie, 216–18, 219, 224, 229
Mauney, Charles, 91
Messner, Roe, 312
  and check bouncing from PTL, 213, 330
  class action lawsuit against, 196, 201
  and costs for Towers Hotel construction, 332
  employed as PTL church contractor, 33
  and Kevin's House, 202–3
  and overselling of Grand Hotel lifetime partnerships, 33–34
  and overselling of PTL lifetime partnerships, 201
  and overselling of Towers Hotel lifetime partnerships, 45, 52, 54, 62–64
  and payments to Jessica Hahn, 146–47, 186
  PTL parsonage work done by, 144
  and PTL payments to Jessica Hahn, 331
  and Towers Hotel construction costs, 127, 131
Michigan Baptist Foundation, 114
Miller, Jerry, 2, 4, 96, 100, 103–4, 157, 160
Miniscribe Corporation, 246
Ministers' Benefit Association, 2, 99, 142, 168, 170
Minneapolis Evangelistic Auditorium, 14
Model Business Corporation Act, 165–66
Moore, Herbert M., 167
Morris Cerullo World Evangelism (MCWE), 265–70, 272–73, 275–86, 343–47
  See also Cerullo, Morris
Moss, Jim, 23
Move That Mountain (Bakker), 8
Mullen, Graham, 193, 287
Murray, Edith, 292
Murray, Phillip, 292

National Association of Securities Dealers (NASD), 248
National Religious Broadcasters, 325

Nelson, Steve, 131
  class action lawsuit against, 196
  and overselling of PTL lifetime partnerships, 149, 153–55, 157, 160–61, 305, 317
  and past-due bills to PTL's vendors, 330
  and selling of Victory Warrior lifetime partnerships, 62
  and the destruction of PTL lifetime partnership reports, 101, 110
  and wire and mail fraud trial of Jim Bakker, 100–104, 107
New Heritage USA (NHUSA), 269, 343
  and lawsuit against Morris Cerullo, 276–86
  opening of, 286
  and the Gold and Platinum Club programs, 270–86, 344–47
New Inspirational Network, 266, 286
North Central Bible College, 9, 12, 14, 137

Oldham, Doug, 63, 104, 153, 202

Panache, 150
Pannell Kerr Forster, 266, 276, 280, 344, 346
Pearson, John R., 98, 100
Penthouse Promotional, 50–51, 53, 301, 318–19, 333
Perry, Harold W., Jr., 283, 344–47
Platinum Card Club, 270–86, 344–47
Ponzi Schemes, 97, 134–35
Potter, Robert
  and sentencing of David and James Taggart, 93
  and sentencing of Jim Bakker, 1, 2, 193
  and sentencing of Richard Dortch, 95
  and wire and mail fraud trial of Jim Bakker, 94, 96, 108
Praise Unlimited, 129
Price, Carol, 156–60
Price Waterhouse, 253
Pridgen, Bill, 44
Prosperity Theology, 15, 18
PTL
  audit and finance committees of, 174, 186, 256, 258
  auditing firms hired by, 4, 243–45
  Peter Bailey memos on financial status of, 113, 116, 119, 121–34
  Jim Bakker's control over, 11
  Bakker family members hired at, 9
  bankruptcy of, 4, 78–89, 256, 264
  board of directors of, 4–5
  building construction funds of, 24–25
  check bouncing of, 212–13, 224
  checking accounts of, 116–19, 212–13

and construction contracts, 201–2
corporate financial structure of, 114–17
corporate structure of, 138
credit cards of, 119, 122, 212, 309, 320–22
crisis fundraising for, 16
declining contributions to, 79, 81, 87, 89, 128–30
and deferred revenue, 128–29
employees of, 7
and Evangelical Council for Financial Accountability (ECFA), 249–62
and executive payroll account, 117–19
Federal Communications Commission investigates, 166
floating of funds by, 122, 127, 130–32, 224
founding of, 22–25
and funding of lifetime partnership programs, 79–80
gift promotionals of, 74, 76
and Jessica Hahn settlement, 81
and legal rights of lifetime partners, 192
overselling of lifetime partnerships by, 2–5, 29–76, 96–98, 100–104, 107–10, 133–34, 149, 153–55, 157–61, 162–63, 179, 181–82, 201, 209, 218, 221–24, 259–62, 295, 298, 301, 306–7, 317–19, 333–36
parsonage account of, 81, 119, 120, 131, 168, 321–22, 330–31
and policies concerning travel expenses, 150
President's Club of, 156–61
prison ministry of, 164–65
and procedure for hiring contractors, 123
property holdings and activities of, 163–65
rationalization of the Bakkers' lifestyle at, 10
recording of bonuses issued by, 141
and shifting of funds for executive compensation, 79–80
James Taggart hired as interior decorator, 92, 93
tax-exempt status of revoked, 4, 22, 231–34
world missions of, 169
and World Outreach Center (WOC), 115–16
See also Board of directors, PTL; Heritage USA
PTL Television Network, 2, 25, 30, 164–65, 265–66
Public Oversight Board, 216–17
Puckett, Donna, 9, 114, 321

Rabon, Rebecca, 292

Racketeering Influenced Corrupt Organizations Act (RICO), 197, 198–99
Reynolds, Rufus W., 77, 79, 81, 87, 89, 153
Roberts, Oral, 325
Robertson, Pat, 16–17, 19, 23, 325
Robinson, William, 196
Rock Hill National Bank, 152, 196, 324
Roman, Lulu, 39, 41, 334
Rubino, Robert, 81
Rule, Hollis C., 153–54, 156, 317

Salinas-Jones, Bill, 272, 279, 281, 283, 285
Salsbury, Kirt, 280–82
Savings and Loan Crisis, 6, 246–47, 288
Schmidt, Barbara, 292
Securities and Exchange Commission, U.S., 7, 220, 288–89
Shedd, Dennis, 264, 265, 268
Sheline, Jack, 280–82
Silver 7000 Club, 53, 55–61, 75, 130, 196, 255, 259, 301, 318–19, 334
Smith, Brenda, 102
Smith, Deborah, 21, 58, 67, 94–95, 96, 98, 100, 105, 128, 129, 134–35, 140, 183, 184, 187, 192
South Carolina Time Share Act, 197, 297
Speakman, Porter, 114, 251
Spears, William J., 196, 222, 230, 255–57, 259, 341–42
Spencer, Evelyn Carter, 324
  and bonuses for Jim Bakker, 188, 302
  elected to PTL board of directors, 172
  and misrepresentations of PTL's financial status, 175, 184
Sporkin, Stanley, 288
Stephens, Sylvia, 171
Strahowski, Rita, 194
Swaggart, Jimmy, 89, 325

Taggart, David
  and blank checks from Peter Bailey, 136
  and bonuses for Jim Bakker, 181, 183, 302
  bonuses for, 80, 179–80, 331–32
  and bonuses for executives of PTL, 189–90
  and changes in operating procedures of PTL board of directors, 143
  class action lawsuit against, 193–200
  compensation of, 86–88, 117–18, 147, 152, 228, 230, 303, 322
  corporate duties of at PTL, 147–53
  and corporate financial structure of PTL, 114–16
  and corporate structure of PTL, 138
  and credit cards of PTL, 119, 149, 300, 320–21

dismissed from PTL, 264
and executive payroll of PTL, 304
hired by Jim Bakker, 92–93
hired by PTL, 171
Internal Revenue Service investigates
PTL compensation of, 176–78
misuses PTL funds, 86–88, 89, 91–92,
148–49, 316
office of, 137
and overselling of Towers Hotel lifetime
partnerships, 112
and payments to Jessica Hahn, 303
and perks for Jim Bakker, 139–40,
147–49, 151–52
and personal loans secured by PTL,
152–53
and PTL bankruptcy trial, 78–89
relationship with Jim Bakker, 141,
147–53
trial and sentencing of, 4, 78, 89–94, 192,
287
and the destruction of PTL lifetime partnership reports, 101
and transfer of funds between PTL accounts, 128, 130
travel receipts of, 150–52
Taggart, Henry, 149
Taggart, James
compensation of, 228, 303, 322
employed as PTL's interior decorator, 92,
93, 128, 150–51, 189
misuses PTL funds, 89, 91–92, 149
trial and sentencing of, 78, 89–94
Teague, Helen, 194–95
Teague, Joseph, 194–95
Teague v. Bakker, 5, 193–200, 204, 209–10,
214, 220, 222, 224, 235, 249, 253,
256, 262
Thyer, Jim, 236, 240–41
Touche and Ross, 4, 205–6
Touche Ross, 196
Towers Hotel, 27–28, 318–19
funds for construction of, 46, 49, 54–55,
60, 67, 80, 112, 124, 127–28, 131,
132, 135–36, 201–2, 332, 337
and Gold and Platinum Club programs,
270–71
overselling of lifetime partnerships in, 3,
40, 45–69, 75–76, 108, 133–34,
162–63, 218, 221–24, 259–60, 295,
301, 306–7, 333, 335–36
promotional brochures for, 298

Treadwell, Timothy, 268
Trinity Broadcasting Systems (TBS), 21–22
Tucker, Karen, 194–95
Tysinger, Harold, 273, 283–84

United States v. Arthur Young and Company,
208
United States v. Bakker, 5, 21, 67, 94–112
United States v. Dortch, 5
United States v. Johnson, 5
United States v. Simon, 207
United States v. Taggart, 5, 89–94

Victory Warriors, 53, 61–65, 75, 101, 103,
131–32, 182, 301, 313–14, 318–19, 335

Wardlow, Knox, Knox, Freeman and Sco-
field, 42, 231
Webster, Evan, 176–77, 320–22
Whitman, Walt, 91
Whittum, Kevin, 202–3
Wigton, Michael J., 178, 231–34, 313
Williams, Jim, 193, 198–99
Woodall, Charles, 140
World Outreach Center (WOC), 27,
115–16
Wyden, Ron, 246

Yorke, John
and alterations of PTL board of directors'
minutes, 189
and changes in operating procedures of
PTL board of directors, 143
and duties as PTL's attorney, 231
and Evangelical Council for Financial Accountability (ECFA), 251
and expansion of PTL board of directors,
139
and Internal Revenue Service investigations of PTL, 176–77, 320–23
on relationship between David Taggart
and Jim Bakker, 147
and overselling of Grand Hotel lifetime
partnerships, 42, 44, 209, 297
and overselling of PTL lifetime partnerships, 235, 333
and PTL executive bonuses, 327–28
and PTL's executive payroll, 227–28

Zimbalist, Efrem, Jr., 169, 172, 175, 184,
188
ZZZZ Best, 246–47